THE LAND OF REST.

*There shall be no night there.*

All Religious Denominations profess to aim for the same object.
So let each have charity for the other.

*See 1 Cor. Ch. 13*

THE

# BOOK OF RELIGIONS;

COMPRISING THE

VIEWS, CREEDS, SENTIMENTS, OR OPINIONS,

OF ALL THE

PRINCIPAL RELIGIOUS SECTS IN THE WORLD

PARTICULARLY OF

ALL CHRISTIAN DENOMINATIONS

IN

EUROPE AND AMERICA;

TO WHICH ARE ADDED

CHURCH AND MISSIONARY STATISTICS,

TOGETHER WITH

BIOGRAPHICAL SKETCHES.

BY JOHN HAYWARD,
AUTHOR OF THE "NEW ENGLAND GAZETTEER,"
&c. &c.

BOSTON:
ALBERT COLBY AND COMPANY.
20 WASHINGTON STREET.
1860.

# PREFACE.

A FEW years since, the Editor of the following pages published a volume of "Religious Creeds and Statistics;" and, as the work, although quite limited, met with general approbation, he has been induced to publish another of the same nature, but on a much larger plan, trusting that it will prove more useful, and more worthy of public favor.

His design has been, to exhibit to his readers, with the utmost impartiality and perspicuity, and as briefly as their nature will permit, the views, creeds, sentiments, or opinions, of all the religious sects or denominations in the world, so far as utility seemed to require such an exhibition; but more especially to give the rise, progress, and peculiarities, of all the principal schemes or systems of religion which exist in the United States at the present day.

The work is intended to serve as a manual for those who are desirous of acquiring, with as little trouble as possible, a correct knowledge of the tenets or systems of religious faith, presented for the consideration of mankind;—to enable them, almost at a glance, to compare one creed or system with another, and each with the holy Scriptures;—to settle the minds of those who have formed no definite opinions on religious subjects;--and to lead us all, by contrasting the sacred truths and sublime beauties of Christianity with the absurd notions of pagan idolaters, of skeptics, and of infidels, to set a just value on the doctrines of HIM WHO SPAKE AS NEVER MAN SPAKE.

To accomplish this design, the Editor has obtained, from the most intelligent and candid among the living defenders of each denomination, full and explicit statements of their religious sentiments—such as they believe and teach. He is indebted to the friends of some new sects or parties in philosophy and religion, for an account of their respective views and opinions. With regard to anterior sects, he has noticed, from the best authorities, as large a number as is thought necessary for the comparison of ancient with modern creeds.

The Church and Missionary Statistics are believed to be as accurate as can be constructed from materials which annually undergo greater or less changes.

The Biographical Sketches are derived from the most authentic sources. While they convey useful knowledge in regard to the fathers and defenders of the various systems of religious faith, they may also stimulate our readers to the practice of those Christian virtues and graces which adorned the lives of many of them, and render their names immortal.

A few only of the works from which valuable aid has been received, can be mentioned:—Mosheim and McLaine's Ecclesiastical History; Gregory and Ruter's Church History; Encyclopædia Americana; Brown's Encyclopedia of Religious Knowledge; Adams's View of Religions, and History of the Jews; Benedict's History of all Religions; Evans's Sketches; Buck's and Henderson's Theological Dictionaries; Eliot's, Allen's, and Blake's Biographical Dictionaries; Davenport; Watson; Grant's Nestorians, Coleman's Christian Antiquities; Ratio Disciplinæ; Haydn's Dictionary of Dates, &c.

To clergymen and laymen of all denominations, who have assisted the Editor in presenting their various views with clearness and fairness; to the secretaries of the several missionary boards; to editors of religious journals, and to other persons who have kindly furnished documents for the Statistics and Biographical Sketches, he tenders acknowledgments of unfeigned gratitude.

While the Editor assures the public that the whole has been prepared with much diligence and care, and with an entire freedom from sectarian zeal or party bias, he cannot but indulge the hope that his "Book of Religions" will prove acceptable and beneficial to the community, as imbodying a great variety of facts on a subject of deep concern, worthy of the exercise of our highest faculties, and requiring our most charitable conclusions.

# INDEX.


A. Page

Abelians, or Abelonians, .....243
Addison, Joseph,............417
Agricola, John, .............370
Allenites, ..................280
American Missions, .........336
Anabaptists, ................190
Ancient American Covenant,.308
Andover Orthodox Creed, ....138
Antinomians, ...............128
Anti-Pedobaptists,...........196
Apostles' Creed,............ 102
Aquarians, ..................168
Arians, .......................18
Arius, ......................368
Armenians,..................303
Arminians,...................115
Arminius, James,............373
Assembly's Catechism,.......141
Athanasian Creed,...........102
Athanasius, ................368
Atheists, ...................217
Augsburg Confession,........302

B.

Bacon, Francis, .............407
Baptists, ...........182, 311, 340
——— Quaker, ...........193
Baptist Missions, English,....339
Baxter, Richard, ............376
Baxterians, .................169
Bereans, ....................109
Beza, Theodore, .............366
Bible Chronology,...........175
Biographical Sketches,.......350
Bishops, Episcopal,..........314
Bourignonists, .... ........201
Boyle, Robert, ..............412
Brown, Robert, .............373
Brownists, ..................200
Bucer, Martin,..............360
Bullinger, Henry, ...........363
Burnet, Gilbert,.............429

C.

Calvin, John, ...............365
Calvinists,...............11, 313
Cambridge Platform,..........48
Campbellites, ................58
Charles V., ..................405
Chauncey, Charles,..........385
Christian Connection, ...295, 313
Christianity, Progress of, .....432
Chronology, Bible, ..........175
Church Government,.........20
Church Statistics, ...........311
Clarke, John, ...............387
Clarke, Richard, ............399
Come-Outers,...............177
Congregationalists, .......20, 313
Courtney, William,..........384
Creed, Andover, ............138
——— Apostles',............102
——— Athanasian,...........102
——— Augsburg, ...........302
——— New Haven, .........142
——— Nicene,..............105
——— Orthodox,............132
Cumberland Presbyterians, ....25

D.

Daleites, ....................272
Dancers, ....................244
Deists, ......................215

Diggers, ..................246
Disciples of Christ, ......58, 314
Disciples of St. John,........284
Dissenters. See *Puritans.*
Doddridge, Philip,...........420
Donatists, ..................281
Dorrelites,..................164
Dutch Reformed Church, .....88

E.

Elizabeth, Princess,..........411
Emancipators, ..............272
English Baptist Missions,.....339
——— Methodist Missions, ..343
Epicureans,.................244
Episcopalians, .......26, 314, 341
Essenes, ...................202

F.

Family of Love, ............259
Fighting Quakers,...........162
Fox, George, ...............377
Free Communion Baptists, ...300
Free-Will Baptists,..190, 312, 341
French Missions,............346
Friends, or Quakers, .....64, 319

G.

Genevieve,.............162, 428
German Missions,...........346
German Reformed Church,....90
Glass, John, ................383
Glassites, ..................126
Government, Church, ........20
Greek Church,..............288

H.

Hale, Matthew, ..............408
Harmless Christians, .........57
Harmonists, ................163
Hicksites, .............74, 319
High Churchmen,...........308
Higginson, Francis, .....310, 374
Hooker, Richard,............385
Hopkins, Samuel, ...........397
Hopkinsians, ................13
Humanitarians, .............19
Huntingdon, Lady Selina,....395
Huss, John, ................354
Hutchinson, Ann, ...........389
Hutchinsonians,.............259

I.

Independents,................20
Indian Missions, ............342
——— Religions, ...........210
——— Statistics,............ 347

J.

Jebb, John,.................401
Jerome of Prague, ..........352
Jews,.............202, 319, 347
Johnsonians,................280
Jumpers,...................181
Justin Martyr, ..............368

K.

Keith, George,..............383
Keithians,..................193
Knipperdolings,.............283
Knox, John,................363

L.

Latter-Day Saints, ..........260
Lavater, John G. C., ........402
Lee, Ann,..................381
Leo X., ....................367
Locke, John, ...............415
London Missionary Society, ..335
Luther, Martin, .............355
Lutherans, ..............9, 320

M.

Mahometans, ...............220
Maimonides, Moses,.....203, 370
Martyr, Peter, ..............362
Materialists, ...............112
Mayhew, Jonathan,..........398
Mendæans, .................284
Melancthon, Philip,..........361
Mennonites, .................57
Menno, Simonis, ............372
Methodists, Episcopal,... 117, 321
——— Protestant ..123, 321

Methodists, Primitive, .......305
Methodists' Missions, ........344
———— Views of Perfection, ..........274
Miller's Views on the Second Coming of Christ, .........170
Millenarians, ...............292
Missionary Statistics, ........333
Missions, American Foreign, ..336
Missions, Indian, ............342
Molinos, Michael, ...........389
Moravians, ..............49, 333
Mormonites, ................260
Muggletonians, .............284
Murray, John, ..............423

N.

Necessarians. See *Materialists.*
Nestorians, .................306
Netherland Missions, ........346
New Haven Orthodox Creed, .142
New Jerusalem Church, .....150
Newton, Isaac, ..............403
Nicene Creed, ..............105
Nonconformists, .............294
Nonjurors, .................294
Non-Resistants, .............247
Novatians, ..................305

O.

Oberlin Views of Sanctification, .....................278
Œcolampadius, John, ........355
Orthodox Creeds, ...........132
Osgoodites, .................166

P.

Pantheists, .................219
Pagans, ......................234
Pedobaptists, ...............193
Pelagians, ..................130
Penn, William, .............378
Perfectionists, ..............274
Pharisees, ..................202
Popes of Rome, .............326
Pre-Adamites, ..............131
Predestinarians, .............132
Presbyterians, ...........22, 322
————, Cumberland, ....25
Presbyterian Missions, .......338
Priestley, Joseph, ...........400
Primitive Christians, ........290
———— Methodists, ........305
Princess Elizabeth, ..........411
Progress of Christianity, .....432
Protestants, .................125
Protestant Methodists, ...123, 321
———— Missions, ..........333
Puritans, ....................200
Purves, James, ..............401
Puseyites, ...................299

Q.

Quakers, or Friends, ..........64
Quaker Baptists, ............193
Quietists, ...................283

R.

Ranters. See *Seekers.*
Re-Anointers, ...............282
Reformation, .................85
Reformed Churches, ..........88
Reformed Dutch Church, .88, 324
———— German Church, ...90
Rhenish Missions, ...........347
Restorationists, ...............91
Rogerenes, .................166
Roman Catholics, ...102, 324, 347
Russian Church, ............288

S.

Sabbatarians, ...............191
Sabellians, ..................125
Sadducees, ..................202
Sanctification, Views on, .....278
Sandemanians, ..............126
Sandeman, Robert, ..........396
Satanians, ..................243
Saybrook Platform, ...........48
Seabury, Samuel, ......... 33, 398
Schools, Theological, ........432
Scottish Missions, .......346, 347
Se-Baptists, .................281
Sectarians, ...................20

Seekers,....................247
Servetus, Michael,...........371
Seventh-Day Baptists,.. .....191, 312, 345
Shakers, ....................75
Simonians, ..................233
Six-Principle Baptists, .......192
Skeptics,....................245
Socinius, Faustus,...........372
Socinians,...................19
Southcotters, ...............255
Spinoza, Benedict,...........380
Statistics of Churches,.......311
——— of Missions,........333
Succession of Bishops,.......315
Supralapsarians,.............243
Swedenborg,..................150
Swedenborgians, ........150, 330

T.

Tao-Se, ....................282
Taylor's (Dr.) Views,........142
Theological Schools,.........432
Tillotson, John, .............402
Transcendentalists,..........301
Trinitarians, ................290
Tunkers, or Tumblers,........55

U.

Unitarians, .............196, 331
United Brethren,.............49
United Society of Believers,...75
Universalists,..... ......95, 331

W.

Waldenses,..................279
Water-Drinkers, ............168
Watts, Isaac, ...............418
Wesley, John, ..............390
Wesleyan Missions,..........343
Westminster Catechism, .....141
Whippers,...................167
Whitefield, George,..........393
Whitefield Methodists,.......293
Wickliffe, John,............ 350
Wickliffites, ................245
Wilhelminians, .............247
Wilkinsonians,..............167
Williams, Roger,............386
Winchester, Elhanan,........425
Worshippers of the Devil,....285

X.

Xavier, Francis,.........161, 372

Y.

Yezidees, or Worshippers of the Devil,....................285

Z.

Zanchius, Jerome,...........366
Zinzendorf, Count,..........383
Zuinglius, Ulricus, ..........359
Zuinglians,.................246

# BOOK OF RELIGIONS

---

## LUTHERANS,

OR

## THE EVANGELICAL LUTHERAN CHURCH.

This denomination adhere to the opinions of Martin Luther, the celebrated reformer.

The Lutherans, of all Protestants, are those who differ least from the Romish church, as they affirm that the body and blood of Christ are materially present in the sacrament of the Lord's supper, though in an incomprehensible manner: this they term *consubstantiation.* They likewise represent some rites and institutions, as the use of images in churches, the vestments of the clergy, the private confession of sins, the use of wafers in the administration of the Lord's supper, the form of exorcism in the celebration of baptism, and other ceremonies of the like nature, as tolerable, and some of them useful. The Lutherans maintain, with regard to the divine decrees, that they respect the salvation or misery of men in consequence of a previous knowledge of their sentiments and characters, and not as founded on the mere will of God. See *Augsburg Confession of Faith.*

Towards the close of the last century, the Lutherans began to entertain a greater liberality of sentiment than they had before adopted, though in many places they persevered longer in despotic principles than other Protestant churches. Their public teachers now enjoy an unbounded liberty of dissenting from the decisions of those symbols of creeds which were once deemed almost infallible rules of faith and practice, and of declaring their dissent in the manner they judge most expedient.

The capital articles which Luther maintained are as follow:—

1. That the holy Scriptures are the only source whence we are to draw our religious sentiments, whether they relate to faith or practice. (See 2 Tim. 3:15—17. Prov. 1: 9. Isa. 8:20. Luke 1:4. John 5:39; 20:31. 1 Cor 4:6, &c.)

2. That justification is the effect of faith, exclusive of good works, and that faith ought to produce good works, purely in obedience to God, and not in order to our justification. (See Gal. 2:21.)

3. That no man is able to make satisfaction for his sins. (See Luke 17:10.)

In consequence of these leading articles, Luther rejected tradition, purgatory, penance, auricular confession, masses, invocation of saints, monastic vows, and other doctrines of the church of Rome.

The external affairs of the Lutheran church are directed by three judicatories, viz., a vestry of the congregation, a district or special conference, and a general synod. The synod is composed of ministers, and an equal number of laymen, chosen as deputies by the vestries of their respective congregations. From this synod there is no appeal.

The ministerium is composed of ministers only, and regulates the internal or spiritual concerns of the church, such as examining, licensing, and ordaining ministers, judging in controversies about doctrine, &c. The synod and ministerium meet annually.

Confession and absolution, in a very simple form, are practised by the American Lutherans; also confirmation, by which baptismal vows are ratified, and the subjects become communicants. Their liturgies are simple and impressive, and the clergy are permitted to use extempore prayer. See *Statistics of Churches.*

# CALVINISTS.

This denomination of Christians, of the Congregational order, are chiefly descendants of the English Puritans, who founded most of the early settlements in New England. They derive their name from John Calvin, an eminent reformer.

The Calvinists are divided into three parties, — *High*, *Strict*, and *Moderate*. The *High* Calvinists favor the Hopkinsian system. The *Moderate* Calvinists embrace the leading features of Calvin's doctrine, but object to some parts, particularly to his views of the doctrines of predestination, and the extent of the design of Christ's death. While they hold to the election of grace, they do not believe that God has reprobated any of his creatures. They believe that the atonement is, in its nature, general, but in its application, particular; and that free salvation is to be preached to sinners indiscriminately. The doctrines of the *Strict* Calvinists are those of Calvin himself, as established at the synod of Dort, A. D. 1618, and are as follow, viz.: —

1. They maintain that God hath chosen a certain number of the fallen race of Adam in Christ, before the foundation of the world, unto eternal glory, according to his immutable purpose, and of his free grace and love, without the least foresight of faith, good works, or any conditions performed by the creature; and that the rest of mankind he was pleased to pass by, and ordain to dishonor and wrath, for their sins, to the praise of his vindictive justice. (See Prov. 16 : 4. Rom. 9 : from ver. 11 to end of chap.; 8 : 30. Eph. 1 : 4. Acts 13 : 48.)

2. They maintain that, though the death of Christ be a most perfect sacrifice, and satisfaction for sins, of infinite value, abundantly sufficient to expiate the sins of the whole world, — and though, on this ground, the gospel is to be

preached to all mankind indiscriminately, yet it was the wil of God that Christ, by the blood of the cross, should efficaciously redeem all those, and those only, who were from eternity elected to salvation, and given to him by the Father. (See Ps. 33 : 11. John 6 : 37; 10 : 11; 17 : 9.)

3. They maintain that mankind are totally depraved, in consequence of the fall of the first man, who being their public head, his sin involved the corruption of all his posterity, and which corruption extends over the whole soul, and renders it unable to turn to God, or to do any thing truly good, and exposes it to his righteous displeasure, both in this world and that which is to come. (See Gen. 8 : 21. Ps. 14 : 2, 3. Rom. 3 : 10, 11, 12, &c.; 4 : 14; 5 : 19. Gal. 3 : 10. 2 Cor. 3 : 6, 7.)

4. They maintain that all whom God hath predestinated unto life, he is pleased, in his appointed time, effectually to call, by his word and Spirit, out of that state of sin and death, in which they are by nature, to grace and salvation by Jesus Christ. (See Eph. 1 : 19; 2 : 1, 5. Phil. 2 : 13. Rom. 3 . 27. 1 Cor. 1 : 31. Titus 3 : 5.)

5. Lastly, they maintain that those whom God has effectually called, and sanctified by his Spirit, shall never finally fall from a state of grace. They admit that true believers may fall partially, and would fall totally and finally, but for the mercy and faithfulness of God, who keepeth the feet of his saints; also, that he who bestoweth the grace of perseverance, bestoweth it by means of reading and hearing the word, meditation, exhortations, threatenings, and promises; but that none of these things imply the possibility of a believer's falling from a state of justification. (See Isa. 53 : 4, 5, 6; 54 : 10. Jer. 32 : 38, 40. Rom. 8 : 38, 39. John 4 : 14; 6 : 39; 10 : 28; 11 : 26. James 1 : 17. 1 Pet. 2 : 25.) See *Orthodox Creeds*, and *Hopkinsians.*

## HOPKINSIANS.

This denomination of Christians derives its name from Samuel Hopkins, D. D., formerly pastor of the first Congregational church in Newport, R. I.

The following is a summary of the distinguishing tenets of the Hopkinsians, together with a few of the reasons they bring forward in support of their sentiments: —

"1. That all true virtue, or real holiness, consists in disinterested benevolence. The object of benevolence is universal being, including God and all intelligent creatures. It wishes and seeks the good of every individual, so far as is consistent with the greatest good of the whole, which is comprised in the glory of God and the perfection and happiness of his kingdom. The law of God is the standard of all moral rectitude or holiness. This is reduced into love to God, and our neighbor as ourselves; and universal good-will comprehends all the love to God, our neighbor, and ourselves, required in the divine law, and, therefore, must be the whole of holy obedience. Let any serious person think what are the particular branches of true piety; when he has viewed each one by itself, he will find that disinterested friendly affection is its distinguishing characteristic. For instance, all the holiness in pious fear, which distinguishes it from the fear of the wicked, consists in love. Again, holy gratitude is nothing but good-will to God and our neighbor, — in which we ourselves are included, — and correspondent affection, excited by a view of the good-will and kindness of God. Universal good-will also implies the whole of the duty we owe to our neighbor; for justice, truth, and faithfulness, are comprised in universal benevolence; so are temperance and chastity. For an undue indulgence of our appetites and passions is contrary to benevolence, as tending to hurt ourselves or others, and so, opposite to the general good, and the divine command, in which all the crime of such indul gence consists. In short, all virtue is nothing but benevolence acted out in its proper nature and perfection; or love to God and our neighbor, made perfect in all its genuine exercises and expressions.

"2. That all sin consists in selfishness. By this is meant an interested, selfish affection, by which a person sets himself up as supreme, and the only object of regard; and nothing is good or lovely in his view, unless suited to promote his own private interest. This self-love is, in its whole nature, and every degree of it, enmity against God; it is not subject to the law of God, and is the only affection that can oppose it. It is the foundation of all spiritual blindness, and, therefore, the source of all the open idolatry in the heathen world, and false religion under the light of the gospel: all this is agreeable to that self-love which opposes God's true character. Under the influence of this principle, men depart from truth, it being itself the greatest practical lie in nature, as it sets up that which is comparatively nothing above universal existence. Self-love is the source of all profaneness and impiety in the world, and of all pride and ambition among men, which is nothing but selfishness, acted out in this particular way. This is the foundation of all covetousness and sensuality, as it blinds people's eyes, contracts their hearts, and sinks them down, so that they look upon earthly enjoyments as the greatest good. This is the source of all falsehood, injustice, and oppression, as it excites mankind by undue methods to invade the property of others. Self-love produces all the violent passions — envy, wrath, clamor, and evil speaking; and every thing contrary to the divine law is briefly comprehended in this fruitful source of all iniquity — self-love.

"3. That there are no promises of regenerating grace made to the doings of the unregenerate. For, as far as men act from self-love, they act from a bad end; for those who have no true love to God, really do no duty when they attend on the externals of religion. And as the unregenerate act from a selfish principle, they do nothing which is commanded; their impenitent doings are wholly opposed to repentance and conversion, therefore not implied in the command to repent, &c.: so far from this, they are altogether disobedient to the command. Hence it appears that there are no promises of salvation to the doings of the unregenerate.

"4. That the impotency of sinners, with respect to believing in Christ, is not natural, but moral; for it is a plain dictate of common sense, that natural impossibility excludes all blame. But an unwilling mind is universally considered as a crime, and not as an excuse, and is the very thing wherein our wickedness consists. That the impotence of the sinner is owing to a disaffection of heart, is evident from the promises of the gospel. When any object of good is proposed and promised to us upon asking, it clearly evinces that there can be no impotence in us, with respect to obtaining it, besides the disapprobation of the will; and that inability which consists in disinclination, never renders any thing improperly the subject of precept or command.

"5. That, in order to faith in Christ, a sinner must approve, in his heart, of the divine conduct, even though God should cast him off forever; which, however, never implies love of misery, nor hatred of happiness. For if the law is good, death is due to those who have broken it. The Judge of all the earth cannot but do right. It would bring everlasting reproach upon his government to spare us, considered merely as in ourselves. When this is felt in our hearts, and not till then, we shall be prepared to look to the free grace of God, through the redemption which is in Christ, and to exercise faith in his blood, 'who is set forth to be a propitiation to declare God's righteousness, that he might be just, and yet be the justifier of him who believeth in Jesus.'

"6. That the infinitely wise and holy God has exerted his omnipotent power in such a manner as he purposed should be followed with the existence and entrance of moral evil into the system. For it must be admitted on all hands, that God has a perfect knowledge, foresight, and view of all possible existences and events. If that system and scene of operation, in which moral evil should never have existed, were actually preferred in the divine mind, certainly the Deity is infinitely disappointed in the issue of his own operations. Nothing can be more dishonorable to God than to imagine that the system which is actually formed by the divine hand, and which was made for his pleasure and glory, is yet not the fruit of wise contrivance and design.

"7. That the introduction of sin is, upon the whole, for the general good. For the wisdom and power of the Deity are displayed in carrying on designs of the greatest good; and the existence of moral evil has, undoubtedly, occasioned a more full, perfect, and glorious discovery of the infinite perfections of the divine nature, than could otherwise have been made to the view of creatures. If the extensive manifestations of the pure and holy nature of God, and his infinite aversion to sin, and all his inherent perfections, in their genuine fruits and effects, is either itself the greatest good, or necessarily contains it, it must necessarily follow that the introduction of sin is for the greatest good.

"8. That repentance is before faith in Christ. By this is not intended, that repentance is before a speculative belief of the being and perfections of God, and of the person and character of Christ; but only that true repentance is previous to a saving faith in Christ, in which the believer is united to Christ, and entitled to the benefits of his mediation and atonement. That repentance is before faith in this sense, appears from several considerations. 1. As repentance and faith respect different objects, so they are distinct exercises of the heart; and therefore one not only may, but must, be prior to the other. 2. There may be genuine repentance of sin without faith in Christ, but there cannot be true faith in Christ without repentance of sin; and since repentance is necessary in order to faith in Christ, it must necessarily be prior to faith in Christ. 3. John the Baptist, Christ, and his apostles, taught that repentance is before faith. John cried, 'Repent, for the kingdom of heaven is at hand;' intimating that true repentance was necessary in order to embrace the gospel of the kingdom. Christ commanded, 'Repent ye, and believe the gospel.' And Paul preached 'repentance toward God, and faith toward our Lord Jesus Christ.'

"9. That, though men became sinners by Adam, according to a divine constitution, yet they have, and are accountable for, no sins but personal; for, 1. Adam's act, in eating the forbidden fruit, was not the *act* of his posterity; therefore they did not sin at the same time he did. 2. The sinfulness of that act could not be *transferred* to them afterwards, because the sinfulness of an act can no more be transferred from one person to another than an act itself. 3. Therefore Adam's act, in eating the forbidden fruit, was not the *cause*, but only the *occasion*, of his posterity's being sinners. God was pleased to make a constitution, that, if Adam remained holy through his state of trial, his posterity should, in consequence, be holy also; but if he sinned, his posterity should, in consequence, be sinners likewise. Adam sinned, and now God brings his posterity into the world sinners. *By* Adam's sin we are become sinners, not *for* it his sin being only the *occasion*, not the *cause*, of our committing sins.

"10. That, though believers are justified *through* Christ's righteousness, yet his righteousness is not *transferred* to them. For, 1. Personal righteousness can no more be transferred from one person to another, than personal sin. 2. If Christ's personal righteousness were transferred to believers, they would be as perfectly holy as Christ, and so stand in no need of forgiveness. 3. But believers are not conscious of having Christ's personal righteousness, but feel and bewail much indwelling sin and corruption. 4. The Scripture represents believers as receiving only the *benefits* of Christ's righteousness in justification, or their being pardoned and accepted for Christ's righteousness' sake; and this is the proper Scripture notion of imputation. Jonathan's righteousness was imputed to Mephibosheth when David showed kindness to him for his father Jonathan's sake."

The Hopkinsians warmly contend for the doctrine of the divine decrees, that of particular election, total depravity, the special influences of the Spirit of God in regeneration, justification by faith alone, the final perseverance of the saints, and the consistency between entire freedom and absolute dependence, and, therefore, claim it as their just due, since the world will make distinctions, to be called HOPKINSIAN CALVINISTS.

The statistics of this denomination are included with those of the *Calvinists*, near the close of this volume.

## ARIANS.

THE followers of Arius, a presbyter of the church of Alexandria, about A. D. 315, who held that the Son of God was totally and essentially distinct from the Father; that he was the first and noblest of those beings whom God had created, the instrument by whose subordinate operation he formed the universe, and, therefore, inferior to the Father, both in nature and dignity; also, that the Holy Ghost was not God, but created by the power of the Son. The Arians owned that the Son was the Word, but denied that Word to have been eternal. They held that Christ had nothing of man in him but the flesh, to which the Word was joined, which was the same as the soul in us.

In modern times, the term *Arian* is indiscriminately applied to those who consider Jesus simply subordinate to the Father. Some of them believe Christ to have been the creator of the world; but they all maintain that he existed previously to his incarnation, though, in his preëxistent state, they assign him different degrees of dignity.

(See Matt. 4:10; 19:17; 27:46. Mark 5:7; 13:32. John 4:23; 14:28; 20:17. Acts 4:24. 1 Cor. 1:4; 11 3; 15:24. Eph. 1.17; 4:6. Phil. 1:3, 4, &c.)

## SOCINIANS.

A SECT so called from Faustus Socinus, who died in Poland, in 1604. There were two who bore the name of Socinus, — uncle and nephew, — and both disseminated the same doctrine; but it is the nephew who is generally considered as the founder of this sect. They maintain that Jesus Christ was a mere man, who had no existence before he was conceived by the Virgin Mary; that the Holy Ghost is no distinct person; but that the Father is truly and properly God. They own that the name of God is given, in the holy Scriptures, to Jesus Christ, but contend that it is only a deputed title, which, however, invests him with a great authority over all created beings. They deny the doctrines of satisfaction and imputed righteousness, and say that Christ only preached the truth to mankind, set before them, in himself, an example of heroic virtue, and sealed his doctrines with his blood. Original sin, and absolute predestination, they esteem scholastic chimeras. Some of them likewise maintain the sleep of the soul, which, they say, becomes insensible at death, and is raised again, with the body, at the resurrection, when the good shall be established in the possession of eternal felicity, while the wicked shall be consigned to a fire that will not torment them eternally, but for a certain duration, proportioned to their demerits. (See Acts 2:22; 17:31. 1 Tim. 2:5.)

## HUMANITARIANS.

THE Humanitarians believe in the simple humanity of Christ, or that he was nothing more than a mere man, born according to the usual course of nature, and who lived and died according to the ordinary circumstances of mankind.

## SECTARIANS.

This term is used among Christians to denote those who form separate communions, and do not associate with one another in religious worship and ceremonies. Thus we call Papists, Lutherans, Calvinists, different sects, not so much on account of their differences in opinion, as because they have established to themselves different fraternities, to which, in what regards public worship, they confine themselves; the several denominations above mentioned having no intercommunity with one another in sacred matters. High, Strict, and Moderate Calvinists, High Church and Low Church, we call only parties, because they have not formed separate communions. Great and known differences in opinion, when followed by no external breach in the society, are not considered constituting distinct sects, though their differences in opinion may give rise to mutual aversion.

The Jewish, Christian, Mahometan, and Pagan world is divided into an almost innumerable variety of sects, each claiming to themselves the title of orthodox, and each charging their opponents with heresy.

Where perfect religious liberty prevails, as in the United States, and where emigrants from all quarters of the globe resort in great numbers, it is not surprising that most of the Christian sects in foreign countries, with some of native origin, should be found in this part of the American continent.

## CHURCH GOVERNMENT.

There are three modes of church government, viz., the *Episcopalian*, from the Latin word *episcopus*, signifying *bishop;* the *Presbyterian*, from the Greek word *presbu-*

*teros*, signifying *senior*, *elder*, or *presbyter;* and the Congregational or Independent mode. Under one of these forms, or by a mixture of their several peculiarities, every church in the Christian world is governed. The Episcopal form is the most extensive, as it embraces the Catholic, Greek, English, Methodist, and Moravian churches.

Episcopalians have three orders in the ministry, viz., bishops, priests, and deacons; they all have liturgies, longer or shorter, which they either statedly or occasionally use. All Episcopalians believe in the existence and the necessity of an apostolic succession of bishops, by whom alone regular and valid ordinations can be performed.

The Presbyterians believe that the authority of their ministers to preach the gospel and to administer the sacraments is derived from the Holy Ghost, by the imposition of the hands of the presbytery. They affirm, however, that there is no order in the church, as established by Christ and his apostles, superior to that of presbyters; that all ministers, being ambassadors of Christ, are equal by their commission; that *presbyter* and *bishop*, though different words, are of the same import; and that prelacy was gradually established upon the primitive practice of making the *moderator*, or speaker of the presbytery, a permanent officer.

The Congregationalists, or Independents, are so called from their maintaining that each congregation of Christians, which meets in one house for public worship, is a complete church, has sufficient power to act and perform every thing relating to religious government within itself, and is in no respect subject or accountable to other churches.

Independents, or Congregationalists, generally ordain their ministers by a council of ministers called for the purpose: but still they hold that the essence of ordination lies in the voluntary choice and call of the people, and that public ordination is no other than a declaration of that call.

## PRESBYTERIANS.

The first settlers of New England were driven away from Old England, in pursuit of religious liberty. They were required to conform to the established Protestant Episcopal church, in all her articles of belief, and modes of worship and discipline: their consciences forbade such conformity: their ministers were displaced: their property was tithed for the support of an ecclesiastical prelacy, which they renounced; and the only relief which they could find, was in abandoning their country for the new world.

Most of the first settlers of New England were Congregationalists, and established the government of individuals by the male communicating members of the churches to which they belonged, and of congregations by sister congregations, met by representation in ecclesiastical councils. A part of the ministers and people of Connecticut, at a very early period of her history, were Presbyterians in their principles of church government. Being intermixed, however, with Congregational brethren, instead of establishing presbyteries in due form, they united with their fellow-Christians in adopting, in 1708, the Saybrook Platform, according to which the churches and pastors are consociated, so as virtually to be under Presbyterian government, under another name.

The first Presbyterian churches duly organized in the United States, were the first Presbyterian church in Philadelphia, and the church at Snow Hill, in Maryland.

The first presbytery in the United States was formed about 1704, by the voluntary association of several ministers, who had received Presbyterian orders in Europe, and who agreed to govern themselves agreeably to the Westminster Confession of Faith, Form of Government, Book of Discipline, and Directory for Worship. (See *Andover Orthodox Creed.*)

The reason why the Presbyterians first settled in Pennsylvania, Maryland, and New Jersey, was undoubtedly this—

that in these places they found toleration, and equal religious rights, while the Episcopacy was established by law in Virginia, Congregationalism in New England, and the Reformed Dutch church, with Episcopacy, in New York.

The doctrines of the Presbyterian church are Calvinistic; and the only fundamental principle which distinguishes it from other Protestant churches is this — that God has authorized the government of his church by presbyters, or elders, who are chosen by the people, and ordained to office by predecessors in office, in virtue of the commission which Christ gave his apostles as ministers in the kingdom of God; and that, among all presbyters, there is an official parity, whatever disparity may exist in their talents or official employments.

All the different congregations, under the care of the general assembly, are considered as the one Presbyterian church in the United States, meeting, for the sake of convenience and edification, in their several places of worship. Each particular congregation of baptized people, associated for godly living, and the worship of Almighty God, may become a Presbyterian church, by electing one or more elders, agreeably to the form prescribed in the book styled the Constitution of the Presbyterian Church, and having them ordained and installed as their session.

They judge that to presbyteries the Lord Jesus has committed the spiritual government of each particular congregation, and not to the whole body of the communicants; and on this point they are distinguished from Independents and Congregationalists. If all were governors, they should not be able to distinguish the overseers or bishops from all the male and female communicants; nor could they apply the command, "Obey them that have the rule over you, and submit yourselves; for they watch for your souls, as they that must give account." (Heb. 13 : 17.) If all are rulers in the church who are communicants, they are at a loss for the meaning of the exhortation, "We beseech you, brethren, to know them that labor among you, *and are over you in the*

*Lord*, and admonish you; and to esteem them very highly in love for their work's sake"

If an aggrieved brother should tell the story of his wrongs to each individual communicant, he would not thereby tell it to the church judicially, so that cognizance could be taken of the affair. It is to the church, acting by her proper organs, and to her overseers, met as a judicatory, that he must bring his charge, if he would have discipline exercised in such a way as God empowered his church to exercise it.

The general assembly is the highest judicatory in the Presbyterian church, and is constituted by an equal number of teaching and ruling elders, elected by each presbytery annually, and specially commissioned to deliberate, vote, and determine, in all matters which may come before that body. Each presbytery may send one bishop and one ruling elder to the assembly: each presbytery, having more than twelve ministers, may send two ministers and two ruling elders, and so, in the same proportion, for every twelve ministerial members.

Every Presbyterian church elects its own pastor; but, to secure the whole church against insufficient, erroneous, or immoral men, it is provided that no church shall prosecute any call, without first obtaining leave from the presbytery under whose care that church may be; and that no licentiate, or bishop, shall receive any call, but through the hands of his own presbytery.

Any member of the Presbyterian church may be the subject of its discipline; and every member, if he judges himself injured by any portion of the church, may, by appeal, or complaint, carry his cause up from the church session to the presbytery, from the presbytery to the synod, and from the synod to the general assembly, so as to obtain the decision of the whole church, met by representation in this high judicatory.

Evangelical ministers of the gospel, of all denominations, are permitted, on the invitation of a pastor, or of the session of a vacant church, to preach in their pulpits; and any person known properly, or made known to a pastor or session, as a communicant in good, regular standing, in any truly Christian denomination of people, is, in most of their churches, affectionately invited to occasional communion. They wish to have Christian fellowship with all the redeemed of the Lord, who have been renewed by his Spirit; but, in ecclesiastical government and discipline, they ask and expect the coöperation of none but Presbyterians. See *Statistics*.

## CUMBERLAND PRESBYTERIANS.

In the year 1800, a very great revival of religion took place within the bounds of the synod of Kentucky, in consequence of which, a greater number of new congregations were formed than it was possible to supply with regularly-educated ministers. To remedy this evil, it was resolved to license men to preach who were apt to teach, and sound in the faith, though they had not gone through any course of classical study. This took place at the Transylvania presbytery; but, as many of its members were dissatisfied with the proposed innovation, an appeal was made to the synod, which appointed a commission to examine into the circumstances of the case, the result of whose report was, a prohibition of the labors of uneducated ministers, which led the opposite party to form themselves into an independent presbytery, which took its name from the district of Cumberland, in which it was constituted.

As to the doctrinal views, they occupy a kind of middle ground between Calvinists and Arminians. They reject the doctrine of eternal reprobation, and hold the universality of redemption, and that the Spirit of God operates on the world, or as coëxtensively as Christ has made the atonement, in such a manner as to leave all men inexcusable.

The Cumberland Presbyterians have about 550 churches and ministers, and about 70,000 members. They have a college at Cumberland, Ky.

## EPISCOPALIANS.

THAT form of Church polity, in which the ministry is divided into the three orders of Bishops, Priests, and Deacons, each having powers and duties, distinct from the others, the Bishops being superior to the Priests and Deacons, and the immediate source of all their authority, is called EPISCOPACY, and those who adhere to this polity, are called EPISCOPALIANS.

It is believed, by Episcopalians, that the Savior, when upon earth, established a Church, or Society, of which He was the Ruler and Head, and with which He promised to be, till the end of the world. They believe, that, during the forty days in which He remained upon earth, after His resurrection, "speaking" to His disciples "of the things pertaining to the kingdom of God," He gave them such directions for the government and management of this Society, or Church, as were necessary; which directions, they implicitly followed: and that, from their subsequent practice, these directions of the Savior, whatever they may have been, are to be ascertained.

"That it was the design of our blessed Redeemer to continue a ministry in the Church, after His ascension, is a truth, for which we ask no better proof, than that furnished by the narratives of the Evangelists, and the practice of the Apostles. If, then, a ministry, divinely authorized, was to exist, it is equally evident, that it would assume some definite form. It would consist, either of a single grade of office, in which every person ordained would have an equal share in its functions and prerogatives; or, of two, three, or more grades, distinguished from each other by degrees of authority and peculiarities of duty." There must, also, exist, *somewhere*, the power of transmitting the ministry, by ordination. Among those, who suppose there is but one grade of office, this power is lodged in every minister. By Episcopalians, the power is confined to the highest order of the ministry, — the Bishops It is evident, that the Savior could not have established both these different modes; and therefore both cannot possibly be correct. "To suppose, that He, who is the Fountain of all wisdom, could have been the Author of such inevitable disorder, — a kind of disorder which must ever keep the axe at the root of that *unity* for which He prayed, — is not only an absurdity, but an opinion equally repudiated by all parties." "It is manifest," therefore, "that whatever may prove itself to be THE form of ministry, established and authorized by Jesus Christ, every other must be altogether void of such authority, and based simply on human appointment."

That this Church, or Society, might endure, it must be provided with a well-arranged organization, or form of government, and consist of officers and members. No society can exist, without this; and the powers and duties of the officers should be well defined, and so adjusted, as to promote, in the best manner, the permanent good of the society. That this Society might endure forever, some provision must be made for the renewal of its officers, so that, when any were taken away, by death, their places might be supplied with suitable successors. That the Savior made all necessary provision for these purposes, there can be no doubt; and that the organization which He directed His Apostles to establish, was Episcopal, is easily susceptible of proof.

Throughout the Bible, different orders in the ministry are recognized or referred to. Under the Jewish dispensation, (which, be it remembered, was established by God Himself,) there were the three orders of High Priest, Priests, and Levites. When the Savior was upon earth, He was the visible Head of the Church, — the "Bishop and Shepherd of our souls," — and the Apostles and seventy Disciples were the other two orders. After his ascension, the Apostles became the visible heads of the Church, the lower orders being Bishops, (called also Priests or Presbyters, and Elders,) and Deacons. When the Apostles were called hence, their successors did not assume the name or title of Apostle, but took that of

Bishop, which thenceforth was applied exclusively to the highest order of the ministry, the other two orders being the Presbyters (Priests or Elders) and Deacons. Thus it has continued to the present day.

It is worthy of remark, that "early writers have been careful to record the ecclesiastical genealogy or succession of the Bishops, in several of the principal Churches. Thus, we have catalogues of the Bishops of Jerusalem, Antioch, Rome, &c.; though it does not appear that the Presbyters and Deacons of those Churches were honored with any similar notice." In like manner, catalogues of temporal Rulers are preserved, when the names of officers subordinate to them are suffered to pass into oblivion. It is easy to trace back the line of Bishops, by name, from our own day, up to the Apostles themselves.

There is no ancient writer on ecclesiastical matters, who does not speak of the division of the ministry into different and distinct Orders, and of certain individuals as Bishops of particular Churches; or who mentions, as existing at the same time, and in the same Churches, any other persons by the same name of Bishops.

But, it is to be observed, that it is not only necessary that a Church should preserve the true Order in the Ministry, but also that it retain the true faith. For a true faith and true Order are both necessary to constitute a Church. All the heretical sects of the ancient Church had the Apostolic Ministry; but, when they departed from the true faith, they were excluded from the communion of the Church. "The Arians, the Donatists, the Novatians, &c. &c., were all Episcopal in their Ministry, and in this respect differed in nothing from the Orthodox Catholic Church. Their grand error lay in the want of that union of Order *and* Faith, which are essential to the being of a Church."

An external commission, conveyed by Episcopal consecration or ordination, is considered necessary to constitute a lawful ministry; and it is therefore declared, by the Church, that "no man shall be accounted or taken to be a lawful

Bishop, Priest, or Deacon, in this Church, or suffered to execute any of said functions," unless he has "had Episcopal consecration or ordination;" and the power of ordaining, or setting apart to the ministry, and of laying on hands upon others, is vested in the Bishops.

The *ministry* is of Divine appointment, and consists of three orders, only, — Bishop, Priest, and Deacon. The *government* is of human regulation, and may be modified as circumstances require. Other officers may be appointed, and the manner in which ministers are invested with their jurisdiction may be varied. To use the language of the Episcopal Church in the United States, in the Preface to her Book of Common Prayer, "It is a most invaluable part of that blessed liberty, wherewith Christ hath made us free, that, in His worship, different forms and usages may, without offence, be allowed, provided the substance of the faith be kept entire; and that, in every Church, what cannot be clearly determined to belong to Doctrine, must be referred to Discipline; and therefore, by common consent and authority, may be altered, abridged, enlarged, amended, or otherwise disposed of, as may seem most convenient for the edification of the people, 'according to the various exigencies of times and occasions.' * * * The particular Forms of Divine Worship, and the Rites and Ceremonies appointed to be used therein, being things in their own nature indifferent and alterable, and so acknowledged, it is but reasonable, that, upon weighty and important considerations, according to the various exigencies of times and occasions, such changes and alterations should be made therein, as to those, who are in places of authority should, from time to time, seem either necessary or expedient."

In the Church of England, there are Archbishops, Deans, and various other officers and titles of office; but these are of local authority, and do not interfere with the three Divinely-appointed orders. To use the language of Hooker, "I may securely, therefore, conclude, that there are, at this day, in the Church of England, no other than the same degrees of ecclesiastical orders, namely, Bishops, Priests, and Deacons, which had their beginning from Christ and His blessed Apostles themselves. As for Deans, Prebendaries, Parsons, Vicars, Curates, Archdeacons, and such like names, being not found in the Scriptures, we have been thereby, through some men's errors, thought to allow ecclesiastical degrees not known nor ever heard of in the better ages of former times. All these are in truth but titles of office," admitted "as the state of the Church doth need, degrees of order still remaining the same as they were from the beginning."

Two hundred years ago, Hooker gave the following challenge, which has never yet been accepted: — "We require you to find but one Church upon the face of the whole earth that hath not been ordered by Episcopal regiment since the time that the blessed Apostles were here conversant." And though, says Bishop Doane, departures from it, since the time of which he spoke, have been but too frequent and too great, "Episcopal regiment" is still maintained as Christ's ordinance, for the perpetuation and government of his Church, and is received as such by eleven twelfths of the whole Christian world. For a period of fifteen hundred years after the Apostolic age, ordination by Presbyters was totally unknown, except in a few crooked cases, where the attempt was made, and followed by instant condemnation from the Church, and the declaration that they were utterly null and void. There was no ministry in existence, before the era of the Reformation, but that which had come down direct from the Apostles, that is, the Episcopal. This is admitted by nearly all the opponents of Episcopacy.

The Episcopal Church in the United States, agrees with that of England, in doctrine, discipline, and worship, with some few unessential variations. Their Ritual, or Form of Worship, is the same, except that some few parts have been omitted for the sake of shortening the service, or for other reasons. Changes became necessary in the prayers for Rulers, in consequence of the independence of the United States.

The different Episcopal parishes in each of the United States, (except in some of the newly-settled parts of the

Country, where two or more States are united for this purpose,) are connected by a Constitution, which provides for a convention of the clergy and lay delegates from each parish in the State or Diocese. This Convention is held annually, and regulates the local concerns of its own Diocese, the Bishop of which, is the President of the Convention. The Conventions of the different Dioceses elect Deputies to a General Convention, which is held once in three years Each Diocese may elect four Clergymen and four Laymen, as delegates, who, when assembled in General Convention, form what is called the "House of Clerical and Lay Deputies," each Order from a Diocese having one vote, and the concurrence of both being necessary to every act of the Convention. The Bishops form a separate House, with a right to originate measures for the concurrence of the House of Clerical and Lay Deputies, each House having a negative upon the other, as in the Congress of the United States. The whole Church is governed by Canons, framed by the General Convention. These Canons regulate the mode of elections of Bishops, declare the age and qualifications necessary for obtaining the orders of Deacon or Priest, the studies to be previously pursued, the examinations which each candidate is to undergo, and all other matters of permanent legislation. Deacon's orders cannot be conferred on any person under the age of twenty-one, nor those of Priest before that of twenty-four. A Bishop must be at least thirty years of age.

Prejudices have prevailed against the Episcopal Church, and probably still exist in the minds of some persons, from an impression, that Episcopacy is not congenial with a republican form of government, and the civil institutions of our Country. But, that this is an erroneous opinion, will be evident, to any one who will carefully and impartially examine the subject. It will be seen, from what has been stated above, that its Constitution is founded on the representative principle, and is strikingly analogous to the form of government of the United States. "In the *permanent* official stations of the Bishops and C ergy in her legislative bodies, our own

Church," says Bishop Hobart, "resembles all other religious communities, whose clergy also are permanent legislators. But, in some respects, she is more conformed than they are to the organization of our civil governments. Of these, it is a characteristic, that legislative power is divided between two branches. And it is a peculiar character of our own Church, that her legislative power is thus divided. Again, a single responsible Executive characterizes our civil constitutions The same feature marks our own Church, in the single Episcopal Executive in each Diocese, chosen, in the first instance, by the Clergy and representatives of the Laity. Nor are these the only points in which the Bishop of our Church may feel pleasure in asserting the free and republican constitution of our government; for, in our ecclesiastical judicatories, the representatives of the laity possess strict coordinate authority, — the power of voting as a separate body, and of annulling, by a majority of votes, the acts of the Bishops and Clergy."

The doctrines of the Episcopal Church are contained in the Thirty-nine Articles of Religion, subjoined to this notice. See Book of Homilies, the Canons of the Church, Archbishop Potter's Discourse on Church Government, Hooker's Ecclesiastical Polity, Daubeny's Guide to the Church, Burton's Early English Church, the Church Dictionaries of Rev. Dr Hook and Rev. Mr. Staunton, Bishop Onderdonk's Episcopacy Examined and Reexamined, and other similar works.

## HISTORICAL NOTICE OF THE CHURCH IN THE UNITED STATES.

Though the greater proportion of the early emigrants to this Country were opposed to the form of religious worship established in the Mother Country, some of them were devoted adherents of that establishment, and Episcopal churches existed, of course, in several of the Colonies, at an early period, although, from the opposition made to them by the other emigrants, and from other causes, the number was not so considerable as might have been expected under different circumstances. At the commencement of the Rev olutionary War, there were not more than eighty parochial clergymen North and East of Maryland; and these, with the exception of those in the towns of Boston and Newport, and the cities of New York and Philadelphia, derived the principal part of their support from England, through the "Society for the Propagation of the Gospel in Foreign Parts," an old and venerable Institution, yet in existence, and still zealously engaged in spreading the Gospel to the utmost parts of the earth. In Maryland and Virginia, the members of the Church were much more numerous, than in the other parts of the Country, and the clergy were supported by a legal establishment.

The distance of this from the Mother Country, and the consequent separation of the members of the Church from their parent stock, which rendered them dependent for the ministry upon emigrations from England, or obliged them to send candidates to that Country, for Holy Orders, operated as a serious obstacle to the increase of the Church here. All the clergy of this Country were attached to the diocese of the Bishop of London, who thus became the only bond of union between them; but his authority could not be effectu ally exerted, at such a distance, in those cases where it was most needed; and, for these and other reasons, several efforts were made by the clergy to obtain an American Episcopate. But the jealousy with which such a measure was regarded by other denominations, and the great opposition with which it consequently met, prevented the accomplishment of the design. When, however, the tie, which had thus bound the members of the Church together in one communion, had been severed, by the independence of the United States, it was necessary that some new bond of union should be adopted; and renewed efforts were made to procure an Episcopate.

The clergy of the Church in Connecticut, at a meeting held in March, 1783, elected the Rev. Samuel Seabury, D. D., their Bishop, and sent him to England, with an application to the Archbishop of Canterbury for his consecration to that holy office. The English Bishops were unable to consecrate him, till an Act of Parliament, authorizing them so to do, could be passed; and he then made application to the Bishops of the Church in Scotland, who readily assented to the request, and he was consecrated by them, in Aberdeen, on the 14th of November, 1784. The Prelates, who were thus the instruments of first communicating the Episcopate to this Country, were, the Right Reverend Robert Kilgour, D. D., Bishop of Aberdeen, the Right Reverend Arthur Petrie, D. D., Bishop of Ross and Moray, and the Right Reverend John Skinner, D. D., Coadjutor Bishop of Aberdeen. Bishop Seabury returned to this Country, immediately after his consecration, and commenced his Episcopal duties without delay.

A few clergymen of New York, New Jersey, and Pennsylvania, having held a meeting at Brunswick, N. J., on the 13th and 14th of May, 1784, for the purpose of consulting in what way to renew a Society for the support of widows and children of deceased clergymen, determined to procure a larger meeting on the 5th of the ensuing October, not only for the purpose of completing the object for which they had then assembled, but also to confer and agree on some general principles of a union of the Church throughout the States. At this latter meeting, a plan of ecclesiastical union was agreed upon, with great unanimity; and a recommendation to the several States, to send delegates to a general meeting, at Philadelphia, in September, 1785, was adopted.

At the meeting, in Philadelphia, in September and October, 1785, there were present, deputies from seven of the thirteen States. This Convention framed an Ecclesiastical Constitution, recommended sundry alterations in the Book of Common Prayer, to adapt it to the local circumstances of the Country, now severed from the parent State, and also took some measures towards procuring the Episcopate from England. An Address was forwarded to the English Bishops, through his Excellency John Adams, then Minister to England, and afterwards President of the United States who zealously used his influence to promote the views of the Convention.

Another Convention was held in Philadelphia, in June, 1786, at which, a Letter was read, from the Archbishops and Bishops of England, in answer to the Address forwarded from the preceding Convention; and another Address to the same Right Reverend Prelates, was adopted, to accompany the Ecclesiastical Constitution now finally agreed upon. This Convention then adjourned, to meet again whenever answers should be received from England. The next meeting was held at Wilmington, in Delaware, in October, 1786, at which, Letters from the English Prelates were read, and also an Act of Parliament, authorizing the consecration of Bishops for foreign places. Sundry further amendments and modifications of the Ecclesiastical Constitution, and Book of Common Prayer, were agreed upon, another Address to the English Prelates was adopted, and testimonials signed for three clergymen, who had been elected Bishops by their respective Dioceses. Two of these clergymen proceeded to England, in the course of the next month; and, after some further delays, all difficulties were finally removed, and the Rev. William White, D. D., of Philadelphia, and the Rev. Samuel Provoost, D. D., of New York, having been elected to the Bishoprics of Pennsylvania and New York, were consecrated to their high and holy office, on the fourth of February, A. D. 1787, in the chapel of the Archiepiscopal palace at Lambeth, by the Most Reverend John Moore, D. D., Archbishop of Canterbury, assisted by the Most Reverend William Markham, D. D., Archbishop of York, the Right Reverend Charles Moss, D. D., Bishop of Bath and Wells, and the Right Reverend Charles Hinchliff, D. D., Bishop of Peterborough. The newly-consecrated Bishops returned to America, April 7, 1787, and soon after, began the exercise of their Episcopal functions in their respective dioceses.

Of these three original Bishops of the Church, Bishop Seabury discharged his Episcopal duties between nine and ten years, and died, February 25, 1796. Bishop White continued to be as a patriarch of the Church for many years, his life having been prolonged to the age of 88, and the discharge of his Episcopal functions having continued forty-nine years. He died, July 17, 1836. Bishop Provoost died, September 6, 1815, in the twenty-ninth year of his Episcopate

The first triennial Convention of the Church was held in July and August, 1789, and the sessions of this body continue to be regularly held every three years. Rev. James Madison, D. D., was consecrated Bishop of Virginia, by the Archbishop of Canterbury, September 19, 1790, and died March 6, 1812. Rev. Thomas John Claggett, D. D., of Maryland, was the first Bishop consecrated in the United States, having been elevated to that holy Order by the Right Reverend Bishops Provoost, Seabury, White, and Madison, in New York, September 17, 1792; since which time, thirty-three Bishops have been consecrated, making the whole number, thirty-eight, of whom twenty are now living. For the succession of Bishops, from the first establishment of the Church, to the present day, see *Statistics*.

The last General Convention was held in New York, in October, 1841, at which time, there were present, twenty-one Bishops, and 79 clerical and 57 lay members. The Bishops reported the consecration of 93 churches, the ordination of 355 clergymen, and the confirmation of 14,767 persons, in the years 1838 to 1841. The whole number of clergymen, at the present time, (1842,) is 1114. Other facts of interest, in relation to the Church in this Country, will be found among the *Statistics* of this volume; and for more full information, the reader is referred to "Swords's Pocket Almanack, Churchman's Register, and Ecclesiastical Calendar," a valuable little manual, published annually, and to the "Churchman's Almanack," also published annually; and for historical notices, reference may be made to Bishop White's "Memoirs of the Protestant Episcopal Church," Journals of the General and State Conventions, Hawks's Ecclesiastical History of different States, and other similar works

## ARTICLES OF RELIGION,

*As established by the Bishops, the Clergy, and Laity of the Protestant Episcopal Church in the United States of America, in Convention, on the twelfth Day of September, in the Year of our Lord, one thousand eight hundred and one.*

"ARTICLE I. *Of Faith in the Holy Trinity.*—There is but one living and true God, everlasting, without body, parts, or passions; of infinite power, wisdom, and goodness; the Maker and Preserver of all things, both visible and invisible. And in unity of this Godhead there be three persons, of one substance, power, and eternity; the Father, the Son, and the Holy Ghost.

"ART. II. *Of the Word, or Son of God, which was made very Man.*—The Son, which is the Word of the Father, begotten from everlasting of the Father, the very and eternal God, of one substance with the Father, took man's nature in the womb of the blessed Virgin, of her substance: so that two whole and perfect natures, that is to say, the Godhead and Manhood, were joined together in one person, never to be divided; whereof is one Christ, very God, and very Man; who truly suffered, was crucified, dead, and buried, to reconcile His Father to us, and to be a sacrifice, not only for original guilt, but also for actual sins of men.

"ART. III. *Of the going down of Christ into Hell.*—As Christ died for us, and was buried, so also is it to be believed, that He went down into hell.

"ART. IV. *Of the Resurrection of Christ.*—Christ did truly rise again from death, and took again His body, with flesh, bones, and all things appertaining to the perfection of man's nature, wherewith He ascended into heaven, and there sitteth, until He return to judge all men at the last day.

"ART. V. *Of the Holy Ghost.*—The Holy Ghost, proceeding from the Father and the Son, is of one substance, majesty, and glory, with the Father and the Son, very and eternal God.

"ART. VI. *Of the Sufficiency of the Holy Scriptures for*

*Salvation.* — Holy Scripture containeth all things necessary to salvation; so that whatsoever is not read therein, nor may be proved thereby, is not to be required of any man, that it should be believed as an article of the faith, or be thought requisite or necessary to salvation. In the name of the Holy Scripture we do understand those Canonical Books of the Old and New Testament, of whose authority was never any doubt in the Church.

"*Of the Names and Number of the Canonical Books.* — Genesis, Exodus, Leviticus, Numeri, Deuteronomium, Joshue, Judges, Ruth, The First Book of Samuel, The Second Book of Samuel, The First Book of Kings, The Second Book of Kings, The First Book of Chronicles, The Second Book of Chronicles, The First Book of Esdras, The Second Book of Esdras, The Book of Hester, The Book of Job, The Psalms, The Proverbs, Ecclesiastes or Preacher, Cantica or Songs of Solomon, Four Prophets the greater, Twelve Prophets the less.

"And the other Books (as Hierome saith) the Church doth read for example of life, and instruction of manners, but yet doth it not apply them to establish any doctrine; such are these following:

"The Third Book of Esdras, The Fourth Book of Esdras, The Book of Tobias, The Book of Judith, The Rest of the Book of Hester, The Book of Wisdom, Jesus the Son of Sirach, Baruch the Prophet, The Song of the Three Children, The Story of Susanna, Of Bel and the Dragon, The Prayer of Manasses, The First Book of Maccabees, The Second Book of Maccabees.

"All the Books of the New Testament, as they are commonly received, we do receive, and account them Canonical.

"Art. VII. *Of the Old Testament.* — The Old Testament is not contrary to the New; for both in the Old and New Testament, everlasting life is offered to mankind by Christ, who is the only Mediator between God and man, being both God and Man. Wherefore they are not to be heard, which feign, that the old fathers did look only for transitory promises

Although the law given from God by Moses, as touching ceremonies and rites, do not bind Christian men, nor the civil precepts thereof ought of necessity to be received in any commonwealth; yet, notwithstanding, no Christian man whatsoever is free from the obedience of the commandments which are called Moral.

"ART. VIII. *Of the Creeds.*—The Nicene Creed, and that which is commonly called the Apostles' Creed, ought thoroughly to be received and believed; for they may be proved by most certain warrants of Holy Scripture.

"ART. IX. *Of Original or Birth-Sin.*—Original sin standeth not in the following of Adam, (as the Pelagians do vainly talk,) but it is the fault and corruption of the nature of every man, that naturally is engendered of the offspring of Adam, whereby man is very far gone from original righteousness, and is, of his own nature, inclined to evil, so that the flesh lusteth always contrary to the Spirit; and therefore, in every person born into this world, it deserveth God's wrath and damnation. And this infection of nature doth remain, yea, in them that are regenerated; whereby the lust of the flesh, called in Greek, Φρόνημα σαρκὸς, which some do expound the wisdom, some sensuality, some the affection, some the desire, of the flesh, is not subject to the law of God. And although there is no condemnation for them that believe and are baptized, yet the Apostle doth confess, that concupiscence and lust hath of itself the nature of sin.

"ART. X. *Of Free Will.*—The condition of man, after the fall of Adam, is such, that he cannot turn and prepare himself, by his own natural strength and good works, to faith, and calling upon God; wherefore we have no power to do good works pleasant and acceptable to God, without the grace of God by Christ preventing us, that we may have a good will, and working with us, when we have that good will.

"ART. XI. *Of the Justification of Man.*—We are accounted righteous before God, only for the merit of our Lord and Savior Jesus Christ by faith, and not for our own works or deservings. Wherefore, that we are justified by faith only, is a most wholesome doctrine, and very full of comfort, as more largely is expressed in the Homily of Justification.

"ART. XII. *Of Good Works.* — Albeit that good works, which are the fruits of faith, and follow after justification, cannot put away our sins, and endure the severity of God's judgment; yet are they pleasing and acceptable to God in Christ, and do spring out, necessarily, of a true and lively faith, insomuch that by them a lively faith may be as evidently known, as a tree discerned by the fruit.

"ART. XIII. *Of Works before Justification.* — Works done before the grace of Christ, and the inspiration of his Spirit, are not pleasant to God, forasmuch as they spring not of faith in Jesus Christ, neither do they make men meet to receive grace, or (as the school authors say) deserve grace of congruity; yea, rather, for that they are not done as God hath willed and commanded them to be done, we doubt not but they have the nature of sin.

"ART. XIV. *Of Works of Supererogation.* — Voluntary works, besides over and above God's commandments, which they call works of supererogation, cannot be taught without arrogancy and impiety; for by them men do declare, that they do not only render unto God as much as they are bound to do, but that they do more for His sake than of bounden duty is required; whereas Christ saith plainly, When ye have done all that are commanded to you, say, We are unprofitable servants.

"ART. XV. *Of Christ alone without Sin.* — Christ, in the truth of our nature, was made like unto us in all things, sin only except, from which He was clearly void, both in His flesh and in His spirit. He came to be a Lamb without spot, who, by sacrifice of Himself once made, should take away the sins of the world; and sin (as Saint John saith) was not in Him. But all we the rest (although baptized and born again in Christ) yet offend in many things; and if we say we have no sin, we deceive ourselves, and the truth is not in us.

"ART. XVI. *Of Sin after Baptism.* — Not every deadly

sin willingly committed after baptism, is sin against the Holy Ghost, and unpardonable. Wherefore the grant of repentance is not to be denied to such as fall into sin after baptism. After we have received the Holy Ghost, we may depart from grace given, and fall into sin, and by the grace of God (we may) arise again, and amend our lives. And therefore they are to be condemned, which say, they can no more sin as long as they live here, or deny the place of forgiveness to such as truly repent.

"Art. XVII. *Of Predestination and Election.* — Predestination to life is the everlasting purpose of God, whereby (before the foundations of the world were laid) He hath constantly decreed, by His counsel, secret to us, to deliver from curse and damnation those whom He hath chosen in Christ out of mankind, and to bring them by Christ to everlasting salvation, as vessels made to honor. Wherefore they, which be endued with so excellent a benefit of God, be called according to God's purpose by His Spirit working in due season: they, through grace, obey the calling: they be justified freely: they be made sons of God by adoption: they be made like the image of His only begotten Son Jesus Christ. they walk religiously in good works; and at length, by God's mercy, they attain to everlasting felicity.

"As the godly consideration of predestination, and our election in Christ, is full of sweet, pleasant, and unspeakable comfort to godly persons, and such as feel in themselves the working of the Spirit of Christ, mortifying the works of the flesh and their earthly members, and drawing up their mind to high and heavenly things, as well because it doth greatly establish and confirm their faith of eternal salvation, to be enjoyed through Christ, as because it doth fervently kindle their love towards God; so, for curious and carnal persons, lacking the Spirit of Christ, to have continually before their eyes the sentence of God's predestination, is a most dangerous downfall, whereby the devil doth thrust them either into desperation, or into wretchlessness of most unclean living, no less perilous than desperation.

4*

"Furthermore, we must receive God's promises in such wise as they be generally set forth to us in Holy Scripture and, in our doings, that will of God is to be followed, which we have expressly declared unto us in the Word of God.

"ART. XVIII. *Of obtaining eternal Salvation only by the Name of Christ.* — They also are to be had accursed, that presume to say, That every man shall be saved by the law or sect which he professeth, so that he be diligent to frame his life according to that law, and the light of nature. For Holy Scripture doth set out unto us only the Name of Jesus Christ, whereby men must be saved.

"ART. XIX. *Of the Church.* — The visible Church of Christ is a congregation of faithful men, in the which the pure Word of God is preached, and the sacraments be duly ministered according to Christ's ordinance, in all those things that of necessity are requisite to the same.

"As the Church of Hierusalem, Alexandria, and Antioch, have erred, so also the Church of Rome hath erred, not only in their living and manner of ceremonies, but also in matters of faith.

"ART. XX. *Of the Authority of the Church.* — The Church hath power to decree rites or ceremonies, and authority in controversies of faith; and yet it is not lawful for the Church to ordain any thing that is contrary to God's Word written; neither may it so expound one place of Scripture, that it be repugnant to another. Wherefore, although the Church be a witness and a keeper of Holy Writ, yet, as it ought not to decree any thing against the same, so besides the same ought it not to enforce any thing to be believed for necessity of salvation.

"ART. XXI. *Of the Authority of General Councils.**

"ART. XXII. *Of Purgatory.* — The Romish doctrine concerning purgatory, pardons, worshipping, and adoration, as well of images as of reliques, and also invocation of

* The 21st of the former Articles is omitted, because it is partly of a ocal and civil nature, and is provided for, as to the remaining parts of t, in other Articles.

saints, is a fond thing vainly invented, and grounded upon no warranty of Scripture, but rather repugnant to the Word of God.

"ART. XXIII. *Of Ministering in the Congregation.* — It is not lawful for any man to take upon him the office of public preaching, or ministering the sacraments in the Congregation, before he be lawfully called, and sent to execute the same. And those we ought to judge lawfully called and sent, which be chosen and called to this work by men who have public authority given unto them in the Congregation, to call and send ministers into the Lord's vineyard.

"ART. XXIV. *Of Speaking in the Congregation in such a Tongue as the People understandeth.* — It is a thing plainly repugnant to the Word of God, and the custom of the primitive Church, to have public prayer in the Church, or to minister the sacraments, in a tongue not understanded of the people.

"ART. XXV. *Of the Sacraments.* — Sacraments ordained of Christ, be not only badges or tokens of Christian men's profession; but rather they be certain sure witnesses, and effectual signs of grace, and God's good will toward us, by the which He doth work invisibly in us, and doth not only quicken, but also strengthen and confirm our faith in Him.

"There are two Sacraments ordained of Christ our Lord in the Gospel, that is to say, Baptism, and the Supper of the Lord.

"Those five commonly called sacraments, that is to say, Confirmation, Penance, Orders, Matrimony, and Extreme Unction, are not to be counted for Sacraments of the Gospel, being such as have grown, partly of the corrupt following of the Apostles, partly are states of life allowed by the Scriptures; but yet have not like nature of Sacraments with Baptism and the Lord's Supper, for that they have not any visible sign or ceremony ordained of God.

"The Sacraments were not ordained of Christ to be gazed upon, or to be carried about, but that we should duly use them. And in such only as worthily receive the same, they have a wholesome effect or operation; but they that receive them unworthily purchase to themselves damnation, as Saint Paul saith.

"ART. XXVI. *Of the Unworthiness of the Ministers, which hinders not the Effect of the Sacraments.* — Although in the visible Church, the evil be ever mingled with the good, and sometime the evil have chief authority in the ministration of the Word and Sacraments; yet, forasmuch as they do not the same in their own name, but in Christ's, and do minister by his commission and authority, we may use their ministry, both in hearing the Word of God, and in receiving the Sacraments. Neither is the effect of Christ's ordinance taken away by their wickedness, nor the grace of God's gifts diminished from such as, by faith, and rightly, do receive the Sacraments ministered unto them, which be effectual, because of Christ's institution and promise, although they be ministered by evil men.

"Nevertheless, it appertaineth to the discipline of the Church, that inquiry be made of evil ministers, and that they be accused by those that have knowledge of their offences; and finally, being found guilty, by just judgment, be deposed.

"ART. XXVII. *Of Baptism.* — Baptism is not only a sign of profession, and mark of difference, whereby Christian men are discerned from others that be not christened; but it is also a sign of regeneration, or new birth, whereby, as by an instrument, they that receive Baptism rightly are grafted into the Church: the promises of the forgiveness of sin, and of our adoption to be the sons of God by the Holy Ghost, are visibly signed and sealed: faith is confirmed, and grace increased by virtue of prayer unto God. The Baptism of young children is in any wise to be retained in the Church, as most agreeable with the institution of Christ.

"ART. XXVIII. *Of the Lord's Supper.* — The Supper of the Lord is not only a sign of the love that Christians ought to have among themselves one to another; but rather it is a Sacrament of our redemption by Christ's death; insomuch that, to such as rightly, worthily, and with faith, receive the same, the Bread which we break is a partaking of the body of Christ; and likewise the Cup of Blessing is a partaking of the blood of Christ.

"Transubstantiation (or the change of the substance of bread and wine) in the Supper of the Lord, cannot be proved by Holy Writ; but it is repugnant to the plain words of Scripture, overthrowing the nature of a sacrament, and hath given occasion to many superstitions.

"The body of Christ is given, taken, and eaten in the Supper, only after a heavenly and spiritual manner. And the mean, whereby the body of Christ is received and eaten in the Supper, is faith.

"The Sacrament of the Lord's Supper was not by Christ's ordinance reserved, carried about, lifted up, or worshipped.

"Art. XXIX. *Of the Wicked, which eat not of the Body of Christ in the Use of the Lord's Supper.*—The wicked, and such as be void of a lively faith, although they do carnally and visibly press with their teeth (as Saint Augustine saith) the Sacrament of the body and blood of Christ; yet in no wise are they partakers of Christ; but rather, to their condemnation, do eat and drink the sign or sacrament of so great a thing.

"Art. XXX. *Of Both Kinds.* — The Cup of the Lord is not to be denied to the lay people; for both the parts of the Lord's Sacrament, by Christ's ordinance and commandment, ought to be ministered to all Christian men alike.

"Art. XXXI. *Of the one Oblation of Christ finished upon the Cross.* — The offering of Christ once made, is that perfect redemption, propitiation, and satisfaction for all the sins of the whole world, both original and actual; and there is none other satisfaction for sin, but that alone. Wherefore the sacrifice of masses, in the which it was commonly said, that the Priest did offer Christ for the quick and the dead, to have remission of pain or guilt, were blasphemous fables, and dangerous deceits.

"Art. XXXII. *Of the Marriage of Priests.*—Bishops,

Priests, and Deacons, are not commanded by God's law either to vow the estate of single life, or to abstain from marriage: therefore it is lawful for them, as for all other Christian men, to marry at their own discretion, as they shall judge the same to serve better to godliness.

"Art. XXXIII. *Of excommunicate Persons, how they are to be avoided.* — That person which, by open denunciation of the Church, is rightly cut off from the unity of the Church, and excommunicated, ought to be taken, of the whole multitude of the faithful, as a heathen and publican, until he be openly reconciled by penance, and received into the Church by a judge that hath authority thereunto.

"Art. XXXIV. *Of the Traditions of the Church.* — It is not necessary that traditions and ceremonies be in all places one, or utterly like; for at all times they have been divers, and may be changed according to the diversity of countries, times, and men's manners, so that nothing be ordained against God's Word. Whosoever, through his private judgment, willingly and purposely doth openly break the traditions and ceremonies of the Church, which be not repugnant to the Word of God, and be ordained and approved by common authority, ought to be rebuked openly, (that other may fear to do the like,) as he that offendeth against the common order of the Church, and hurteth the authority of the magistrate, and woundeth the consciences of the weak brethren.

"Every particular or national Church hath authority to ordain, change, and abolish ceremonies or rites of the Church, ordained only by man's authority, so that all things be done to edifying.

"Art. XXXV. *Of Homilies.* — The second Book of Homilies, the several titles whereof we have joined, under this article, doth contain a godly and wholesome doctrine, and necessary for these times, as doth the former Book of Homilies, which were set forth in the time of Edward the Sixth; and therefore we judge them to be read in Churches oy the Ministers, diligently and distinctly, that they may be understanded of the people.

"*Of the Names of the Homilies.* — 1. Of the right Use of the Church. 2. Against Peril of Idolatry. 3. Of repairing and keeping clean of Churches. 4. Of Good Works; first of Fasting. 5. Against Gluttony and Drunkenness. 6. Against Excess of Apparel. 7. Of Prayer. 8. Of the Place and Time of Prayer. 9. That Common Prayers and Sacraments ought to be ministered in a known Tongue. 10. Of the reverent Estimation of God's Word. 11. Of Alms-doing. 12. Of the Nativity of Christ. 13. Of the Passion of Christ. 14. Of the Resurrection of Christ. 15. Of the worthy receiving of the Sacrament of the Body and Blood of Christ. 16. Of the Gifts of the Holy Ghost. 17. For the Rogation-Days. 18. Of the State of Matrimony. 19. Of Repentance. 20. Against Idleness. 21. Against Rebellion.

"[This article is received in this Church, so far as it declares the Books of Homilies to be an explication of Christian doctrine, and instructive in piety and morals. But all references to the constitution and laws of England are considered as inapplicable to the circumstances of this Church, which also suspends the order for the reading of said Homilies in Churches, until a revision of them may be conveniently made, for the clearing of them, as well from obsolete words and phrases, as from the local references.]

"Art. XXXVI. *Of Consecration of Bishops and Ministers.* — The Book of Consecration of Bishops, and Ordering of Priests and Deacons, as set forth by the General Convention of this Church, in 1792, doth contain all things necessary to such consecration and ordering; neither hath it any thing that, of itself, is superstitious and ungodly: and, therefore, whosoever are consecrated or ordered according o said form, we decree all such to be rightly, orderly, and awfully, consecrated and ordered.

"Art. XXXVII. *Of the Power of the Civil Magis-*

*trates.* — The power of the civil magistrate extendeth to all men, as well clergy as laity, in all things temporal; but hath no authority in things purely spiritual. And we hold it to be the duty of all men, who are professors of the Gospel, to pay respectful obedience to the civil authority, regularly and legitimately constituted.

"Art. XXXVIII. *Of Christian Men's Goods which are not common.* — The riches and goods of Christians are not common, as touching the right, title, and possession, of the same, as certain Anabaptists do falsely boast. Notwithstanding, every man ought, of such things as he possesseth, liberally to give alms to the poor, according to his ability.

"Art. XXXIX. *Of a Christian Man's Oath.* — As we confess that vain and rash swearing is forbidden Christian men by our Lord Jesus Christ, and James his Apostle; so we judge that Christian religion doth not prohibit, but that a man may swear when the magistrate requireth, in a cause of faith and charity, so it be done according to the prophet's teaching, in justice, judgment, and truth."

## CAMBRIDGE AND SAYBROOK PLATFORMS.

The Cambridge Platform of church government, and the Confession of Faith of the New England churches, adopted in 1680; the Saybrook Platform, adopted in 1708; and the Heads of Agreement, assented to by the Presbyterians and Congregationalists in England in 1690, — form a volume, and cannot, therefore, be inserted in this work.

The form of church government, however, embraced in those Platforms, is essentially the same as that now in use by the Orthodox Congregationalists at the present day, and the Confession of Faith the same in substance to that we term the "Andover Orthodox Creed."

## MORAVIANS,

OR

## UNITED BRETHREN

A NAME given to the followers of Nicholas Lewis, count of Zinzendorf, who, in the year 1721, settled at Bartholdorf, in Upper Lusatia. There he made proselytes of two or three Moravian families, and, having engaged them to leave their country, received them at Bartholdorf, in Germany. They were directed to build a house in a wood, about half a league from that village, where, in 1722, this people held their first meeting.

This society increased so fast, that, in a few years, they had an orphan-house and other public buildings. An adjacent hill, called the Huth-Berg, gave the colonists occasion to call this dwelling-place Herrnhut, which may be interpreted *the guard* or *protection of the Lord.* Hence this society are sometimes called *Herrnhuters.*

The Moravians avoid discussions respecting the speculative truths of religion, and insist upon individual experience of the practical efficiency of the gospel in producing a real change of sentiment and conduct, as the only essentials in religion. They consider the manifestation of God in Christ as intended to be the most beneficial revelation of the Deity to the human race; and, in consequence, they make the life, merits, acts, words, sufferings, and death, of the Savior the principal theme of their doctrine, while they carefully avoid entering into any theoretical disquisitions on the mysterious essence of the Godhead, simply adhering to the words of Scripture. Admitting the sacred Scriptures as the only source of divine revelation, they nevertheless believe that the Spirit of God continues to lead those who believe in Christ into all further truth, not by revealing new doctrines, but by teaching those who sincerely desire to learn, daily, better to understand and apply the truths which the Scriptures contain. They believe that, to live agreeably to the gospel, it is essential to aim, in all things, to fulfil the will of God Even in their temporal concerns, they endeavor to ascertain the will of God. They do not, indeed, expect some miraculous manifestation of his will, but only endeavor to test the purity of their purposes by the light of the divine word. Nothing of consequence is done by them, as a society, until such an examination has taken place; and, in cases of difficulty, the question is decided by lot, to avoid the undue preponderance of influential men, and in the humble hope that God will guide them right by its decision, where their limited understanding fails them. In former times, the marriages of the members of the society were, in some respects, regarded as a concern of the society, as it was part of their social agreement that none should take place without the approval of the elders; and the elders' consent or refusal was usually determined by lot. But this custom was at length abandoned; and nothing is now requisite to obtain the consent of the elders, but propriety of conduct in the parties. They consider none of their peculiar regulations essential, but all liable to be altered or abandoned, whenever it is found necessary, in order better to attain their great object — the promotion of piety.

What characterizes the Moravians most, and holds them up to the attention of others, is their missionary zeal. In this they are superior to any other body of people in the world. "Their missionaries," as one observes, "are all of them volunteers; for it is an inviolable maxim with them to *persuade* no man to engage in missions. They are all of one mind as to the doctrines they teach, and seldom make an attempt where there are not half a dozen of them in the mission. Their zeal is calm, steady, persevering. They would reform the world, but are careful how they quarrel with it. They carry their point by address, and the insinuations of modesty and mildness, which commend them to all men, and give offence to none. The habits of silence, quietness, and decent reserve, mark their character."

The following is a sketch of the mode of life of the Mora

vians, or United Brethren, where they form separate communities, which, however, is not always the case; for, in many instances, societies belonging to the Unity are situated in larger and smaller cities and towns, intermingled with the rest of the inhabitants, in which cases their peculiar regulations are, of course, out of the question. In their separate communities, they do not allow the permanent residence of any persons as householders who are not members in full communion, and who have not signed the written instrument of brotherly agreement, upon which their constitution and discipline rest; but they freely admit of the temporary residence among them of such other persons as are willing to conform to their external regulations. According to these, all kinds of amusements considered dangerous to strict morality are forbidden, as balls, dancing, plays, gambling of any kind, and all promiscuous assemblies of youth of both sexes. These, however, are not debarred from forming, under proper advice and parental superintendence, that acquaintance which their future matrimonial connections may require. In the communities on the European continent, whither, to this day, numbers of young persons of both sexes resort, in order to become members of the society from motives of piety and a desire to prepare themselves to become missionaries among the heathen, and where, moreover, the difficulties of supporting a family greatly limit the number of marriages, a stricter attention to this point becomes necessary. On this account, the unmarried men and boys, not belonging to the families of the community, reside together, under the care of an elder of their own class, in a building called the *single brethren's house*, where usually divers trades and manufactures are carried on, for the benefit of the house or of the community, and which, at the same time, furnishes a cheap and convenient place for the board and lodging of those who are employed as journeymen, apprentices, or otherwise, in the families constituting the community. Particular daily opportunities of edification are there afforded them; and such a house is the place of resort where the young men and boys of the families spend their leisure time, it being a general rule, that every member of the society shall devote himself to some useful occupation. A similar house, under the guidance of a female superintendent, and under similar regulations, is called the *single sisters' house*, and is the common dwelling-place of all unmarried females, not members of any family, or not employed as servants in the families of the community. Even these regard the sisters' house as their principal place of association at leisure hours. Industrious habits are here inculcated in the same way. In the communities of the United Brethren in America, the facilities of supporting families, and the consequent early marriages, have superseded the necessity of single brethren's houses; but they all have sisters' houses of the above description, which afford a comfortable asylum to aged unmarried females, while they furnish an opportunity of attending to the further education and improvement of the female youth after they have left school. In the larger communities, similar houses afford the same advantages to such widows as desire to live retired, and are called *widows' houses.* The individuals residing in these establishments pay a small rent, by which, and by the sums paid for their board, the expenses of these houses are defrayed, assisted occasionally by the profits on the sale of ornamental needle-work, &c., on which some of the inmates subsist. The aged and needy are supported by the same means. Each division of sex and station just alluded to, viz., widows, single men and youths, single women and girls past the age of childhood, is placed under the special guidance of elders of their own description, whose province it is to assist them with good advice and admonition, and to attend, as much as may be, to the spiritual and temporal welfare of each individual. The children of each sex are under the immediate care of the superintendent of the single choirs, as these divisions are termed. Their instruction in religion, and in all the necessary branches of human knowledge, in good schools, carried on separately for each sex, is under the special superintendence of the stated minister of each community, and of the board of elders Similar special elders are charged to attend to the spiritual welfare of the married people. All these elders, of both sexes, together with the stated minister, to whom the preaching of the gospel is chiefly committed, (although all other elders who may be qualified participate therein,) and with the persons to whom the economical concerns of the community are intrusted, form together the board of elders, in which rests the government of the community, with the concurrence of the committee elected by the inhabitants for all temporal concerns. This committee superintends the observance of all regulations, has charge of the police, and decides differences between individuals. Matters of a general nature are submitted to a meeting of the whole community, consisting either of all male members of age, or of an intermediate body elected by them. Public meetings are held every evening in the week. Some of these are devoted to the reading of the Scriptures, others to the communication of accounts from the missionary stations, and others to the singing of hymns or selected verses. On Sunday mornings, the church litany is publicly read, and sermons are delivered to the congregation, which, in many places, is the case likewise in the afternoon. In the evening, discourses are delivered, in which the texts for that day are explained and brought home to the particular circumstances of the community. Besides these regular means of edification, the festival days of the Christian church, such as Easter, Pentecost, Christmas, &c., are commemorated in a special manner, as well as some days of peculiar interest in the history of the society. A solemn church music constitutes a prominent feature of their means of edification, music in general being a favorite employment of the leisure of many. On particular occasions, and before the congregation meets to partake of the Lord's supper, they assemble expressly to listen to instrumental and vocal music, interspersed with hymns, in which the whole congregation joins, while they partake together of a cup of coffee, tea, or chocolate, and light cakes, in token of fellowship and brotherly union. This solemnity is called a *love-feast*, and is in imitation of the custom of the agapæ in the primitive Christian churches. The Lord's supper is celebrated at stated intervals, generally by all communicant members together, under very solemn but simple rites.

Easter morning is devoted to a solemnity of a peculiar kind. At sunrise, the congregation assembles in the graveyard; a service, accompanied by music, is celebrated, expressive of the joyful hopes of immortality and resurrection, and a solemn commemoration is made of all who have, in the course of the last year, departed this life from among them, and "gone home to the Lord" — an expression they often use to designate death.

Considering the termination of the present life no evil, but the entrance upon an eternal state of bliss to the sincere disciples of Christ, they desire to divest this event of all its terrors. The decease of every individual is announced to the community by solemn music from a band of instruments. Outward appearances of mourning are discountenanced. The whole congregation follows the bier to the graveyard, (which is commonly laid out as a garden,) accompanied by a band, playing the tunes of well-known verses, which express the hopes of eternal life and resurrection; and the corpse is deposited in the simple grave during the funeral service The preservation of the purity of the community is intrusted to the board of elders and its different members, who are to give instruction and admonition to those under their care, and make a discreet use of the established church discipline. In cases of immoral conduct, or flagrant disregard of the regulations of the society, this discipline is resorted to. If expostulations are not successful, offenders are for a time restrained from participating in the holy communion, or called before the committee. For pertinacious bad conduct, or flagrant excesses, the culpable individual is dismissed from the society. The ecclesiastical church officers, generally speaking, are the bishops, — through whom the regular succession of ordination, transmitted to the United Brethren through the ancient church of the Bohemian and Moravian Brethren, is preserved, and who alone are authorized to ordain ministers, but possess no authority in the government of the church, except such as they derive from some other office, being, most frequently, the presidents of some board of elders, — the civil seniors, — to whom, in subordination to the board of elders of the Unity, belongs the management of the external relations of the society, — the presbyters, or ordained stated ministers of the communities, and the deacons. The degree of deacon is the first bestowed upon young ministers and missionaries, by which they are authorized to administer the sacraments. Females, although elders among their own sex, are never ordained; nor have they a vote in the deliberations of the board of elders, which they attend for the sake of information only.

The Moravians that first visited the United States, settled at Savannah, Ga., in 1735.

## TUNKERS.

A DENOMINATION of Seventh-Day Baptists, which took its rise in the year 1724. It was founded by a German, who, weary of the world, retired to an agreeable solitude, within sixty miles of Philadelphia, for the more free exercise of religious contemplation. Curiosity attracted followers, and his simple and engaging manners made them proselytes. They soon settled a little colony, called Ephrata, in allusion to the Hebrews, who used to sing psalms on the border of the River Euphrates. This denomination seem to have obtained their name from their baptizing their new converts by plunging. They are also called *Tumblers,* from the manner in which they perform baptism, which is by putting the person, while kneeling, head first under water, so as to resemble the motion of the body in the action of tumbling. They use the trine immersion, with laying on the hands and prayer, even when the person baptized is in the water. Their habit seems to be peculiar to themselves, consisting of a long tunic or coat, reaching down to their heels, with a sash or girdle round the waist, and a cap or hood hanging from the shoulders. They do not shave the head or beard.

The men and women have separate habitations and distinct governments. For these purposes, they erected two large wooden buildings, one of which is occupied by the brethren, the other by the sisters, of the society; and in each of them there is a banqueting-room, and an apartment for public worship; for the brethren and sisters do not meet together even at their devotions.

They used to live chiefly upon roots and other vegetables, the rules of their society not allowing them flesh, except upon particular occasions, when they hold what they call a love-feast; at which time, the brethren and sisters dine together in a large apartment, and eat mutton, but no other meat. In each of their little cells they have a bench fixed, to serve the purpose of a bed, and a small block of wood for a pillow. They allow of marriages, but consider celibacy as a virtue.

The principal tenet of the Tunkers appears to be this — that future happiness is only to be obtained by penance and outward mortifications in this life, and that, as Jesus Christ, by his meritorious sufferings, became the Redeemer of mankind in general, so each individual of the human race, by a life of abstinence and restraint, may work out his own salvation. Nay, they go so far as to admit of works of supererogation, and declare that a man may do much more than he is in justice or equity obliged to do, and that his superabundant works may, therefore, be applied to the salvation of others.

This denomination deny the eternity of future punishments, and believe that the dead have the gospel preached to them by our Savior, and that the souls of the just are employed to preach the gospel to those who have had no revelation in this life They suppose the Jewish Sabbath, sabbatical year, and year of jubilee, are typical of certain periods after the general judgment, in which the souls of those who are not then admitted into happiness are purified from their corruption. If any, within those smaller periods, are so far humbled as to acknowledge the perfections of God, and to own Christ as their only Savior, they are received to felicity; while those who continue obstinate are reserved in torments, until the grand period, typified by the jubilee, arrives, in which all shall be made happy in the endless fruition of the Deity.

They also deny the imputation of Adam's sin to his posterity. They disclaim violence, even in cases of self-defence, and suffer themselves to be defrauded, or wronged, rather than go to law.

Their church government and discipline are the same with other Baptists, except that every brother is allowed to speak in the congregation; and their best speaker is usually ordained to be the minister. They have deacons and deaconesses from among their ancient widows and exhorters, who are all licensed to use their gifts statedly.

The Tunkers are not so rigid in their dress and manner of life as formerly; still they retain the faith of their fathers, and lead lives of great industry, frugality, and purity.

## MENNONITES,

OR

## HARMLESS CHRISTIANS.

The Mennonites derive their name from Menno Simons, an illustrious reformer. This people came to the United States from Holland, and first settled in Pennsylvania, where a large body of them now reside.

It is a universal maxim of this denomination, that practical piety is the essence of religion, and that the surest mark of the true church is the sanctity of its members. They all unite in pleading for toleration in religion, and debar none from their assemblies who lead pious lives, and own the Scriptures for the word of God. They teach that infants are not the proper subjects of baptism; that ministers of the gospel ought to receive no salary; and that it is not lawful to swear, or wage war, upon any occasion. They also maintain that the terms *person* and *Trinity* are not to be used in speaking of the Father, Son, and Holy Ghost.

The Mennonites meet privately, and every one in the assembly has the liberty to speak, to expound the Scriptures, to pray, and sing.

The Mennonites do not baptize by immersion, though they administer the ordinance to none but adult persons. Their common method is this: The person who is to be baptized, kneels; the minister holds his hands over him, into which the deacon pours water, and through which it runs on the crown of the kneeling person's head; after which follow imposition of hands and prayer.

Mr. Van Beuning, the Dutch ambassador, speaking of these *Harmless Christians*, as they choose to call themselves, says, "The Mennonites are good people, and the most commodious to a state of any in the world; partly, because they do not aspire to places of dignity; partly, because they edify the community by the simplicity of their manners, and application to arts and industry; and partly, because we fear no rebellion from a sect who make it an article of their faith never to bear arms."

## DISCIPLES OF CHRIST;

SOMETIMES CALLED

## CAMPBELLITES, OR REFORMERS

The rise of this society, if we only look back to the drawing of the lines of demarkation between it and other professors, is of recent origin. About the commencement of the present century, the Bible alone, without any human addition in the form of creeds or confessions of faith, began to be preached by many distinguished ministers of different denominations, both in Europe and America.

With various success, and with many of the opinions of the various sects imperceptibly carried with them from the denominations to which they once belonged, did the advocates of the Bible cause plead for the union of Christians of every name, on the broad basis of the apostles' teaching. But it was not until the year 1823, that a restoration of the *original gospel* and *order of things* began to be advocated in a periodical, edited by Alexander Campbell, of Bethany, Virginia, entitled "The Christian Baptist."

He and his father, Thomas Campbell, renounced the Presbyterian system, and were immersed, in the year 1812 They, and the congregations which they had formed, united with the Redstone Baptist association, protesting against all human creeds as bonds of union, and professing subjection to the Bible alone. This union took place in the year 1813. But, in pressing upon the attention of that society and the public the all-sufficiency of the *sacred* Scriptures for every thing necessary to the perfection of Christian character, — whether in the private or social relations of life, in the church, or in the world, — they began to be opposed by a strong creed-party in that association. After some ten years debating and contending for the Bible alone, and the apostles' doctrine, Alexander Campbell, and the church to which he belonged, united with the Mahoning association, in the Western Reserve of Ohio; that association being more favorable to his views of reform.

In his debates on the subject and action of baptism with Mr. Walker, a seceding minister, in the year 1820, and with Mr. M'Calla, a Presbyterian minister of Kentucky, in the year 1823, his views of reformation began to be developed, and were very generally received by the Baptist society, as far as these works were read

But in his "Christian Baptist," which began July 4, 1823

his views of the need of reformation were more fully exposed and, as these gained ground by the pleading of various ministers of the Baptist denomination, a party in opposition began to exert itself, and to oppose the spread of what they were pleased to call heterodoxy. But not till after great numbers began to act upon these principles, was there any attempt towards separation. After the Mahoning association appointed Mr. Walter Scott an evangelist, in the year 1827, and when great numbers began to be immersed into Christ, under his labors, and new churches began to be erected by him and other laborers in the field, did the Baptist associations begin to declare non-fellowship with the brethren of the reformation. Thus by constraint, not of choice, they were obliged to form societies out of those communities that split, upon the ground of adherence to the apostles' doctrine. The distinguishing characteristics of their views and practices are the following: —

They regard all the sects and parties of the Christian world as having, in greater or less degrees, departed from the simplicity of faith and manners of the first Christians, and as forming what the apostle Paul calls "the apostasy." This defection they attribute to the great varieties of speculation and metaphysical dogmatism of the countless creeds, formularies, liturgies, and books of discipline, adopted and inculcated as bonds of union and platforms of communion in all the parties which have sprung from the Lutheran reformation. The effect of these synodical covenants, conventional articles of belief, and rules of ecclesiastical polity, has been the introduction of a new nomenclature, — a human vocabulary of religious words, phrases, and technicalities, which has displaced the style of the living oracles, and affixed to the sacred diction ideas wholly unknown to the apostles of Christ.

To remedy and obviate these aberrations, they propose to ascertain from the holy Scriptures, according to the commonly-received and well-established rules of interpretation, the ideas attached to the leading terms and sentences found in the holy Scriptures, and then to use the words of the Holy Spirit in the apostolic acceptation of them.

By thus expressing the ideas communicated by the Holy Spirit, in the terms and phrases learned from the apostles, and by avoiding the artificial and technical language of scholastic theology, they propose to restore a pure speech to the household of faith; and, by accustoming the family of God to use the language and dialect of the heavenly Father, they expect to promote the sanctification of one another through the truth, and to terminate those discords and debates which have always originated from the words which man's wisdom teaches, and from a reverential regard and esteem for the style of the great masters of polemic divinity; believing that speaking the same things in the same style, is the only certain way to thinking the same things.

They make a very marked difference between faith and opinion; between the testimony of God and the reasonings of men; the words of the Spirit and human inferences. Faith in the testimony of God, and obedience to the commandments of Jesus, are their bond of union, and not an agreement in any abstract views or opinions upon what is written or spoken by divine authority. Hence all the speculations, questions, debates of words, and abstract reasonings, found in human creeds, have no place in their religious fellowship. Regarding Calvinism and Arminianism, Trinitarianism and Unitarianism, and all the opposing theories of religious sectaries, as *extremes* begotten by each other, they cautiously avoid them, as equidistant from the simplicity and practical tendency of the promises and precepts, of the doctrine and facts, of the exhortations and precedents, of the Christian institution.

They look for unity of spirit and the bonds of peace in the practical acknowledgment of one faith, one Lord, one immersion, one hope, one body, one Spirit, one God and Father of all; not in unity of opinions, nor in unity of forms, ceremonies, or modes of worship.

The holy Scriptures of both Testaments they regard as

containing revelations from God, and as all necessary to make the man of God perfect, and accomplished for every good word and work; the New Testament, or the living oracles of Jesus Christ, they understand as containing the Christian religion; the testimonies of Matthew, Mark, Luke, and John, they view as illustrating and proving the great proposition on which our religion rests, viz., *that Jesus of Nazareth is the Messiah, the only-begotten and well-beloved Son of God, and the only Savior of the world;* the Acts of the Apostles as a divinely-authorized narrative of the beginning and progress of the reign or kingdom of Jesus Christ, recording the full development of *the gospel* by the Holy Spirit sent down from heaven, and the procedure of the apostles in setting up the church of Christ on earth; the Epistles as carrying out and applying the doctrine of the apostles to the practice of individuals and congregations, and as developing the tendencies of the gospel in the behavior of its professors; and all as forming a complete standard of Christian faith and morals, adapted to the interval between the ascension of Christ and his return with the kingdom which he has received from God; the Apocalypse, or Revelation of Jesus Christ to John, in Patmos, as a figurative and prospective view of all the fortunes of Christianity, from its date to the return of the Savior.

Every one who sincerely believes the testimony which God gave of Jesus of Nazareth, saying, "*This is my Son, the beloved, in whom I delight,*" or, in other words, believes what the evangelists and apostles have testified concerning him, from his conception to his coronation in heaven as Lord of all, and who is willing to obey him in every thing, they regard as a proper subject of immersion, and no one else. They consider immersion into the name of the Father, Son, and Holy Spirit, after a public, sincere, and intelligent confession of the faith in Jesus, as necessary to admission to the privileges of the kingdom of the Messiah, and as a solemn pledge, on the part of Heaven, of the actual remission of all past sins, and of adoption into the family of God.

The Holy Spirit is promised only to those who believe and obey the Savior. No one is taught to expect the reception of that heavenly Monitor and Comforter, as a resident in his heart, till he obeys the gospel.

Thus, while they proclaim faith and repentance, or faith and a change of heart, as preparatory to immersion, remission, and the Holy Spirit, they say to all penitents, or all those who believe and repent of their sins, as Peter said to the first audience addressed after the Holy Spirit was bestowed, after the glorification of Jesus, "Be immersed, every one of you, in the name of the Lord Jesus, for the remission of sins, and you shall receive the gift of the Holy Spirit." They teach sinners that God commands *all men*, every where, to reform, or to turn to God; that the Holy Spirit strives with them, so to do, by the apostles and prophets; that God beseeches them to be reconciled, through Jesus Christ; and that it is the duty of all men to believe the gospel, and turn to God.

The immersed believers are congregated into societies, according to their propinquity to each other, and taught to meet every first day of the week, in honor and commemoration of the resurrection of Jesus, and to break the loaf, which commemorates the death of the Son of God, to read and hear the living oracles, to teach and admonish one another, to unite in all prayer and praise, to contribute to the necessities of saints, and to perfect holiness in the fear of the Lord.

Every congregation chooses its own overseers and deacons, who preside over and administer the affairs of the congregations; and every church, either from itself, or in coöperation with others, sends out, as opportunity offers, one or more evangelists, or proclaimers of the word, to preach the word, and to immerse those who believe, to gather congregations, and to extend the knowledge of salvation where it is necessary, as far as their means allow. But every church regards these evangelists as its servants; and, therefore, they have no control over any congregation, each congregation being subject to its own choice of presidents or elders, whom they have appointed. Perseverance in all the work of faith, labor of ove, and patience of hope, is inculcated, by all the disciples, as essential to admission into the heavenly kingdom.

Such are the prominent outlines of the faith and practices of those who wish to be known as the Disciples of Christ; but no society among them would agree to make the preceding items either a confession of faith or a standard of practice, but, for the information of those who wish an acquaintance with them, are willing to give, at any time, a reason for their faith, hope, and practice.

---

## FRIENDS, OR QUAKERS.

This class of Christians arose in England about the middle of the 17th century. They were at first called *Seekers*, from their seeking the truth; and afterwards *Quakers*, for directing their enemies to tremble at the word of the Lord. They prefer the more endearing appellation of Friends, which has been transmitted to them by their predecessors.

George Fox was the first who publicly advocated their principles in England, and the celebrated William Penn in America.

The following is a summary of the doctrines and discipline of the society of Friends, published in London in 1800, and sanctioned by the orthodox society of Friends in this country.

Doctrine. — "We agree, with other professors of the Christian name, in the belief of one eternal God, the Creator and Preserver of the universe, and in Jesus Christ, his Son, the Messiah, and Mediator of the new covenant.

"When we speak of the gracious display of the love of God to mankind, in the miraculous conception, birth, life, miracles, death, resurrection, and ascension, of our Savior, we prefer the use of such terms as we find in Scripture; and, contented with that knowledge which Divine Wisdom hath seen meet to reveal, we attempt not to explain those mysteries which remain under the veil; nevertheless, we acknowledge and assert the divinity of Christ, who is the wisdom and power of God unto salvation.

"To Christ, alone, we give the title of the Word of God, and not to the Scriptures; although we highly esteem these sacred writings, in subordination to the Spirit, from which they were given forth; and we hold, with the apostle Paul, that they are able to make wise unto salvation, through faith which is in Christ Jesus.

"We reverence those most excellent precepts which are recorded, in Scripture, to have been delivered by our great Lord; and we firmly believe that they are practicable, and binding on every Christian, and that, in the life to come, every man will be rewarded according to his works. And, further, it is our belief that, in order to enable mankind to put in practice these sacred precepts, many of which are contradictory to the unregenerate will of man, every man, coming into the world, is endued with a measure of the light, grace, or good spirit, of Christ, by which, as it is attended to, he is enabled to distinguish good from evil, and to correct the disorderly passions and corrupt propensities of his nature, which mere reason is altogether insufficient to overcome. For all that belongs to man is fallible, and within the reach of temptation; but this divine grace, which comes by Him who hath overcome the world, is, to those who humbly and sincerely seek it, an all-sufficient and present help in time of need. By this, the snares of the enemy are detected, his allurements avoided, and deliverance is experienced, through faith in its effectual operation; whereby the soul is translated out of the kingdom of darkness, and from under the power of Satan, into the marvellous light and kingdom of the Son of God.

"Being thus persuaded that man, without the Spirit of Christ inwardly revealed, can do nothing to the glory of God, or to effect his own salvation, we think this influence especially necessary to the performance of the highest act of which the human mind is capable, — even the worship of the Father of lights and of spirits, in spirit and in truth; therefore we consider as obstruction to pure worship, all forms which divert the attention of the mind from the secret influence of this unction from the Holy One. Yet, although true worship is not confined to time and place, we think it incumbent on Christians to meet often together, in testimony of their dependence on the heavenly Father, and for a renewal of their spiritual strength: nevertheless, in the performance of worship, we dare not depend, for our acceptance with him, on a formal repetition of the words and experiences of others; but we believe it to be our duty to lay aside the activity of the imagination, and to wait in silence, to have a true sight of our condition bestowed upon us; believing even a single sight, arising from such a sense of our infirmities, and of the need we have of divine help, to be more acceptable to God than any performances, however specious, which originate in the will of man.

"From what has been said respecting worship, it follows that the ministry we approve must have its origin from the same source; for that which is needful for man's own direction, and for his acceptance with God, must be eminently so to enable him to be helpful to others. Accordingly, we believe that the renewed assistance of the light and power of Christ is indispensably necessary for all true ministry, and hat this holy influence is not at our command, or to be procured by study, but is the free gift of God to chosen and devoted servants. Hence arises our testimony against preaching for hire, in contradiction to Christ's positive command, 'Freely ye have received, freely give;' and hence our conscientious refusal to support such ministry by tithes or other means.

"As we dare not encourage any ministry but that which we believe to spring from the influence of the Holy Spirit, so neither dare we attempt to restrain this influence to persons of any condition in life, or to the male sex alone; but, as male and female are one in Christ, we allow such of the female sex as we believe to be endued with a right qualification for the ministry, to exercise their gifts for the genera. edification of the church; and this liberty we esteem a peculiar mark of the gospel dispensation, as foretold by the prophet Joel, and noticed by the apostle Peter.

"There are two ceremonies in use among most professors of the Christian name — water baptism, and what is termed the Lord's supper. The first of these is generally esteemed the essential means of initiation into the church of Christ, and the latter of maintaining communion with him. But, as we have been convinced that nothing short of his redeeming power, inwardly revealed, can set the soul free from the thraldom of sin, by this power alone we believe salvation to be effected. We hold that, as there is one Lord, and one faith, so his baptism is one, in nature and operation; that nothing short of it can make us living members of his mystical body; and that the baptism with water, administered by his forerunner John, belonged, as the latter confessed, to an inferior and decreasing dispensation.

"With respect to the other rite, we believe that communion between Christ and his church is not maintained by that, nor any other external performance, but only by a real participation of his divine nature, through faith; that this is the supper alluded to in Revelation, 'Behold, I stand at the door and knock; if any man hear my voice, and open the door, I will come in to him, and will sup with him, and he with me;' and that, where the substance is attained, it is unnecessary to attend to the shadow, which doth not confer grace, and concerning which, opinions so different, and animosities so violent, have arisen.

"Now, as we thus believe that the grace of God, which comes by Jesus Christ, is alone sufficient for salvation, we can neither admit that it is conferred on a few only, whilst others are left without it, nor, thus asserting its universality, can we limit its operation to a partial cleansing of the soul from sin, even in this life. We entertain worthier notions, both of the power and goodness of our heavenly Father, and believe that he doth vouchsafe to assist the obedient to experience a total surrender of the natural will to the guidance of his pure, unerring Spirit, through whose renewed assistance they are enabled to bring forth fruits unto holiness, and to stand perfect in their present rank.

"There are not many of our tenets more generally known than our testimony against oaths, and against war. With respect to the former of these, we abide literally by Christ's positive injunction, delivered in his Sermon on the Mount, 'Swear not at all.' From the same sacred collection of the most excellent precepts of moral and religious duty, from the example of our Lord himself, and from the correspondent convictions of his Spirit in our hearts, we are confirmed in the belief that wars and fightings are, in their origin and effects, utterly repugnant to the gospel, which still breathes peace and good-will to men. We also are clearly of the judgment, that, if the benevolence of the gospel were generally prevalent in the minds of men, it would effectually prevent them from oppressing, much more enslaving, their brethren, (of whatever color or complexion,) for whom, as for themselves, Christ died; and would even influence their conduct in their treatment of the brute creation, which would no longer groan, the victims of their avarice, or of their false ideas of pleasure.

"Some of our tenets have, in former times, as hath been shown, subjected our friends to much suffering from government, though to the salutary purposes of government our principles are a security. They inculcate submission to the laws in all cases wherein conscience is not violated. But we hold that, as Christ's kingdom is not of this world, it is not the business of the civil magistrate to interfere in matters of religion, but to maintain the external peace and good order of the community. We, therefore, think persecution, even in the smallest degree, unwarrantable. We are careful in requiring our members not to be concerned in illicit trade, nor in any manner to defraud the revenue.

"It is well known that the society, from its first appearance, has disused those names of the months and days, which having been given in honor of the heroes or false gods of the heathen, originated in their flattery or superstition; and the custom of speaking to a single person in the plural number, as having arisen also from motives of adulation. Compliments, superfluity of apparel, and furniture, outward shows of rejoicing and mourning, and the observation of days and times, we esteem to be incompatible with the simplicity and sincerity of a Christian life; and public diversions, gaming, and other vain amusements of the world, we cannot but condemn. They are a waste of that time which is given us for nobler purposes, and divert the attention of the mind from the sober duties of life, and from the reproofs of instruction, by which we are guided to an everlasting inheritance.

"To conclude: Although we have exhibited the several tenets which distinguish our religious society, as objects of our belief, yet we are sensible that a true and living faith is not produced in the mind of man by his own effort, but is the free gift of God in Christ Jesus, nourished and increased by the progressive operation of his Spirit in our hearts, and our proportionate obedience. Therefore, although, for the preservation of the testimonies given us to bear, and for the peace and good order of the society, we deem it necessary that those who are admitted into membership with us should be previously convinced of those doctrines which we esteem essential, yet we require no formal subscription to any articles, either as a condition of membership, or a qualification for the service of the church. We prefer the judging of mer by their fruits, and depending on the aid of Him, who, by his prophet, hath promised to be 'a spirit of judgment to him that sitteth in judgment.' Without this there is a danger of receiving numbers into outward communion, without any addition to that spiritual sheepfold, whereof our blessed Lord declared himself to be both the door and the shepherd; that is, such as know his voice, and follow him in the paths of obedience. (See Heb. 12:24. 1 Cor. 1:24. John 1:1. 2 Pet. 1:21. 2 Tim. 2:15. Matt. 16:27. John 1:9—16, 33. 1 John 2:20, 27. Heb. 10:25. Rom 8:

26. Jer. 23:30—32. Matt. 10:8. Joel 2.28, 29. Acts 2:16, 17. Eph. 4:5. John 3:30. 2 Pet. 1:4. Rev. 3 20. Matt. 5:48. Eph. 4:13. Col. 4:12. Matt. 5:34 39, 44, &c.; 26:52, 53. Luke 22:51. John 18:11. Eph 2:8. John 7:17. Isa. 28:6. John 10:7, 11.)

"Discipline.—The purposes which our discipline hath chiefly in view, are, the relief of the poor; the maintenance of good order; the support of the testimonies which we believe it is our duty to bear to the world; and the help and recovery of such as are overtaken in faults.

"In the practice of discipline, we think it indispensable that the order recommended by Christ himself be invariably observed. 'If thy brother shall trespass against thee, go and tell him his fault between thee and him alone; if he shall hear thee, thou hast gained thy brother; but if he will not hear thee, then take with thee one or two more, that in the mouth of two or three witnesses, every word may be established; and if he shall neglect to hear them, tell it unto the church.'

"To effect the salutary purposes of discipline, meetings were appointed, at an early period of the society, which, from the times of their being held, were called *quarterly meetings*. It was afterward found expedient to divide the districts of those meetings, and to meet more frequently; from whence arose *monthly meetings*, subordinate to those held quarterly. At length, in 1669, a *yearly meeting* was established, to superintend, assist, and provide rules for the whole; previously to which, *general meetings* had been occasionally held.

"A monthly meeting is usually composed of several particular congregations, situated within a convenient distance from each other. Its business is to provide for the subsistence of the poor, and for the education of their offspring; to judge of the sincerity and fitness of persons appearing to be convinced of the religious principles of the society, and desiring to be admitted into membership; to excite due attention to the discharge of religious and moral duty; and to deal with disorderly members. Monthly meetings also grant to such of their members as remove into other monthly meetings, certificates of their membership and conduct, without which they cannot gain membership in such meetings Each monthly meeting is required to appoint certain persons, under the name of *overseers*, who are to take care that the rules of our discipline be put in practice, and, when any case of complaint, or disorderly conduct, comes to their knowledge, to see that private admonition, agreeably to the gospel rule before mentioned, be given, previously to its being laid before the monthly meeting.

"When a case is introduced, it is usual for a small committee to be appointed to visit the offender, to endeavor to convince him of his error, and to induce him to forsake and condemn it. If they succeed, the person is by minute declared to have made satisfaction for the offence; if not, he is disowned as a member of the society.

"In disputes between individuals, it has long been the decided judgment of the society, that its members should not sue each other at law. It therefore enjoins all to end their differences by speedy and impartial arbitration, agreeably to rules laid down. If any refuse to adopt this mode, or, having adopted it, to submit to the award, it is the direction of the yearly meeting that such be disowned.

"To monthly meetings, also, belongs the allowing of marriages; for our society hath always scrupled to acknowledge the exclusive authority of the priests in the solemnization of marriage. Those who intend to marry appear together, and propose their intention to the monthly meeting, and, if not attended by their parents and guardians, produce a written certificate of their consent, signed in the presence of witnesses. The meeting then appoints a committee to inquire whether they be clear of other engagements respecting marriage; and if, at a subsequent meeting, to which the parties also come and declare the continuance of their intention, no objections be reported, they have the meeting's consent to solemnize their intended marriage. This is done in a public meeting for worship, toward the close whereof the parties stand up, and solemnly take each other for husband and wife. A certificate of the proceedings is then publicly read, and signed by the parties, and afterward by the relations and others as witnesses. Of such marriage the monthly meeting keeps a record, as also of the births and burials of its members. A certificate of the date, of the name of the infant, and of its parents, signed by those present at the birth, is the subject of one of these last-mentioned records, and an order for the interment, countersigned by the grave-maker, of the other. The naming of children is without ceremony Burials are also conducted in a simple manner. The body, followed by the relations and friends, is sometimes, previously to interment, carried to a meeting; and at the grave a pause is generally made; on both which occasions it frequently falls out, that one or more friends present have somewhat to express for the edification of those who attend; but no religious rite is considered as an essential part of burial.

"Several monthly meetings compose a quarterly meeting. At the quarterly meeting are produced written answers from the monthly meetings, to certain queries respecting the conduct of their members, and the meetings' care over them. The accounts thus received are digested into one, which is sent also in the form of answers to queries, by representatives, to the yearly meeting. Appeals from the judgment of monthly meetings are brought to the quarterly meetings, whose business also it is to assist in any difficult case, or where remissness appears in the care of the monthly meetings over the individuals who compose them.

"The yearly meeting has the general superintendence of the society in the country in which it is established; and therefore, as the accounts which it receives discover the state of inferior meetings, as particular exigencies require, or as the meeting is impressed with a sense of duty, it gives forth its advice, makes such regulations as appear to be requisite, or excites to the observance of those already made, and sometimes appoints committees to visit those quarterly meet ings which appear to be in need of immediate advice. Appeals from the judgment of quarterly meetings are here finally determined; and a brotherly correspondence, by epistles, is maintained with other yearly meetings.

"In this place it is proper to add that, as we believe women may be rightly called to the work of the ministry, we also think that to them belongs a share in the support of our Christian discipline, and that some parts of it, wherein their own sex is concerned, devolve on them with peculiar propriety; accordingly, they have monthly, quarterly, and yearly meetings of their own sex, held at the same time and in the same place with those of the men, but separately, and without the power of making rules; and it may be remarked that, during the persecutions, which, in the last century, occasioned the imprisonment of so many of the men, the care of the poor often fell on the women, and was by them satisfactorily administered.

"In order that those who are in the situation of ministers may have the tender sympathy and counsel of those of either sex, who, by their experience in the work of religion, are qualified for that service, the monthly meetings are advised to select such, under the denomination of *elders*. These, and ministers approved by their monthly meetings, have meetings peculiar to themselves, called *meetings of ministers and elders*, in which they have an opportunity of exciting each other to a discharge of their several duties, and of extending advice to those who may appear to be weak, without any needless exposure. Such meetings are generally held in the compass of each monthly, quarterly, and yearly meeting. They are conducted by rules prescribed by the yearly meeting, and have no authority to make any alteration or addition to them. The members of them unite with their brethren in the meetings for discipline, and are equally accountable to the latter for their conduct.

"Thus have we given a view of the foundation and establishment of our discipline; by which it will be seen that it is not, as hath been frequently insinuated, merely the work of modern times, but was the early care and concern of our pious predecessors. We cannot better close this short sketch of it, than by observing that, if the exercise of discipline should in some instances appear to press hard upon those, who, neglecting the monitions of divine counsel in their hearts, are also unwilling to be accountable to their brethren, yet, if that great, leading, and indispensable rule, enjoined by our Lord, be observed by those who undertake to be active in it, —'Whatsoever ye would that men should do to you, do ye even so to them,'—it will prevent the censure of the church from falling on any thing but that which really obstructs the progress of truth. Discipline will then promote, in an eminent degree, that love of our neighbor which is the mark of discipleship, and without which a profession of love to God, and to his cause, is a vain pretence. 'He,' said the beloved disciple, 'that loveth not his brother, whom he hath seen, how can he love God, whom he hath not seen? And this commandment have we from him, that he who loveth God, love his brother also.'"

The Friends are divided in sentiment; there are, in fact, two sects, denominated *Orthodox* and *Hicksites*.

Some opinion of Elias Hicks's sentiments, in regard to the Trinity, may be formed by an extract from one of his publications, (Sermons, vol. iv. pp. 288, 289.)

"He that laid down his life, and suffered his body to be crucified by the Jews, without the gates of Jerusalem, is Christ, the only Son of the most high God. But that the *outward person which suffered* was properly the Son of God, we utterly deny. Flesh and blood cannot enter into heaven. By the analogy of reason, spirit cannot beget a material body, because the thing begotten must be of the same nature with its father. Spirit cannot beget any thing but spirit: it cannot beget flesh and blood. '*A body hast thou prepared me*,' said the Son: *then the Son was not the body*, though the body was the Son's."

## SHAKERS,

OR

## THE UNITED SOCIETY OF BELIEVERS.

The editor gives an account of the religious tenets, &c., of this society, in the precise words of his worthy friends and correspondents at Enfield, N. H.: —

"Respected Friend,

"Having received your circular, requesting information concerning our society, we freely notice it, and are most willing to give you any information respecting us.

"It appears your request extends sufficiently far to embrace an exposition of our moral and religious tenets, our faith, principles, and manner of life, our secular concerns, &c.

"We have seen several historical sketches of our society by different writers; but it is very rare to find one free from misrepresentations of some kind, which must be owing either to ignorance or prejudice. Therefore, in our communications, we may be somewhat particular on some points; in any of which, if there be any thing found agreeable to your desires, you are welcome to it; and, as it is presumed your publication is intended for information, among other truths, we hope to see something relative to us, different from most of the descriptions of former writers.

"In obtaining information of one society, you get a general understanding of all; for we are of one heart and one mind. Our faith is one, our practice is one.

"We are acknowledged and distinguished as a peculiar people, singular from all others; which peculiarity arises wholly from these two principles — our faith and manner of life, which comprise our motives in separating from the course and practice of the world, the manner in which our property is held, &c. &c.

"It is a fact acknowledged by all professed Christians, that here are two creations, an old and a new; or, which is the same thing, two kingdoms, the kingdom of this world, and the kingdom of Christ. It is also a truth as frankly granted, that these two creations, or kingdoms, are headed, the one by the first Adam, denominated the *old man*, and the other by the second Adam, Christ Jesus, denominated the *new man* — two different personages, possessing very different spirits, and executing very different works. As positive as the preceding declarations are, that there exist two distinct creations, and which are headed by two distinct characters, so positive are the following: — that the subjects of each kingdom bear a strong resemblance to their respective king, and plainly represent the particular kingdom they inhabit; for, 'As we have borne the image of the earthly, we shall also bear the image of the heavenly.' (1 Cor. 15 : 49.)

"Also that no person can have demands upon, and privileges in, these two men and creations at one and the same time. We must either hold to the old, and have nothing to do with the new, or we must come out and forsake the old, and come into the new. We must either put off the old man, Adam, and his works, which are well known to be multiplying and supporting of an earthly kingdom, which is the kingdom of this world, or we must put on the new man, Christ Jesus, and his works, which are well known to be a life without spot, chaste, virgin, and unstained by indulgences in any of those things which a beloved worthy said constitutes the world. (1 John 2 : 15, 16.) To these principles of faith we are strict, and may be called rigid, adherents; equally tenacious in the practical part of the new man, and in the same degree pointed against the old.

"The second part of this subject of singularity in us consists in the manner in which we hold our property, which, perhaps, is well known to be in common, after the order of the primitive church in the days of the apostles, in which state we have lived rising forty years, 'of one heart and one soul;' not any of us saying that 'aught of the things which he possessed was his own,' (Acts 4 : 32;) 'buying as though we possessed not,' (1 Cor. 7 : 30;) and 'having nothing, and yet possessing all things.' (2 Cor. 6 : 10.) In consequence hereof, we are retired from the world, as not of that kingdom; 'My kingdom is not of this world,' &c., (John 18 : 36;) by which we enjoy a closer communion with our God, and by which we follow the instruction of the Spirit, which saith, 'Come ye out from among them, and be ye separate,' &c. (2 Cor. 6 : 17.)

"Our society contains three distinct families, comprising 233 souls; 103 males, and 130 females. The number of persons over 70 is 18; between 60 and 70, 21; between 21 and 60, 125; under 21, 63. The oldest person is 88. Deaths since the gathering of the society, in 1792, 85.

"Our village is situated in the N. W. corner of the town, on the western shore of ***Mascomy Pond***, a pleasant sheet of water, of nearly five miles in length, and half a mile average width. Our village and home are pleasant to us, and are said to be so by travellers. It is about ten miles S. E. from Dartmouth College, forty N. W. from Concord, and one hundred from Boston.

"In all the families there are nearly thirty buildings, unadorned, except with neatness, simplicity, and convenience, besides many out-buildings. Among the buildings are one house of public worship, one convenient school-house, three dwelling-houses, one for each family, sufficiently large to accommodate us as places for cooking, eating, sleeping, and retirement from labor, and shops for the different branches of work. Our privilege for mills is very small; consequently our machinery cannot be extensive. Yet the little water that is running in small brooks, which can be conveniently collected into artificial ponds, is improved, by their emptying from one to another, and by the interspersion of mills upon their discharging streams. We have three saw-mills, two grist-mills, and some other machinery.

"As strangers, who many times wish to call, are frequently much straitened and embarrassed by not knowing where to call, or what to say, we should be pleased to have it particularly noticed, that we have one building designated from the est by the sign, "Trustees' Office," over the door, where strangers are received, where our commercial business is transacted, and where civil people wishing for information may freely obtain it, or be directed where it can be obtained.

"In our occupation we are agriculturists and mechanics. The products of the garden may be said to be as important as any; which are principally seeds, herbs, &c., from which this section of the country is chiefly supplied. Our manufactures are wooden ware, such as tubs, pails, half-bushel and other measures, boxes, &c.; also, whips, corn-brooms, eather, and various other articles.

"We keep from 1200 to 1500 sheep, mostly Saxon and Merino, which afford wool for our own wear, and is likewise a source of small trade with us. We keep about eighty cows, which supply us with milk for a dairy, for our own consumption only.

"The education of our youth and children has been a subject of much conversation among many people. It has been reported, that the children which we frequently take in and bring up with us, are kept in ignorance, having no opportunity of improving their minds by a literary education. But the weight of this censure is gradually growing less, by the contrary proof to the hundreds of visitors who flock into our school, and who are not at all sparing of their high encomiums upon it. It is conducted partially on the Lancasterian system, and is said to surpass any of the common schools about us. Our school-room is furnished with books and apparatus of a superior kind, which, we presume, is not equalled by any school in the country, save the one among our people at Canterbury, which, perhaps, is not in any respect inferior.

"In this society are two physicians. Each family has its respective elders or ministers; among these and other individuals of the society, are public speakers, whom you would denominate the clergy.

"You see, from what we have here written, that we have aken up many subjects, and several of them explicitly treated upon, although short; from which, together with the pam phlet accompanying this letter, we conclude you may be able to get considerable of an understanding, and which you are at liberty to cull at your pleasure. But it is sincerely to be hoped, if you publish any thing concerning us, you will be careful to preserve the true ideas of our communications."

From the pamphlet above mentioned we make the following extracts: —

"FAITH AND PRINICPLES OF THE SOCIETY.

"1. A life of *innocence* and *purity*, according to the example of Jesus Christ and his first true followers; implying entire abstinence from all sensual and carnal gratifications.

"2. Love. — 'By this shall all men know that ye are my disciples, if ye have love one to another. Love is the fulfilling of the law.' This is our bond of union.

"3. Peace. — 'Follow peace with all men,' is a divine precept; hence our abstinence from war and bloodshed, from all acts of violence towards our fellow-men, from all the party contentions and politics of the world, and from all the pursuits of pride and worldly ambition. 'My kingdom (said Christ) is not of this world.'

"4. Justice. — 'Render to every man his due. Owe no man any thing, but to love one another.' We are to be just and honest in all our dealings with mankind, to discharge all just dues, duties, and equitable claims, as seasonably and effectually as possible.

"5. Holiness. — 'Without which no man shall see the Lord.' Which signifies to be *consecrated*, or set apart from a common to a sacred use. Hence arise all our doctrines and practical rules of dedicating our persons, services, and property, to social and sacred uses, having adopted the example of the first gospel church, in establishing and supporting one *consecrated* and *united* interest by the voluntary choice of every member, as a sacred privilege, and not by any undue constraint or persuasion.

"6. Goodness. — Do good to all men, as far as opportunity and ability may serve, by administering acts of charity and kindness, and promoting light and truth among mankind 'Whatsoever ye would that men should do to you, do ye even so to them.'

"7. Truth.—This principle is opposed to falsehood, lying, deceit, and hypocrisy, and implies fidelity, reality, good, earnest sincerity, and punctuality in keeping vows and promises. These principles are the genuine basis of our institution, planted by its first founders, exhibited in all our public writings, justified by Scripture and fair reason, and practically commended as a system of morality and religion, adapted to the best interest and happiness of man, both here and hereafter.

"MANNER OF ADMITTING MEMBERS.

"1. All persons who unite with this society, in any degree, must do it freely and voluntarily, according to their own faith and unbiased judgment.

"2. In the testimony of the society, both public and private, no flattery nor any undue influence is used, but the most plain and explicit statements of its faith and principles are laid before the inquirer, so that the whole ground may be comprehended, as far as possible, by every candidate for admission.

"3. No considerations of property are ever made use of, by this society, to induce any person to join it, nor to prevent any one from leaving it; because it is our faith, that no act of devotion, or service, that does not flow from the free and voluntary emotions of the heart, can be acceptable to God, as an act of true religion.

"4. No believing husband, or wife, is allowed, by the principles of this society, to separate from an unbelieving partner, except by mutual agreement, unless the conduct of the unbeliever be such as to warrant a separation by the laws of God and man. Nor can any husband, or wife, who has otherwise abandoned his or her partner, be received into communion with the society.

"5. Any person becoming a member, must rectify all his wrongs, and, as fast and as far as it is in his power, discharge all just and legal claims, whether of creditors or filial heirs. Nor can any person, not conforming to this rule, long remain in union with the society. But the society is not responsible for the debts of any individual, except by agreement because such responsibility would involve a principle ruinous to the institution.

"6. No difference is to be made in the distribution of parental estate among the heirs, whether they belong to the society or not; but an equal partition must be made, as far as may be practicable, and consistent with reason and justice.

"7. If an unbelieving wife separate from a believing husband, by agreement, the husband must give her a just and reasonable share of the property; and if they have children who have arrived to years of understanding sufficient to judge for themselves, and who choose to go with their mother, they are not to be disinherited on that account. Though the character of this institution has been much censured on this ground, yet we boldly assert that the rule above stated has never, to our knowledge, been violated by this society.

"8. Industry, temperance, and frugality, are prominent features of this institution. No member who is able to labor, can be permitted to live idly upon the labors of others. All are required to be employed in some manual occupation, according to their several abilities, when not engaged in other necessary duties."

"The rules of government in the society are adapted to the different orders of which it is composed. In all (as far as respects adults) it is spiritual; its powers and authorities growing out of the *mutual faith, love, and confidence*, of all the members, and harmoniously concurring in the general form and manner of government established by the first founders of the society.

"The leading authority of the society is vested in a

ministry, generally consisting of four persons, including both sexes. These, together with the elders and trustees, constitute the general government of the society in all its branches, and, being supported by the general union and approbation of the members, are invested with power to appoint their successors and other subordinate officers, as occasion may require; to counsel, advise, and direct, in all matters, whether of a spiritual or temporal nature; to superintend the concerns of the several families, and establish all needful orders, rules, and regulations, for the direction and protection of the several branches of the society; but no rule can be made, nor any member assume a lead, contrary to the original faith and known principles of the society. And nothing which respects the government, order, and general arrangement, of the society is considered as fully established until it has received the general approbation of the society, or of that branch thereof which it more immediately concerns.

"This community is divided into several different branches, commonly called *families*. This division is generally made for the sake of convenience, and is often rendered necessary on account of local situation and occurrent circumstances; but the proper division and arrangement of the community, without respect to local situation, are into three classes, or progressive degrees of order.

"Those children taken into the society are treated with care and tenderness, receive a good school education, and, according to their genius, are trained to industry and virtuous habits, restrained from vice, and, at a suitable age, led into the knowledge of the sacred Scriptures, and practically taught the divine precepts contained in them, particularly those of Jesus Christ and the apostles.

"During a period of more than forty years, since the permanent establishment of this society at New Lebanon and Watervliet, there never has been a legal claim entered by any person for the recovery of property brought into the society but all claims of that nature, if any have existed, have been amicably settled, to the satisfaction of the parties concerned. Complaints and legal prosecutions have not, hitherto, come from persons who brought property into the institution, but from those who came destitute of property, and who, generally speaking, have been no benefit to the society in any way, but, on the contrary, after having enjoyed its hospitality, and brought no small share of trouble upon the people, have had the assurance to lay claim to wages which they never earned, or property to which they never had any just or legal claim.

"No person can be received into this order until he shall have settled all just and legal claims, both of creditors and filial heirs; so that whatever property he may possess, may be justly and truly his own. Minors cannot be admitted as covenant members of this order; yet they may be received under its immediate care and protection. And when they shall have arrived at lawful age, if they should choose to continue in the society, and sign the covenant of the order, and support its principles, they are then admitted to all the privileges of members. The members of this order are all equally entitled to the benefits and privileges thereof, without any difference made on account of what any one may have contributed to the interest of the society. All are equally entitled to their support and maintenance, and to every necessary comfort, whether in health, sickness, or old age, so long as they continue to maintain the principles, and conform to the orders, rules, and regulations, of the institution They, therefore, give their property and services for the most valuable of all temporal considerations — an ample security, during life, for every needful support, if they continue faithful to their contract and covenant, the nature of which they clearly understand before they enter into it.

"We believe it will be generally granted that the history of the world does not furnish a single instance of any religious institution which has stood fifty years without a visible declension of the principles of the institution, in the general purity and integrity of its members. This has been generally acknowledged by the devotees of such institutions and facts have fully verified it. But we would appeal to the candid judgment of those who have known this institution from the beginning, and have had a fair opportunity of observing the progress of its improvement, whether they have, in reality, found any declension, either in the external order and regulations of the society, or in the purity and integrity of its members, in the general practice of the moral and Christian duties; and whether they have not, on the contrary, discovered a visible and manifest increase in all these respects. And hence they may judge for themselves, whether the moral character of the society, and its progressive improvement, can be ascribed to any other cause than the blessing, protection, and government, of Divine Power and Wisdom."

This denomination is also styled the *millennial church.* Although celibacy is enjoined by the Shakers upon their members, yet their numbers rather increase, by converts from the world.

There are fifteen societies of Shakers in the United States, located in the following places: — Alfred, New Gloucester, and Poland, Me.; Canterbury and Enfield, N. H.; Shirley, Harvard, Tyringham, and Hancock, Mass.; Enfield, Conn.; Watervliet and New Lebanon, N. Y.; Union Village and Watervliet, Ohio; Pleasant Hill and South Union, Ky. The number of Shakers in the United States is about 6000.

This sect of Christians arose at Manchester, in England; and ANN LEE has the credit of being its founder. They derive their name from their manner of worship, which is performed by singing, dancing, and clapping their hands in regular time, to a novel, but rather pleasant kind of music. This sect was persecuted in England, and came to America in 1774. They first settled in Watervliet, near Albany, N. Y. They have, or think they have, revelations from Heaven, or gifts from the Holy Spirit, which direct them in the choice of their leaders, and in other important concerns. Their dress and manners are similar to those of the society of Friends; hence they are often called *Shaking Quakers.* They display great skill and science in agriculture, horticulture, and the mechanic arts; and their honesty, industry, hospitality, and neatness, are proverbial. These people choose their locations with great taste and judgment. A *Shaker village* always presents a scene of beauty.

We close this article with an extract from a speech of the Hon. Johr Breathitt, late governor of Kentucky.

"Much has been urged against Shakerism, much has been said against their covenant; but, I repeat it, *that* individual who is prepared to sign the church covenant, stands in an enviable situation: his situation is, indeed, an enviable one, who, devoted to God, is prepared to say of his property, 'Here it is, little or much; take it, and leave me unmolested to commune with my God. Indeed, I dedicate myself to what? not to a fanatical tenet; O, no! to a subject far beyond; to the worship of Almighty God, the great Creator and Governor of the universe. Under the influence of his love, I give my all: only let me worship according to my faith, and in a manner I believe acceptable to my God!'

"I say again, the world cannot produce a parallel to the situation which such a man exhibits — resigned to the will of Heaven, free from all the feelings of earthly desire, and pursuing, quietly, the peaceful tenor of his way."

## REFORMATION.

This term is used, by way of eminence, to denote that great change which took place in the Christian world, under the ministry of Luther, Calvin, Zuinglius, Melancthon, and others, who successfully opposed some of the doctrines, and many of the practices, of the Roman church. It commenced at Wittemberg, in Saxony, in 1517, and greatly weakened the Papal authority.

It was from causes seemingly fortuitous, and from a source very inconsiderable, that all the mighty effects of the reformation flowed. Leo X., when raised to the Papal throne, in 1513, found the revenues of the church exhausted by the vast projects of his two ambitious predecessors. His own temper, naturally liberal and enterprising, rendered him incapable of severe and patient economy; and his schemes for aggrandizing the family of Medicis, his love of splendor, and his munificence in rewarding men of genius, involved him daily in new expenses, in order to provide a fund for which, he tried every device that the fertile invention of priests had fallen upon, to drain the credulous multitude of their wealth. Among others, he had recourse to a sale of indulgences.

The Romish church believe that pious persons may do works of supererogation, that is to say, more good works than are necessary for their own salvation. All such works, according to their doctrine, are deposited, together with the infinite merits of Jesus Christ, in one inexhaustible treasury. The keys of this were committed to St. Peter, and to his successors the popes, who may open it at pleasure, and, by transferring a portion of this superabundant merit to any particular person for a sum of money, may convey to him either pardon for his own sins, or a release for any one, for whom he feels an interest, from the pains of purgatory. Such indulgences were offered as a recompense for those who engaged in the wars of the crusades against the Infidels. Since those times, the power of granting indulgences has been greatly abused in the church of Rome. Pope Leo X., finding that the sale of indulgences was likely to be lucrative, granted to Albert, elector of Mentz and archbishop of Magdeburg, the benefit of the indulgences of Saxony, and the neighboring parts, and farmed out those of other countries to the highest bidders; who, to make the best of their bargain, procured the ablest preachers to cry up the value of the commodity. The form of these indulgences was as follows.—"May our Lord Jesus Christ have mercy upon thee, and absolve thee by the merits of his most holy passion. And I, by his authority, that of his blessed apostles, Peter and Paul and of the most holy pope, granted and committed to me in these parts, do absolve thee, first, from all ecclesiastical censures, in whatever manner they may have been incurred; then from all thy sins, transgressions, and excesses, how enormous soever they may be; even from such as are reserved for the cognizance of the holy see, and as far as the keys of the holy church extend. I remit to you all punishment which you deserve in purgatory on their account; and I restore you to the holy sacraments of the church, to the unity of the faithful, and to that innocence and purity which you possessed at baptism; so that, when you die, the gates of punishment shall be shut, and the gates of the paradise of delight shall be opened; and if you shall not die at present, this grace shall remain in full force when you are at the point of death. In the name of the Father, Son, and the Holy Ghost."

According to a book, called the "Tax of the Sacred Roman Chancery," in which are the exact sums to be levied for the pardon of each particular sin, some of the fees are thus stated: — For simony, 10*s.* 6*d.;* for sacrilege, 10*s.* 6*d.;* for taking a false oath, 9*s.;* for robbing, 12*s.;* for burning a neighbor's house, 12*s.;* for defiling a virgin, 9*s.;* for murdering a layman, 7*s.* 6*d.;* for keeping a concubine, 10*s.* 6*d.;* for laying violent hands on a clergyman, 10*s.* 6*d.*

The terms in which the retailers of these abominable licenses described their advantages to the purchasers, and the arguments with which they urged the necessity of obtaining them, were so extravagant that they appear almost incredible. "If any man," said they, "purchase letters of indulgence, his soul may rest secure with respect to its salvation. The souls confined in purgatory, for whose redemption indulgences are purchased, as soon as the money is paid, instantly escape from that place of torment, and ascend into heaven." They said that the efficacy of indulgences was so great, that the most heinous sins would be remitted and expiated by them, and the person be freed both from punishment and guilt: this was the unspeakable gift of God, in order to reconcile man to himself; the cross erected by the preachers of indulgences was equally efficacious with the cross of Christ. "Lo," said they, "the heavens are open; if you enter not now, when will you enter? For twelve pence you may redeem the soul of your father out of purgatory; and are you so ungrateful that you will not rescue the soul of your parent from torment? If you had but one coat, you ought to strip yourself of that instantly, and sell it, in order to purchase such benefit," &c.

It was against these preachers of licentiousness, and their diabolical conduct, that Luther began first to declaim.

## REFORMED CHURCHES.

The Reformed churches comprehend the whole Protestant churches in Europe and America, whether Lutheran, Calvinistic, Independent, Quaker, Baptist, or any other denomination who dissent from the church of Rome. The term *Reformed* is now, however, more particularly employed to distinguish the Calvinists from the Lutherans.

The Reformed churches in America are the two following:—

### REFORMED DUTCH CHURCH.

This is the oldest body of Presbyterians in America: it descended immediately from the church of Holland; and, for about a century from its commencement in this country, it hung in colonial dependence on the Classis of Amsterdam, and the Synod of North Holland, and was unable to ordain a minister, or perform any ecclesiastical function of the kind, without a reference to the parent country and mother church.

The origin of this church will lead us back to the earliest

history of the city and state of New York; for they were first settled by this people, and by them a foundation was laid for the first churches of this persuasion, the most distinguished of which were planted at New York, (then called New Amsterdam,) Flatbush, Esopus, and Albany. The church at New York was probably the oldest, and was founded at, or before, the year 1639; this is the earliest period to which its records conduct us. The first minister was the Rev. Evarardus Bogardus. But when he came from Holland, does not appear. Next to him were two ministers by the name of Megapolensis, John and Samuel.

The first place of worship built by the Dutch in the colony of New Netherlands, as it was then called, was erected in the fort at New York, in the year 1642. The second, it is believed, was a chapel built by Governor Stuyvesant, in what is now called the Bowery. In succession, churches of this denomination arose on Long Island, in Schenectady, on Staten Island, and in a number of towns on the Hudson River, and several, it is believed, in New Jersey. But the churches of New York, Albany, and Esopus, were the most important, and the ministers of these churches claimed and enjoyed a kind of episcopal dignity over the surrounding churches.

The Dutch church was the established religion of the colony, until it surrendered to the British in 1664; after which its circumstances were materially changed. Not long after the colony passed into the hands of the British, an act was passed, which went to establish the Episcopal church as the predominant party; and for almost a century after, the Dutch and English Presbyterians, and all others in the colony, were forced to contribute to the support of that church.

The first judicatory higher than a consistory, among this people, was a Cœtus, formed in 1747. The object and powers of this assembly were merely those of advice and fraternal intercourse. It could not ordain ministers, nor judicially decide in ecclesiastical disputes, without the consent of the Classis of Amsterdam.

The first regular Classis among the Dutch was formed in 1757. But the formation of this Classis involved this infan church in the most unhappy collisions, which sometimes threatened its very existence. These disputes continued for many years, by which two parties were raised in the church, one of which was for, and the other against, an ecclesiastical subordination to the judicatories of the mother church and country. These disputes, in which eminent men on both sides were concerned, besides disturbing their own peace and enjoyment, produced unfavorable impressions towards them among their brethren at home.

In 1766, John H. Livingston, D. D., then a young man, went from New York to Holland, to prosecute his studies in the Dutch universities. By his representations, a favorable disposition was produced towards the American church in that country; and, on his return, in full convention of both parties, an amicable adjustment of their differences was made, and a friendly correspondence was opened with the church in Holland, which was continued until the revolution of the country under Bonaparte.

The Dutch church suffered much in the loss of its members, and in other respects, by persisting to maintain its service in the Dutch language after it had gone greatly into disuse. The solicitation for English preaching was long resisted, and Dr. Laidlie, a native of Scotland, was the first minister in the Dutch church in North America, who was expressly called to officiate in the English language.

## REFORMED GERMAN CHURCH.

As the Dutch Reformed church in this country is an exact counterpart of the church of Holland, so the German Reformed is of the Reformed or Calvinistic church of Germany. The people of this persuasion were among the early settlers of Pennsylvania: here their churches were first formed; but they are now to be found in nearly all the states south and west of the one above named. The German Reformed churches in this country remained in a scattered and neglected state until 1746, when the Rev. Michael Schlatter, who was sent from Europe for the purpose, collected them together, and put their concerns in a more prosperous train. They have since increased to a numerous body, and are assuming an important stand among the American Presbyterians.

This denomination is scattered over the Middle, Western, and Southern States, but is most numerous in the states of Ohio and Pennsylvania. The population of this church in the United States is estimated at 300,000; 180 ministers, 600 congregations, and 30,000 communicants.

## RESTORATIONISTS.

The Restorationists are those who believe that all men will ultimately become holy and happy. They maintain that God created only to bless, and that, in pursuance of that purpose, he sent his Son to "be for salvation to the ends of the earth;" that Christ's kingdom is moral in its nature, and extends to moral beings in every state or mode of existence; that the probation of man is not confined to the present life, but extends through the mediatorial reign; and that, as Christ died for all, so, before he shall have delivered up the kingdom to the Father, all shall be brought to a participation of the knowledge and enjoyment of that truth which maketh free from the bondage of sin and death. They believe in a general resurrection and judgment, when those who have improved their probation in this life will be raised to more perfect felicity, and those who have misimproved their opportunities on earth will come forward to shame and condemnation, which will continue till they become truly penitent; that punishment itself is a mediatorial work, a discipline, perfectly consistent with mercy; that it is a means employed by Christ to humble and subdue the stubborn will, and prepare the mind to receive a manifestation of the goodness of God, which leadeth the sinner to true repentance. (See Gen. 12: 3; 22 : 18. Gal. 3 : 8. Isa. 45 : 22, 23. Phil. 2: 10, 11. Rev. 5 : 13. 1 Tim. 2 : 1—6. Col. 1 : 20. Eph. 1 : 7—11. Rom. 5 : 12—21; 8: 20, 21. 1 Cor. 15 : 24—28.)

They contend that this doctrine is not only sustained by particular texts, but grows necessarily out of some of the first principles of divine revelation. They maintain that it is immediately connected with the perfections of the Deity; that God, being infinitely benevolent, must have desired the happiness of all his offspring; that his infinite wisdom would enable him to form a perfect plan, and his almighty power will secure its accomplishment. They contend that the mission of Christ is abortive on any other plan, and that nothing short of the "restitution of all things" can satisfy the ardent desires of every pious soul. On this system alone can they reconcile the attributes of justice and mercy, and secure to the Almighty a character worthy of our imitation.

They insist that the words rendered *everlasting*, *eternal*, and *forever*, which are, in a few instances, applied to the misery of the wicked, do not prove that misery to be endless, because these terms are loose in their signification, and are frequently used in a limited sense; that the original terms, being often used in the plural number, clearly demonstrate that the period, though indefinite, is limited in its very nature. They maintain that the meaning of the term must always be sought in the subject to which it is applied, and that there is nothing in the nature of punishment which will justify an endless sense. They believe that the doctrine of the restoration is the most consonant to the perfections of the Deity, the most worthy of the character of Christ, and the only doctrine which will accord with pious and devout feelings, or harmonize with the Scriptures. They teach their followers that ardent love to God, active benevolence to man, and personal meekness and purity, are the natural results of these views

Though the Restorationists, as a separate sect, have arisen within a few years, their sentiments are by no means new Clemens Alexandrinus, Origen, Didymus of Alexandria, Gregory Nyssen, and several others, among the Christian fathers of the first four centuries, it is said, believed and advocated the restoration of all fallen intelligences. A branch of the German Baptists, before the reformation, held this doctrine, and propagated it in Germany. Since the reformation, this doctrine has had numerous advocates; and some of them have been among the brightest ornaments of the church. Among the Europeans, we may mention the names of Jeremy White, of Trinity College, Dr. Burnet, Dr. Cheyne, Chevalier Ramsay, Dr. Hartley, Bishop Newton, Mr. Stonehouse, Mr. Petitpierre, Dr. Cogan, Mr. Lindsey, Dr. Priestley, Dr. Jebb, Mr. Relly, Mr. Kenrick, Mr. Belsham, Dr. Southworth, Smith, and many others. In fact, the restoration is the commonly-received doctrine among the English Unitarians at the present day. In Germany, a country which, for several centuries, has taken the lead in all theological reforms, the Orthodox have espoused this doctrine. The restoration was introduced into America about the middle of the eighteenth century, though it was not propagated much till about 1775 or 1780, when John Murray and Elhanan Winchester became public advocates of this doctrine, and by their untiring labors extended it in every direction. From that time to the present, many men have been found, in all parts of our country, who have rejoiced in this belief. This doctrine found able advocates in the learned Dr. Chauncy, of Boston, Dr. Rush, of Philadelphia, and Dr. Smith, of New York: Mr. Foster, of New Hampshire, may also be mentioned as an advocate of the restoration.

Most of the writers whose names are given above, did not belong to a sect which took the distinctive name of Restorationists. They were found in the ranks of the various sects into which the Christian world has been divided. And those who formed a distinct sect were more frequently denominated Universalists than Restorationists. In 1785, a convention was organized at Oxford, Massachusetts, under the auspices of Messrs. Winchester and Murray.* And as all who had embraced universal salvation believed that the effects of sin and the means of grace extended into a future life, the terms *Restorationist* and *Universalist* were then used as synonymous; and those who formed that convention adopted the latter as their distinctive name.

During the first twenty-five years, the members of the Universalist convention were believers in a future retribution. But, about the year 1818, Hosea Ballou, now of Boston, advanced the doctrine that all retribution is confined to this world. That sentiment, at first, was founded upon the old Gnostic notion that all sin originates in the flesh, and that death frees the soul from all impurity. Subsequently, some of the advocates for the no-future punishment scheme adopted the doctrine of materialism, and hence maintained that the soul was mortal; that the whole man died a temporal death, and that the resurrection was the grand event which would introduce all men into heavenly felicity.

Those who have since taken to themselves the name of Restorationists, viewed these innovations as corruptions of the gospel, and raised their voices against them. But a majority of the convention having espoused those sentiments, no reformation could be effected. The Restorationists, believing these errors to be increasing, and finding in the connection what appeared to them to be a want of engagedness in the cause of true piety, and in some instances an open opposition to the organization of churches, and finding that a spirit of levity and bitterness characterized the public labors of their brethren, and that practices were springing up totally repugnant to the principles of Congregationalism, resolved to obey the apostolic injunction, by coming out from among them, and forming an independent association. Accordingly a convention, consisting of Rev. Paul Dean, Rev. David Pickering, Rev. Charles Hudson, Rev. Adin Ballou, Rev. Lyman Maynard, Rev. Nathaniel Wright, Rev. Philemon R Russell, and Rev. Seth Chandler, and several laymen, met at

Mendon, Massachusetts, August 17, 1831, and formed themselves into a distinct sect, and took the name of *Universal Restorationists.*

The Restorationists are Congregationalists on the subject of church government.

The differ nce between the Restorationists and Universalists relates principally to the subject of a future retribution. The Universalists believe that a full and perfect retribution takes place in this world, that our conduct here cannot affect our future condition, and that the moment man exists after death, he will be as pure and as happy as the angels. From these views the Restorationists dissent. They maintain that a just retribution does not take place in time; that the conscience of the sinner becomes callous, and does not increase in the severity of its reprovings with the increase of guilt; that men are invited to act with reference to a future life; that, if all are made perfectly happy at the commencement of the next state of existence, they are not rewarded according to their deeds; that, if death introduces them into heaven, they are saved by death, and not by Christ; and if they are made happy by being raised from the dead, they are saved by physical, and not by moral means, and made happy without their agency or consent; that such a sentiment weakens the motives to virtue, and gives force to the temptations of vice; that it is unreasonable in itself, and opposed to many passages of Scripture. (See Acts 24 : 25; 17 : 30, 31. Heb. 9 : 27, 28. Matt. 11 : 23, 24. 2 Pet. 2 : 9. 2 Cor. 5 : 8—11. John 5 : 28, 29. Matt. 10 : 28. Luke 12 : 4, 5; 16 : 19—31. 1 Pet. 3. 18—20.)

## UNIVERSALISTS.

The grand distinguishing characteristic of this class of Christians is their belief in the final holiness and happiness of the whole human family. Some of them believe that all punishment for sin is endured in the present state of existence, while others believe it extends into the future life; but all agree that it is administered in a spirit of kindness, is intended for the good of those who experience it, and that it will finally terminate, and be succeeded by a state of perfect and endless holiness and happiness.

## DOCTRINE.

The following is the "Profession of Belief," adopted by the General Convention of Universalists in the United States, at the session holden in 1803. It has never been altered, and it is perfectly satisfactory to the denomination.

"ART. I. We believe that the Holy Scriptures of the Old and New Testaments contain a revelation of the character of God, and of the duty, interest, and final destination, of mankind.

"ART. II. We believe that there is one God, whose nature is love; revealed in one Lord Jesus Christ, by one Holy Spirit of grace, who will finally restore the whole family of mankind to holiness and happiness.

"ART. III. We believe that holiness and true happiness are inseparably connected, and that believers ought to be careful to maintain order, and practise good works; for these things are good and profitable unto men."

## HISTORY.

Universalists claim that the salvation of all men was taught by Jesus Christ and his apostles. It was also taught and defended by several of the most eminent Christian fathers; such as Clemens Alexandrinus, Origen, &c. In the third and fourth centuries, this doctrine prevailed extensively, and, for aught which appears to the contrary, was then accounted orthodox. It was at length condemned, however, by the fifth general council, A. D. 553; after which, we find few traces of it through the dark ages, so called.

It revived at the period of the reformation, and since that

time has found many able and fearless advocates;—in Switzerland, Petitpierre and Lavater; in Germany, Seigvolk, Everhard, Steinbart, and Semler; in Scotland, Purves, Douglass, and T. S. Smith; in England, Coppin, Jeremy White, Dr. H. More, Dr. T. Burnet, Whiston, Hartley, Bishop Newton, Stonehouse, Barbauld, Lindsey, Priestley, Belsham, Carpenter, Relly, Vidler, Scarlett, and many others

At the present day, Universalism prevails more extensively than elsewhere in England, Germany, and the United States

In England, the Unitarian divines, generally, believe in the final salvation of all men. Dr. Lant Carpenter says, "Most of us, however, believe that a period will come to each individual, when punishment shall have done its work — when the awful sufferings with which the gospel threatens the impenitent and disobedient, will have humbled the stubborn, purified the polluted, and eradicated malignity, impiety, hypocrisy, and every evil disposition; that a period will come (which it may be the unspeakable bliss of those who enter the joy of their Lord to accelerate, which, at least, it will be their delight to anticipate,) when he who 'must reign till he hath put *all enemies* under his feet,' 'shall have put down all rule, and all authority, and power.' 'The LAST ENEMY, death, shall be DESTROYED.' 'Every tongue shall confess that Jesus Christ is Lord, to the glory of God the Father,' 'who wills that all men should be saved, and come to the knowledge of the truth,'— that truth which sanctifies the heart,— that knowledge which is life eternal,— and God shall be ALL IN ALL."

In Germany, nearly every theologian is a believer in the final salvation of all men. Speaking of Professor Tholuck, Professor Sears says, "The most painful disclosures remain yet to be made. This distinguished and excellent man, in common with the *great majority of the Evangelical divines* of Germany, though he professes to have serious doubts, and is cautious in avowing the sentiment, believes that all men and fallen spirits will finally be saved." Mr. Dwight, in his recent publication, says, "The doctrine of the eternity of future punishments is almost universally rejected. I have seen but one person in Germany who believed it, and but one other whose mind was wavering on this subject." Universalism may, therefore, be considered the prevailing religion in Germany.

In the United States, Universalism was little known until about the middle of the last century; and afterwards it found but few advocates during several years. Dr. George de Benneville, of Germantown, Penn., Rev. Richard Clarke, of Charleston, S. C., and Jonathan Mayhew, D. D., of Boston, were, perhaps, the only individuals who publicly preached the doctrine before the arrival of Rev. John Murray, in 1770. Mr. Murray labored almost alone until 1780, when Rev. Elhanan Winchester, a popular Baptist preacher, embraced Universalism, though on different principles. About ten years afterwards, Rev. Hosea Ballou embraced the same doctrine, but on principles different from those advocated by Mr. Murray or Mr. Winchester. To the efforts of these three men is to be attributed much of the success which attended the denomination in its infancy. Although they differed widely from each other in their views of punishment, yet they labored together in harmony and love, for the advancement of the cause which was dear to all their hearts. The seed which they sowed has since produced an abundant harvest.

The ministry of the Universalist denomination in the United States, hitherto, has been provided for, not so much by the means of schools, as by the unaided, but irresistible influence of the gospel of Christ. This has furnished the denomination with its most successful preachers. It has turned them from other sects and doctrines, and brought them out from forests and fields, and from secular pursuits of almost every kind, and driven them, with inadequate literary preparation, to the work of disseminating the truth. This state of things has been unavoidable, and the effect of it is visible. It has made the ministry of the Universalist denomination very different from that of any other sect in the country; studious of the Scriptures, confident in the truth of their distinguishing doctrine, zealous, firm, industrious; depending more on the truths communicated for their success, than on the manner in which they are stated. It has had the effect, also, to give the ministry a polemic character — the natural result of unwavering faith in the doctrine believed, and of an introduction into the desk without scholastic training. But the attention of the denomination, in various parts of the country, has of late been turned to the education of the ministry; and conventions and associations have adopted resolves requiring candidates to pass examinations in certain branches of literature. The same motives have governed many in their effort to establish literary and theological institutions. The desire to have the ministry respectable for literary acquirements, is universal.

A few years since, a small number separated from the denomination, and adopted the appellation of *Restorationists*. To prevent misapprehension, it may be repeated, that, although a few have thus seceded, yet a difference of opinion in regard to the duration of punishment has not disturbed the harmony of the denomination generally, nor is it regarded as sufficient cause for breach of fellowship, or alienation of heart and affection.

The Universalists quote the following texts of Scripture, among others, in support of their sentiments: — Gen. 22: 18. Ps. 22: 27; 86: 9. Isa. 25: 6, 7, 8; 45: 23, 24. Jer. 31: 33, 34. Lam. 3: 31—33. John 12: 32. Acts 3: 21. Rom. 5: 18, 21; 8: 38, 39; 11: 25—36. 1 Cor. 15: 22—28, and 51—57. 2 Cor. 5: 18, 19. Gal. 3: 8. Eph. 1: 9, 10 Phil. 2: 9—11. Col. 1: 19, 20. 1 Tim. 2: 1—6. Heb. 8: 10, 11. Rev. 5: 13; 21: 3, 4.

We copy the following from the *Trumpet and Universalist Magazine* of June 4, 1836. It is by the Rev. Hosea Ballou, of Boston, in answer to the question, "Who are Universalists?"

"There seems to be an evident propriety in calling all who believe in the final holiness and happiness of all mankind, *Universalists.* There appears no good reason why those who believe in a limited punishment, in the future state, should have a less or a greater claim to be called Universalists, than those who entertain a hope that all sin and misery end when the functions of life cease in the mortal body As they both agree in the belief that God is the Savior of all men, if this belief entitle one to the name of Universalist. of course it gives the other the same title. The Rev. John Murray was called a Universalist, and he called himself by this name, although he admitted there might be suffering hereafter, in consequence of blindness or unbelief. It is true, he did not allow that the sinner was punished for sin, either here or in the future world, in his own person, because he maintained that the whole penalty of the divine law, for the sin of the whole world, was suffered by the Lord Jesus, as the head of every man. He allowed, notwithstanding, that the natural consequences of sin would inevitably follow transgression, as we see is the case by every day's observation. So, likewise, was the Rev. Elhanan Winchester called a Universalist, and he called himself so, although his views respecting a state of retribution, and the sufferings to which the wicked in the world to come will be subjected, were widely different from those entertained by Mr. Murray. Mr. Winchester believed in a place of material fire and brimstone, where the wicked would endure a torment as intense as has been represented by those Christians who believe in endless misery. But, as he believed that all these sufferings will end, though they might continue for many thousand years, and that those miserable wretches will at last be subdued and reconciled to the divine government, and be happy, he was denominated a Universalist.

"The Rev. Dr. Huntington is ranked a Universalist, equally with those who have been named; but he believed in no punishment hereafter, being Calvinistic in his views of the demerit of sin, and of the atonement made by Christ

" From the commencement of the denomination of Universalists in this country, there has been a difference of opinion respecting the doctrine of rewards and punishments, among both the clergy and the laity belonging to the connection. But this difference was not considered, in those times, a good reason for a distinction of either name, denomination, or fellowship. All united in the cheering hope that, in the fulness of the dispensation of times, sin will be finished, transgression ended, and all moral intelligences reconciled to God, in true holiness and everlasting happiness. A view so grand and glorious, so full of comfort, of joy, and of peace, and so triumphant, was sufficiently powerful to draw together all who enjoyed it, and to hold them together as a denomination distinct from all those who hold the unmerciful doctrine of endless punishment.

" When the General Convention of the New England States, professing the doctrine of universal salvation, appointed a committee to draft articles of faith and a constitution, by which it might be known and distinguished from other religious sects, care was taken to appoint on that committee brethren whose views differed respecting the subject of a future state of rewards and punishments. The worthy and fondly-remembered brother Walter Ferriss, who penned that instrument, was a believer in future rewards and punishments; but he so wrote that confession of faith as to comprehend the full belief of universal salvation, without making any distinction between the belief of future punishment, or no future punishment. And it is well remembered that this circumstance was, at the time of accepting the report of the committee, viewed as one of its excellences.

" It seems improper to give so much weight to different opinions, which differ not in principle, but in circumstances only, as to constitute them walls of separation and disfellowship. If one believe that all misery ends with this mortal state, and another believe that it may continue twenty years after, and then come to an end, is there any real difference as to principle? All believe that our heavenly Father holds all times and seasons, and all events, in his own power, and that he worketh all things after the counsel of his own will. And, moreover, all believe that God will have all men to be saved, and to come unto the knowledge of the truth. This constitutes us all Universalists, and calls on us to keep the unity of the spirit, and to walk in the bonds of peace."

---

## ROMAN CATHOLICS.

THE following Creeds and Rule of Faith contain the fundamental principles of the Latin or Roman church.

### APOSTLES' CREED.

"I believe in God the Father almighty, Creator of heaven and earth; and in Jesus Christ, his only Son, our Lord, who was conceived by the Holy Ghost, born of the Virgin Mary, suffered under Pontius Pilate, was crucified, dead, and buried; he descended into hell; the third day he rose again from the dead; he ascended into heaven, sitteth at the right hand of God the Father almighty; from thence he shall come to judge the living and the dead. I believe in the Holy Ghost; the holy Catholic church; the communion of saints; the forgiveness of sins, the resurrection of the body; and life everlasting. AMEN."

It is doubtful who composed the above Creed. It was not in common use in the church until the end of the fifth century. See *King's History of the Apostles' Creed.*

### THE SYMBOL, OR CREED OF ST. ATHANASIUS.

"Whosoever will be saved, before all things it is necessary that he hold the Catholic faith;

"Which faith except every one do keep entire and inviolate, without doubt he shall perish everlastingly.

"Now, the Catholic faith is this—that we worship one God in Trinity, and Trinity in Unity.

"Neither confounding the persons, nor dividing the substance.

"For one is the person of the Father, another of the Son, another of the Holy Ghost.

"But the Godhead of the Father, and of the Son, and of the Holy Ghost, is all one, the glory equal, the majesty co-eternal.

"Such as the Father is, such is the Son, and such is the Holy Ghost.

"The Father is uncreated, the Son is uncreated, and the Holy Ghost uncreated.

"The Father incomprehensible, the Son incomprehensible, and the Holy Ghost incomprehensible.

"The Father eternal, the Son eternal, and the Holy Ghost eternal.

"And yet they are not three Eternals, but one Eternal.

"As also they are not three Uncreated, nor three Incomprehensibles; but one Uncreated, and one Incomprehensible.

"In like manner, the Father is almighty, the Son almighty, and the Holy Ghost almighty.

"And yet they are not three Almighties, but one Almighty

"So the Father is God, the Son is God, and the Holy Ghost is God.

"And yet they are not three Gods, but one God.

"So likewise the Father is Lord, the Son is Lord, and the Holy Ghost is Lord.

"And yet they are not three Lords, but one Lord,

"For, as we are compelled by the Christian truth to acknowledge every person by himself to be God and Lord,

"So we are forbidden by the Catholic religion to say there are three Gods or three Lords.

"The Father is made of no one, neither created nor begotten.

"The Son is from the Father alone, not made, nor created, but begotten

"The Holy Ghost is from the Father and the Son, not made, nor created, nor begotten, but proceeding.

"So there is one Father, not three Fathers; one Son, not three Sons; one Holy Ghost, not three Holy Ghosts.

"And in this Trinity there is nothing before or after, nothing greater or less; but the whole three Persons are coeternal to one another, and coëqual.

"So that in all things, as has been already said above, the Unity is to be worshipped in Trinity, and the Trinity in Unity

"He, therefore, that will be saved, must thus think of the Trinity.

"Furthermore, it is necessary to everlasting salvation, that he also believe rightly the incarnation of our Lord Jesus Christ.

"Now, the right faith is, that we believe and confess that our Lord Jesus Christ, the Son of God, is both God and Man.

"He is God of the substance of his Father, begotten before the world; and he is Man of the substance of his mother, born in the world.

"Perfect God and perfect Man; of a rational soul, and human flesh subsisting.

"Equal to the Father according to his Godhead, and less than the Father according to his Manhood.

"Who, although he be both God and Man, yet he is not two, but one Christ.

"One, not by the conversion of the Godhead into flesh, but by the taking of the Manhood unto God.

"One altogether, not by confusion of substance, but by unity of person.

"For as the rational soul and the flesh is one man, so God and Man is one Christ.

"Who suffered for our salvation, descended into hell, rose again the third day from the dead.

"He ascended into heaven: he sitteth at the right hand of God the Father almighty; thence he shall come to judge the living and dead.

"At whose coming all men shall rise again with their bodies, and shall give an account of their own works.

"And they that have done good shall go into life everlasting, and they that have done evil into everlasting fire.

"This is the Catholic faith, which except a man believe faithfully and steadfastly, he cannot be saved.

"Glory be to the Father, and to the Son, and to the Holy Ghost. As it was in the beginning, is now, and ever shall be, one God, world without end. AMEN."

This Creed is said to have been drawn up in the fourth century. "It obtained in France about A. D. 850, and was received in Spain and Germany about one hundred and eighty years later. We have clear proofs of its being sung alternately in the English churches in the tenth century. It was in common use in some parts of Italy in 960, and was received at Rome about A. D. 1014." This Creed is retained by the church of England, but the Protestant Episcopal churches in the United States have rejected it.

## THE NICENE CREED.

"Credo in unum Deum, Patrem omnipotentem, Factorem cœli et terræ, visibilium omnium et invisibilium. Et in unum Dominum Jesum Christum, Filium Dei unigenitum. Et ex Patre natum, ante omnia sæcula. Deum de Deo, Lumen de Lumine, Deum verum de Deo vero, genitum, non factum; consubstantialem Patri, per quem omnia facta sunt. Qui propter nos homines, et propter nostram salutem, descendit de cœlis. Et incarnatus est de Spiritu Sancto ex Maria Virgine; ET HOMO FACTUS EST: crucifixus etiam pro nobis sub Pontio Pilato, passus, et sepultus est. Et resurrexit tertia die, secundum Scripturas. Et ascendit in cœlum, sedet ad dexteram Patris. Et iterum venturus est cum gloria judicare vivos et mortuos; cujus regni non erit finis. Et in Spiritum Sanctum, Dominum et Vivificantem; qui ex Patre Filioque procedit. Qui cum Patre et Filio simul adoratur et conglorificatur; qui locutus est per Prophetas. Et unam,

Sanctam, Catholicam, et Apostolicam Ecclesiam. Confiteor unum Baptisma, in remissionem peccatorum. Et expecto resurrectionem mortuorum. Et vitam venturi sæculi. Amen"

TRANSLATION.

"I believe in one God, the Father almighty, Maker of heaven and earth, of all things visible and invisible. And in one Lord Jesus Christ, the only-begotten Son of God. And born of the Father, before all ages. God of God, Light of Light, true God of true God, begotten, not made; consubstantial to the Father, by whom all things were made. Who for us men, and for our salvation, came down from heaven. And was incarnated by the Holy Ghost of the Virgin Mary; AND HE WAS MADE MAN: was crucified also under Pontius Pilate; he suffered, and was buried. And the third day he rose again, according to the Scriptures. And he ascended into heaven. Sits at the right hand of the Father. And he is to come again with glory to judge the living and the dead; of whose kingdom there shall be no end. And in the Holy Ghost, the Lord and Giver of Life, who proceeds from the Father and the Son, who, together with the Father and the Son, is adored and glorified; who spoke by the Prophets. And One, Holy, Catholic, and Apostolical Church. I confess one Baptism, for the remission of sins And I look for the resurrection of the dead; and the life of the world to come. Amen."

This Creed was adopted at Constantinople, A. D. 381. I is used in the Protestant Episcopal churches in England, and occasionally in those of the United States.

The foregoing Creeds are copied from Catholic books.

The Catholics, both in Europe and America, acknowledge the following Rule is "all that, and only that, belongs to Catholic belief, which is revealed in the word of God, and which is proposed by the Catholic church to all its members to be believed with divine faith."

"Guided by this certain criterion," they say, "we profess to believe,

1. "That Christ has established a church upon earth, and that this church is that which holds communion with the see of Rome, being one, holy, Catholic, and apostolical.

2. "That we are obliged to hear this church; and, therefore, that she is infallible, by the guidance of Almighty God, in her decisions regarding faith.

3. "That St. Peter, by divine commission, was appointed the head of this church, under Christ, its Founder; and that the pope, or bishop of Rome, as successor to St. Peter, has always been, and is, at present, by divine right, head of this church.

4. "That the canon of the Old and New Testament, as proposed to us by this church, is the word of God; as also such traditions, belonging to faith and morals, which, being originally delivered by Christ to his apostles, have been preserved by constant succession.

5. "That honor and veneration are due to the angels of God and his saints; that they offer up prayers to God for us; that it is good and profitable to have recourse to their inter cession; and that the relics, or earthly remains, of God's particular servants, are to be held in respect.

6. "That no sins ever were, or can be, remitted, unless by the mercy of God, through Jesus Christ; and, therefore, that man's justification is the work of divine grace.

7. "That the good works which we do, receive their whole value from the grace of God; and that, by such works, we not only comply with the precepts of the divine law, but hat we thereby likewise merit eternal life.

8. "That, by works done in the spirit of penance, we can make satisfaction to God for the temporal punishment which often remains due, after our sins, by the divine goodness, have been forgiven us.

9. "That Christ has left to his church a power of

granting indulgences, that is, a relaxation from such temporal chastisement only, as remains due after the divine pardon of sin; and that the use of such indulgences is profitable to sinners.

10. "That there is a purgatory, or middle state; and that the souls of imperfect Christians, therein detained, are helped by the prayers of the faithful.

11. "That there are seven sacraments, all instituted by Christ—baptism, confirmation, eucharist, penance, extreme unction, holy order, matrimony.

12. "That, in the most holy sacrament of the eucharist, there is truly, really, and substantially, the body and blood, together with the soul and divinity, of our Lord Jesus Christ.

13. "That, in this sacrament, there is, by the omnipotence of God, a conversion, or change, of the whole substance of the bread into the body of Christ, and of the whole substance of the wine into his blood, which change we call TRANSUBSTANTIATION.

14. "That, under either kind, Christ is received whole and entire.

15. "That, in the mass, or sacrifice of the altar, is offered to God a true, proper, and propitiatory, sacrifice for the living and the dead.

16. "That, in the sacrament of penance, the sins we fall into after baptism are, by the divine mercy, forgiven us.

"These are the great points of Catholic belief, by which we are distinguished from other Christian societies; and these, only, are the real and essential tenets of our religion. We admit, also, the other grand articles of revealed and natural religion, which the gospel and the light of reason have manifested to us. To these we submit, as men and as Christians, and to the former as obedient children of the Catholic church."

## BEREANS.

The Bereans are a sect of Protestant dissenters from the church of Scotland, who take their title from, and profess to follow the example of, the ancient Bereans, in building their system of faith and practice upon the Scriptures alone, without regard to any human authority whatever. The Bereans first assembled, as a separate society of Christians, in the city of Edinburgh, in the autumn of 1773. Mr. Barclay, a Scotch clergyman, was the founder of this sect.

The Bereans agree with the great majority of Christians respecting the doctrine of the Trinity, which they hold as a fundamental article; and they also agree, in a great measure, with the professed principles of our Orthodox churches, respecting predestination and election, though they allege that these doctrines are not consistently taught. But they differ from the majority of all sects of Christians in various other important particulars, such as, —

1. Respecting our knowledge of the Deity. Upon this subject, they say the majority of professed Christians stumble at the very threshold of revelation; and, by admitting the doctrine of natural religion, natural conscience, natural notices, &c., not founded upon revelation, or derived from it by tradition, they give up the cause of Christianity at once to the infidels, who may justly argue, as Mr. Paine, in fact, does, in his "Age of Reason," that there is no occasion for any revelation or word of God, if man can discover his nature and perfections from his works alone. But this, the Bereans argue, is beyond the natural powers of human reason; and, therefore, our knowledge of God is from revelation alone: and, without revelation, man would never have entertained an idea of his existence.

2. With regard to faith in Christ, and assurance of salvation through his merits, they differ from almost all other sects whatsoever. These they reckon inseparable, or rather the same, because (they say) "God hath expressly declared, He

that believeth shall be saved; and, therefore, it is not only absurd, but impious, and, in a manner, calling God a liar, for a man to say, 'I believe the gospel, but have doubts, nevertheless, of my own salvation.'" With regard to the various distinctions and definitions that have been given of different kinds of faith, they argue that there is nothing incomprehensible or obscure in the meaning of this word, as used in Scripture; but that, as faith, when applied to human testimony, signifies neither more nor less than the mere simple belief of that testimony as true, upon the authority of the testifier, so, when applied to the testimony of God, it signifies precisely "the belief of his testimony, and resting upon his veracity alone, without any kind of collateral support from concurrence of any other evidence or testimony whatever." And they insist that, as this faith is the gift of God alone, so the person to whom it is given is as conscious of possessing it, as the being to whom God gives life is of being alive; and, therefore, he entertains no doubts, either of his faith, or his consequent salvation through the merits of Christ, who died and rose again for that purpose. In a word, they argue that the gospel would not be what it is held forth to be, — glad tidings of great joy, — if it did not bring full personal assurance of eternal salvation to the believer; which assurance, they insist, is the present infallible privilege and portion of every individual believer of the gospel.

3. Consistently with the above definition of faith, they say that the sin against the Holy Ghost, which has alarmed and puzzled so many in all ages, is nothing else but unbelief; and that the expression, "it shall not be forgiven, neither in this world nor that which is to come," means only that a person dying in infidelity would not be forgiven, neither under the former dispensation by Moses, (the then present dispensation, kingdom, or government, of God,) nor under the gospel dispensation, which, in respect of the Mosaic, was a kind of future world, or kingdom to come.

4. The Bereans interpret a great part of the Old Testament prophecies, and, in particular, the whole of the Psalms,

excepting such as are merely historical or laudatory, to be typical or prophetical of Jesus Christ, his sufferings, atonement, mediation, and kingdom; and they esteem it a gross perversion of these psalms and prophecies, to apply them to the experiences of private Christians. In proof of this, they not only urge the words of the apostle, that no prophecy is of any private interpretation, but they insist that the whole of the quotations from the ancient prophecies in the New Testament, and particularly those from the Psalms, are expressly applied to Christ. In this opinion, many other classes of Protestants agree with them.

5. Of the absolute, all-superintending sovereignty of the Almighty, the Bereans entertain the highest idea, as well as of the uninterrupted exertion thereof over all his works, in heaven, earth, and hell, however unsearchable by his creatures. A God without election, they argue, or choice in all his works, is a God without existence, a mere idol, a nonentity. And to deny God's election, purpose, and express will, in all his works, is to make him inferior to ourselves.

The Bereans consider infant baptism as a divine ordinance, instituted in the room of circumcision, and think it absurd to suppose that infants, who, all agree, are admissible to the kingdom of God in heaven, should, nevertheless, be incapable of being admitted into his visible church on earth.

They commemorate the Lord's supper generally once a month; but, as the words of the institution fix no particular period, they sometimes celebrate it oftener, and sometimes at more distant periods, as it may suit their general convenience They meet every Lord's day, for the purpose of preaching, praying, and exhorting to love and good works. With regard to admission and exclusion of members, their method is very simple: when any person, after hearing the Berean doctrines, professes his belief and assurance of the truths of the gospel, and desires to be admitted into their communion, he is cheerfully received upon his profession, whatever may have been his former manner of life. But, if such a one should afterwards draw back from his good profession or practice, they first admonish him, and, if that has no effect, they leave him to himself. They do not think that they have any power to deliver a backsliding brother to Satan; that text, and other similar passages, such as, "Whatsoever ye shall bind on earth shall be bound in heaven," &c., they consider as restricted to the apostles, and to the inspired testimony alone, and not to be extended to any church on earth, or any number of churches, or of Christians, whether decided by a majority of votes, or by unanimous voices. Neither do they think themselves authorized, as a Christian church, to inquire into each other's political opinions, any more than to examine into each other's notions of philosophy.

They both recommend and practise, as a Christian duty, submission to lawful authority; but they do not think that a man, by becoming a Christian, or joining their society, is under any obligation, by the rules of the gospel, to renounce his right of private judgment upon matters of public or private importance. Upon all such subjects, they allow each other to think and act as each may see it his duty; and they require nothing more of the members, than a uniform and steady profession of the apostolic faith, and a suitable walk and conversation. (See Acts 17:11. Rom. 10:9.)

The Berean doctrines have found converts in various parts of Europe and America.

## MATERIALISTS.

Materialists are those who maintain that the soul of man is material, or that the principle of perception and thought is not a substance distinct from the body, but the result of corporeal organization. There are others called by this name who have maintained that there is nothing but matter in the universe.

The followers of the late Dr. Priestley are considered as

Materialists, or philosophical Necessarians. According to the doctor's writings, he believed, —

1. That man is no more than what we now see of him; his being commenced at the time of his conception, or perhaps at an earlier period. The corporeal and mental faculties, inhering in the same substance, grow, ripen, and decay together; and whenever the system is dissolved, it continues in a state of dissolution, till it shall please that Almighty Being who called it into existence, to restore it to life again. For if the mental principle were, in its own nature, immaterial and immortal, all its peculiar faculties would be so too; whereas we see that every faculty of the mind, without exception, is liable to be impaired, and even to become wholly extinct, before death. Since, therefore, all the faculties of the mind, separately taken, appear to be mortal, the substance or principle, in which they exist, must be pronounced mortal too. Thus we might conclude that the body was mortal, from observing that all the separate senses and limbs were liable to decay and perish.

This system gives a real value to the doctrine of the resurrection from the dead, which is peculiar to revelation; on which alone the sacred writers build all our hope of future life; and it explains the uniform language of the Scriptures, which speak of one day of judgment for all mankind, and represent all the rewards of virtue, and all the punishments of vice, as taking place at that awful day, and not before. In the Scriptures, the heathen are represented as without hope, and all mankind as perishing at death, if there be no resurrection of the dead.

The apostle Paul asserts, in 1 Cor. 15 : 16, that "if the dead rise not, then is not Christ risen; and if Christ be not raised, your faith is vain, ye are yet in your sins: then they also who are fallen asleep in Christ are perished." And again, verse 32, "If the dead rise not, let us eat and drink, for to-morrow we die." In the whole discourse, he does not even mention the doctrine of happiness or misery without the body.

If we search the Scriptures for passages expressive of the state of man at death, we shall find such declarations as expressly exclude any trace of sense, thought, or enjoyment (See Ps. 6 : 5. Job 14 · 7, &c.)

2. That there is some fixed law of nature respecting the will, as well as the other powers of the mind, and every thing else in the constitution of nature; and consequently that it is never determined without some real or apparent cause foreign to itself, i. e., without some motive of choice; or that motives influence us in some definite and invariable manner, so that every volition, or choice, is constantly regulated and determined by what precedes it; and this constant determination of mind, according to the motives presented to it, is what is meant by its *necessary determination.* This being admitted to be fact, there will be a necessary connection between all things past, present, and to come, in the way of proper cause and effect, as much in the intellectual as in the natural world; so that, according to the established laws of nature, no event could have been otherwise than it *has been,* or *is to be,* and therefore all things past, present, and to come, are precisely what the Author of Nature really intended them to be, and has made provision for.

To establish this conclusion, nothing is necessary but that throughout all nature the same consequences should invariably result from the same circumstances. For if this be admitted, it will necessarily follow that, at the commencement of any system, since the several parts of it, and their respective situations, were appointed by the Deity, the first change would take place according to a certain rule established by himself, the result of which would be a new situation; after which the same laws containing another change would succeed, according to the same rules, and so on forever; every new situation invariably leading to another, and every event, from the commencement to the termination of the system, being strictly connected, so that, unless the fundamental laws of the system were changed, it would be impossible that any event should have been otherwise than it was. In all these cases, the circumstances preceding any change are called the causes of that change; and, since a determinate event, or effect, constantly follows certain circumstances, or causes, the connection between cause and effect is concluded to be invariable, and therefore necessary.

It is universally acknowledged that there can be no effect without an adequate cause. This is even the foundation on which the only proper argument for the being of a God rests. And the Necessarian asserts that if, in any given state of mind, with respect both to dispositions and motives, two different determinations, or volitions, be possible, it can be on no other principle, than that one of them should come under the description of an effect without a cause; just as if the beam of a balance might incline either way, though loaded with equal weights. And if any thing whatever — even a thought in the mind of man — could arise without an adequate cause, any thing else — the mind itself, or the whole universe — might likewise exist without an adequate cause.

This scheme of philosophical necessity implies a chain of causes and effects established by infinite wisdom, and terminating in the greatest good of the whole universe; evils of all kinds, natural and moral, being admitted, as far as they contribute to that end, or are in the nature of things inseparable from it. Vice is productive, not of good, but of evil, to us, both here and hereafter, though good may result from it to the whole system; and, according to the fixed laws of nature, our present and future happiness necessarily depends on our cultivating good dispositions.

## ARMINIANS.

Those persons who follow the doctrines of Arminius, who was pastor at Amsterdam, and afterwards professor of divinity at Leyden. Arminius had been educated in the opinions of Calvin; but, thinking the doctrine of that great man, with regard to free will, predestination, and grace, too severe. he began to express his doubts concerning them in the year 1591, and, upon further inquiry, adopted the sentiments of those whose religious system extends the love of the Supreme Being and the merits of Jesus Christ to all mankind.

The distinguishing tenets of the Arminians may be comprised in the five following articles relative to predestination, universal redemption, the corruption of man, conversion, and perseverance, viz. : —

"1. That God determined to bestow pardon and present salvation on all who repent and believe in Christ, and final salvation on all who persevere to the end, and to inflict everlasting punishment on those who should continue in their unbelief, and resist his divine succors; so that election was conditional, and reprobation, in like manner, the result of foreseen infidelity and persevering wickedness. (See Ezek. 18 : 30—32. Acts 17 : 24—30. Matt. 23 : 37. Rom. 2 : 4, 5; 5 : 18. 1 Tim. 11 : 1—4. 2 Pet. 1 : 10; 3 : 9.)

"2. That Jesus Christ, by his sufferings and death, made an atonement for the sins of all mankind in general, and of every individual in particular; that, however, none but those who believe in him can be partakers of divine benefits. (See John 2 : 2; 3 : 16, 17. Heb. 2 : 9. Isa. 50 : 19, 20. 1 Cor. 8 : 11.)

"3. That true faith cannot proceed from the exercise of our natural faculties and powers, nor from the force and operation of free will; since man, in consequence of his natural corruption, is incapable either of thinking or doing any good thing; and that, therefore, it is necessary, in order to his conversion and salvation, that he be regenerated and renewed by the operation of the Holy Ghost, which is the gift of God through Jesus Christ.

"4. That this divine grace, or energy, of the Holy Ghost, begins and perfects every thing that can be called good in man, and, consequently, all good works are to be attributed to God alone; that, nevertheless, this grace is offered to all, and does not force men to act against their inclinations, but may be resisted, and rendered ineffectual, by the perverse wil of the impenitent sinner. Some modern Arminians interpret this and the last article with a greater latitude. (See Isa. 1 : 16. Deut. 10 : 16. Eph. 4 : 22.)

"5. That God gives to the truly faithful, who are regenerated by his grace, the means of preserving themselves in this state."

The first Arminians, indeed, had some doubt with respect to the closing part of the latter article; but their followers uniformly maintain, "that the regenerate may lose true, justifying faith, fall from a state of grace, and die in their sins." (See Heb. 6 : 4—6. 2 Pet. 2 : 20, 21. Luke 21 : 35. 2 Pet. 3 : 17.)

---

## METHODISTS,

OR

## THE METHODIST EPISCOPAL CHURCH.

This denomination arose in England, in 1729, and derived their name from the exact regularity of their lives. In 1741, they divided into two parties, under George Whitefield and John Wesley. The former adopted the sentiments of Calvin, and the latter those of Arminius. The Arminian class compose the great body of Methodists in this country and in Great Britain. Both of those men were eminently distinguished for the variety and extent of their labors.

The following are the articles of religion, as published in the "Doctrines and Discipline of the Methodist Episcopal Church:" —

"1. There is but one living and true God, everlasting, without body or parts, of infinite power, wisdom, and goodness; the Maker and Preserver of all things, visible and invisible. And in unity of this Godhead, there are three persons, of one substance, power and eternity — the Father, the Son, and the Holy Ghost.

"2. The Son, who is the Word of the Father, the very and eternal God, of one substance with the Father, took man's nature in the womb of the blessed Virgin; so that two whole and perfect natures, that is to say, the Godhead and manhood, were joined together in one person, never to be divided, whereof is one Christ, very God and very man, who truly suffered, was crucified, dead, and buried, to reconcile his Father to us, and to be a sacrifice, not only for original guilt, but also for the actual sins of men.

"3. Christ did truly rise again from the dead, and took again his body, with all things appertaining to the perfection of man's nature, wherewith he ascended into heaven, and there sitteth, until he return to judge all men at the last day.

"4. The Holy Ghost, proceeding from the Father and the Son, is of one substance, majesty, and glory, with the Father and the Son, very and eternal God.

"5. The holy Scriptures contain all things necessary to salvation; so that whatsoever is not read therein, nor may be proved thereby, is not to be required of any man, that it should be believed as an article of faith, or be thought requisite or necessary to salvation. By the name of the holy Scriptures, we do understand those canonical books of the Old and New Testament, of whose authority was never any doubt in the church. [Here follow the names of the canonical books of the Scriptures.]

"6. The Old Testament is not contrary to the New; for, both in the Old and New Testament, everlasting life is offered to mankind by Christ, who is the only Mediator between God and man, being both God and man. Wherefore they are not to be heard, who feign that the old fathers did look only for transitory promises. Although the law given from God by Moses, as touching ceremonies and rites, doth not bind Christians, nor ought the civil precepts thereof of necessity to be received in any commonwealth, yet, notwithstanding, no Christian whatsoever is free from the obedience of the commandments which are called moral.

"7. Original sin standeth not in the following of Adam, (as the Pelagians do vainly talk,) but it is the corruption of the nature of every man, that naturally is engendered of the off-spring of Adam, whereby man is very far gone from original righteousness, and of his own nature inclined to evil, and that continually.

"8. The condition of man, after the fall of Adam, is such, that he cannot turn and prepare himself, by his own natural strength and works, to faith, and calling upon God; wherefore we have no power to do good works, pleasant and acceptable to God, without the grace of God by Christ preventing us, that we may have a good will, and working with us when we have that good will.

"9. We are accounted righteous before God, only for the merit of our Lord and Savior Jesus Christ by faith, and not for our own works or deservings. Wherefore, that we are justified by faith only, is a most wholesome doctrine, and very full of comfort.

"10. Although good works, which are the fruits of faith, and follow after justification, cannot put away our sins, and endure the severity of God's judgments, yet are they pleasing and acceptable to God in Christ, and spring out of a true and lively faith, insomuch that by them a lively faith may be as evidently known, as a tree is discerned by its fruit.

"11. Voluntary works, being over and above God's commandments, which are called works of supererogation, cannot be taught without arrogancy and impiety. For by them men do declare that they do not only render unto God as much as they are bound to do, but they do more for his sake than of bounden duty is required; whereas Christ saith plainly, 'When ye have done all that is commanded you, say, We are unprofitable servants.'

"12. Not every sin willingly committed after justification, is the sin against the Holy Ghost, and unpardonable. Wherefore, the grant of repentance is not to be denied to such as fall into sin after justification; after we have received the Holy Ghost, we may depart from grace given, and fall into sin, and, by the grace of God, rise again, and amend our lives. And, therefore, they are to be condemned who say they can no more sin as long as they live here, or deny the place of forgiveness to such as truly repent.

"13. The visible church of Christ is a congregation of faithful men, in which the pure word of God is preached, and the sacraments duly administered according to Christ's ordinance, in all those things that of necessity are requisite to the same.

"14. The Romish doctrine concerning purgatory, pardon, worshipping and adoration as well of images as of relics, and also invocation of saints, is a fond thing, vainly invented, and grounded upon no warrant of Scripture, but repugnant to the word of God.

"15. It is a thing plainly repugnant to the word of God, and the custom of the primitive church, to have public prayer in the church, or to minister the sacraments, in a tongue not understood by the people.

"16. Sacraments ordained of Christ are not only badges or tokens of Christian men's profession, but rather they are certain signs of grace, and God's good-will towards us, by the which he doth work invisibly in us, and doth not only quicken, but also strengthen and confirm, our faith in him.

"There are two sacraments ordained of Christ our Lord in the gospel; that is to say, baptism and the supper of the Lord.

"Those five commonly called *sacraments* — that is to say, confirmation, penance, orders, matrimony, and extreme unction — are not to be counted for sacraments of the gospel, being such as have partly grown out of the *corrupt* following of the apostles, and partly are states of life allowed in the Scriptures, but yet have not the like nature of baptism and the Lord's supper, because they have not any visible sign or ceremony ordained of God.

"The sacraments were not ordained of Christ to be gazed upon, or to be carried about, but that we should duly use them. And in such only as worthily receive the same, they have a wholesome effect or operation; but they that receive them unworthily, purchase to themselves condemnation, as St. Paul saith. (1 Cor. 11:29.)

"17. Baptism is not only a sign of profession, and mark of difference, whereby Christians are distinguished from others that are not baptized, but it is also a sign of regeneration, or the new birth. The baptism of young children is to be retained in the church.

"18. The supper of the Lord is not only a sign of the love that Christians ought to have among themselves one to another, but rather is a sacrament of our redemption by Christ's death; insomuch that to such as rightly, worthily, and with faith, receive the same, the bread which we break is a partaking of the body of Christ, and likewise the cup of blessing is a partaking of the blood of Christ.

"Transubstantiation, or the change of the substance of bread and wine in the supper of our Lord, cannot be proved by Holy Writ, but is repugnant to the plain words of Scripture, overthroweth the nature of a sacrament, and hath given occasion to many superstitions.

"The body of Christ is given, taken, and eaten, in the supper, only after a heavenly and scriptural manner. And the means whereby the body of Christ is received and eaten in the supper, is faith.

"The sacrament of the Lord's supper was not by Christ's ordinance reserved, carried about, lifted up, or worshipped.

"19. The cup of the Lord is not to be denied to the lay people; for both the parts of the Lord's supper, by Christ's ordinance and commandment, ought to be administered to all Christians alike.

"20. The offering of Christ, once made, is that perfect redemption, propitiation, and satisfaction, for all the sins of the whole world, both original and actual; and there is none other satisfaction for sin but that alone. Wherefore the sacrifice of masses, in the which it is commonly said that the priest doth offer Christ for the quick and the dead, to have remission of pain or guilt, is a blasphemous fable and dangerous deceit.

"21. The ministers of Christ were not commanded by God's

law either to vow the estate of single life, or to abstract from marriage; therefore it is lawful for them, as for all other Christians, to marry at their own discretion, as they shall judge the same to serve best to godliness.

"22. It is not necessary that rites and ceremonies should in all places be the same, or exactly alike; for they have been always different, and may be changed according to the diversity of countries, times, and men's manners, so that nothing be ordained against God's word. Whosoever, through his private judgment, willingly and purposely doth openly break the rites and ceremonies of the church to which he belongs, which are not repugnant to the word of God, and are ordained and approved by common authority, ought to be rebuked openly, that others may fear to do the like, as one that offendeth against the common order of the church, and woundeth the consciences of weak brethren.

"Every particular church may ordain, change, and abolish, rites and ceremonies, so that all things may be done to edification.

"23. The president, the congress, the general assemblies, the governors, and the councils of state, *as the delegates of the people*, are the rulers of the United States of America according to the division of power made to them by the Constitution of the United States, and by the constitutions of their respective states. And the said states are a sovereign and independent nation, and ought not to be subject to any foreign jurisdiction.*

"24. The riches and goods of Christians are not common, as touching the right, title, and possession, of the same, as

* "As far as it respects civil affairs, we believe it the duty of Christians, and especially all Christian ministers, to be subject to the supreme authority of the country where they may reside, and to use all laudable means to enjoin obedience to the powers that be; and therefore it is expected that all our preachers and people, who may be under the British or any other government, will behave themselves as peaceable and orderly subjects."

some do falsely boast. Notwithstanding every man ought, of such things as he possesseth, liberally to give alms to the poor, according to his ability.

"25. As we confess that vain and rash swearing is forbidden Christian men by our Lord Jesus Christ and James his apostle, so we judge that the Christian religion doth not prohibit but that a man may swear when the magistrate requireth, in a cause of faith and charity, so it be done according to the prophet's teaching, in justice, judgment, and truth."

## METHODISTS,

OR

## THE METHODIST PROTESTANT CHURCH.

THE Protestant Methodists adhere to the Wesleyan Methodist doctrines, but discard certain parts of the discipline, particularly those concerning episcopacy and the manner of constituting the general conference. They seceded from the *Methodist Episcopal Church* in 1830, and formed a constitution and discipline of their own.

The following preamble and articles precede the constitution: —

"We, the representatives of the associated Methodist churches, in general convention assembled, acknowledging the Lord Jesus Christ as the only HEAD of the church, and the word of God as the sufficient rule of faith and practice, in all things pertaining to godliness, and being fully persuaded that the representative form of church government is the most scriptural, best suited to our condition, and most congenial with our views and feelings as fellow-citizens with the saints, and of the household of God; and whereas, a written constitution, establishing the form of government, and securing to the ministers and members of the church their rights and privileges, is the best safeguard of Christian liberty: We, therefore, trusting in the protection of Almighty God, and acting in the name and by the authority of our constituents, do ordain and establish, and agree to be governed by, the following elementary principles and constitution: —

"1. A Christian church is a society of believers in Jesus Christ, and is a divine institution.

"2. Christ is the only Head of the church, and the word of God the only rule of faith and conduct.

"3. No person who loves the Lord Jesus Christ, and obeys the gospel of God our Savior, ought to be deprived of church membership.

"4. Every man has an inalienable right to private judgment in matters of religion, and an equal right to express his opinion in any way which will not violate the laws of God, or the rights of his fellow-men.

"5. Church trials should be conducted on gospel principles only; and no minister or member should be excommunicated except for immorality, the propagation of unchristian doctrines, or for the neglect of duties enjoined by the word of God.

"6. The pastoral or ministerial office and duties are of divine appointment, and all elders in the church of God are equal; but ministers are forbidden to be lords over God's heritage, or to have dominion over the faith of the saints.

"7. The church has a right to form and enforce such rules and regulations only as are in accordance with the holy Scriptures, and may be necessary or have a tendency to carry into effect the great system of practical Christianity.

"8. Whatever power may be necessary to the formation of rules and regulations, is inherent in the ministers and members of the church; but so much of that power may be delegated, from time to time, upon a plan of representation, as they may judge necessary and proper.

"9. It is the duty of all ministers and members of the church, to maintain godliness, and to oppose all moral evil

"10. It is obligatory on ministers of the gospel to be

faithful in the discharge of their pastoral and ministerial duties, and it is also obligatory on the members to esteem ministers highly for their works' sake, and to render them a righteous compensation for their labors.

"11. The church ought to secure to all her official bodies the necessary authority for the purposes of good government; but she has no right to create any distinct or independent sovereignties."

We omit the constitution, as the preceding elementary principles sufficiently develop the peculiarities of this denomination.

## PROTESTANTS.

A NAME first given, in Germany, to those who adhered to the doctrine of Luther; because, in 1529, they protested against a decree of the emperor Charles V., and the diet of Spires, declaring that they appealed to a general council. The same name has also been given to the Calvinists, and is now become a common denomination for all sects which differ from the church of Rome.

## SABELLIANS.

A SECT, in the third century, that embraced the opinions of Sabellius, a philosopher of Egypt, who openly taught that there is but one person in the Godhead.

The Sabellians maintained that the Word and the Holy Spirit are only virtues, emanations, or functions of the Deity, and held that he who is in heaven is the Father of all things;

that he descended into the Virgin, became a child, and was born of her as a Son; and that, having accomplished the mystery of our salvation, he diffused himself on the apostles in tongues of fire, and was then denominated the *Holy Ghost.* This they explained by resembling God to the sun; the illuminated virtue or quality of which was the Word, and its warming virtue the Holy Spirit. The Word, they taught, was darted, like a divine ray, to accomplish the work of redemption; and that, being re-ascended to heaven, the influences of the Father were communicated after a like manner to the apostles.

## SANDEMANIANS.

So called from Mr. Robert Sandeman, a Scotchman, who published his sentiments in 1757. He afterwards came to America, and established societies at Boston, and other places in New England, and in Nova Scotia.

This sect arose in Scotland about the year 1728, where it is distinguished at the present day by the name of *Glassites*, after its founder, Mr. John Glass, a minister of the established church.

The Sandemanians consider that faith is neither more nor less than a simple assent to the divine testimony concerning Jesus Christ, delivered for the offences of men, and raised again for their justification, as recorded in the New Testament. They also maintain that the word *faith*, or belief, is constantly used by the apostles to signify what is denoted by it in common discourse, viz., a persuasion of the truth of any proposition, and that there is no difference between believing any common testimony and believing the apostolic testimony, except that which results from the testimony itself, and the divine authority on which it rests.

They differ from other Christians in their weekly adminis

ration of the Lord's supper; their love-feasts, of which every member is not only allowed, but required, to partake, and which consist of their dining together at each other's houses in the interval between the morning and afternoon service; their kiss of charity, used on this occasion, at the admission of a new member, and at other times, when they deem it necessary and proper; their weekly collection, before the Lord's supper, for the support of the poor, and defraying other expenses; mutual exhortation; abstinence from blood and things strangled; washing each other's feet, when, as a deed of mercy, it might be an expression of love, the precept concerning which, as well as other precepts, they understand literally; community of goods, so far as that every one is to consider all that he has in his possession and power liable to the calls of the poor and the church; and the unlawfulness of laying up treasures upon earth, by setting them apart for any distant, future, or uncertain use. They allow of public and private diversions, so far as they are not connected with circumstances really sinful; but, apprehending a lot to be sacred, disapprove of lotteries, playing at cards, dice, &c.

They maintain a plurality of elders, pastors, or bishops, in each church, and the necessity of the presence of two elders in every act of discipline, and at the administration of the Lord's supper.

In the choice of these elders, want of learning and engagement in trade are no sufficient objections, if qualified according to the instructions given to Timothy and Titus; but second marriages disqualify for the office; and they are ordained by prayer and fasting, imposition of hands, and giving the right hand of fellowship.

In their discipline they are strict and severe, and think themselves obliged to separate from communion and worship of all such religious societies as appear to them not to profess the simple truth for their only ground of hope, and who do not walk in obedience to it. (See John 13: 14, 15; 16: 13. Acts 6: 7. Rom. 3: 27; 4: 4, 5; 16: 16. 1 Cor. 16: 20. 2 Cor. 4: 13. 1 Pet. 1: 22.)

## ANTINOMIANS.

As we elsewhere give the sentiments of the ancient *Bereans*, *Pelagians*, and *Sabellians*, it is proper to notice those of Agricola, an eminent doctor in the Lutheran church, who flourished about the middle of the sixteenth century. The word *Antinomian* is derived from two Greek words, signifying *against law.*

It will be observed that the above names are used to denote sentiments or opinions, rather than sects or denominations.

The principal doctrines of the Antinomians, together with a short specimen of the arguments made use of in their defence, are comprehended in the following summary: —

"1. That the law ought not to be proposed to the people as a rule of manners, nor used in the church as a means of instruction; and that the gospel alone is to be inculcated and explained, both in the churches and in the schools of learning.

"For the Scriptures declare that Christ is not the lawgiver; as it is said, 'The law was given by Moses; but grace and truth came by Jesus Christ.' Therefore the ministers of the *gospel* ought not to teach the *law.* Christians are not ruled by the law, but by the spirit of regeneration; according as it is said, 'Ye are not under the law, but under grace.' Therefore the law ought not to be taught in the church of Christ.

"2. That the justification of sinners is an immanent and eternal act of God, not only preceding all acts of sin, but the existence of the sinner himself.

"For nothing new can arise in God; on which account, he calls things that are not, as though they were; and the apostle saith, 'Who hath blessed us with all spiritual blessings in heavenly places, in Christ Jesus, before the foundation of he world.' Besides, Christ was set up from everlasting, not only as the Head of the church, but as the surety of his people; by virtue of which engagement, the Father lecreed never to impute unto them their sins. (See 2 Cor. 5: 19.)

" 3. That justification by faith is no more than a manifestation to us of what was done before we had a being.

" For it is thus expressed, in Heb. 11: 1: 'Now, faith is the substance of things hoped for, the evidence of things not seen.' We are justified only by Christ; but by faith we perceive it, and by faith rejoice in it, as we apprehend it to be our own.

" 4. That men ought not to doubt of their faith, nor question whether they believe in Christ.

" For we are commanded to 'draw near in full assurance of faith.' (Heb. 10: 22.) 'He that believeth on the Son of God, hath the witness in himself,' (2 John 5: 10;) i. e., he has as much evidence as can be desired.

" 5. That God sees no sin in believers; and they are not bound to confess sin, mourn for it, or pray that it may be forgiven.

" For God has declared, (Heb. 10: 17,) 'Their sins and iniquities I will remember no more.' And in Jer. 50: 20, 'In those days, and in that time, saith the Lord, the iniquity of Israel shall be sought for, and there shall be none; and the sins of Judah, and they shall not be found; for I will pardon them whom I reserve.'

" 6. That God is not angry with the elect, nor doth he punish them for their sins.

" For Christ has made ample satisfaction for their sins. See Isaiah 53: 5, 'He was wounded for our transgressions, he was bruised for our iniquities,' &c. And to inflict punishment once upon the surety, and again upon the believer, is contrary to the justice of God, as well as derogatory to the satisfaction of Christ.

" 7. That by God's laying our iniquities upon Christ, he became as completely sinful as we, and we as completely righteous as Christ.

" For Christ represents our persons to the Father; and we represent the person of Christ to him. The loveliness of

Christ is transferred to us. On the other hand, all that is hateful in our nature is put upon Christ, who was forsaken by the Father for a time. See 2 Cor. 5 : 21, 'He was made sin for us, who knew no sin; that we might be made the righteousness of God in him.'

"8. That believers need not fear either their own sins or the sins of others, since neither can do them any injury.

"See Rom. 8 : 33, 34, 'Who shall lay any thing to the charge of God's elect?' &c. The apostle does not say that they never transgress, but triumphs in the thought that no curse can be executed against them.

"9. That the new covenant is not made properly with us, but with Christ for us; and that this covenant is all of it a promise, having no conditions for us to perform; for faith, repentance, and obedience, are not conditions on our part, but Christ's; and he repented, believed, and obeyed for us.

"For the covenant is so expressed, that the performance lies upon the Deity himself. 'For this is the covenant that I will make with the house of Israel, after those days, saith the Lord; I will put my laws into their mind, and write them in their hearts; and I will be to them a God, and they shall be to me a people.' Heb. 8 : 10.

"10. That sanctification is not a proper evidence of justification.

"For those who endeavor to evidence their justification by their sanctification, are looking to their own attainments, and not to Christ's righteousness, for hopes of salvation."

## PELAGIANS

A DENOMINATION which arose in the fifth century, so called from Pelagius, a monk, who looked upon the doctrines which were commonly received, concerning the original corruption of human nature, and the necessity of divine grace to enlighten the understanding and purify the heart, as prejudicial to the progress of holiness and virtue, and tending to establish mankind in a presumptuous and fatal security. He maintained the following doctrines :—

"1. That the sins of our first parents were imputed to them only, and not to their posterity; and that we derive no corruption from their fall, but are born as pure and unspotted as Adam came out of the forming hand of his Creator.

"2. That mankind, therefore, are capable of repentance and amendment, and of arriving to the highest degrees of piety and virtue, by the use of their natural faculties and powers. That, indeed, external grace is necessary to excite their endeavors, but that they have no need of the internal succors of the divine Spirit.

"3. That Adam was, by nature, mortal, and, whether he had sinned or not, would certainly have died.

"4. That the grace of God is given in proportion to our merits.

"5. That mankind may arrive at a state of perfection in this life.

"6. That the law qualified men for the kingdom of heaven, and was founded upon equal promises with the gospel."

## PRE-ADAMITES.

This denomination began about the middle of the sixteenth century. Their principal tenet is, *that there must have been men before Adam.* One proof of this they bring from Rom. 5: 12, 13, 14. The apostle says, "*Sin was in the world till the law;*" meaning the law given to Adam. But sin, it is evident, was not imputed, though it might have been committed, till the time of the pretended first man. "*For sin is not imputed when there is no law.*"

The election of the Jews, they say, is a consequence of th same system. It began at Adam, who is called their fathei or founder. God is also their Father, having espoused the Judaical church. The Gentiles are only adopted children, as being Pre-Adamites. Men (or Gentiles) are said to be made by the word of God. (Gen. 1 : 26, 27.) Adam, the founder of the Jewish nation, whose history alone Moses wrote, is introduced in the second chapter, as the workmanship of God's own hands, and as created apart from other men.

They argue thus : — Cain, having killed his brother Abel, was afraid of being killed himself. By whom ? He married — yet Adam had then no daughter. What wife could he get ? He built a town — what architects, masons, carpenters, and workmen, did he employ ? The answer to all these questions is in one word — Pre-Adamites.

This reasoning is opposed by sundry texts of Scripture. (See Gen. 1 : 26; 2 : 7; 3 : 20. Mark 10 : 6. 1 Cor. 15 45, 47.)

## PREDESTINARIANS

Are those who believe that God, for his own glory, hath foreordained whatsoever comes to pass. (See Matt. 25 : 34. Rom. 8 : 29, 30. Eph. 1 : 3, 6, 11. 2 Tim. 1 : 9. 2 Thess. 11 : 13. 1 Pet. 1 : 1, 2. John 6 : 37; 17 : 2—24. Rev. 13 : 8; 17 : 8. Dan. 4 : 35. 1 Thess. 5 : 19. Matt. 11 26. Exod. 4 : 21. Prov. 16 : 4. Acts 13 48.)

## ORTHODOX CREEDS.

Orthodoxy literally signifies *correct opinions.* The word 's generally used to denote those who are attached to the Trinitarian scheme of Christian doctrine.

The following article is found in the "Spirit of the Pilgrims," vol. v. No. 1, and is supposed to have been written by the late Rev. BENJAMIN B. WISNER, D. D., pastor of the Old South church, Boston.

The following summary contains the more material parts of the Orthodox faith. Those who embrace this system believe, —

"That, since the fall of Adam, men are, in their natural state, altogether destitute of true holiness, and entirely depraved.

"That men, though thus depraved, are justly required to love God with all the heart, and justly punishable for disobedience; or, in other words, they are complete moral agents, proper subjects of moral government, and truly accountable to God for their actions.

"That in the unspeakable wisdom and love of God was disclosed a plan of redemption for sinful men.

"That, in the development of this plan, God saw fit to reveal so much concerning the nature and the mode of the divine existence, as that he is manifested to his creatures as the Father, the Son, and the Holy Ghost; and that these three, each partaking of all the attributes of the Deity, and being entitled to receive divine worship and adoration, are the one living and true God.

"That the Son of God, laying aside the glory which he had with the Father from everlasting, came down from heaven, took upon himself man's nature, and by his humiliation, sufferings, and death, made an atonement for the sins of the world.

"That, in consequence of this atonement, the offer of pardon and eternal life was freely made to all; so that those who truly repent of sin, and believe in the Lord Jesus Christ, will be saved.

"That men are naturally so averse to God and holiness, that, if left to themselves, they reject the offers of salvation, and neither repent of sin nor truly believe in a Savior

"That God, being moved with infinite love and compassion, sends forth the Holy Spirit, according to his sovereign pleasure, by whose beneficent energy an innumerable multitude of the human family are renewed, sanctified, and prepared for heaven; while others are suffered to pursue the course which they have freely chosen, and in which they obstinately persevere till the day of salvation is past.

"That God, in his providential dispensations, in the bestowment of his saving mercy, and in his universal government, exhibits his adorable perfections, in such a manner as will call forth the admiration and love of all holy beings forever.

"That believers are justified by faith, through the efficacy of the atonement, so that all claims of human merit, and all grounds of boasting, are forever excluded.

"That the law of God is perpetually binding upon all moral beings, and upon believers not less than other men, as a rule of life; and that no repentance is genuine unless it bring forth fruits meet for repentance, and no faith is saving unless it produce good works.

"That those who have been renewed by the Spirit will be preserved by the power of God, and advanced in holiness unto final salvation. And,

"That Christ, as the great King of the universe, the Lord and Proprietor of created beings, will judge the world at the last day, when the righteous will be received to life eternal, and the wicked will be consigned to endless punishment"

"Since the reformation from Popery, those who profess to admit these doctrines, and others necessarily connected with them, and forming a part of the same system, have been denominated Orthodox, while to those who openly reject them, or any considerable part of them, this appellation has been denied.

"It is not to be inferred, however, that the Orthodox have been, or are, entirely *unanimous* on the subject of religion. In matters comparatively unessential, and in their modes of stating, explaining, and establishing essential truths, there has always been more or less a diversity. Thus persons may disagree as to the form of church government, or as to the mode of administering ordinances, and yet have an equal claim to be entitled Orthodox. Or persons may disagree in their interpretation of particular passages of Scripture, and as to the manner in which these bear on the doctrines of religion, without forfeiting their title to the some honorable appellation. For instance, one person may regard a particular passage as proof conclusive of the divinity of Christ, while another may be in doubt respecting it, or may apply it differently, and yet both be firm believers in the divinity of Christ. Many passages which the old writers quoted as proof-texts, have, in the progress of critical science, been differently interpreted; and yet the evidence in support of the Orthodox system, so far from being weakened in this way, has been constantly gaining strength.

"Again: persons may disagree, to a certain extent, at least, in their statements and explanations of the most essential doctrines, and yet be properly and equally Orthodox. In illustration of this remark, several examples will be given.

"All Orthodox Christians believe in the full inspiration of the sacred Scriptures; or that the holy men, through whose instrumentality the world originally received these Scriptures, spake and wrote "as they were moved by the Holy Ghost." They believe in this as a *fact* of the utmost importance. But there have been various modes of stating, explaining, and illustrating this fact. Some, for instance, have spoken of two or three kinds of inspiration; others have insisted that there can be but one kind; while others have thought it better to state the subject in general terms, without attempting very minutely to define or explain them.

"All Orthodox Christians believe in the doctrine of the Trinity, or that the one God exists in a threefold distinction, commonly called persons, — the Father, the Son, and the Holy Ghost. They believe this as a revealed fact, and as an essential part of the Christian doctrine. But how differently has this fact been stated by different individuals! What different explanations have been put upon it! While not a few have preferred to leave the subject — as God seems to have left it — altogether unexplained.

"All Orthodox Christians believe in the universality of God's eternal purposes, in the certainty of their execution, and that they are so executed as not to obstruct or impair the free agency of man. But respecting the *manner* of God's executing his purposes, — whether by the instrumentality of motives, or by a direct efficiency, — persons having equal claims to the appellation of Orthodox, have not been agreed.

"All the Orthodox believe in the natural and entire depravity of man; or that, in consequence of the sin of his first progenitors, and previous to regeneration, every thing within him, going to constitute moral character, is sinful. But how many theories have been framed to account for the connection of our sin with that of Adam! And how many explanations have been put upon the doctrine of entire depravity! Some have made this depravity to extend to all the powers of the soul; others have restricted it to our voluntary exercises and actions; while others have confined it chiefly to a moral taste, disposition, or instinct, which is regarded as back of our voluntary exercises, and the source of them.

"All the Orthodox believe in the doctrine of atonement; but all do not state or explain this important doctrine after the same manner. Some suppose the atonement of Christ to consist wholly in his obedience, others wholly in his sufferings, and others in both his obedience and sufferings. Some hold that Christ suffered the penalty of the law for sinners, and others that he only opened a way in which, on condition of repentance, this penalty may be remitted. Some think the atonement made only for the elect, while others regard it as the propitiation for the sins of the whole world.

"The doctrine of instantaneous regeneration by the special operations of the Holy Spirit, is believed by all who have any claim to be called Orthodox. But this doctrine, like the others mentioned, is variously stated and explained. Some consider man as entirely active in regeneration, others as entirely passive, and others as not entirely the one or the other. Some believe there is a holy principle implanted in regeneration, which ever afterwards remains in the heart of the subject, while others believe the change to consist in the commencement of holy exercises, which may be subsequently interrupted, though not finally lost. As to the manner in which the Spirit operates in regeneration, there is also a difference of opinion; some holding that he changes the heart by a direct efficiency, and others that this is done by the more powerful presentation and impression of motives.

"Another doctrine of the Orthodox system is, that of justification by faith in Christ. But this, also, has been differently stated and explained. Some think the believer justified by Christ's righteousness, others by the influence of his sufferings and death, and others by the joint efficacy of both his obedience and sufferings. Some believe justification to be the same as forgiveness, while others regard it as implying, not only forgiveness, but also a title to eternal life.

"It is evident, from the examples here given, that, although Orthodoxy denotes a general system of important doctrines or facts on the subject of religion, it is not to be inferred, either by friends or foes, that Orthodox Christians are tied up to precisely the same views of subjects, or that there exists no diversity of sentiment among them. There is, and always has been, a diversity of sentiment, in regard not only to modes and forms, but to the statement, proofs, and explanations, of the most important doctrines. Some of them, to be sure, are little more than verbal; but others are *real*, are fitted to excite interest, and are entitled to very serious consideration. Still, as they are all held in avowed consistency with that great series of facts which go to constitute the Orthodox system, they should not be regarded as placing their advocates beyond the proper limits of Orthodoxy. They constitute a wide field of important discussion, over which those who agree in holding the Head, — in holding the great doctrines of redemption by the blood of Christ, and of sanctification by the Holy Spirit, — may freely and fraternally traverse. Modes and forms, the interpretation of passages, and explanations of particular doctrines, (so long as essential doctrines are not discarded,) may be discussed without the interruption of brotherly affection, and without the imputation and reproach of heresy. One person may hold that all Scripture is given by the inspiration of *suggestion;* and another that, while some parts are the fruit of immediate suggestion, others may more properly be attributed to the inspiration of *superintendence;* and neither should charge the other with denying the inspiration of the Scriptures, or with being a heretic, or an infidel. One person may insist that the passage in 1 John 5 : 7, is authentic Scripture, and strong proof of the doctrine of the Trinity ; and another may doubt this, or deny it altogether ; and neither should be charged with intentionally corrupting the Scriptures, or with being a Unitarian. One person may hold that God executes his immutable and eternal decrees by a direct efficiency, and another that he does it by the intervention of motives, and yet one be no more an Arminian than the other."

## ANDOVER ORTHODOX CREED

EVERY person appointed or elected a professor in the Theological Institution at Andover, in the state of Massachusetts, shall, on the day of his inauguration into office, publicly make and subscribe the following CREED and DECLARATION : —

### CREED.

"I believe that there is one, and but one, living and true GOD ; that the word of GOD, contained in the Scriptures of the Old and New Testament, is the only perfect rule of faith and practice ; that, agreeably to those Scriptures, GOD is a Spirit, infinite, eternal, and unchangeable, in his being, wisdom, power, holiness, justice, goodness, and truth ; that in the Godhead are three Persons, the FATHER, the SON, and the HOLY GHOST; and that these THREE are ONE GOD, the same in substance, equal in power and glory; that God created man, after his own image, in knowledge, righteousness, and holiness; that the glory of GOD is man's chief end, and the enjoyment of GOD his supreme happiness; that this enjoyment is derived solely from conformity of heart to the moral character and will of GOD; that ADAM, the federal head and representative of the human race, was placed in a state of probation, and that, in consequence of his disobedience, all his descendants were constituted sinners; that, by nature, every man is personally depraved, destitute of holiness, unlike and opposed to GOD; and that, previously to the renewing agency of the DIVINE SPIRIT, all his moral actions are adverse to the character and glory of GOD; that, being morally incapable of recovering the image of his CREATOR, which was lost in ADAM, every man is justly exposed to eternal damnation; so that, except a man be born again, he cannot see the kingdom of GOD; that GOD, of his mere good pleasure, from all eternity, elected some to everlasting life, and that he entered into a covenant of grace, to deliver them out of this state of sin and misery by a REDEEMER; that the only REDEEMER of the elect is the eternal SON of GOD, who, for this purpose, became man, and continues to be GOD and man, in two distinct natures, and one person, forever; that CHRIST, as our Redeemer, executeth the office of a Prophet, Priest, and King; that, agreeably to the covenant of redemption, the SON of GOD, and he alone, by his sufferings and death, has made atonement for the sins of all men; that repentance, faith, and holiness, are the personal requisites in the gospel scheme of salvation; that the righteousness of CHRIST is the only ground of a sinner's justification; that this righteousness is received through faith; and that this faith is the gift of GOD; so that our salvation is wholly of grace; that no means whatever can change the heart of a sinner, and make it holy; that regeneration and sanctification are effects of the creating and renewing agency of the HOLY SPIRIT, and that supreme love to GOD constitutes the essen tial difference between saints and sinners; that, by convincing us of our sin and misery, enlightening our minds, working faith in us, and renewing our wills, the HOLY SPIRIT makes us partakers of the benefits of redemption; and that the ordinary means by which these benefits are communicated to us, are the word, sacraments, and prayer; that repentance unto life, faith to feed upon CHRIST, love to GOD, and new obedience, are the appropriate qualifications for the Lord's supper; and that a Christian church ought to admit no person to its holy communion, before he exhibit credible evidence of his godly sincerity; that perseverance in holiness is the only method of making our calling and election sure, and that the final perseverance of saints, though it is the effect of the special operation of GOD on their hearts, necessarily implies their own watchful diligence; that they who are effectually called, do, in this life, partake of justification, adoption, and sanctification, and the several benefits which do either accompany or flow from them; that the souls of believers are, at their death, made perfect in holiness, and do immediately pass into glory; that their bodies, being still united to CHRIST, will, at the resurrection, be raised up to glory, and that the saints will be made perfectly blessed in the full enjoyment of GOD, to all eternity; but that the wicked will awake to shame and everlasting contempt, and, with devils, be plunged into the lake that burneth with fire and brimstone forever and ever. I moreover believe that GOD, according to the counsel of his own will, and for his own glory, hath foreordained whatsoever comes to pass, and that all beings, actions, and events, both in the natural and moral world, are under his providential direction; that GOD's decrees perfectly consist with human liberty, GOD's universal agency with the agency of man, and man's dependence with his accountability; that man has understanding and corporeal strength to do all that GOD requires of him; so that nothing but the sinner's aversion to holiness prevents his salvation; that it is the prerogative of GOD to bring good out of evil, and that he will cause the wrath and rage of wicked men and devils to praise him; and that all the evil which has existed, and will forever exist, in the moral system, will eventually be made to promote a most important purpose, under the wise and perfect administration of that ALMIGHTY BEING, who will cause all things to work for his own glory, and thus fulfil all his pleasure."

DECLARATION.

' And, furthermore, I do solemnly promise that I will open and explain the Scriptures to my pupils with integrity and faithfulness; that I will maintain and inculcate the Christian faith, as expressed in the creed, by me now repeated, together with all the other doctrines and duties of our holy religion, so far as may appertain to my office, according to the best light GOD shall give me, and in opposition, not only to Atheists and Infidels, but to Jews, Papists, Mahometans, Arians, Pelagians, Antinomians, Arminians, Socinians, Sabellians, Unitarians, and Universalists, and to all heresies and errors, ancient and modern, which may be opposed to the gospel of CHRIST, or hazardous to the souls of men; that, by my instruction, counsel, and example, I will endeavor to promote true piety and godliness; that I will consult the good of this INSTITUTION, and the peace of the churches of our Lord Jesus Christ on all occasions; and that I will religiously conform to the constitution and laws of this SEMINARY, and to the statutes of this foundation."

The foregoing creed is considered a summary of what is commonly called the ASSEMBLY'S CATECHISM.

The *Westminster Assembly* met in London, in the reign of Charles I, A. D. 1643. It was a synod of learned divines, assembled by order of parliament, for the purpose of settling the government, liturgy, and doctrine, of the church of England.

## NEW HAVEN ORTHODOX CREED.

CONSIDERABLE anxiety existed, a few years since, in regard to the Orthodoxy of the Rev. Dr. TAYLOR, professor of divinity at Yale College, at New Haven, in the state of Connecticut. The following letter from Dr. TAYLOR to the Rev. Dr. HAWES, of Hartford, contains a full exposition of the religious views of that distinguished theologian: —

YALE COLLEGE, *Feb.* 1, 1832.

"Dear Brother:

"I thank you for yours of the 23d ult., in which you express your approbation of my preaching during the protracted meetings at Hartford. This expression of fraternal confidence is grateful to me, not because I ever supposed that we differed in our views of the great doctrines of the gospel, but because, for some reason or other, an impression has been made, to some extent, *that I am unsound in the faith.* This impression, I feel bound to say, in my own view, is wholly groundless and unauthorized. You think, however, that 'I owe it to myself, to the institution with which I am connected, and to the Christian community, to make a frank and full statement of my views of some of the leading doctrines of the gospel, and that this cannot fail to relieve the minds of many, who are now suspicious of my Orthodoxy.'

"Here I must be permitted to say, that the repeated and full statements of my opinions, which I have already made to the public, would seem to be sufficient to prevent or remove such suspicions. The course you propose, however, may furnish information to some who would desire it before they form an opinion, as well as the means of correcting the misrepresentations of others. I therefore readily comply with your request, and submit to your disposal the following statement of my belief on some of the leading doctrines of the gospel. I believe, —

"1. That there are three persons in one God, — the Father, the Son, and the Holy Ghost.

"2. That the eternal purposes of God extend to all actual events, sin not excepted; or that God foreordains whatsoever comes to pass, and so executes these purposes, as to leave the free moral agency of man unimpaired.

"3. That all mankind, in consequence of the fall of Adam, are born destitute of holiness, and are by nature totally depraved; in other words, that all men, from the commencement of moral agency, do, without the interposition of divine grace, sin, and only sin, in all their moral conduct.

"4. That an atonement for sin has been made for all mankind by the Lord Jesus Christ; that this atonement was necessary to magnify the law, and to vindicate and unfold the justice of God in the pardon of sin; and that the sinner who believes in the Lord Jesus Christ is freely justified on the ground of his atoning sacrifice, and on that ground alone.

"5. That the change in regeneration is a *moral* change, consisting in a new, holy disposition, or governing purpose of the heart, as a permanent principle of action; in which change, the sinner transfers the *supreme* affection of his heart from all inferior objects to the living God, chooses him as the portion of his soul, and his service and glory as his supreme good, and thus, in respect to moral character, becomes *a new man.*

"6. That this moral change is never produced in the human heart by *moral suasion*, i. e., by the mere influence of truth and motives, as the Pelagians affirm, but is produced by the influence of the Holy Spirit, operating on the mind through the truth, and in perfect consistency with the nature of moral action, and laws of moral agency.

"7. That all men (in the words of the article of your church) may accept of the offers of salvation freely made to them in the gospel, but that no one will do this, except he be drawn by the Father.

"8. That the necessity of the influence of the Holy Spirit in regeneration results solely from the voluntary perverseness of the sinner's heart, or disinclination to serve God, which, while it leaves him a complete moral agent, and without excuse for neglecting his duty, suspends his actual salvation on the sovereign will of God.

"9. That the renewing grace of God is *special*, in distinction from that which is common, and is resisted by the sinful mind, inasmuch as it is that which is designed to secure, and does infallibly secure, the conversion of the sinner.

"10. That all who are renewed by the Holy Spirit are elected or chosen of God from eternity, that they should be holy, not on account of foreseen faith, or good works, but according to the good pleasure of his will.

"11. That all who are renewed by the Holy Spirit, will, through his continual influence, persevere in holiness to the end, and obtain eternal life.

"Such is my faith in respect to some of the leading doctrines of the gospel. These doctrines I preach; these I teach in the theological department of this Seminary; these I have repeatedly published to the world. With what truth or justice any regard me as a 'teacher of theology, introducing heresy into our churches,' the candid can judge.

"But it may be asked, whether, after all, there are not some points on which I differ from my brethren generally, or, at least, from some of them. I answer, — It would be strange if any two men should be found to agree exactly in all the minute matters of religious opinion. With respect, however, to what is properly considered the Orthodox or Calvinistic SYSTEM of doctrines, as including the great FACTS of Christianity, and as opposed to, and distinguished from, the Unitarian, Pelagian, and Arminian *systems*, I suppose there is between the Orthodox ministry and myself an entire agreement. In respect to comparatively minor points, and philosophical theories, and modes of defending the Calvinistic system of doctrines, there has always been, as you are aware, a diversity of opinion, with freedom of discussion, among the Calvinists in this country, especially in New England, but which has never impaired their fellowship or mutual confidence. To these topics of difference, greater or less importance has been attached by different individuals. In respect to some of these, (and, in respect to them, I suppose myself to agree with a large majority of our Calvinistic clergy,) I will now briefly but frankly state what I do *not*, and what I do, believe.

"I do *not* believe that the posterity of Adam are, in the proper sense of the language, guilty of his sin; or that the ill desert of that sin is truly theirs; or that they are punished for that sin. But I do believe that, by the wise and holy constitution of God, all mankind, in consequence of Adam's sin, become sinners by their own act.

"I do *not* believe that the nature of the human mind, which God creates, is itself sinful; or that God punishes men for the nature which he creates; or that sin pertains to any thing in the mind which precedes all conscious mental exercise or action, and which is neither a matter of consciousness nor of knowledge. But I do believe that sin, universally, is no other than selfishness, or a *preference* of one's self to all others, — of some inferior good to God; that this free, voluntary preference is a permanent principle of action in all the unconverted; and that this is sin, and all that in the Scriptures is meant by sin. I also believe that such is the *nature* of the human mind, that it becomes the occasion of universal sin in men in all the appropriate circumstances of their existence, and that, therefore, they are truly and properly said to be sinners *by nature.*

"I do *not* believe that sin can be proved to be the necessary means of the greatest good, and that, as such, God prefers it, on the whole, to holiness in its stead; or that a God of sincerity and truth punishes his creatures for doing that which he, on the whole, prefers they should do, and which, as the means of good, is the best thing they can do. But I do believe that holiness, as the means of good, may be better than sin; that it may be true that God, all things considered, prefers holiness to sin in all instances in which the latter takes place, and, therefore, sincerely desires that all men should come to repentance, though, for wise and good reasons, he *permits*, or does not prevent, the existence of sin. I do *not* believe that it can be proved that an omnipotent God would be *unable* to secure more good by means of the perfect and universal obedience of his creatures, if they would render it, than by means of their sin. But I do believe that it may involve a dishonorable limitation of his power to suppose that he could not do it.*

"I do *not* believe that the grace of God can be truly said to be *irresistible*, in the primary, proper import of this term. But I do believe that, in all cases, it *may be* resisted by man as a free moral agent, and that, when it becomes effectual to conversion, as it infallibly does in the case of all the elect, it is *unresisted*

"I do *not* believe that the grace of God is necessary, as Arminians and some others maintain, to render man an accountable agent, and responsible for rejecting the offers of eternal life. But I do believe that man would be such an agent, and thus responsible, were no such grace afforded, and that otherwise 'grace would be no more grace.'

"I do *not* believe that it is necessary that the sinner, in using the means of regeneration, should commit sin in order to become holy. But I do believe that, as a moral agent, he is qualified so to use these means, i. e., the truth of God when present to his mind, as to become holy at once; that he is authorized to believe that, through the grace of the Holy Spirit, this *may be* done; and that, except in so doing, he cannot be truly and properly said to *use* the means of regeneration.

"I do *not* believe that we are authorized to assure the sin-

* "The question is, not whether God, all things considered, has purposed the existence of sin rather than to prevent it; but for what *reason* has he purposed it? Some affirm this *reason* to be, *that sin is the necessary means of the greatest good.* Now, what I claim, and all that I claim, is, that *no one can prove this to be the reason* why God has purposed the existence of sin, and that some other may be *the true reason*, without affirming what the true reason is."

ner, as Arminians do, and some others also, that the Holy Spirit is always ready to convert him. But I do believe that we are authorized to assure any sinner that it *may be true* that the Holy Spirit is now ready to convert him; 'that God PERADVENTURE will now give him repentance;' and that thus, in view of the possible intervention of divine influence, we remove what would otherwise be a ground of fatal discouragement to the sinner, when we exhort him to immediate repentance.

"I have dwelt the more on some of these particulars, because much pains has been taken, by some individuals, to make the impression that I have departed from the true faith respecting the influences of the Holy Spirit, even denying his influences altogether. So far is this from the fact, that, as you well know, no one attaches higher importance to this doctrine than I do, preaches it more decisively, or appreciates more highly its practical relations and bearings In my own view, the power of the gospel on the mind of the sinner very much consists in the two great facts of his complete moral agency as the basis of his obligation, of his guilt, and of his duty; — and of his dependence on the sovereign grace of God, resulting from his voluntary perverseness in sin. Without the latter, we could, in my opinion, neither show the Christian what thanks he owes his Deliverer from sin, nor awaken the sinner to flee from the wrath to come. This doctrine seems to be indispensable to destroy the presumptuous reliance of the sinner on future repentance, as it shows him how fearfully he provokes an offended God to withhold the grace on which all depends. At the same time, one thing is indubitably certain, viz., that God never revealed the doctrine of the sinner's dependence on his Spirit, to prevent the sinner from doing his duty at once God does not call sinners to instant compliance with the terms of life, and then assure them that such compliance is utterly out of the question, and to be wholly despaired of. The opposite impression, however, is not uncommon; and it is an error not less fatal to immediate repentance, than the fond hope of repenting hereafter. Both are to be destroyed; and he who does not preach the gospel in that manner which tends to destroy both, preaches it but imperfectly.

"In the earlier revivals of this country, great prominence was given, in the preaching, to the doctrine of dependence, in the forms of regeneration, election, &c. This was what was to be expected from the Calvinistic preachers of the time, in view of the prevalence of Arminianism. In the more recent revivals, however, a similar prominence seems to be given to moral agency, in the forms of present obligation to duty, its present practicability, &c. The preaching, thus distinguished in its more prominent characteristics, has been undeniably owned and blessed by the Spirit of God, although we are very apt to believe that what is true of one kind of preaching at one time, must be true of it at another. Now, I believe that both the doctrines of dependence and moral accountability must be *admitted by the public mind*, to secure upon that mind the full power of the gospel. I also believe that greater or less *prominence* should be given to the one or the other of these doctrines, according to the prevailing state of public opinion. When, at the earlier periods alluded to, the doctrine of dependence was dwelt on chiefly, (I do not suppose exclusively,) the public mind believed enough—I might say too much—concerning the free moral agency of man, and had not so well learned as since to pervert the doctrine of dependence to justify the waiting attitude of a passive recipient. And, then, both doctrines told with power on the mind and the conscience, and, through God, were attended with great and happy results. But the prominence given to the doctrine of dependence, in preaching, was continued, until, if I mistake not, it so engrossed the public attention, and so obscured or weakened the doctrine of responsibility, that many fell into the opposite error of quietly waiting for God's interposition. Hence, when this prevailing error is again corrected by a more prominent exhibition of man's responsibility, in the form of immediate obligation, &c., the power of both doctrines is again combined on he public mind, and we see the same or even greater results in revivals of religion. Nor would it be strange if the latter kind of preaching should, in its turn, prevail so exclusively and so long, that the practical influence of the doctrine of dependence should be greatly impaired, to be followed with another dearth of revivals and a quiet reliance of sinful men on their own self-sufficiency. On this subject, I have often, in view of the tendency of the human mind to vacillate from one extreme to the other, expressed my apprehensions. In some of my brethren, whom I love and respect, I see what I esteem a *disproportioned* estimate of the importance of preaching dependence; in others, whom I equally respect, I see what I regard as a *disproportioned* estimate of the importance of preaching moral responsibility. In regard to myself, I can say that I have aimed, in this respect, rightly to divide the word of truth, and that those discourses in which I have best succeeded in bringing the two doctrines to bear, in their combined force, on the mind, have been more blessed to the awakening and conversion of sinners, than almost any others which I preach. When both doctrines are wisely and truly presented, the sinner has no resting-place. He cannot well avoid a sense of guilt while proposing to remain in his sins, for he sees that he is a free moral agent, under all the responsibilities of such an agent to immediate duty. He cannot well presume on his resolution of future repentance, for he sees that sovereign, injured grace may at once abandon him to hopeless sin. He is thus shut up to the faith, — to the immediate performance of his duty. In accordance with these views, I aim, in my instructions to those who are preparing for the ministry, to inculcate the importance of a consistent, well-proportioned exhibition of the two great doctrines of the sinner's dependence and responsibility, that, in this respect, they may hold the minds of their hearers under the full influence of that gospel which is the power of God to salvation.

"I have thus stated, more minutely, perhaps, than you anticipated, my views and opinions. I could wish that they might be satisfactory to all our Orthodox brethren. I have no doubt that they will be to very many, and to some who have been alarmed by groundless rumors concerning my unsoundness in the faith. With respect to what I have called *leading doctrines*, I regard these as among the cardinal truths of the Christian system. They are truths to which I attach the highest importance, and in which my faith is more and more confirmed, the more I examine the word of God. To *some* of those of which I have spoken as *comparatively minor points*, I attach a high importance in their practical bearings and doctrinal connections. They are points, however, in regard to which there is more or less diversity of opinion among the Orthodox; and, as it is not my intention nor my practice to denounce others as heretics, merely because they differ from me in these matters, so I should be pleased with the reciprocation of the like catholicism on their part."

## SWEDENBORGIANS,

OR

## THE NEW JERUSALEM CHURCH.

Emanuel Swedenborg, the father of this sect, was the son of a bishop of West Gothnia, in the kingdom of Sweden, whose name was Swedberg, a man of considerable learning and celebrity in his time. The son was born at Stockholm, January 29, 1688, and died in London, 1772. He enjoyed early the advantages of a liberal education, and, being naturally endowed with uncommon talents for the acquirement of learning, his progress in the sciences was rapid and extensive, and he soon distinguished himself by several publications in the Latin language, which gave proof of equal genius and erudition. It may reasonably be supposed that, under the care of his pious and reverend father, our author's religious instruction was not neglected. This, indeed, appears plain from the general tenor of his life and writings, which are marked with strong and lively characters of a mind deeply impressed with a sense of the divine Being, and of all the relative duties thence resulting. He was ennobled in the year 1719, by Queen Ulrica Eleonora, and named Swedenborg, from which time he took his seat with the nobles of the equestrian order, in the triennial assembly of the states.

Baron Swedenborg had many eccentricities; but perhaps the most remarkable circumstance respecting him was his asserting that, during the uninterrupted period of twenty-seven years, he enjoyed open intercourse with the world of departed spirits, and during that time was instructed in the internal sense of the sacred Scriptures, hitherto undiscovered.

## ARTICLES OF FAITH

*Of the New Church, signified by the New Jerusalem in the Revelation.*

"1. That Jehovah God, the Creator and Preserver of heaven and earth, is Love Itself and Wisdom Itself, or Good Itself and Truth Itself: That he is One both in Essence and in Person, in whom, nevertheless, is the Divine Trinity of Father, Son, and Holy Spirit, which are the Essential Divinity, the Divine Humanity, and the Divine Proceeding, answering to the soul, the body, and the operative energy, in man: And that the Lord and Savior Jesus Christ is that God.

"2. That Jehovah God himself descended from heaven, as Divine Truth, which is the Word, and took upon him Human Nature for the purpose of removing from man the powers of hell, and restoring to order all things in the spiritual world, and all things in the church: That he removed from man the powers of hell, by combats against and victories over them; in which consisted the great work of Redemption: That by the same acts, which were his temptations, the last of which was the passion of the cross, he united, in his Humanity, Divine Truth to Divine Good, or Divine Wisdom to Divine Love, and so returned into his Divinity in which he was from eternity, together with, and in, his Glorified Humanity; whence he forever keeps the infernal powers in subjection to himself: And that all who believe in him, with the understanding, from the heart, and live accordingly, will be saved.

"3. That the Sacred Scripture, or Word of God, is Divine Truth itself; containing a Spiritual Sense heretofore unknown, whence it is divinely inspired, and holy in every syllable; as well as a Literal Sense, which is the basis of its Spiritual Sense, and in which Divine Truth is in its fulness, its sanctity, and its power; thus that it is accommodated to the apprehension both of angels and men: That the spiritual and natural senses are united, by correspondences, like soul and body, every natural expression and image answering to, and including, a spiritual and divine idea: And thus that the Word is the medium of communication with heaven, and of conjunction with the Lord.

"4. That the government of the Lord's Divine Love and Wisdom is the Divine Providence; which is universal, exercised according to certain fixed laws of Order, and extending to the minutest particulars of the life of all men, both of the good and of the evil: That in all its operations it has respect to what is infinite and eternal, and makes no account of things transitory, but as they are subservient to eternal ends; thus that it mainly consists, with man, in the connection of things temporal with things eternal; for that the continual aim of the Lord, by his Divine Providence, is to join man to himself and himself to man, that he may be able to give him the felicities of eternal life: And that the laws of permission are also laws of the Divine Providence; since evil cannot be prevented without destroying the nature of man as an accountable agent; and because, also, it cannot be removed unless it be known, and cannot be known unless it appear. Thus that no evil is permitted but to prevent a greater; and all is overruled, by the Lord's Divine Providence, for the greatest possible good.

"5. That man is not life, but is only a recipient of life

from the Lord, who, as he is Love Itself and Wisdom Itself, is also Life Itself; which life is communicated by influx to all in the spiritual world, whether belonging to heaven or to hell, and to all in the natural world; but is received differently by every one, according to his quality and consequent state of reception.

"6. That man, during his abode in the world, is, as to his spirit, in the midst between heaven and hell, acted upon by influences from both, and thus is kept in a state of spiritual equilibrium between good and evil; in consequence of which he enjoys free will, or freedom of choice, in spiritual things as well as in natural, and possesses the capacity of either turning himself to the Lord and his kingdom, or turning himself away from the Lord, and connecting himself with the kingdom of darkness: And that, unless man had such freedom of choice, the Word would be of no use, the church would be a mere name, man would possess nothing by virtue of which he could be conjoined to the Lord, and the cause of evil would be chargeable on God himself.

"7. That man at this day is born into evil of all kinds, or with tendencies towards it: That, therefore, in order to his entering the kingdom of heaven, he must be regenerated, or created anew; which great work is effected in a progressive manner, by the Lord alone, by charity and faith as mediums, during man's coöperation: That, as all men are redeemed, all are capable of being regenerated, and consequently saved, every one according to his state: And that the regenerate man is in communion with the angels of heaven, and the unregenerate with the spirits of hell: But that no one is condemned for hereditary evil, any further than as he makes it his own by actual life; whence all who die in infancy are saved, special means being provided by the Lord in the other life for that purpose.

"8. That Repentance is the first beginning of the Church in man; and that it consists in a man's examining himself, both in regard to his deeds and his intentions, in knowing and acknowledging his sins, confessing them before the Lord, supplicating him for aid, and beginning a new life: That, to this end, all evils, whether of affection, of thought, or of life, are to be abhorred and shunned as sins against God, and because they proceed from infernal spirits, who in the aggregate are called the Devil and Satan; and that good affections, good thoughts, and good actions, are to be cherished and performed, because they are of God and from God: That these things are to be done by man as of himself; nevertheless, under the acknowledgment and belief, that it is from the Lord, operating in him and by him: That so far as man shuns evils as sins, so far they are removed, remitted, or forgiven; so far also he does good, not from himself, but from the Lord; and in the same degree he loves truth, has faith, and is a spiritual man: And that the Decalogue teaches what evils are sins.

"9. That Charity, Faith, and Good Works, are unitedly necessary to man's salvation; since charity, without faith, is not spiritual, but natural; and faith, without charity, is not living, but dead; and both charity and faith, without good works, are merely mental and perishable things, because without use or fixedness: And that nothing of faith, of charity, or of good works, is of man; but that all is of the Lord, and all the merit is his alone.

"10. That Baptism and the Holy Supper are sacraments of divine institution, and are to be permanently observed; Baptism being an external medium of introduction into the Church, and a sign representative of man's purification and regeneration; and the Holy Supper being an external medium to those who receive it worthily, of introduction, as to spirit, into heaven, and of conjunction with the Lord; of which also it is a sign and seal.

"11. That, immediately after death, which is only a putting off of the material body, never to be resumed, man rises again in a spiritual or substantial body, in which he continues to live to eternity; in heaven, if his ruling affections, and hence his life, have been good; and in hell, if his ruling affections, and thence his life, have been evil.

"12. That Now is the time of the Second Advent of the Lord which is a Coming, not in Person, but in the power and glory of his Holy Word: That it is attended, like his first Coming, with the restoration to order of all things in the spiritual world, where the wonderful divine operation, commonly expected under the name of the Last Judgment, has in consequence been performed; and with the preparing of the way for a New Church on the earth, — the first Christian Church having spiritually come to its end or consummation, through evils of life and errors of doctrine, as foretold by the Lord in the Gospels: And that this New or Second Christian Church, which will be the Crown of all Churches, and will stand forever, is what was representatively seen by John, when he beheld the holy city, New Jerusalem, descending from God out of heaven, prepared as a bride adorned for her husband."

The leading theological works of Swedenborg are, the *Heavenly Arcana*, in twelve octavo volumes, giving an explanation of the books of Genesis and Exodus, being a key to what he calls the internal or spiritual sense of the sacred Scriptures. The next in importance is the *Apocalypse Explained*, in six octavo volumes, containing a full explanation of that book.

From his last work, *The True Christian Religion*, we make the following extracts, to show some of his peculiar views and style of writing: —

"CONCERNING THE SPIRITUAL WORLD.

"The spiritual world has been treated of in a particular work concerning Heaven and Hell, in which many things of that world are described; and, because every man, after death, comes into that world, the state of men there is also described. Who does not know, or may not know, that man lives after death? both because he is born a man, created an image of God, and because the Lord teaches it in his word

But what life he is to live, has been hitherto unknown. It has been believed that then he would be a soul, of which they entertained no other idea than as of ether, or air; thus that it is breath, or spirit, such as man breathes out of his mouth when he dies, in which, nevertheless, his vitality resides; but that it is without sight, such as is of the eye, without hearing, such as is of the ear, and without speech, such as is of the mouth; when yet, man, after death, is equally a man, and such a man, that he does not know but that he is still in the former world. He walks, runs, and sits, as in the former world; he lies down, sleeps, and wakes up, as in the former world; he eats and drinks, as in the former world; he enjoys conjugial delight, as in the former world; in a word, he is a man as to all and every particular; whence it is manifest, that death is not an extinction, but a continuation, of life, and that it is only a transition.

"That man is equally a man after death, although he does not then appear to the eyes of the material body, may be evident from the angels seen by Abraham, Hagar, Gideon, Daniel, and some of the prophets, — from the angels seen in the Lord's sepulchre, and afterwards, many times, by John, concerning whom in the Revelation, — and especially from the Lord himself, who showed that he was a man by the touch and by eating, and yet he became invisible to their eyes. Who can be so delirious, as not to acknowledge that, although he was invisible, he was still equally a man? The reason why they saw him was, because then the eyes of their spirit were opened; and, when these are opened, the things which are in the spiritual world appear as clearly as those which are in the natural world. The difference between a man in the natural world and a man in the spiritual world is, that the latter is clothed with a substantial body, but the former with a material body, in which, inwardly, is his substantial body; and a substantial man sees a substantial man as clearly as a material man sees a material man; but a substantial man cannot see a material man, nor a material man a substantial man, on account of the difference between material and substantial, which is such as may be described, but not in a few words.

"From the things seen for so many years, I can relate the following: That there are lands in the spiritual world, as well as in the natural world, and that there are also plains, and valleys, and mountains, and hills, and likewise fountains and rivers; that there are paradises, gardens, groves, and woods; that there are cities, and in them palaces and houses; and also that there are writings and books; that there are employments and tradings; and that there are gold, silver, and precious stones; in a word, that there are all things whatsoever that are in the natural world; but those in heaven are immensely more perfect. But the difference is, that all things that are seen in the spiritual world are created in a moment by the Lord, as houses, paradises, food, and other things; and that they are created for correspondence with the interiors of the angels and spirits, which are their affections and thoughts thence; but that all things that are seen in the natural world exist and grow from seed.

"Since it is so, and I have daily spoken there with the nations and people of this world, — thus not only with those who are in Europe, but also with those who are in Asia and in Africa, thus with those who are of various religions, — I shall add, as a conclusion to this work, a short description of the state of some of them. It is to be observed, that the state of every nation and people in general, as well as of each individual in particular, in the spiritual world, is according to the acknowledgment of God, and the worship of him; and that all who in heart acknowledge a God, and, after this time, those who acknowledge the Lord Jesus Christ to be God, the Redeemer and Savior, are in heaven; and that those who do not acknowledge him are under heaven, and are there instructed; and that those who receive are raised up into heaven, and that those who do not receive are cast down into hell."

Swedenborg says, "The Dutch are easily distinguished

from others in the spiritual world, because they appear in garments like those which they wore in the natural world, with the distinction, that those appear in finer ones, who have received faith and spiritual life. The reason why they are clothed in the like garments is, because they remain constantly in the principles of their religion; and all in the spiritual world are clothed according to them; wherefore, those there who are in divine truths, have white garments, and of fine linen.

"The cities in which the Dutch live are guarded in a singular manner: all the streets in them are covered with roofs, and there are gates in the streets, so that they may not be seen from the rocks and hills round about: this is done on account of their inherent prudence in concealing their designs, and not divulging their intentions; for such things, in the spiritual world, are drawn forth by inspection. When any one comes for the purpose of exploring their state, and is about to go out, he is led to the gates of the streets, which are shut, and thus is led back, and led to others, and this even to the highest degree of vexation, and then he is let out this is done that he may not return. Wives, who affect dominion over their husbands, live at one side of the city, and do not meet their husbands, except when they are invited, which is done in a civil manner; and then they also lead them to houses, where consorts live without exercising dominion over each other, and show them how clean and elegant their houses are, and what enjoyment of life they have, and that they have these things from mutual and conjugal love. Those wives who attend to these things, and are affected by them, cease to exercise dominion, and live together with their husbands; and then they have a habitation assigned to them nearer to the middle, and are called angels: the reason is, because truly conjugal love is heavenly love, which is without dominion.

"With respect to the English nation, the best of them are in he centre of all Christians, because they have interior intel ectual light. This does not appear to any one in the natura world, but it appears conspicuously in the spiritual world. This light they derive from the liberty of speaking and writing, and thereby of thinking. With others, who are not in such liberty, that light, not having any outlet, is obstructed. That light, indeed, is not active of itself, but it is made active by others, especially by men of reputation and authority. As soon as any thing is said by them, that light shines forth.

"For this reason, they have moderators appointed over them in the spiritual world; and priests are given to them, of high reputation and eminent talents, in whose opinions, from this their natural disposition, they acquiesce.

"There are two great cities, like London, into which most of the English come after death: it has been given me to see the former city, and also to walk over it. The middle of that city is where the merchants meet in London, which is called the Exchange: there the moderators dwell. Above that middle is the east, below it is the west, on the right side is the south, on the left side is the north. In the eastern quarter, those dwell who have preëminently led a life of charity. there are magnificent palaces. In the southern quarter the wise dwell, with whom there are many splendid things. In the northern quarter, those dwell who have preëminently loved the liberty of speaking and writing. In the western quarter, those dwell who boast of justification by faith alone. On the right there, in this quarter, is the entrance into this city, and also a way out of it: those who live ill are sent out there. The ministers who are in the west, and teach that faith alone, dare not enter the city through the great streets, but through narrow alleys; since no other inhabitants are tolerated in the city itself, than those who are in the faith of charity. I have heard them complaining of the preachers from the west, that they compose their sermons with such art and eloquence, and introduce into them the strange doctrine of justification by faith, that they do not know whether good ought to be done or not. They preach faith as intrinsic good, and separate this from the good of charity, which they call meritorious, and thus not acceptable to God. But, when those who dwell in the eastern and southern quarters of the city hear such sermons, they go out of the temples; and the preachers afterwards are deprived of the priestly office."

"CONCERNING THE POPISH SAINTS IN THE SPIRITUAL WORLD.

"It is known that man has innate or hereditary evil from parents; but it is known to few in what that dwells, in its fulness: it dwells in the love of possessing the goods of all others, and in the love of ruling; for this latter love is such, that, as far as the reins are given to it, so far it bursts forth, until it burns with the desire of ruling over all, and, at length, wishes to be invoked and worshipped as a god. This love is the serpent, which deceived Eve and Adam; for it said to the woman, *God doth know, in the day that ye eat of the fruit of that tree, your eyes will be opened,* AND THEN YE WILL BE AS GOD. (Gen. iii. 4, 5.) As far, therefore, as man, without restraint, rushes into this love, so far he averts himself from God, and turns to himself, and becomes a worshipper of himself; and then he can invoke God with a warm mouth from the love of self, but with a cold heart from contempt of God. And then, also, the divine things of the church may serve for means; but, because the end is dominion, the means are regarded no more than as they are subservient to it. Such a person, if he is exalted to the highest honors, is, in his own imagination, like Atlas bearing the terraqueous globe upon his shoulders, and like Phœbus, with his horses, carrying the sun around the world.

"Since man hereditarily is such, therefore all who, by papal bulls, have been made saints, in the spiritual world are removed from the eyes of others, and concealed, and all intercourse with their worshippers is taken away from them the reason is, lest that most pernicious root of evil should be excited in them, and they should be brought into such fantastic deliriums as there are with demons. Into such deliri ums those come, who, while they live in the world, zealously aspire to be made saints after death, that they may be invoked.

"Many of the Roman Catholic persuasion, especially the monks, when they come into the spiritual world, inquire for the saints, particularly the saint of their order; but they do not find them, at which they wonder; but afterwards they are instructed that they are mixed together, either with those who are in heaven, or with those who are in the earth below; and that, in either case, they know nothing of the worship and invocation of themselves, and that those who do know, and wish to be invoked, fall into deliriums, and talk foolishly. The worship of saints is such an abomination in heaven, that, if they only hear it, they are filled with horror; since, as far as worship is ascribed to any man, so far it is withheld from the Lord; for thus, he alone is not worshipped; and, if the Lord alone is not worshipped, a discrimination is made, which destroys communion, and the happiness of life flowing from it. That I might know what the Roman Catholic saints are, in order that I might make it known, as many as a hundred were brought forth from the earth below, who knew of their canonization. They ascended behind my back, and only a few before my face; and I spoke with one of them, who, they said, was Xavier. He, while he talked with me, was like a fool; yet he could tell, that, in his place, where he was shut up with others, he was not a fool, but that he becomes a fool as often as he thinks that he is a saint, and wishes to be invoked. A like murmur I heard from those who were behind my back. It is otherwise with the saints, so called, in heaven: these know nothing at all of what is done on earth; nor is it given them to speak with any of the Roman Catholic persuasion, who are in that superstition, lest any idea of that thing should enter into them.

"From this their state, every one may conclude that invocations of them are only mockeries; and, moreover, I can assert, that they do not hear their invocations on earth, any more than their images do at the sides of the streets, nor any more than the walls of the temple, nor any more than the birds that build their nests in towers. It is said by their servants on earth, that the saints reign in heaven, together with the Lord Jesus Christ; but this is a figment and a falsehood; for they no more reign with the Lord, than a hostler with a king, a porter with a grandee, or a footman with a primate; for John the Baptist said, concerning the Lord, *that he was not worthy to unloose the latchet of his shoe*, (Mark 1 : 7. John 1 : 27.) What, then, are those who are such?

"There appears, sometimes, to the people of Paris, who are in the spiritual world, in a society, a certain woman of a common stature, in shining raiment, and of a face, as it were, holy; and she says that she is Genevieve; but, when any begin to adore her, then her face is immediately changed, and also her raiment, and she becomes like an ordinary woman, and reproves them for wishing to adore a woman, who, among her companions, is in no higher estimation than as a maid-servant, wondering that the men of the world should be captivated by such trifles.

"To the above, I shall add this, which is most worthy of attention. Once, Mary, the Mother of the Lord, passed by, and was seen overhead in white raiment; and then, stopping a while, she said that she was the mother of the Lord, and that he was indeed born of her; but that he, being made God, put off all the human from her, and that, therefore, she now adores him as her God; and that she is unwilling that any one should acknowledge him for her son, since in him all is divine."

## FIGHTING QUAKERS.

The term *Fighting* or *Wet* Quaker is applied to those who retain the Quaker faith, but adopt the manners and costume of other denominations. The celebrated Nathaniel

Greene was one of this character, as were many of the people of Rhode Island, where religious liberty first erected its standard in America.

"When the British army had possession of Philadelphia, a committee of three of the leading men of the society of Friends had permission to go to the head-quarters of General Washington, relative to some matters of inconvenience of some of their brethren, within Washington's command. The general listened to them with his usual courtesy and wisdom, but could not determine the business till the next day. In the mean time, he told them he would put them under the protection of an officer of their own society, and thereupon sent for General Nathaniel Greene; and when he arrived, in full uniform, he introduced 'the Friends' to each other. After a little silence, Friend James Pemberton turned slowly to General Greene, and said, 'Dost thou profess to be one of our persuasion?' 'O, yes,' said the general; 'I was so educated.' The committee looked at each other, and upon the general's sword, when one of them said, 'May I ask General Greene what part of our land thou wast born and brought up in?' 'O, yes, yes,' replied Greene; 'I'm from RHODE ISLAND.' 'Oho,' rejoined more than one of them, 'yes, yes, a RHODE ISLAND QUAKER! Yes, Friend Greene, we are satisfied with thy explanation, and will accept of thy kind offer.' Greene betrayed a momentary flush of disconcertion, at which, it was said, Washington's countenance half smiled at the *Rhode Island Quaker!*"

## HARMONISTS.

MR. GEORGE RAPP and other emigrants arrived from Germany, and settled in the interior of Pennsylvania, about the year 1805. They formed an economy on the primitive plan of having "all things in common." They appear to have prospered. In 1814 they sold their property in Pennsylvania and removed to Indiana, to form a new establishment, on an improved plan. They profess the Protestant religion, but admit of universal toleration. They cultivate the learned languages and professions, and maintain strict morals, with a due observation of the Sabbath. They keep watch by turns at night; and, after crying the hour, add, "A day is past, and a step made nearer our end. Our time runs away, and the joys of heaven are our reward." (See Acts 4 : 32.)

## DORRELITES.

A SECTARY, by the name of Dorrel, appeared in Leyden, Mass., about fifty years ago, and made some proselytes. The following are some of his leading sentiments: — Jesus Christ is, as to substance, a spirit, and is God. He took a body, died, and never rose from the dead. None of the human race will ever rise from their graves. The resurrection, spoken of in Scripture, is only one from sin to spiritual life, which consists in perfect obedience to God. Written revelation is a type of the substance of the true revelation, which God makes to those whom he raises from spiritual death. The substance is God revealed in the soul. Those who have it are perfect, are incapable of sinning, and have nothing to do with the Bible. The eternal life, purchased by Christ, was an eternal succession of natural generation. Heaven is light, and hell is darkness. God has no wrath. There is no opposition between God and the devil, who have equal power in their respective worlds of light and darkness. Those who are raised are free from all civil laws; are not bound by the marriage covenant; and the perfect have a right to promiscuous intercourse. Neither prayer nor any other worship is necessary. There is no law but that of nature. There is no future judgment, nor any knowledge n the future state, of what is done in this world. God has no forethought, no knowledge of what passes in the dark world, which is hell, nor any knowledge of what has taken place, or will take place, in this world. Neither God nor the devil has any power to control man. There are two kinds of perfection — that of the head, and that of the members. The leader is perfect as the head; but none of his followers can be so, in this sense, so long as the leader continues. All covenants which God has heretofore entered into with man, are at an end, and a new covenant made with the leader, (Dorrel,) in which he has all power to direct, and all the blessings of which must be looked for through him. Neither Moses nor Christ wrought any miracles. I (says Dorrel) stand the same as Jesus Christ in all respects. My disciples stand in the same relation to me, as the disciples of Christ did to him. I am to be worshipped in the same manner as Christ was to be worshipped, as God united to human flesh. This sect was broken up in the following manner: —

One of Dorrel's lectures was attended by Captain Ezekiel Foster, of Leyden, a man of good sense, of a strong, muscular frame, and a countenance which bespoke authority. When Dorrel came to the declaration of his extraordinary powers, he had no sooner uttered the words, 'No arm can hurt my flesh,' than Foster rose, indignant at the imposture he was practising on his deluded followers, and knocked down Dorrel with his fist. Dorrel, in great trepidation, and almost senseless, attempted to rise, when he received a second blow, at which he cried for mercy. Foster engaged to forbear, on condition that he would renounce his doctrines, but continued beating him. Soon a short parley ensued, when Dorrel consented, and did renounce his doctrines in the hearing of all his astonished followers. He further told them, that his object was to see what fools he could make of mankind. His followers, ashamed and chagrined at being made the dupes of such an unprincipled fellow, departed in peace to their homes. Dorrel promised his assailant, upon the penalty of his life never to attempt any similar imposition upon the people.

## OSGOODITES.

These people profess to believe in one God, who is fully acquainted with all his own works; but they believe there are some things done by wicked agents, of which God has no knowledge. They reject the idea of Christ's divinity, and of any thing special in regeneration. They pretend to miraculous gifts, such as healing the sick, and praying down the judgments of God upon those who oppose them. They deny any thing peculiarly sacred in the Christian Sabbath, although they generally meet on that day for religious worship, but without much regard to order. They reject the ordinances of baptism and the Lord's supper. They are opposed to Bible societies, and other moral and religious institutions of the day, particularly to temperance societies.

This sect arose about the year 1812, in the county of Merrimack, N. H., where a few societies exist. Jacob Osgood is their leader

## ROGERENES.

This is a sect calling themselves Seventh-Day Baptists, that arose in New England about the year 1674. John and James Rogers were their leaders. They were peculiar in their language, dress, and manners; they employed no physician, nor used any medicine: they paid no regard to the Christian Sabbath, and disturbed and abused those that did. It is said that a few of this people still remain. See the *Battle-Axe*, a work published by them a few years ago, at their printing establishment, at Groton, Conn.

## WHIPPERS.

This denomination sprang up in Italy, in the thirteenth century, and was thence propagated through almost all the countries of Europe. The society that embraced this new discipline, ran in multitudes, composed of persons of both sexes, and all ranks and ages, through the public streets, with whips in their hands, lashing their naked bodies with the most astonishing severity, with a view to obtain the divine mercy for themselves and others, by their voluntary mortification and penance. This sect made their appearance anew in the fourteenth century, and taught, among other things, that flagellation was of equal virtue with baptism and other sacraments; that the forgiveness of all sins was to be obtained by it from God, without the merit of Jesus Christ; that the old law of Christ was soon to be abolished, and that a new law, enjoining the baptism of blood, to be administered by whipping, was to be substituted in its place.

A new denomination of Whippers arose in the fifteenth century, who rejected the sacraments and every branch of external worship, and placed their only hopes of salvation in *faith* and *flagellation.*

## WILKINSONIANS.

The followers of Jemima Wilkinson, who was born in Cumberland, R. I. In 1776, she asserted that she was taken sick, and actually died, and that her soul went to heaven. Soon after, her body was reanimated with the spirit and power of Christ, upon which she set up as a public teacher, and declared she had an immediate revelation for all she delivered, and was arrived to a state of absolute perfection. It is also said she pretended to foretell future events, to discern the secrets of the heart, and to have the power of healing diseases; and if any person who had made application to her was not healed, she attributed it to his want of faith. She asserted that those who refused to believe these exalted things concerning her, will be in the state of the unbelieving Jews, who rejected the counsel of God against themselves; and she told her hearers that was the eleventh hour, and the last call of mercy that ever should be granted them; for she heard an inquiry in heaven, saying, "Who will go and preach to a dying world?" or words to that import; and she said she answered, "Here am I — send me;" and that she left the realms of light and glory, and the company of the heavenly host, who are continually praising and worshipping God, in order to descend upon earth, and pass through many sufferings and trials for the happiness of mankind. She assumed the title of the *universal friend of mankind.*

Jemima made some converts in Rhode Island and New York, and died in 1819. She is said to have been a very beautiful, but artful woman.

## AQUARIANS.

Water-Drinkers, a branch of the *Encratites*, a sect in the second century, who abstained from marriage, wine, and animal food; who carried their aversion to wine so far, that they substituted water in the holy communion, though some refused it only in their *morning* ceremonies. It is well known that the ancient Christians mingled water with their wine for sacred use, partly, perhaps, for economy, and partly from sobriety; but Cyprian gives a mystical reason — because the wine and water represent Christ and his people united.

## BAXTERIANS.

The Baxterian strikes into a middle path between Arminianism and Calvinism, and thus endeavors to unite both schemes. With the Calvinist, he professes to believe that a certain number, determined upon in the divine councils, will be infallibly saved; and with the Arminian, he joins in rejecting the doctrine of reprobation, as absurd and impious;—admits that Christ, in a certain sense, died for all, and supposes that such a portion of grace is allotted to *every* man, as renders it his own fault if he does not attain to eternal life.

This conciliatory system was espoused by the famous Nonconformist, Richard Baxter, who was celebrated for the acuteness of his controversial talents, and the utility of his practical writings.

Among Baxterians are ranked both Watts and Doddridge. Dr. Doddridge, indeed, has this striking remark — "That a Being who is said not to tempt any one, and even swears that he desires not the death of a sinner, should *irresistibly* determine millions to the commission of every sinful action of their lives, and then, with all the pomp and pageantry of a universal judgment, condemn them to eternal misery, on account of these actions, that hereby he may promote the happiness of others who are, or shall be, irresistibly determined to virtue, in the like manner, is of all incredible things to me the most incredible!"

In the scale of religious sentiment, Baxterianism seems to be, with respect to the subject of divine favor, what Arianism is with respect to the person of Christ. It appears to have been considered by some pious persons as a safe middle way between two extremes.

# MILLER'S VIEWS
## ON THE
## SECOND COMING OF CHRIST.

THE following letter from Rev. WILLIAM MILLER to Rev JOSHUA V. HIMES contains a synopsis of Mr. Miller's views on this interesting subject:—

"Rev. J. V. Himes:

"My dear brother: You have requested a synopsis of my views of the Christian faith. The following sketch will give you some idea of the religious opinions I have formed, by a careful study of the word of God:—

"I believe all men, coming to years of discretion, do and will disobey God; and this is, in some measure, owing to corrupted nature by the sin of our parent. I believe God will not condemn us for any pollution in our father; but the soul that sinneth shall die. All pollution of which we may be partakers from the sins of our ancestors, in which we could have no agency, can and will be washed away in the blood and sacrifice of Jesus Christ, without our agency. But all sins committed by us as rational, intelligent agents, can only be cleansed by the blood of Jesus Christ, through our repentance and faith. I believe in the salvation of all men who receive the grace of God by repentance and faith in the mediation of Jesus Christ. I believe in the condemnation of all men who reject the gospel and mediation of Christ, and thereby lose the efficacy of the blood and righteousness of our Redeemer, as proffered to us in the gospel. I believe in practical godliness, as commanded us in the Scriptures, (which are our only rule of faith and practice,) and that they only will be entitled to heaven and future blessedness, who obey and keep the commandments of God, as given us in the Bible, which is the word of God. I believe in God, the Father of our Lord Jesus Christ, who is a Spirit, omnipresent, omniscient, having all power, Creator, Preserver. and self existent. As being holy, just, and beneficent, I believe in Jesus Christ, the Son of God, having a body in fashion and form like man, divine in his nature, human in his person, godlike in his character and power. He is a Savior for sinners, a Priest to God, a Mediator between God and man, and King in Zion. He will be all to his people, God with us forever. The spirit of the Most High is in him, the power of the Most High is given him, the people of the Most High are purchased by him, the glory of the Most High shall be with him, and the kingdom of the Most High is his on earth.

"I believe the Bible is the revealed will of God to man, and all therein is necessary to be understood by Christians in the several ages and circumstances to which they may refer;—for instance, what may be understood to-day, might not have been necessary to have been understood a thousand years ago; for its object is to reveal things new and old, that the man of God may be thoroughly furnished for, and perfected in, every good word and work, for the age in which he lives. I believe it is revealed in the best possible manner for all people, in every age and under every circumstance, to understand, and that it is to be understood as literal as it can be and make good sense; and that in every case where the language is figurative, we must let the Bible explain its own figures. We are in no case allowed to speculate on the Scriptures, and suppose things which are not clearly expressed, nor reject things which are plainly taught. I believe all of the prophecies are revealed to try our faith, and to give us hope, without which we could have no reasonable hope. I believe that the Scriptures do reveal unto us, in plain language, that Jesus Christ will appear again on this earth; that he will come in the glory of God, in the clouds of heaven, with all his saints and angels; that he will raise the dead bodies of all his saints who have slept, change the bodies of all that are alive on the earth that are his, and both these living and raised saints will be caught up to meet the Lord in the air. There the saints will be judged and presented to the Father, without spot or wrinkle. Then the gospel kingdom will be given up to God the Father. Then will the Father give the bride to the Son Jesus Christ; and when the marriage takes place, the church will become the 'New Jerusalem,' the 'beloved city.' And while this is being done in the air, the earth will be cleansed by fire, the elements will melt with fervent heat, the works of men will be destroyed, the bodies of the wicked will be burned to ashes, the devil and all evil spirits, with the souls and spirits of those who have rejected the gospel, will be banished from the earth, shut up in the pit or place prepared for the devil and his angels, and will not be permitted to visit the earth again until a thousand years. This is the first resurrection, and first judgment. Then Christ and his people will come down from the heavens, or middle air, and live with his saints on the new earth in a new heaven, or dispensation, forever, even forever and ever. This will be the restitution of the right owners to the earth.

"Then will the promise of God to his Son be accomplished—'I will give him the heathen for his inheritance, and the utmost parts of the earth for his possession.' Then 'the whole earth shall be full of his glory.' And then will the holy people take possession of their joint heirship with Christ, and his promise be verified, 'The meek shall inherit the earth,' and the kingdom of God will have come, and 'his will done in earth as in heaven.' After a thousand years shall have passed away, the saints will all be gathered and encamped in the beloved city. The sea, death, and hell, will give up their dead, which will rise up on the breadths of the earth, out of the city, a great company like the sand of the sea-shore. The devil will be let loose, to go out and deceive this wicked host. He will tell them of a battle against the saints, the beloved city; he will gather them in the battle around the camp of the saints. But there is no battle; the devil has deceived them. The saints will judge them; the justice of God will drive them from the earth into the lake of fire and brimstone, where they will be tormented day and night, forever and ever. 'This is the second death.' After the second resurrection, second judgment, the righteous will then possess the earth forever.

"I understand that the judgment day will be a thousand years long. The righteous are raised and judged in the commencement of that day, the wicked in the end of that day. I believe that the saints will be raised and judged about the year 1843, according to Moses' prophecy, Lev. ch. 26; Ezek. ch. 39; Daniel, ch. 2, 7, 8—12; Hos. 5 : 1—3; Rev., the whole book; and many other prophets have spoken of these things. Time will soon tell if I am right, and soon he that is righteous will be righteous still, and he that is filthy will be filthy still. I do most solemnly entreat mankind to make their peace with God, to be ready for these things. 'The end of all things is at hand.' I do ask my brethren in the gospel ministry to consider well what they say before they oppose these things. Say not in your hearts, 'My Lord delayeth his coming.' Let all do as they would wish they had if it does come, and none will say they have not done right if it does not come. I believe it will come; but if it should not come, then I will wait and look until it does come. Yet I must pray, 'Come, Lord Jesus, come quickly.'

"This is a synopsis of my views. I give it as a matter of faith. I know of no scripture to contradict any view given in the above sketch. Men's theories may oppose. The ancients believed in a temporal and personal reign of Christ on earth. The moderns believe in a temporal, spiritual reign as a millennium. Both views are wrong; both are too gross and carnal. I believe in a glorious, immortal, and personal reign of Jesus Christ, with all his people, on the purified earth forever. I believe the millennium is between the two resurrections and two judgments, the righteous and the wicked, the just and the unjust. I hope the dear friends of Christ will lay by all prejudice, and look at and examine these three views by the only rule and standard, the Bible.

"WILLIAM MILLER.

## A BIBLE CHRONOLOGY, FROM ADAM TO CHRIST.

BY WILLIAM MILLER.

| No. | Names of Patriarchs, Kings, &c. | Age. | A. M. | B. C. | Book. | Chap. | Verse |
|---|---|---|---|---|---|---|---|
| | Creation, | | 1 | 4157 | Gen. | i. ii. | |
| 1. | Adam, | 130 | 130 | 4027 | " | v. | 3 |
| 2. | Seth, | 105 | 235 | 3922 | " | " | 6 |
| 3. | Enos, | 90 | 325 | 3832 | " | " | 9 |
| 4. | Cainan, | 70 | 395 | 3762 | " | " | 12 |
| 5. | Mahalaleel, | 65 | 460 | 3697 | " | " | 15 |
| 6. | Jared, | 162 | 622 | 3535 | " | " | 18 |
| 7. | Enoch, | 65 | 687 | 3470 | " | " | 21 |
| 8. | Methuselah, | 187 | 874 | 3283 | " | " | 25 |
| 9. | Lamech, | 182 | 1056 | 3101 | " | " | 28 |
| 10. | Noah, | 600 | 1656 | 2501 | " | vii. | 6 |
| | The Flood, | 1 | 1657 | 2500 | " | viii | 13 |
| 11. | Shem, | 2 | 1659 | 2498 | " | xi. | 10 |
| 12. | Arphaxad, | 35 | 1694 | 2463 | " | " | 12 |
| 13. | Salah, | 30 | 1724 | 2433 | " | " | 14 |
| 14. | Heber, | 34 | 1758 | 2399 | " | " | 16 |
| 15. | Peleg, | 30 | 1788 | 2369 | " | " | 18 |
| 16. | Reu, | 32 | 1820 | 2337 | " | " | 20 |
| 17. | Serug, | 30 | 1850 | 2307 | " | " | 22 |
| 18. | Nahor, | 29 | 1879 | 2278 | " | " | 24 |
| 19. | Terah's life, | 205* | 2084 | 2073 | " | " | 32 |
| 20. | Exode, &c. | 430† | 2514 | 1643 | Exod. | xii. 40, | 41 |
| 21 | Wilderness, | 40 | 2554 | 1603 | Josh. | v. 6; xiv. | 7 |
| 22 | Joshua, | 25‡ | 2579 | 1578 | | xxiv. | 29 |
| 1. | Elders and Anarchy,§ | 18 | 2597 | 1560 | See Josephus. | | |
| 2. | Under Cushan, | 8 | 2605 | 1552 | Judges | iii. | 8 |
| 3. | Othniel, | 40 | 2645 | 1512 | " | " | 11 |
| 4. | Eglon, | 18 | 2663 | 1494 | " | " | 14 |
| 5. | Ehud, | 80 | 2743 | 1414 | " | " | 30 |
| 6. | Jabin, | 20 | 2763 | 1394 | " | iv. | 3 |
| 7. | Barak, | 40 | 2803 | 1354 | " | v. | 31 |
| 8. | Midianites, | 7 | 2810 | 1347 | " | vi. | 1 |
| 9. | Gideon, | 40 | 2850 | 1307 | " | viii. | 28 |
| 10. | Abimelech, | 3 | 2853 | 1304 | " | ix. | 22 |
| 11. | Tola, | 23 | 2876 | 1281 | " | x. | 2 |
| 12. | Jair, | 22 | 2898 | 1259 | " | " | 3 |
| 13. | Philistines, | 18 | 2916 | 1241 | " | " | 8 |

* The Exode did not begin until Terah's death; then Abraham left Haran, and the Exode began, as is clearly proved by Acts 7:4.

† Exode in Egypt from Abraham to wilderness state.

‡ Joshua was a young man when he came out of Egypt, (Exod. 33:11;) could not have been more than 45 years old then; 85 when he entered Canaan, and 110 when he died, leaves 25 years.

§ Judges begin. See Judges 2:7—15.

BIBLE CHRONOLOGY, CONTINUED.

| No. | Names of Patriarchs, Kings, &c. | Age. | A. M. | B. C. | Book. | Chap. | Verse |
|---|---|---|---|---|---|---|---|
| 14. | Jephthah, ............. | 6 | 2922 | 1235 | Judges | xii. | 7 |
| 15. | Ibzan, ................ | 7 | 2929 | 1228 | " | " | 9 |
| 16. | Elon, ................. | 10 | 2939 | 1218 | " | " | 11 |
| 17. | Abdon, ................ | 8 | 2947 | 1210 | " | " | 14 |
| 18. | Philistines, ........... | 40 | 2987 | 1170 | " | xiii. | 1 |
| 19. | Eli, .................. | 40* | 3027 | 1130 | 1 Sam. | iv. | 18 |
| 20. | Samuel, prophet, ....... | 24† | 3051 | 1106 | " | vii. | 2—17 |
| 1. | Kings — Saul, ......... | 40 | 3091 | 1066 | Acts | xiii. | 21 |
| 2. | David, ................ | 40 | 3131 | 1026 | 2 Sam. | v. | 4 |
| 3. | Solomon, .............. | 40 | 3171 | 986 | 1 Kings | xi. | 42 |
| 4. | Rehoboam, ............. | 17 | 3188 | 969 | 2 Chron. | xii. | 13 |
| 5. | Abijam, ............... | 3 | 3191 | 966 | 1 Kings | xv. | 2 |
| 6. | Asa, .................. | 41 | 3232 | 925 | " | " | 10 |
| 7. | Jehoshaphat, ........... | 25 | 3257 | 900 | " | xxii. | 42 |
| 8. | Jehoram, .............. | 5 | 3262 | 895 | 2 Kings | viii. | 17 |
| 9. | Ahaziah, .............. | 1 | 3263 | 894 | " | " | 26 |
| 10. | Athaliah, his mother, .... | 6 | 3269 | 888 | " | xi. | 3, 4 |
| 11. | Joash, ................ | 40 | 3309 | 848 | " | xii. | 1 |
| 12. | Amaziah, ..... ....... | 29 | 3338 | 819 | " | xiv. | 2 |
| | Interregnum,‡ ........ | 11 | 3349 | 808 | " | xv. | 1, 2 |
| 13. | Azariah, .............. | 52 | 3401 | 756 | " | " | 2 |
| 14. | Jotham, ............... | 16 | 3417 | 740 | " | " | 33 |
| 15. | Ahaz, ................ | 16 | 3433 | 724 | " | xvi. | 2 |
| 16. | Hezekiah, ............. | 29 | 3462 | 695 | " | xviii. | 2 |
| 17. | Manasseh, ............. | 55 | 3517 | 640 | " | xxi. | 1 |
| 18. | Amon, ................ | 2 | 3519 | 638 | " | " | 19 |
| 19. | Josiah, ............... | 31 | 3550 | 607 | " | xxii. | 1 |
| 20. | Jehoahaz, 3 months, ..... | | 3550 | 607 | " | xxiii. | 31 |
| 21. | Jehoiakim, ............ | 11 | 3561 | 596 | " | " | 36 |
| | The 70 years of Captivity began here, ended 1st year of Cyrus, ... | 70 | 3631 | 526 | " / 2 Chron. | xxiv. / xxxvi. | 2—16 / 5 —10; 15—23 |
| | Cyrus, ................ | 6 | 3637 | 520 | Rollin | i. | p. 354 |
| | Cambyses, ............. | 7 | 3644 | 513 | " | i. | p. 366 |
| | Darius Hystaspes, ....... | 36 | 3680 | 477 | " | ii. | p. 9 |
| | Xerxes, ............... | 13 | 3693 | 464 | " | ii. | p. 9 |
| | Artaxerxes Longimanus,. | 7 | 3700 | 457 | Ezra | vii. | 10—13 |
| | Birth of Christ,§ ........ | 457 | 4157 | | | | |
| | Add present year, 1840, .. | 1840 | 5997 | | | | |
| | To 1843, .............. | 3 | 6000 | | | | |

* This ends the Judges, — 448 years. Acts 13 : 20 ; also, chap. 8.

† Samuel could not have been more than 38 when Eli died. Then, Israel was lamenting the loss of the ark more than 20 years. Samuel judged Israel some years after, and became old, and his sons judged Israel. He must have been 62 or 63 when Saul was made king.

‡ See 2 Kings, chapters 14 and 15.

§ See Ferguson's Astronomy ; also, Prideaux's Connection.

Mr. Miller adduces the following texts of Scripture in support of his sentiments: — Rev. 22 : 20. Ps. 130 : 6. 1 Thess. 3 : 13. Ps. 50 : 4. Rev. 11 : 15. Isa. 2 : 19—21. John 5 : 28. 1 Thess. 4 : 17. 2 Thess. 1 : 5—7. 1 Cor. 15 : 52. Rev 5 : 9. Dan. 7 : 9—14. Rev. 14 : 14—16. Matt. 26 : 64. Isa. 27 : 13. Matt. 24 : 29. Rev. 20 : 11. Isa. 66 : 15, 16. Mal. 4 : 1. Isa. 5 : 24. Rev. 19 : 18. Ezek. 39 : 17—20. Dan. 2 35, 44. Isa. 17 : 13. Rev. 13 : 1—7; 20 : 10. Isa. 24 : 20, 23. 2 Pet. 3 : 13. Rev. 19 : 8; 21 : 2. Heb. 4 : 9—11; 6 : 2, 3. Isa. 35 : 10; 65 17. Rev. 20 : 6; 20 : 9. Zech. 8 : 5. Rev. 3 : 12; 5 : 10 20 : 2, 3, 7; 21 : 1; 20 : 8, 9, 13. Rom. 7 : 5. 1 Pet. 4 6. Ps. 59 : 6—14. Jer. 4 : 12. Rev. 21 : 12, 27. Zech. 14 : 9—11. 1 Cor. 6 : 2. Rev. 20 : 9, 14, 15. Mal. 4 : 2. Isa. 4 : 3—5. Hos. 13 : 14. Rom. 8 : 17. Rev. 21 : 23; 22 : 5. Jer. 31 : 12—14. Eph. 1 : 10. Tit. 2 : 13. Rev. 4 : 11. Eph. 6 : 13. Heb. 10 : 36, 37.

The believers in Mr. Miller's theory are numerous, and converts to his doctrines are increasing.

Mr. Miller was born at Hampton, N. Y., Feb. 15, 1782. He is a farmer, of common school education, and possesses strong intellectual and colloquial powers. He is a man of unexceptionable character, is a member of the Baptist church, in good standing, and has a license to preach the gospel. For the last fifteen years, he has almost exclusively devoted himself to investigating Scripture prophecies, and in promulgating his peculiar views of them to the world.

The Rev J. V. Himes and Rev. J. Litch, No. 14 Devonshire Street, Boston, publish the *Signs of the Times*, a weekly paper, devoted to Miller's views. They also publish Miller's works, and a variety of other books, embracing similar sentiments

## COME-OUTERS.

This is a term which has been applied to a considerable number of persons in various parts of the Northern States, principally in New England, who have recently *come out* of the various religious denominations with which they were connected; — hence the name. They have not themselves assumed any distinctive name, not regarding themselves as a sect, as they have not formed, and do not contemplate forming, any religious organization. They have no creed, believing that every one should be left free to hold such *opinions* on religious subjects as he pleases, without being held accountable for the same to any human authority. Hence, as might be expected, they hold a diversity of opinions on many points of belief upon which agreement is considered essential by the generality of professing Christians. Amongst other subjects upon which they differ is that of the authority of the Scriptures of the Old and the New Testaments, some among them holding the prevailing belief of their divine inspiration, whilst others regard them as mere human compositions, and subject them to the same rules of criticism as they do any other book, attaching to them no authority any further than they find evidence of their truth. They believe the commonly-received opinion of the plenary inspiration of the writers of those books to be unfounded, not claimed by the writers themselves, and therefore *unscriptural*, as well as unreasonable. Whilst, then, they believe the authors of the Gospels to have been fallible men, liable to err both in relation to matters of fact and opinion, they believe they find in their writings abundant evidence of their honesty. Therefore they consider their testimony satisfactory as regards the main facts there stated of the life of Jesus Christ, at least so far, that there can be no difficulty in deducing therefrom the great principles of the religion which he taught. They *all* believe him to have been a divinely-inspired teacher, and his religion, therefore, to be a revelation of eternal truth. They regard him as the only authorized expositor of his own religion, and believe that to apply in practice its principles as promulgated by him, and as exemplified in his life, is all that is essential to constitute a Christian, according to his testimony, (Matt. 7:24,) — "*Whosoever heareth these sayings of mine, and doeth them, I will liken him unto a wise man which built his house upon a rock,*" &c. Hence they believe that to make it essential to Christianity to assent to all the opinions expressed by certain men, good men though they were, who wrote either before or after his time, involves a denial of the words of Christ. They believe that, according to his teachings, true religion consists in purity of heart, holiness of life, and not in opinions; that *Christianity, as it existed in the mind of Christ, is a life rather than a belief.*

This class of persons *agree* in the opinion that *he only is a Christian who has the spirit of Christ;* that all such as these are members of his church, and that it is composed of none others; therefore that membership in the Christian church is not, and cannot, in the nature of things, be determined by any human authority. Hence they deem all attempts to render the church identical with any outward organizations as utterly futile, not warranted by Christ himself, and incompatible with its spiritual character. Having no organized society, they have no stations of authority or superiority, which they believe to be inconsistent with the Christian idea, (Matt. 23:8,) — "But be not ye called Rabbi: for one is your Master, even Christ; and all ye are brethren." (Matt. 20:25, 26,) — "Ye know that the princes of the Gentiles exercise dominion over them, and they that are great exercise authority upon them. *But it shall not be so among you.*"

As might be inferred from the foregoing, they discard all outward ordinances as having no place in a spiritual religion the design of which is to purify the heart, and the extent of whose influence is to be estimated by its legitimate effects in producing a life of practical righteousness, and not by any mere arbitrary sign, which cannot be regarded as a certain indication of the degree of spiritual life, and must consequently be inefficient and unnecessary.

Their views of worship correspond, as they believe, with the spiritual nature of the religion they profess. They believe that true Christian worship is independent of time and place; that it has no connection with forms, and ceremonies, and external arrangements, any further than these are the exponents of a divine life; that it spontaneously arises from the pure in heart at all times and in all places: in short, they regard the terms *Christian worship* and *Christian obedience* as synonymous, believing that he gives the highest and only conclusive evidence of worshipping the Creator, who exhibits in his life the most perfect obedience to his will. These views they consider in perfect harmony with the teachings of Jesus, particularly in his memorable conversation with the woman of Samaria.

They also agree in the belief that the religion of Christ asserts the equality of all men before God; that it confers upon no man, or class of men, a monopoly of Heaven's favors; neither does it give to a portion of his children any means of knowing his will not common to the race. They believe the laws of the soul are so plain that they may be easily comprehended by all who sincerely seek to know them, without the intervention of any human teacher or expounder. Hence they regard no teaching as authoritative but that of the Spirit of God, and reject all priesthoods but the universal priesthood which Christianity establishes. They believe that every one whose soul is imbued with a knowledge of the truth is qualified to be its minister, and it becomes his duty and his pleasure, by his every word and action, to preach it to the world. It follows, then, that, as Christ prepares and appoints his own ministers, and as they receive their commissions only from him, they are accountable to him alone for their exercise, and not to any human authority whatsoever. They therefore reject all human ordinations, appointments, or control, or any designation by man of an order of men to preach the gospel, as invasions of his rightful prerogative.

Amongst the prevailing sins, against which they feel bound to bear testimony, are slavery and war; and it is alleged as the main reason why many of them have disconnected themselves from the professedly Christian denominations to which they belonged, that those bodies gave their sanction to those anti-Christian practices. They believe slaveholding to be sinful under all circumstances, and that, therefore, it should be immediately abandoned. They believe, not only that national wars are forbidden by Christianity, but that the taking of human life for any purpose, by governments or individuals, is incompatible with its spirit. A large proportion of them, also, consider all resort to punishment, as a penalty for crime, equally inconsistent with the law of love. Hence they deem it their duty to withhold their voluntary sanction or support from human governments, and all institutions which claim the right to exercise powers which they thus regard as unlawful.

In various places, these persons hold meetings on the first day of the week, which are conducted consistently with their views of Christian freedom and equality. It is understood that the object of thus meeting together, is to promote their spiritual welfare. For this purpose, they encourage a free interchange of sentiment on religious subjects, without any restraint or formality. They have no prescribed exercises, but every one is left free to utter his thoughts as he may feel inclined; and even those who differ from them in opinion are not only at liberty, but are invited, to give expression to their thoughts. They believe this to be the only mode of holding religious meetings consistent with the genius of their religion, and for an example of like gatherings they refer to those of the primitive Christians. They meet on *the first day of the week*, not because they believe it incumbent to devote that portion of time more than any other to objects regarded as peculiarly religious, — for they regard all days as equally holy, and equally devoted to the service of the Lord, — but merely because they have become habituated to abstain from their ordinary occupations on that day, and it is, therefore, the most convenient time for them to assemble.

The practical acknowledgment of the moral equality of the sexes is another distinguishing characteristic of these people. They regard woman as equally qualified to hold any station in society from which she is not excluded by her physical disability; and that she alone must decide for herself what position she shall occupy, or what duties in the community she shall perform; the control of woman never, as they conceive, having been delegated to man by the Creator. Therefore they consider her equal in all mental and intellectual pursuits. And when they associate together for religious and benevolent objects, they exercise the various duties pertaining to them indiscriminately.

The number of persons who hold a similarity of opinions on these subjects cannot be known. It is, at present, comparatively small, but rapidly increasing.

## JUMPERS.

Persons so called from the practice of jumping during the time allotted for religious worship. This singular practice began, it is said, in the western part of Wales, about the year 1760. It was soon after defended by Mr. William Williams, (the Welsh poet, as he is sometimes called,) in a pamphlet, which was patronized by the abettors of jumping in religious assemblies. Several of the more zealous itinerant preachers encouraged the people to cry out, "*Gogoniant,*" (the Welsh word for *glory*,) "Amen," &c. &c., to put themselves in violent agitations, and, finally, to jump until they were quite exhausted, so as often to be obliged to fall down on the floor, or the field, where this kind of worship was held.

# BAPTISTS.

This denomination of Christians holds that a personal profession of faith and an immersion in water are essential to baptism. There are several bodies of Baptists in the United States, which will be found under their different names. The *Regular* or *Associated Baptists* are, in sentiment, moderate Calvinists, and form the most numerous body of Baptists in this country.

The Baptists being Independent, or Congregational, in their form of church government, their ecclesiastical assemblies disclaim all right to interfere with the concerns of individual churches. Their public meetings, by delegation from different churches, are held for the purpose of mutual advice and improvement, but not for the general government of the whole body.

The following Declaration of Faith, with the Church Covenant, was recently published by the Baptist Convention of New Hampshire, and is believed to express, with little variation, the general sentiments of the Regular or Associated Baptists: –

"I. Of the Scriptures. — We believe the Holy Bible was written by men divinely inspired, and is a perfect treasure of heavenly instruction; that it has God for its Author, salvation for its end, and truth, without any mixture of error, for its matter; that it reveals the principles by which God will judge us, and therefore is, and shall remain to the end of the world, the true centre of Christian union, and the supreme standard by which all human conduct, creeds, and opinions, should be tried.

"II. Of the true God. — That there is one, and only one, true and living God, whose name is JEHOVAH, the Maker and Supreme Ruler of heaven and earth; inexpressibly glorious in holiness; worthy of all possible honor, confidence, and love; revealed under the personal and relative distinctions of the Father, the Son, and the Holy Ghost equal in every divine perfection, and executing distinct bu harmonious offices in the great work of redemption.

"III. OF THE FALL OF MAN. — That man was created in a state of holiness, under the law of his Maker, but by voluntary transgression fell from that holy and happy state; in consequence of which all mankind are now sinners, not by constraint, but choice; being by nature utterly void of that holiness required by the law of God, wholly given to the gratification of the world, of Satan, and of their own sinful passions, and therefore under just condemnation to eternal ruin, without defence or excuse.

"IV. OF THE WAY OF SALVATION. — That the salvation of sinners is wholly of grace, through the mediatorial offices of the Son of God, who took upon him our nature, yet without sin; honored the law by his personal obedience, and made atonement for our sins by his death; being risen from the dead, he is now enthroned in heaven; and uniting in his wonderful person the tenderest sympathies with divine perfections, is every way qualified to be a suitable, a compassionate, and an all-sufficient Savior.

"V. OF JUSTIFICATION. — That the great gospel blessing which Christ, of his fulness, bestows on such as believe in him, is justification; that justification consists in the pardon of sin and the promise of eternal life, on principles of righteousness; that it is bestowed, not in consideration of any works of righteousness which we have done, but solely through his own redemption and righteousness; that it brings us into a state of most blessed peace and favor with God, and secures every other blessing needful for time and eternity.

"VI. OF THE FREENESS OF SALVATION. — That the blessings of salvation are made free to all by the gospel; that it is the immediate duty of all to accept them by a cordial and obedient faith; and that nothing prevents the salvation of the greatest sinner on earth, except his own voluntary refusal to submit to the Lord Jesus Christ; which refusal will subject him to an aggravated condemnation.

"VII. OF GRACE IN REGENERATION. — That, in order to

be saved, we must be regenerated, or born again; that regeneration consists in giving a holy disposition to the mind, and is effected in a manner above our comprehension or calculation, by the power of the Holy Spirit, so as to secure our voluntary obedience to the gospel; and that its proper evidence is found in the holy fruit which we bring forth to the glory of God.

"VIII. OF GOD'S PURPOSE OF GRACE. — That election is he gracious purpose of God, according to which he regenerates, sanctifies, and saves sinners; that, being perfectly consistent with the free agency of man, it comprehends all the means in connection with the end; that it is a most glorious display of God's sovereign goodness, being infinitely wise, holy, and unchangeable; that it utterly excludes boasting, and promotes humility, prayer, praise, trust in God, and active imitation of his free mercy; that it encourages the use of means in the highest degree; that it is ascertained by its effects in all who believe the gospel; is the foundation of Christian assurance; and that to ascertain it with regard to ourselves, demands and deserves our utmost diligence.

"IX. OF THE PERSEVERANCE OF SAINTS. — That such only are real believers as endure unto the end; that their persevering attachment to Christ is the grand mark which distinguishes them from superficial professors; that a special Providence watches over their welfare; and they are kept by the power of God through faith unto salvation.

"X. HARMONY OF THE LAW AND GOSPEL. — That the law of God is the eternal and unchangeable rule of his moral government; that it is holy, just, and good; and that the inability which the Scriptures ascribe to fallen men to fulfil its precepts, arises entirely from their love of sin; to deliver them from which, and to restore them, through a Mediator, to unfeigned obedience to the holy law, is one great end of the gospel, and of the means of grace connected with the establishment of the visible church.

"XI. OF A GOSPEL CHURCH. — That a visible church of Christ is a congregation of baptized believers, associated by covenant in the faith and fellowship of the gospel; observing the ordinances of Christ; governed by his laws; and exercising the gifts, rights, and privileges, invested in them by his word; that its only proper officers are bishops, or pastors, and deacons, whose qualifications, claims, and duties, are defined in the Epistles to Timothy and Titus.

"XII. Of Baptism and the Lord's Supper. — That Christian baptism is the immersion of a believer in water, in the name of the Father, Son, and Spirit; to show forth, in a solemn and beautiful emblem, our faith in a crucified, buried, and risen Savior, with its purifying power; that it is prerequisite to the privileges of a church relation, and to the Lord's supper, in which the members of the church, by the use of bread and wine, are to commemorate together the dying love of Christ, — preceded always by solemn self-examination.

"XIII. Of the Christian Sabbath. — That the first day of the week is the Lord's day, or Christian Sabbath, and is to be kept sacred to religious purposes, by abstaining from all secular labor and recreations; by the devout observance of all the means of grace, both private and public; and by preparation for that rest which remaineth for the people of God.

"XIV. Of Civil Government. — That civil government is of divine appointment, for the interests of good order of human society; and that magistrates are to be prayed for, conscientiously honored, and obeyed, except in things opposed to the will of our Lord Jesus Christ, who is the only Lord of the conscience, and the Prince of the kings of the earth.

"XV. Of the Righteous and the Wicked. — That there is a radical and essential difference between the righteous and the wicked; that such only as through faith are justified in the name of the Lord Jesus, and sanctified by the Spirit of our God, are truly righteous in his esteem; while all such as continue in impenitence and unbelief are in his sight wicked, and under the curse; and this distinction holds among men both in and after death.

"XVI. Of the World to come. — That the end of this world is approaching; that, at the last day, Christ will descend from heaven, and raise the dead from the grave to final retribution; that a solemn separation will then take place; that the wicked will be adjudged to endless punishment, and the righteous to endless joy; and that this judgment will fix forever the final state of men, in heaven or hell, on principles of righteousness.

"Church Covenant. — Having been, as we trust, brought by divine grace to embrace the Lord Jesus Christ, and to give up ourselves wholly to him, we do now solemnly and joyfully covenant with each other, TO WALK TOGETHER IN HIM WITH BROTHERLY LOVE, to his glory as our common Lord. We do, therefore, in his strength engage,

"That we will exercise a mutual care, as members one of another, to promote the growth of the whole body in Christian knowledge, holiness, and comfort; to the end that we may stand perfect and complete in all the will of God.

"That, to promote and secure this object, we will uphold the public worship of God and the ordinances of his house, and hold constant communion with each other therein; that we will cheerfully contribute of our property for the support of the poor, and for the maintenance of a faithful ministry of the gospel among us.

"That we will not omit closet and family religion at home, nor allow ourselves in the too common neglect of the great duty of religiously training up our children, and those under our care, with a view to the service of Christ and the enjoyment of heaven.

"That we will walk circumspectly in the world, that we may win their souls; remembering that God hath not given us the spirit of fear, but of power, and of love, and of a sound mind, that we are the light of the world and the salt of the earth, and that a city set on a hill cannot be hid.

"That we will frequently exhort, and, if occasion shall require, admonish, one another, according to Matthew 18th, in the spirit of meekness; considering ourselves, lest we also be tempted; and that, as in baptism, we have been buried with Christ, and raised again, so there is on us a special obligation henceforth to walk in newness of life.

"And may the God of peace, who brought again from the dead our Lord Jesus, that great Shepherd of the sheep, through the blood of the everlasting covenant, make us perfect in every good work to do his will; working in us that which is well pleasing in his sight, through Jesus Christ; to whom be glory forever and ever. AMEN."

(See Matt. 3:5, 6, 11, 13—16; 20:22, 23; 21:25; 28: 19. Mark 1:4, 5, 8, 9, 10; 11:30; 16:15, 16. Luke 3: 3, 7, 12, 16, 21; 7:29, 30; 12:50; 20:4. John 1:28, 31, 33; 3:22, 23; 4:1, 2. Acts 1:5, 22; 2:38, 41; 8:12, 13, 36—39; 9:18; 10:37, 47, 48; 13:24; 16:15, 33; 18:8, 25; 19:4, 5; 22:16. Rom. 6:3, 4. 1 Cor. 1:13—17; 10:2; 12:13; 15:29. Gal. 3:27. Eph. 4:5. Col. 2:12. Heb. 6:2. 1 Pet. 3:21.)

"This denomination claims an immediate descent from the apostles, and asserts that the constitution of their churches is from the authority of Jesus Christ himself, and his immediate successors. Many others, indeed, deduce their origin as a sect from much later times, and affirm that they first sprang up in Germany in the sixteenth century. This denomination of Christians is distinguished from others by their opinions respecting the mode and subjects of baptism. Instead of administering the ordinance by sprinkling or pouring water, they maintain that it ought to be administered only by immersion: such, they insist, is the meaning of the Greek word *baptizo*, to wash or dip, so that a command to baptize is a command to immerse. They also defend their practice from the phrase *buried with him in baptism*, from the first administrators' repairing to rivers, and the practice of the primitive church, after the apostles.

"With regard to the *subjects* of baptism, this denomination alleges that it ought not to be administered to children or infants at all, nor to adults in general; but to those only who profess repentance for sin and faith in Christ. Our Savior's commission to his apostles, by which Christian baptism was instituted, is to *go and teach all nations, baptizing them*, &c.; that is, not to baptize all they meet with, but first to examine and instruct them, and whoever will receive instruction, to baptize in the *name of the Father, and of the Son, and of the Holy Ghost.* This construction of the passage is confirmed by another passage — '*Go ye into all the world, and preach the gospel to every creature; he that believeth, and is baptized, shall be saved.*' To such persons, and to such only, this denomination says, baptism was administered by the apostles and the immediate disciples of Christ; for those who were baptized in primitive times are described as repenting of their sins, and believing in Christ. (See Acts 2:38, 8:37, and other passages of Scripture.)

"They further insist that all positive institutions depend entirely upon the will and declaration of the institutor; and that, therefore, reasoning by analogy from previous abrogated rites is to be rejected, and the express commands of Christ respecting the mode and subjects of baptism ought to be our only rule.

"They observe that the meaning of the word *baptizo* signifies immersion or dipping only; that John baptized *in* Jordan; that he chose a place where there was *much* water; that Jesus came up *out of* the water; that Philip and the eunuch went down both *into* the water; that the terms *washing, purifying, burying in baptism*, so often mentioned in Scripture, allude to this mode; that immersion *only* was the practice of the apostles and the first Christians; and that it was only laid aside from the love of novelty, and the coldness of our climate. These positions, they think, are so clear from Scripture, and the history of the church, that they stand in need of but little argument to support them"

There are some interesting facts connected with the histoy of the Baptists in America. In 1631, the Rev. Roge Williams, who had been a clergyman of the church of Eng land, but, disliking its formalities, seceded, and ranged him self with the Nonconformists, fled to America from the per secutions which then raged in England. The great princi ples of civil and religious liberty were not then understood in the western world, and, as Mr. Williams was a man of in trepid firmness in advocating those principles, we are not surprised at the excitement and opposition which his doctrines awakened. He settled first in Salem, New England, the magistracy of which condemned his opinions, and subsequently sentenced him to banishment. Under that cruel act of legislation, he was driven from his family, in the midst of winter, to seek for refuge among the wild Indians. After great sufferings, having conciliated the Indians, he commenced the formation of a colony, to which he gave the name of *Providence*, situate in Rhode Island, a name which it still bears.

Thus he became the founder of a new order of things. Several of his friends afterwards joined him, and in that infant settlement he sustained the twofold character of minister and lawgiver. He formed a constitution on the broad principle of civil and religious liberty, and thus became the first ruler that recognized equal rights. Nearly a century and a half after that, when the Americans achieved their independence, thirteen of the states united in forming a government for themselves, and adopted that principle; thus America became, what the little colony of Providence had been before, a refuge for the persecuted for conscience sake. It has been well observed that the millions in both hemispheres who are now rejoicing in the triumph of liberal principles, should unite in erecting a monument to perpetuate the memory of Roger Williams, the first governor who held liberty of conscience, as well as of person, to be the birthright of man.

In the year 1639, Mr. Williams formed the *first* Baptist

church in America, at Providence. Throughout succeeding years, few changes, comparatively, were experienced in the movements of the Baptist denomination on this vast continent. Baptist churches multiplied exceedingly, until they assumed a leading attitude among the religious communities of America. They have amply provided for an efficient and learned ministry, and the extraordinary revivals with which they have been frequently favored, invest them with a moral strength and glory which cannot be contemplated but with astonishment and admiration.

## ANABAPTISTS.

THOSE who maintain that baptism ought always to be performed by immersion. The word is compounded of *ana* "new," and *baptistes*, "a Baptist," signifying that those who have been baptized in their infancy, ought to be baptized *anew*. It is a word which has been indiscriminately applied to Christians of very different principles and practices. The English and Dutch Baptists do not consider the word as at all applicable to their sect, because those persons whom they baptize they consider as never having been baptized before, although they have undergone what they term the ceremony of sprinkling in their infancy.

## FREE-WILL BAPTISTS.

THE first church gathered, of this order, was in New Durham, N. H., in the year 1780, principally by the instrumentality of Elder Benjamin Randall, who then resided in that town. Soon after, several branches were collected which united with this church; and several preachers, of different persuasions, were brought to see the beauties of a *free salvation*, and united as fellow-laborers with Elder Randall.

They believe that, by the death of Christ, salvation was provided for all men; that, through faith in Christ, and sanctification of the Spirit, — though by nature entirely sinners, — all men may, if they improve every means of grace in their power, become new creatures in this life, and, after death, enjoy eternal happiness; that all who, having actually sinned, die in an unrenewed state, will suffer eternal misery.

Respecting the divine attributes of the Father, Son, and Holy Spirit, they in substance agree with other Orthodox Christians. They hold the holy Scriptures to be their only rule of religious faith and practice, to the exclusion of all written creeds, covenants, rules of discipline, or articles of organization. They consider that elders and deacons are the officers of the church designed in the Scriptures, and maintain that piety, and a call to the work, are the essential qualifications of a minister, without regard to literary attainments.

## SEVENTH-DAY BAPTISTS,

OR

## SABBATARIANS,

ARE those who keep the seventh day of the week as the Sabbath. They are to be found principally, if not wholly, among the Baptists. They object to the reasons which are generally alleged for keeping the first day, and assert that the change from the seventh to the first was effected by Constantine, on his conversion to Christianity, A. D. 321. The three following propositions contain a summary of their principles as to this article of the Sabbath, by which they stand distinguished: —

1. That God hath required the seventh or last day of every week to be observed by mankind, universally, for the weekly Sabbath.

2. That this command of God is perpetually binding on man till time shall be no more.

3. That this sacred rest of the seventh-day Sabbath is not by divine authority changed from the seventh and last to the first day of the week, and that the Scripture doth nowhere require the observation of any other day of the week for the weekly Sabbath, but the seventh day only. They hold, in common with other Christians, the distinguishing doctrines of Christianity.

## SIX-PRINCIPLE BAPTISTS.

THIS appellation is given to those who hold the imposition of hands, subsequent to baptism, and generally on the admission of candidates into the church, as an indispensable prerequisite for church membership and communion. They support their peculiar principle chiefly from Heb. 6: 1, 2 — "Therefore, leaving the principles of the doctrine of Christ, let us go on unto perfection; not laying again the foundation of repentance from dead works, and faith toward God, of the doctrine of baptism, and of laying on of hands, and of resurrection of the dead, and of eternal judgment." As these two verses contain six distinct propositions, one of which is the laying on of hands, these brethren have, from thence, acquired the name of ***Six-Principle Baptists***, to distinguish them from others, whom they sometimes call ***Five-Principle Baptists***. They have fourteen churches in Massachusetts and Rhode Island.

## QUAKER BAPTISTS,

OR

## KEITHIANS

A PARTY from the society of Friends, in Pennsylvania, separated in the year 1691. It was headed by the famous GEORGE KEITH. They practised baptism, and received the Lord's supper, but retained the language, dress, and manners, of the Friends, or Quakers.

---

## PEDOBAPTISTS

ARE those who practise the baptism of children, without regard to personal faith.

Pedobaptists, in common with all others, claim for their practice an apostolical origin; and, although they differ much in theological opinions, in forms of church government, and modes of worship, yet they all adopt substantially the same mode of reasoning in their defence of pedobaptism. They say that the church, under both the old and new dispensations, has ever been the same, although under a different form; that infants, as well as parents, were admitted into the church under the earlier dispensations, the rite of circumcision being the sign of their introduction into it; and that the Christian dispensation (as the Savior came not to destroy, but to fulfil, the law and the prophets) did not annul or abridge any of the privileges of the church that were possessed under the dispensations of former times. But as the right of children, who are bound to their parents by the strongest natural tie, to be solemnly and visibly dedicated to God, and to come within the pale and under the watch of the church, is a blessing and a privilege, we are entitled to ask for the passages in the New Testament which require its abandonment. We ake it for granted, that children are to be publicly dedicated to God, now, as in former times, unless some positive directions can be shown to the contrary. It appearing, therefore, that children may be dedicated to God, by their parents, in some public and visible way, and there remaining no outward ceremony, under the Christian dispensation, suitable to that purpose, but baptism, we infer that baptism is designed to take the place of circumcision, and that children may be baptized. And these views are thought to be encouraged by the affectionate saying of Christ, "Suffer little children to come unto me, and forbid them not, for of such is the kingdom of God." (Mark 10 : 14.)

A second argument in favor of infant baptism is derived from the repeated accounts, in the Acts, of the baptism of whole families. The families referred to are those of Lydia, a seller of purple in the city of Thyatira, of the jailer, in the same city, and of Cornelius, the centurion, of Cæsarea. Instances of this kind are not to be considered as conclusively proving the Scripture authority of infant baptism of themselves; but they form a presumptive argument, in its favor, of great weight.

And, further, it may be shown, from ecclesiastical history, that the baptism of infants was practised in the time of the primitive Christians. This being the fact, the conclusion seems to follow irresistibly, that they received the practice from the apostles, and that it was, therefore, known and recognized by the Savior himself; and, if it were known and recognized by him, or even introduced, subsequently and solely, by those he commissioned, it must be received, in either case, as the will of Christ, and as a law of the Christian dispensation.

Again, they say that the particular mode of baptism can not be determined from the meaning of the word *baptizo*, which may mean either to immerse or to lave, according to the particular connection in which it is found. (See Mark 7 : 4. Heb. 9 : 10.)

None of the accounts of baptism, which are given in the

New Testament, necessarily imply that it was performed by immersion. It is true the Savior and the eunuch, when they were baptized, went up out of, or rather *from*, the water, but the inference that they went *under* the water, which is sometimes drawn from these expressions, does not appear to be sufficiently warranted.

The circumstances attending the baptism of the jailer and his family are of such a nature as to render the opinion of its being performed by immersion improbable. The baptism was evidently performed at midnight, and within the limits of the prison, — a time and a situation evidently implying some other mode than plunging. Similar views will hold in respect to the baptism of the three thousand at the season of Pentecost.

As, therefore, there are no passages of Scripture which positively require immersion, but various scriptural considerations against it, besides its being always inconvenient, and not unfrequently impracticable, the Pedobaptists have ever thought it fit and requisite, as a general rule, to practise baptism by sprinkling or laving.

The Greek church, in all its branches, — whether in the frozen regions of Siberia, or in the torrid zone, — practise trine immersion. All Pedobaptists require of adults, who seek for baptism, a personal profession of their faith, and so far agree with the Baptists. They also, with the Baptists, allow immersion to be valid baptism; but, in opposition to them, the Baptists deny that any other mode of administering this rite is valid. (See Exod. 14 : 22. Isa. 44 : 3. Matt. 3 : 11; 19 : 13. Mark 7 : 4. Acts 2 : 39; 19 : 2, 5. Rom. 4 : 11; 11 : 17. 1 Cor. 7 : 14; 10 : 2. Eph. chap. 2. Heb. 9 : 10, 13, 14.)

The term *Pedobaptist* is derived from two Greek words — *pais*, a child, and *baptismos*, baptism. This mode of baptism is practised by nearly the whole Christian world, except the Baptists and Friends.

## ANTI-PEDOBAPTISTS.

A NAME given to those who object to the baptism of nfants. The word is derived from the Greek words signifying *against*, *a child*, and *I baptize.*

## UNITARIANS.

THOSE Christians who are usually designated by this name in the United States, and who are also called *Liberal Christians,* are mostly Congregationalists, and are found principally in New England.

They acknowledge no other rule of faith and practice than the holy Scriptures, which they consider it the duty of every man to search for himself, prayerfully, and with the best exercise of his understanding. They reject all creeds of human device, as generally unjust to the truth of God and the mind of man, tending to produce exclusiveness, bigotry, and divisions, and at best of doubtful value. They regard, however, with favor the earliest creed on record, commonly called the Apostles', as approaching nearest to the simplicity of the gospel, and as imbodying the grand points of the Christian faith.

They adopt the words of St. Paul, (1 Cor. 8 : 6,) "*To us there is but one God, the Father, of whom are all things, and we in him; and one Lord Jesus Christ, by whom are all things, and we by him.*" They make great account of the doctrine of God's paternal character and government, and continually set it forward as the richest source of consolation, and the most powerful motive to repentance and improvement.

Receiving and trusting in Christ as their Lord, Teacher, Mediator, Intercessor, Savior, they hold in less esteem han many other sects, nice theological questions and speculations concerning his precise rank, and the nature of his relation to God. They feel that by honoring him as *the Son of God*, they honor him as he desired to be honored; and that by obeying and imitating him, they in the best manner show their love.

They believe that the Holy Ghost is not a distinct person in the Godhead, but that *power of God*, that *divine influence*, by which Christianity was established through miraculous aids, and by which its spirit is still shed abroad in the hearts of men.

They advocate the most perfect toleration. They regard CHARITY as the crowning Christian grace, — the end of the commandment of God. They consider a pure and lofty morality as not only inseparable from true religion, but the most acceptable service that man can render to his Maker, and the only indubitable evidence of a believing heart.

They believe that sin is its own punishment, and virtue its own rewarder; that the moral consequences of a man's good or evil conduct go with him into the future life, to afford him remorse or satisfaction; that God will be influenced in all his dealings with the soul by mercy and justice, punishing no more severely than the sinner deserves, and always for a benevolent end. Indeed, the greater part of the denomination are Restorationists.

Unitarians consider that, besides the Bible, all the Ante-Nicene fathers — that is, all Christian writers for three centuries after the birth of Christ — give testimony in their favor, against the modern popular doctrine of the Trinity. As for *antiquity*, it is their belief that it is really on their side.

In the *First Epistle of Clement to the Corinthians*, which was written towards the close of the first century, — and the evidence for the genuineness of which is stronger than for that of any other of the productions attributed to the apostolical fathers, — the supremacy of the Father is asserted or implied throughout, and Jesus is spoken of in terms mostly borrowed from the Scriptures. He is once called the "sceptre of the majesty of God;" and this highly-figurative expression is the most exalted applied to him in the whole Epistle.

Justin Martyr, the most distinguished of the ancient fathers of the church, who flourished in the former part of the second century, and whose writings (with the exception of those attributed to the *apostolic* fathers) are the earliest Christian records next to the New Testament, expressly says, "We worship God, the Maker of the universe, offering up to him prayers and thanks. But, assigning to Jesus, who came to teach us these things, and for this end was born, the '*second place*' after God, we not without reason honor him."

The germ and origin of the doctrine of the Trinity, the Unitarians find in the speculations of those Christianized philosophers of the second century, whose minds were strongly tinctured with the Platonic philosophy, combined with the *emanation system*, as taught at Alexandria, and held by Philo. From this time they trace the gradual formation of the doctrine through successive ages down to Athanasius and Augustine; the former of whom, A. D. 362, was the first to insist upon the equality of the Holy Ghost with the Father and the Son; and the latter, about half a century afterwards, was the first to insist upon their numerical unity.

In all ages of the church, there have been many learned and pious men who have rejected the Trinity as unscriptural and irrational. The first attempt, at the council of Nice, to establish and make universal the Trinitarian creed, caused disturbances and dissensions in the church, which continued for ages, and produced results the most deplorable to every benevolent mind which exalts *charity* over faith.

Soon after the reformation, the Unitarian faith was avowed by Martin Cellarius, who was then finishing his studies at Wittenberg, where Luther was professor. In 1546, the Unitarian opinions made a considerable movement in Italy, and several persons of learning and eminence were put to death. In 1553, Michael Servetus was burned foı this heresy, at Geneva. The elder Socinus made his escape from this persecution, and spread his views throughout several countries of Europe, more particularly in Poland, where a large part of the Reformed clergy embraced them, and were separated, in 1565, from the communion of the Calvinists and Lutherans.

In England, the number of Unitarians was considerable, according to Strype, as early as 1548; and in 1550, he represents the Unitarian doctrine as spreading so fast that the leading Churchmen were alarmed, and "thought it necessary to suppress its expression by rigid measures." These "rigid measures," such as imprisonment and burning, were successful for a time. But afterwards, the "heresy" gained new and able supporters, such as Biddle, Firmin, Dr. S. Clarke, Dr. Lardner, Whiston, Emlyn, Sir Isaac Newton, &c., and has been spreading to this day.

In the north of Ireland, the Unitarians compose several presbyteries. There are also congregations of Unitarians in Dublin, and in other southern cities of the kingdom.

In Scotland, there are chapels of this character in Edinburgh, Glasgow, and other principal places.

In the United States, Unitarian opinions were not prevalent till towards the close of the last century. Since that time, however, they have advanced rapidly, and have been embraced by some of the wisest and best men in the land.

Of late years, the Congregational Unitarians have generally abstained from controversy, in the United States. They have, however, published and circulated extensively a large number of tracts, of a doctrinal and practical character. They have at the present time assumed a *positive* condition, gained a strong and permanent hold amongst the Christian sects, and are manifesting new signs of vitality and usefulness.

The following proof-texts are some of those upon which the Unitarians rest their belief in the inferiority of the Son to he Father: — John 8: 17, 18. John 17: 3. Acts 10: 38 1 Tim. 2: 5. 1 John 4: 14. Rom. 8: 34 1 Cor 11: 3

John 10 . 29. John 14 : 28. Matt. 19 : 17. John 17 : 21 John 20 : 17. 1 Cor. 8 : 5, 6. John 10 : 25 ; 7 : 16, 17 8 : 28 ; 5 : 19, 20 ; 8 : 49, 50. Matt. 20 : 23. John 6 : 38 57 ; 5 : 30. Mark 13 : 32. Luke 6 : 12. John 11 : 41, 42 Matt. 27 : 46. Acts 2 : 22—24. Phil. 2 : 11. Col. 1 : 15 Rev. 3 . 14. Heb. 3 : 3. Matt. 12 : 18. Luke 2 : 52.

## BROWNISTS.

A DENOMINATION which sprung up in England towards the close of the sixteenth century. They derive their name from their leader, Robert Brown.

This denomination did not differ in point of doctrine from the church of England, or from the other Puritans ; but they apprehended, according to Scripture, that every church ought to be confined within the limits of a single congregation, and that the government should be democratical. They maintained the discipline of the church of England to be Popish and antichristian, and all her ordinances and sacraments invalid. Hence they forbade their people to join with them in prayer, in hearing the word, or in any part of public worship. They not only renounced communion with the church of England, but with all other churches, except such as were of the same model.

## PURITANS.

THIS name was given to a party which appeared in England in the year 1565, who opposed the liturgy and ceremonies of the church of England.

They acquired this denomination from their professed design to establish a purer form of worship and discipline.

Those who were first styled *Puritans* were Presbyterians, out the term was afterwards applied to others who differec from the church of England.

Those who separated from the church of England were also styled *Dissenters.*

## BOURIGNONISTS.

The followers of Antoinette Bourignon, a lady in France, who pretended to particular inspirations. She was born at Lisle, in 1616. At her birth, she was so deformed that it was debated some days in the family whether it was not proper to stifle her as a monster; but, her deformity diminishing, she was spared, and afterwards obtained such a degree of beauty, that she had her admirers. From her childhood to her old age she had an extraordinary turn of mind. She set up for a reformer, and published a great number of books, filled with very singular notions; the most remarkable of which are entitled "The Light of the World," and "The Testimony of Truth." In her confession of faith, she professes her belief in the Scriptures, the divinity and atonement of Christ. She believed, also, that man is perfectly free to resist or receive divine grace; that God is ever unchangeable love towards all his creatures, and does not inflict any arbitrary punishment, but that the evils they suffer are the natural consequence of sin; that religion consists not in outward forms of worship, nor systems of faith, but in an entire resignation to the will of God. She held many extravagant notions, among which, it is said, she asserted that Adam, before the fall, possessed the principles of both sexes, that, in an ecstasy, God represented Adam to her mind in his original state, as also the beauty of the first world, and how he had drawn from it the chaos; and that every thing was bright, transparent, and darted forth life and ineffable glory, with a number of other wild ideas. She dressed like a her mit, and travelled through France, Holland, England, and Scotland. She died at Franeker, in the province of Frise, October 30, 1680.

## JEWS.

A COMPLETE system of the religious doctrines of the Jews is contained in the five books of Moses, their great lawgiver, who was raised up to deliver them from their bondage in Egypt, and to conduct them to the possession of Canaan, the promised land.

The principal sects among the Jews, in the time of our Savior, were the Pharisees, who placed religion in external ceremony; the Sadducees, who were remarkable for their incredulity; and the Essenes, who were distinguished by an austere sanctity.

The Pharisees and Sadducees are frequently mentioned in the New Testament; and an acquaintance with their principles and practices serves to illustrate many passages in the sacred history. At present, the Jews have two sects — the Caraites, who admit no rule of religion but the law of Moses; and the Rabbinists, who add to the laws the traditions of the Talmud, a collection of the doctrines and morality of the Jews. The expectation of a Messiah is the distinguishing feature of their religious system. The word *Messiah* signifies one anointed, or installed into an office by an unction.

Christians believe that Jesus Christ is the Messiah, in whom all the Jewish prophecies are accomplished. The Jews, infatuated with the idea of a temporal Messiah, who is to subdue the world, still wait for his appearance.

The most remarkable periods in the history of the Jews are the call of Abraham, the giving of the law by Moses, their establishment in Canaan under Joshua, the building of the temple by Solomon, the division of the tribes, their captivity in Babylon, their return under Zerubbabel and he destruction of their city and temple by Titus, afterwards emperor, A. D. 70.

Maimonides, an illustrious rabbi, drew up for the Jews, in the eleventh century, a confession of faith, which all Jews admit. It is as follows: —

"1. I believe, with a true and perfect faith, that God is the Creator, whose name be blessed, Governor, and Maker, of all creatures, and that he hath wrought all things, worketh and shall work forever.

"2. I believe, with a perfect faith, that the Creator, whose name be blessed, is *one*, and that such a unity as in him can be found in none other, and that he alone hath been our God, is, and forever shall be.

"3. I believe, with a perfect faith, that the Creator, whose name be blessed, is not corporeal, nor to be comprehended with any bodily property, and that there is no bodily essence that can be likened unto him.

"4. I believe, with a perfect faith, the Creator, whose name be blessed, to be the first and the last, that nothing was before him, and that he shall abide the last forever.

"5. I believe, with a perfect faith, that the Creator, whose name be blessed, is to be worshipped, and none else.

"6. I believe, with a perfect faith, that all the words of the prophets are true.

"7. I believe, with a perfect faith, the prophecies of Moses, our master, — may he rest in peace; — that he was the father and chief of all wise men that lived before him, or ever shall live after him.

"8. I believe, with a perfect faith, that all the law which at this day is found in our hands, was delivered by God himself to our master, Moses. God's peace be with him.

"9. I believe, with a perfect faith, that the same law is never to be changed, nor another to be given us of God, whose name be blessed.

"10. I believe, with a perfect faith, that God, whose name be blessed, understandeth all the works and thoughts of men, as it is written in the prophets. He fashioneth their hearts alike; he understandeth all their works.

"11. I believe, with a perfect faith, that God will recompense good to them that keep his commandments, and will punish them who transgress them.

"12. I believe, with a perfect faith, that the Messiah is yet to come; and, although he retard his coming, yet I will wait for him till he come.

"13. I believe, with a perfect faith, that the dead shall be restored to life, when it shall seem fit unto God the Creator, whose name be blessed, and memory celebrated, world without end. AMEN."

This people constitute one of the most singular and interesting portions of mankind. For about three thousand years, they have existed as a distinct nation; and, what is remarkable, by far the greatest part of this time they have been in bondage and captivity.

The calling of Abraham, the father and founder of this nation; the legislation of Moses; the priesthood of Aaron; the Egyptian bondage; the conquest of Canaan, and the history of the Jews to the coming of the Messiah; their cruel and injurious treatment of this august and innocent personage, – are facts which the Scriptures disclose, and with which, it is presumed, every reader is well acquainted.

For about eighteen hundred years, this wonderful people have maintained their peculiarities of religion, language, and domestic habits, among Pagans, Mahometans, and Christians, and have suffered a continued series of reproaches, privations, and miseries, which have excited the admiration and astonishment of all who have reflected on their condition.

The siege and destruction of Jerusalem by Titus, the Roman general, was one of the most awful and distressing scenes that mortals ever witnessed; and the details, as given by Josephus, are enough to make humanity shudder. During the siege, which lasted nearly five months, upwards of eleven hundred thousand Jews perished. John and Simon, he two generals of the Hebrews, who were accounted the ringleaders of the rebellious nation, with seven hundred of the most beautiful and vigorous of the Jewish youth, were reserved to attend the victor's triumphal chariot. The number taken captive, during this fatal contest, amounted to ninety-seven thousand; many of whom were sent into Syria, and the other provinces, to be exposed in public theatres, to fight like gladiators, or to be devoured by wild beasts. The number of those destroyed in the whole war, of which the taking of the holy city was the bloody and tremendous consummation, is computed to have been one million four hundred and sixty thousand.

In addition to the terrors of the Roman sword, this devoted nation was exposed to famine, pestilence, and the implacable fury of contending parties among themselves, which all conspired together to make the siege of Jerusalem surpass, in horror, every account of any other siege in the records of the world.

A small portion, indeed, of this wretched, ruined nation were permitted to remain, and establish themselves in Judea, who, by degrees, reorganized a regular system of government, which became the centre of Jewish operations, not only for those in Judea, but for such as were dispersed in other nations. But the yoke of foreign masters was so grievous and burdensome, that they were continually restless and impatient; and, in consequence of a general revolt under the emperor Adrian, in 134, they were a second time slaughtered in multitudes, and were driven to madness and despair. Bither, the place of their greatest strength, was compelled to surrender, and Barchochba, their leader, who pretended to be the Messiah, was slain, and five hundred and eighty housand fell by the sword in battle, besides vast numbers who perished by famine, sickness, fire, and other calamities.

Kings have enacted the severest laws against them, and employed the hand of executioners to ruin them. The seditious multitudes, by murders and massacres, have committed outrages against them, if possible, still more violent and tragical. Besides their common share in the sufferings of society, they have undergone a series of horrid and unutterable calamities, which no other description of men has ever experienced in any age, or in any country. Princes and people, Pagans, Mahometans, and Christians, disagreeing in so many things, have united in the design of exterminating this fugitive and wretched race, but have not succeeded. They have been banished, at different times, from France, Germany, Spain, Bohemia, Hungary, and England; and from some of these kingdoms they have been banished and recalled many times in succession.

The Romans and Spaniards have probably done more than any other nations to oppress and destroy this people; and the inquisition has doomed multitudes of them to torture and death.

At different times, they were accused of poisoning wells, rivers, and reservoirs of water, and, before any proof of these strange and malicious charges was produced, the populace in many parts of Germany, Italy, and France, have fallen upon them with merciless and murderous severity. At one time, the German emperor found it necessary to issue an edict for their banishment, to save them from the rage of his exasperated and unrestrained subjects.

As the Jews have generally been the *bankers* and *brokers* of the people among whom they have resided, and have made a show of much wealth, this has tempted their avaricious adversaries to impose upon them enormous taxes and ruinous fines.

Muley Archy, a prince of one of the Barbary states, by seizing the property of a rich Jew, was enabled to dispossess his brother of the throne of Morocco.

The English parliament of Northumberland, in 1188, for the support of a projected war, assessed the Jews with 60,000 pounds, while only 70,000 were assessed upon the Christians; which proves either that the Jews were immensely rich, or that the parliament was extremely tyrannical.

The English king John was unmercifully severe upon this

afflicted people. In 1210, regardless of the costly freedom he had sold them, he subjected them all, as a body, to a fine of 66,000 marks. The ransom required by this same unfeeling king, of a rich Jew of Bristol, was 10,000 marks of silver; and on his refusing to pay this ruinous fine, he ordered one of his teeth to be extracted every day; to which the unhappy man submitted seven days, and on the eighth day he agreed to satisfy the king's rapacity. Isaac of Norwich was, not long after, compelled to pay a similar fine. But the king, not satisfied with these vast sums extorted from these injured Israelites, in the end confiscated all their property, and expelled them from the kingdom.

About the beginning of the 16th century, the Jews in Persia were subjected to a tax of two millions of gold. Long would be the catalogue of injuries of this kind, which this outcast and hated nation has sustained. Numerous are the cases in which those who have become deeply in debt to them for borrowed money, have procured their banishment, and the confiscation of their property, as the readiest way to cancel their demands; and, as they have ever been addicted to usurious practices, they have, by this means, furnished plausible pretexts to their foes to fleece and destroy them.

The fraternal disposition of this people led them to seek the society of each other; and, notwithstanding the wideness of their dispersion, in process of time, they, by uniting under different leaders, formed two communities of considerable extent, known by the name of the eastern and western Jews. The western Jews inhabited Egypt, Judea, Italy, and other parts of the Roman empire; the eastern Jews settled in Babylon, Chaldea, Persia, &c. The head of the western division was known by the name of the patriarch, while he who presided over the eastern Jews, was called the prince of the captivity. The office of patriarch was abolished, by imperial laws, about 429, from which time the western Jews were solely under the rule of the chiefs of their synagogues, whom they called primates. But the princes of the captivity had a longer and more splendid sway. They resided at

Babylon, or Bagdad, and exercised an extensive authority over their brethren, as far down as the 12th century. About this period, a Jewish historian asserts that he found, at Bagdad, the prince of the captivity, lineally descended from David, and permitted, by the caliph, to exercise the rights of sovereignty over the Jews from Syria to Indostan.

The existence of a succession of these imaginary potentates, from the destruction of Jerusalem by the Romans, the Jews have ever been strenuous in maintaining, partly to aggrandize their nation, and partly to deprive Christians of the benefit of an argument furnished by the prophecy of Jacob,* concerning the termination of the Jewish polity and independence, soon after the coming of the Messiah.

Notwithstanding the world, in general, has shown a spirit of hostility and contempt for the remnant of Israel, yet they have found a few, in every age, who, either from motives of policy or justice, have treated them with kindness and respect. The first Mahometan caliphs, a number of the Roman pontiffs, and some of the Asiatic and European sovereigns, have shown them friendship and protection. Don Solomon, a learned and illustrious Jew of Portugal, in the 12th century, was raised to the highest military command in that kingdom. Casimir the Great, of Poland, in the 14th century, received the Jews as refugees into his kingdom, and granted them extensive privileges; and from that time to the present, they have been more numerous in that country than in any other in Europe.

For many centuries, this persecuted race found a favorite asylum in Holland, and, by their dexterity and success in commerce, became very affluent.

Cromwell, seeing the benefit which the Netherlands had derived from this money-making and money-lending community, was very desirous to recall them to England, from which they had been exiled about three hundred and fifty years. The celebrated Manasses Ben Israel had many interviews with the Protector; and so high were the expectations of the Israelites, from the clemency and authority of this illustrious statesman, that they began to look up to him as the promised Messiah. And, although Cromwell's friendly proposals, as to their recall, were overruled by the bigoted and intolerant policy of the times, yet, from that period, they have found favor and protection in England, and have been much more numerous and prosperous there than formerly.

In France and the United States, the Jews are admitted to equal rights with all other citizens, which cannot be said of any other nations in Christendom. In the United States, they have acquired this freedom, of course, with all other citizens of this free country. In France, they were admitted to it by Bonaparte; and afterwards, in 1807, by his directions, they convened a Grand Sanhedrim, consisting, according to ancient custom, of 70 members, exclusive of the president. The number and distinction of the spectators of this Sanhedrim greatly added to the solemnity of the scene. This venerable assembly passed and agreed to various articles respecting the Mosaic worship, and their civil and ecclesiastical concerns.

The extreme aversion of the Jews to every thing which bears the Christian name, and their obstinate attachment to their ancient religion, have, in former years, discouraged all attempts to convert them to the Christian faith. And not only has their conversion been neglected, but for many centuries they have been persecuted, plundered, and destroyed, by those who have called themselves Christians; they have not been permitted to enter their churches as worshippers, nor their dwellings as guests, nor reside in their territories, where Pagans and Mahometans have found an unmolested abode. While we, then, blame the blindness and incredulity of the descendants of Abraham, let us lament the folly and unkindness of the professed disciples of the mild and compassionate Redeemer. But a different spirit is now prevailing in many parts of Christendom, and a new era, as to the tribes of Israel, seems about to burst upon the world. Societies are formed in Europe and America for their benefit, and a disposition is said to be increasing, among the Jews, favorable to that Messiah and that religion which they have so long hated and rejected.

The history of this people certainly forms a striking evidence of the truth of divine revelation. They are a living and perpetual miracle, continuing to subsist as a distinct and peculiar race for upwards of three thousand years, intermixed among almost all the nations of the world, flowing forward in a full and continued stream, like the waters of the Rhone, without mixing with the waves of the expansive lake through which the passage lies to the ocean of eternity.

## INDIAN RELIGIONS.

"Lo, the poor Indian! whose untutored mind
Sees God in clouds, or hears him in the wind;
His soul proud science never taught to stray
Far as the solar walk, or milky way;
Yet simple nature to his hope has given,
Behind the cloud-topped hill, an humbler heaven—
Some safer world in depth of woods embraced,
Some happier island in the watery waste,
Where slaves once more their native land behold,
No fiends torment, no Christians thirst for gold.
To be, contents his natural desire;
He asks no angel's wing, no seraph's fire;
But thinks, admitted to that equal sky,
His faithful dog will bear him company."—Pope.

The natives of Canada have an idea of the Supreme Being; and they all, in general, agree in looking upon him as the First Spirit, and the Governor and the Creator of the world. It is said that almost all the nations of the Algonquin language give this Sovereign Being the appellation of the Great Hare. Some, again, call him Michabou, and others Atahocan. Most of them hold the opinion that he was born upon the waters, together with his whole court, entirely composed of four-footed animals, like himself; that he formed the earth of a grain of sand, which he took from the bottom of the ocean; and that he created man of the bodies of the dead animals. There are, likewise, some who mention a god of the waters, who opposed the designs of the Great Hare, or, at least, refused to be assisting to him. This god is, according to some, the Great Tiger. They have a third, called Matcomek, whom they invoke in the winter season.

The Agreskoui of the Hurons, and the Agreskouse of the Iroquois, is, in the opinion of these nations, the Sovereign Being, and the god of war. These Indians do not give the same original to mankind with the Algonquins; they do not ascend so high as the first creation. According to them, there were, in the beginning, six men in the world; and, if you ask them who placed them there, they answer you, they do not know.

The gods of the Indians have bodies, and live much in the same manner as themselves, but without any of those inconveniences to which they are subject. The word *spirit*, among them, signifies only a being of a more excellent nature than others.

According to the Iroquois, in the third generation there came a deluge, in which not a soul was saved; so that, in order to repeople the earth, it was necessary to change beasts into men.

Beside the First Being, or the Great Spirit, they hold an infinite number of genii, or inferior spirits, both good and evil, who have each their peculiar form of worship.

They ascribe to these beings a kind of immensity and omnipresence, and constantly invoke them as the guardians of mankind. But they never address themselves to the evil genii, except to beg of them to do them no hurt.

They believe in the immortality of the soul, and say that the region of their everlasting abode lies so far westward, that the souls are several months in arriving at it, and have vast difficulties to surmount. The happiness which they hope to enjoy is not believed to be the ecompense of virtue only; but to have been a good hunter, brave in war, &c., are the merits which entitle them to this paradise, which they, and the other American natives, figure as a delightful country, blessed with perpetual spring, whose forests abound with game, whose rivers swarm with fish, where famine is never felt, and uninterrupted plenty shall be enjoyed without labor or toil.

The natives of New England believed not only a plurality of gods, who made and governed the several nations of the world, but they made deities of every thing they imagined to be great, powerful, beneficial, or hurtful to mankind. Yet they conceived an Almighty Being, who dwells in the south-west regions of the heavens, to be superior to all the rest. This Almighty Being they called Kichtan, who at first, according to their tradition, made a man and woman out of a stone, but, upon some dislike, destroyed them again; and then made another couple out of a tree, from whom descended all the nations of the earth; but how they came to be scattered and dispersed into countries so remote from one another, they cannot tell. They believed their Supreme God to be a good being, and paid a sort of acknowledgment to him for plenty, victory, and other benefits.

But there is another power, which they called *Hobamocko,* (the devil,) of whom they stood in greater awe, and worshipped merely from a principle of fear.

The immortality of the soul was universally believed among them. When good men die, they said, their souls go to Kichtan, where they meet their friends, and enjoy all manner of pleasures; when wicked men die, they go to Kichtan also, but are commanded to walk away, and wander about in restless discontent and darkness forever.

After the coming of the white people, the Indians in New Jersey, who once held a plurality of deities, supposed there were only three, because they saw people of three kinds of complexion, viz., English, negroes, and themselves.

It was a notion generally prevailing among them, that the same God who made them did not make us, but that they were created after the white people; and it is probable they supposed their God gained some special skill by seeing the white people made, and so made them better; for it is certain they considered themselves and their methods of living, which they said their God expressly prescribed for them, vastly preferable to the white people and their methods.

With regard to a future state of existence, many of them imagined that the Chichung, i. e., the shadow, or what survives the body, will, at death, go southward, to some unknown, but curious place, — will enjoy some kind of happiness, such as hunting, feasting, dancing, or the like; and what they suppose will contribute much to their happiness in the next state, is, that they shall never be weary of these entertain ments.

Those who have any notion about rewards and sufferings in a future state, seem to imagine that most will be happy, and that in the delightful fields, chasing the game, or reposing themselves with their families; but the poor, frozen sinners cannot stir one step towards that sunny region. Nevertheless, their misery has an end; it is longer or shorter, according to the degree of their guilt; and, after its expiation, they are permitted to become inhabitants of the Indian paradise.

The Indians of VIRGINIA gave the names of *Okee*, *Quioccos*, or *Kiwasa*, to the idol which they worshipped. These names might possibly be so many epithets, which they varied according to the several functions they ascribed to this deity, or the different notions they might form to themselves of it in their religious exercises and common discourses. Moreover, they were of opinion that this idol is not one sole being, but that there were many more of the same nature, besides the tutelary gods. They gave the general name of Quioccos to all these genii, or beings, so that the name of Kiwasa might be particularly applied to the idol in question

These savages consecrated chapels and oratories to this deity, in which the idol was often represented under a variety of shapes. They even kept some of these in the most retired parts of their houses, to whom they communicated their affairs, and consulted them upon occasion. In this case, they made use of them in the quality of tutelary gods, from whom they supposed they received blessings on their families.

The sacerdotal vestment of their priests was like a woman's petticoat plaited, which they put about their necks, and tied over the right shoulder; but they always kept one arm out, to use it as occasion required. This cloak was made round at bottom, and descended no lower than the middle of the thigh; it was made of soft, well-dressed skins, with the hair outwards.

These priests shaved their heads close, the crown excepted, where they left only a little tuft, that reached from the top of the forehead to the nape of the neck, and even on the top of the forehead. They here left a border of hair, which, whether it was owing to nature, or the stiffness contracted by the fat and colors with which they daubed themselves, bristled up, and came forward like the corner of a square cap.

The natives of Virginia had a great veneration for their priests; and the latter endeavored to procure it, by daubing themselves all over in a very frightful manner, dressing themselves in a very odd habit, and tricking up their hair after a very whimsical manner. Every thing they said was considered as an oracle, and made a strong impression on the minds of the people; they often withdrew from society, and lived in woods or in huts, far removed from any habitation. They were difficult of access, and did not give themselves any trouble about provisions, because care was always taken to set food for them near their habitations. They were always addressed in cases of great necessity. They also acted in the quality of physicians, because of the great knowledge they were supposed to have of nature. In fine, peace or war was determined by their voice; nor was any thing of importance undertaken without first consulting them.

They had not any stated times nor fixed days, on which they celebrated their festivals, but they regulated them only by the different seasons of the year; as, for instance, they celebrated one day at the arrival of their wild birds, another upon the return of the hunting season, and for the maturity of their fruits; but the greatest festival of all was at harvest time. They then spent several days in diverting themselves, and enjoyed most of their amusements, such as martial dances and heroic songs.

After their return from war, or escaping some danger, they lighted fires, and made merry about them, each having his gourd-bottle, or his little bell, in his hand. Men, women, and children, often danced in a confused manner about these fires. Their devotions, in general, consisted only of acclamations of joy, mixed with dances and songs, except in seasons of sorrow and affliction, when they were changed into howlings. The priests presided at this solemnity, dressed in their sacerdotal ornaments, part of which were the gourd-bottle, the petticoat above mentioned, and the serpents' or weasels' skins, the tails of which were dexterously tied upon their heads like a tiara, or triple crown. These priests began the song, and always opened the religious exercise, to which they often added incantations, part of the mysteries of which were comprehended in the songs. The noise, the gestures, the wry faces, in a word, every thing, contributed to render these incantations terrible.

## DEISTS.

**The** Deists believe in a God, but reject a written revelation from him. They are extravagant in their encomiums on natural religion, though they differ much respecting its nature, extent, obligation, and importance. Dr. Clarke, in his treatise on Deism, divides them into four classes, according to the number of articles comprised in their creed.

The first are such as pretend to believe the existence of an eternal, infinite, independent, intelligent Being, and who, to avoid the name of Epicurean Atheists, teach also that this Supreme Being made the world; though, at the same time, they agree with the Epicureans in this—that they fancy God does not at all concern himself in the government of the world, nor has any regard to, or care of, what is done therein.

The second sort of Deists are those who believe not only the being, but also the providence, of God, with respect to the *natural* world, but who, not allowing any difference between moral good and evil, deny that God takes any notice of the morally good or evil actions of men; these things depending, as they imagine, on the arbitrary constitution of human laws.

A third sort of Deists there are, who, having right apprehensions concerning the natural attributes of God and his all-governing providence, and some notion of his moral perfections also, yet, being prejudiced against the notion of the immortality of the soul, believe that men perish entirely at death, and that one generation shall perpetually succeed another, without any further restoration or renovation of things.

A fourth and last sort of Deist are such as believe the existence of a Supreme Being, together with his providence in the government of the world; also all the obligations of natural religion, but so far only as these things are discoverable by the light of nature alone, without believing any divine revelation.

These, the learned author observes, are the only true Deists; but, as their principles would naturally lead them to embrace the Christian revelation, he concludes there is now no consistent scheme of Deism in the world. Dr. Clarke then adds, "The heathen philosophers—those few of them who taught and lived up to the obligations of natural religion—had, indeed, a consistent scheme of Deism, as far as it went. But the case is not so now; the same scheme is not any longer consistent with its own principles; it does not now lead men to embrace revelation, as it then taught them to hope for it. Deists in our days, who reject revelation when offered to them, are not such men as Socrates and Cicero were; but, under pretence of Deism, it is plain they are generally ridiculers of all that is truly excellent in natural religion itself. Their trivial and vain cavils; their mocking and ridiculing without and before examination; their directing the whole stress of objections against particular customs, or particular and perhaps uncertain opinions or explications of opinions, without at all considering the main body of religion; their loose, vain, and frothy discourses; and, above all, their vicious and immoral lives, — show, plainly and undeniably, that they are not real Deists, but mere Atheists, and, consequently, not capable to judge of the truth of Christianity."

Dr. Paley observes, "Of what a revelation discloses to mankind, one, and only one, question can be properly asked. — Was it of importance to mankind to know or to be better assured of? In this question, when we turn our thoughts to the great Christian doctrine of a resurrection from the dead and a future judgment, no doubt can be possibly entertained He who gives me riches or honors does nothing; he who even gives me health, does little in comparison with that which lays before me just grounds for expecting a restoration to life, and a day of account and retribution, which thing Christianity hath done for millions."

## ATHEISTS.

The Atheists are those who deny the existence of God; this is called *speculative* Atheism. Professing to believe in God, and yet acting contrary to this belief, is called *practical* Atheism. Absurd and irrational as Atheism is, it has had its votaries and martyrs. In the seventeenth century, Spinosa was its noted defender. Lucilio Venini, a native of Naples, also publicly taught Atheism in France; and, being convicted of it at Toulouse, was condemned and executed in 1619. It has been questioned, however, whether any man ever seriously adopted such a principle.

Archbishop Tillotson says, "I appeal to any man of reason, whether any thing can be more unreasonable than obstinately to impute an effect to chance, which carries in the very face of it all the arguments and characters of a wise design and contrivance. Was ever any considerable work in which there were required a great variety of parts, and a regular and orderly disposition of those parts, done by chance? Will chance fit means to ends, and that in ten thousand instances, and not fail in any one? How often might a man, after he had jumbled a set of letters in a bag, fling them out upon the ground, before they would fall into an exact poem! yea, or so much as make a good discourse in prose! And may not a little book be as easily made by chance as the great volume of the world? How long might a man be in sprinkling colors upon canvass with a careless hand, before they would happen to make the exact picture of a man! And is a man easier made by chance than his picture? How long might twenty thousand blind men, who should be sent out from several remote parts of England, wander up and down before they would all meet upon Salisbury Plain, and fall into rank and file in the exact order of an army! And yet this is much more easy to be imagined than how the innumerable blind parts of matter should rendezvous themselves into a world. A man that sees Henry the Seventh's chapel at Westminster, might with as good reason maintain (yea, with much better, considering the vast difference betwixt that little structure and the huge fabric of the world) that it was never contrived or built by any means, but that the stones did by chance grow into those curious figures into which they seem to have been cut and graven; and that, upon a time, (as tales usually begin,) the materials of that building — the stone, mortar, timber, iron, lead, and glass — happily met together, and very fortunately ranged themselves into that delicate order in which we see them now, so close compacted, that it must be a very great chance that parts them again. What would the world think of a man that should advance such an opinion as this, and write a book for it? If they would do him right, they ought to look upon him as mad; but yet with a little more reason than any man can have to say that the world was made by chance, or that the first men grew up out of the earth as plants do now. For can any thing be more ridiculous, and against all reason, than to ascribe the production of men to the first fruitfulness of the earth, without so much as one instance and experiment, in any age or history, to countenance so monstrous a supposition? The thing is, at first sight, so gross and palpable, that no discourse about it can make it more apparent. And yet these shameful beggars of principles give this precarious account of the original of things; assume to themselves to be the men of reason, the great wits of the world, the only cautious and wary persons, that hate to be imposed upon, that must have convincing evidence for every thing, and can admit of nothing without a clear demonstration of it

Lord Bacon remarks, that "A *little* philosophy inclineth a man's mind to Atheism, but depth in philosophy bringeth men's minds about to religion; for, while the mind of man looketh upon second causes scattered, it may rest in them, and go no farther; but when it beholdeth *the chain* of them confederated and linked together, it must needs fly to Providence and Deity."

## PANTHEISTS.

Abner Kneeland's "Philosophical Creed," as he terms it, is probably a good definition of the views of those who consider the universe as an immense animal,

"Whose body nature is, and God the soul."

Mr. Kneeland says, "I believe in the existense of a

universe of suns and planets, among which there is one sun belonging to our planetary system, and that other suns, being more remote, are called stars; but that they are indeed suns to other planetary systems. I believe that the whole universe is NATURE, and that the word NATURE embraces the whole universe, and that God and Nature, so far as we can attach any rational idea to either, are perfectly synonymous terms. Hence I am not an Atheist, but a PANTHEIST; that is, instead of believing there is no God, I believe that, in the abstract, all is God; and that all power that is, is in God, and that there is no power except that which proceeds from God. I believe that there can be no will or intelligence where there is no sense, and no sense where there are no organs of sense; and hence sense, will, and intelligence, is the effect, and not the cause, of organization. I believe in all that logically results from those premises, whether good, bad, or indifferent. Hence I believe that God is all in all; and that it is in God we live, move, and have our being; and that the whole duty of man consists in living as long as he can, and in promoting as much happiness as he can while he lives."

## MAHOMETANS.

MAHOMETANISM is a scheme of religion formed and propagated by *Mahomet*, who was born at Mecca, A. D. 569, and died at Medina, in 632.

His system is a compound of Paganism, Judaism, and Christianity; and the Koran, which is their Bible, is held in grea. reverence. It is replete with absurd representations and is supposed to have been written by a Jew. The most eloquent passage is allowed to be the following, where God is introduced, bidding the waters of the deluge to cease:— "Earth, swallow up the waters; heaven, draw up those thou hast poured out; immediately the waters retreated, the command of God was obeyed, the ark rested on the mountains, and these words were heard — 'Woe to the wicked!'"

This religion is still professed and adhered to by the Turks and Persians, and by several nations in Asia and Africa. The best statistical writers estimate the number of Mahometans in the world at about one hundred and forty millions.

Mahomet descended from an honorable tribe, and from the noblest family of that tribe; yet his original lot was poverty. By his good conduct, he obtained the hand of a widow of wealth and respectability, and was soon raised to an equality with the richest people in Mecca.

Soon after his marriage, he formed the scheme of establishing a new religion, or, as he expressed it, of replanting the only true and ancient one professed by Adam, Noah, Abraham, Moses, Jesus, and all the prophets, by destroying the gross idolatry into which most of his countrymen had fallen, and weeding out the corruptions and superstitions which the later Jews and Christians had, as he thought, introduced into their religion, and reducing it to its original purity, which consisted chiefly in the worship of one God.

The Mahometans divide their religion into two general parts, faith and practice, of which the first is divided into six distinct branches — belief in God, in his angels, in his Scriptures, in his prophets, in the resurrection and final judgment, and in God's absolute decrees. The points relating to practice are, prayer, with washings, alms, fasting, pilgrimage to Mecca, and circumcision.

They believe that both Mahomet and those among his followers who are reckoned orthodox, had, and continue to have, just and true notions of God, and that his attributes appear so plain from the Koran itself, and all the Mahometan divines, that it would be loss of time to refute those who suppose the God of Mahomet to be different from the true God, and only a fictitious deity, or idol of his own creation

They believe that the existence of angels, and their purity, are absolutely required to be believed in the Koran; and he is reckoned an infidel who denies there are such beings, or hates any of them, or asserts any distinction of sexes among them. They believe them to have pure and subtile bodies, created of fire; that they neither eat, drink, nor propagate their species; that they have various forms and offices, some adoring God in different postures, others singing praises to him, or interceding for mankind. They hold that some of them are employed in writing down the actions of men others in carrying the throne of God, and other services.

As to the Scriptures, the Mahometans are taught by the Koran, that God, in divers ages of the world, gave revelations of his will in writing to several prophets, the whole and every one of which it is absolutely necessary for a good Moslem to believe. The number of these sacred books were, according to them, one hundred and four; of which ten were given to Adam, fifty to Seth, thirty to Edris or Enoch, ten to Abraham, and the other four, being the Pentateuch, the Psalms, the Gospel, and the Koran, were successively delivered to Moses, David, Jesus, and Mahomet; which last being the seal of the prophets, those revelations are now closed, and no more are to be expected. All these divine books, except the four last, they agree now to be entirely lost, and their contents unknown, though the Sabians have several books which they attribute to some of the antediluvian prophets. And of those four, the Pentateuch, Psalms, and Gospel, they say, have undergone so many alterations and corruptions, that, though there may possibly be some part of the true word of God therein, yet no credit is to be given to the present copies in the hands of the Jews and Christians.

They believe that the number of the prophets which have been from time to time sent by God into the world, amounts to no less than 224,000, according to one Mahometan tradition; or to 124,000, according to another; among whom 313 were apostles, sent with special commissions to reclaim mankind from infidelity and superstition; and six of them brought new laws or dispensations, which successively abrogated the preceding: these were Adam, Noah, Abraham, Moses, Jesus, and Mahomet. All the prophets in general the Mahometans believe to have been freed from great sins and errors of consequence, and professors of one and the same religion, that is, Islamism, notwithstanding the different laws and institutions which they observed. They allow of degrees among them, and hold some of them to be more excellent and honorable than others. The first place they give to the revealers and establishers of new dispensations, and the next to the apostles.

They believe in a general resurrection and a future judgment.

The time of the resurrection the Mahometans allow to be a perfect secret to all but God alone; the angel Gabriel himself acknowledging his ignorance in this point, when Mahomet asked him about it. However, they say the approach of that day may be known from certain signs which are to precede it.

After the examination is past, and every one's work weighed in a just balance, they say that mutual retaliation will follow, according to which every creature will take vengeance one of another, or have satisfaction made them for the injuries which they have suffered. And, since there will then be no other way of returning like for like, the manner of giving this satisfaction will be by taking away a proportional part of the good works of him who offered the injury, and adding it to those of him who suffered it; which being done, if the angels (by whose ministry this is to be performed) say, "*Lord we have given to every one his due, and there remaineth oj this person's good works so much as equalleth the weight of an ant,*" God will, of his mercy, cause it to be doubled unto him, that he may be admitted into paradise; but if, on the contrary, his good works be exhausted, and there remain evil works only, and there be any who have not yet received satisfaction from him, God will order that an equal weight of their sins be added unto his, that he may be punished for them in their stead, and he will be sent to hell laden with both. This will be the method of God's dealing with mankind. As to brutes, after they shall have likewise taken vengeance of one another, he will command them to be changed into dust; wicked men being reserved to more grievous punishment, so that they shall cry out, on hearing this sentence passed on the brutes, "*Would to God that we were dust also!*"

The trials being over, and the assembly dissolved, the Manometans hold that those who are to be admitted into paradise will take the right hand way, and those who are destined into hell-fire will take the left; but both of them must first pass the bridge called in Arabic *al Sirat*, which, they say, is laid over the midst of hell, and described to be finer than a hair, and sharper than the edge of a sword; so that it seems very difficult to conceive how any one shall be able to stand upon it; for which reason most of the sect of the Motazalites reject it as a fable; though the orthodox think it a sufficient proof of the truth of this article, that it was seriously affirmed by him who never asserted a falsehood, meaning their prophet, who, to add to the difficulty of the passage, has likewise declared that this bridge is beset on each side with briers and hooked thorns, which will, however, be no impediment to the good; for they shall pass with wonderful ease and swiftness, like lightning, or the wind, Mahomet and his Moslems leading the way; whereas the wicked, what with the slipperiness and extreme narrowness of the path, the entangling of the thorns, and the extinction of the light which directed the former to paradise, will soon miss their footing, and fall down headlong into hell, which is gaping beneath them.

As to the punishment of the wicked, the Mahometans are taught that hell is divided into seven stories or apartments, one below another, designed for the reception of as many distinct classes of the damned.

The first, which they call *Jehenan*, they say, will be the receptacle of those who acknowledged one God, that is, the wicked Mahometans; who, after having been punished according to their demerits, will at length be released; the second, named *Ladha*, they assign to the Jews; the third, named *al Hotama,* to the Christians; the fourth, named *al Sair,* to the Sabians; the fifth, named *Sakar,* to the Magians; the sixth, named *al Jahin,* to the idolaters; and the seventh, which is the lowest and worst of all, and is called *al Howyat,* to the hypocrites, or those who outwardly professed some religion, but in their hearts were of none. Over each of these apartments they believe there will be set a guard of angels, nineteen in number; to whom the damned will confess the just judgment of God, and beg them to intercede with him for some alleviation of their pain, or that they may be delivered by being annihilated.

Mahomet has, in his Koran and traditions, been very exact in describing the various torments of hell, which, according to him, the wicked will suffer, both from intense heat and excessive cold. The degrees of these pains will also vary in proportion to the crimes of the sufferer, and the apartment he is condemned to; and he who is punished the most lightly of all will be shod with shoes of fire, the fervor of which will cause his skull to boil like a caldron. The condition of these unhappy wretches, as the same prophet teaches, cannot be properly called either *life* or *death;* and their misery will be greatly increased by their despair of being ever delivered from that place, since, according to that frequent expression in the Koran, *they must remain therein forever.* It must be remarked, however, that the infidels alone will be liable to eternity of damnation; for the Moslems, or those who have embraced the true religion, and have been guilty of heinous sins, will be delivered thence after they shall have expiated their crimes by their sufferings. The time which these believers shal. be detained there, according to a tradition handed down from their prophet, will not be less than nine hundred years, nor more than seven thousand. And, as to the manner of their delivery, they say that they shall be distinguished by the marks of prostration on those parts of their bodies with which they used to touch the ground in prayer, and over which the fire will therefore have no power; and that, being known by this characteristic, they will be released by the mercy of God, at the intercession of Mahomet and the blessed whereupon those who shall have been dead will be restored to life, as has been said; and those whose bodies shall have contracted any sootiness or filth, from the flames and smoke of hell, will be immersed in one of the rivers of paradise, called the *River of Life*, which will wash them whiter than pearls.

The righteous, as the Mahometans are taught to believe, having surmounted the difficulties, and passed the sharp bridge above mentioned, before they enter paradise, will be refreshed by drinking at the *Pond* of their prophet, who describes it to be an exact square, of a month's journey in compass; its water, which is supplied by two pipes from al Cawthay, one of the rivers of paradise, being whiter than milk or silver, and more odoriferous than musk, with as many cups set round it as there are stars in the firmament; of which water whoever drinks will thirst no more forever. This is the first taste which the blessed will have of their future and now near-approaching felicity.

Though paradise be so very frequently mentioned in the Koran, yet it is a dispute among the Mahometans, whether it be already created, or to be created hereafter; the Motazalites and some other sectaries asserting that there is not at present any such place in nature, and that the paradise which the righteous will inhabit in the next life will be different from that from which Adam was expelled. However, the orthodox profess the contrary, maintaining that it was created even before the world, and describe it from their prophet's traditions in the following manner: —

They say it is situated in the seventh heaven, and next under the throne of God; and, to express the amenity of the place, tell us that the earth of it is of the finest wheat-flour, or of the purest musk, or, as others will have it, of saffron; that its stones are pearls and jacinths, the walls of its building enriched with gold and silver, and that the trunks of all its trees are of gold; among which the most remarkable is the tree called *tuba*, or the tree of happiness. Concerning this tree, they fable that it stands in the palace of Mahomet though a branch of it will reach to the house of every true believer; that it will be laden with pomegranates, grapes, dates, and other fruits of surprising bigness, and of tastes unknown to mortals; so that, if a man desire to eat of any particular kind of fruit, it will immediately be presented him; or, if he choose flesh, birds ready dressed will be set before him, according to his wish. They add that the boughs of this tree will spontaneously bend down to the hand of the person who would gather of its fruits, and that it will supply the blessed not only with food, but also with silken garments, and beasts to ride on ready saddled and bridled, and adorned with rich trappings, which will burst forth from its fruits; and that this tree is so large, that a person mounted on the fleetest horse, would not be able to gallop from one end of its shade to the other in one hundred years.

As plenty of water is one of the greatest additions to the pleasantness of any place, the Koran often speaks of the rivers of paradise as a principal ornament thereof: some of these rivers, they say, flow with water, some with milk, some with wine, and others with honey; all taking their rise from the root of the tree tuba.

But all these glories will be eclipsed by the resplendent and ravishing girls of paradise, called, from their large black eyes, *Hur al oyun*, the enjoyment of whose company will be a principal felicity of the faithful. These, they say, are created, not of clay, as mortal women are, but of pure musk; being, as their prophet often affirms in his Koran, free from all natural impurities, of the strictest modesty, and secluded from public view in pavilions of hollow pearls, so large that, as some traditions have it, one of them will be no less than sixty miles square.

The name which the Mahometans usually give to this happy mansion is *al Jannat*, or "the Garden;" and sometimes they call it the "Garden of Paradise," the "Garden of Eden," the "Garden of Abode," the "Garden of Pleasure," and the like; by which several appellations some understand so many different gardens, or at least places of different degrees of felicity, (for they reckon no less than one hundred such in all,) the very meanest whereof will afford its inhabitants so many pleasures and delights, that one would conclude they must even sink under them, had not Mahomet declared that, in order to qualify the blessed for a full enjoyment of them, God will give to every one the abilities of one hundred men.

The orthodox doctrine is, that whatever hath or shall come to pass in this world, whether it be good or whether it be bad, proceedeth entirely from the divine will, and is irrevocably fixed and recorded from all eternity in the preserved table; God having secretly predetermined not only the adverse and prosperous fortune of every person in this world, in the most minute particulars, but also his faith or infidelity, his obedience or disobedience, and consequently his everlasting happiness or misery after death; which fate or predestination it is not possible by any foresight or wisdom to avoid.

The pilgrimage to Mecca is so necessary a point of practice, that, according to a tradition of Mahomet, he who dies without performing it, may as well die a Jew or a Christian; and the same is expressly commanded in the Koran.

What is principally reverenced in Mecca, and gives sanctity to the whole, is a square stone building, called the *Caaba*. Before the time of Mahomet, this temple was a place of worship for the idolatrous Arabs, and is said to have contained no less than three hundred and sixty different images, equalling in number the days of the Arabian year. They were all destroyed by Mahomet, who sanctified the Caaba, and appointed it to be the chief place of worship for all true believers. The Mussulmen pay so great a veneration to it, that they believe a single sight of its sacred walls, without any particular act of devotion, is as meritorious in the sight of God as the most careful discharge of one's duty, for the space of a whole year, in any other temple.

The Mahometans have an established priesthood and a

numerous body of clergymen: their spiritual head, in Turkey, whose power is not inferior to the Roman Pontiff, or the Grecian Patriarch, is denominated the *Mufti*, and is regarded as the oracle of sanctity and wisdom. Their houses of worship are denominated mosques, many of which are very magnificent, and very richly endowed. The revenues of some of the royal mosques are said to amount to the enor mous sum of 60,000 pounds sterling. In the city of Fez, the capital of the emperor of Morocco, there are near one thousand mosques, fifty of which are built in a most magnificent style, supported by marble pillars. The circumference of the grand mosque is near a mile and a half, in which near a thousand lamps are lighted every night. The Mahometan priests, who perform the rites of their public worship, are called *Imams;* and they have a set of ministers called *Sheiks*, who preach every *Friday*, the Mahometan Sabbath, much in the manner of Christian preachers. They seldom touch upon points of controversy in their discourses, but preach upon moral duties, upon the dogmas and ceremonies of their religion, and declaim against vice, luxury, and corruption of manners.

The rapid success which attended the propagation of this new religion was owing to causes that are plain and evident, and must remove, or rather prevent, our surprise, when they are attentively considered. The terror of Mahomet's arms, and the repeated victories which were gained by him and his successors, were, no doubt, the irresistible arguments that persuaded such multitudes to embrace his religion, and submit to his dominion. Besides, his law was artfully and marvellously adapted to the corrupt nature of man, and, in a most particular manner, to the manners and opinions of the Eastern nations, and the vices to which they were naturally addicted; for the articles of faith which it proposed were few in number, and extremely simple; and the duties it required were neither many nor difficult, nor such as were incompatible with the empire of appetites and passions. It is to be observed, further, that the gross ignorance under which the Arabians, Syrians, Persians, and the greatest part of the Eastern nations, labored at this time, rendered many an easy prey to the artifice and eloquence of this bold adventurer To these causes of the progress of Mahometanism we may add the bitter dissensions and cruel animosities that reigned among the Christian sects — dissensions that filled a great part of the East with carnage, assassinations, and such detestable enormities as rendered the very name of Christianity odious to many. Other causes of the sudden progress of that religion will naturally occur to such as consider attentively its spirit and genius, and the state of the world at this time

To show the subtlety of Mahomet's mind, and the extreme ignorance of his followers, we give the story of that impostor's night journey from Mecca to Jerusalem, and from thence to heaven.

The story, as related in the Koran, and believed by the Mahometans, is this: "At night, as he lay in his bed, with his best beloved wife Ayesha, he heard a knocking at his door; upon which, arising, he found there the angel Gabriel, with seventy pair of wings, expanded from his sides, whiter than snow, and clearer than crystal, and the beast Alborak standing by him; which, they say, is the beast on which the prophets used to ride, when they were carried from one place to another, upon the execution of any divine command. Mahomet describes it to be a beast as white as milk, and of a mixed nature, between an ass and a mule, and also of a size between both; but of such extraordinary swiftness as to equal even lightning itself.

"As soon as Mahomet appeared at the door, the angel Gabriel kindly embraced him, saluted him in the name of God, and told him that he was sent to bring him unto God, into heaven, where he should see strange mysteries, which were not lawful to be seen by any other man. He prayed him, then, to get upon Alborak; but the beast, having lain idle and unemployed from the time of Christ to Mahomet, was grown so mettlesome and skittish, that he would not stand still for Mahomet to mount him, till at length he was forced to bribe him to it by promising him a place in paradise. When he was firmly seated on him, the angel Gabriel led the way, with the bridle of the beast in his hand, and carried the prophet from Mecca to Jerusalem in the twinkling of an eye. On his coming thither, all the departed prophets and saints appeared at the gate of the temple to salute him, and, thence attending him into the chief oratory, desired him to pray for them, and then withdrew. After this, Mahomet went out of the temple with the angel Gabriel, and found a ladder of light, ready fixed for them, which they immediately ascended, leaving Alborak tied to a rock till their return.

"On their arrival at the first heaven, the angel knocked at the gate; and, informing the porter who he was, and that he had brought Mahomet, the friend of God, he was immediately admitted. This first heaven, he tells us, was all of pure silver; from whence he saw the stars hanging from it by chains of gold, each as big as Mount Noho, near Mecca, in Arabia On his entrance, he met a decrepit old man, who, it seems, was our first father, Adam; and, as he advanced, he saw a multitude of angels in all manner of shapes — in the shape of birds, beasts, and men. We must not forget to observe that Adam had the piety immediately to embrace the prophet, giving God thanks for so great a son, and then recommended himself to his prayers. From this first heaven he tells us that he ascended into the second, which was at the distance of five hundred years' journey above it, and this he makes to be the distance of every one of the seven heavens, each above the other. Here the gates being opened to him as before, at his entrance he met Noah, who, rejoicing much at the sight of him, recommended himself to his prayers. This heaven was all of pure gold, and there were twice as many angels in it as in the former; for he tells us that the number of angels in every heaven increased as he advanced. From this second heaven he ascended into the third, which was made of precious stones, where he met Abraham, who also recommended himself to his prayers; Joseph, the son of Jacob, did the same in the fourth heaven, which was all of emerald; Moses in the fifth, which was all of adamant; and John the Baptist in the sixth, which was all of carbuncle; whence he ascended into the seventh, which was of divine light; and here he found Jesus Christ. However, it is observed that here he alters his style; for he does not say that Jesus Christ recommended himself to his prayers, but that he recommended himself to the prayers of Jesus Christ.

"The angel Gabriel, having brought him thus far, told him that he was not permitted to attend him any farther, and therefore directed him to ascend the rest of the way to the throne of God by himself. This he performed with great difficulty, passing through rough and dangerous places, till he came where he heard a voice saying unto him, 'O Mahomet, salute thy Creator;' whence ascending higher, he came into a place where he saw a vast expansion of light, so exceedingly bright, that his eyes could not bear it. This, it seems, was the habitation of the Almighty, where his throne was placed; on the right side of which, he says, God's name and his own were written in these Arabic words: 'La ellah ellallah Mahomet reful ollah;' that is, 'There is no God but God, and Mahomet is his prophet,' which is at this day the creed of the Mahometans. Being approached to the divine presence, he tells us that God entered into a familiar converse with him, revealed to him many hidden mysteries, made him understand the whole of his law, gave him many things in charge concerning his instructing men in the knowledge of it, and, in conclusion, bestowed on him several privileges above the rest of mankind. He then returned, and found the angel Gabriel waiting for him in the place where he left him. The angel led him back along the seven heavens, through which he had brought him, and set him again upon the beast Alborak, which stood tied to the rock near Jerusalem. Then he conducted him back to Mecca, in the same manner as he brought him thence; and all this within the space of the tenth part of one night."

Dr. Joseph White thus concludes one of his discourses on

Mahometanism: "What raises Christ and his religion far above all the fictions of Mahomet, is that awful alternative of hopes and fears, that looking-for of judgment, which our Christian faith sets before us. At that day, when time, the great arbiter of truth and falsehood, shall bring to pass the accomplishment of the ages, and the Son of God shall make his enemies his footstool, — then shall the deluded followers of the great Impostor, disappointed of the expected intercession of their prophet, stand trembling and dismayed at the approach of the glorified Messiah. Then shall they say, 'Yonder cometh in the clouds that Jesus whose religion we labored to destroy; whose temples we profaned; whose servants and followers we cruelly oppressed! Behold, he cometh, but no longer the humble son of Mary; no longer a mere mortal prophet, the equal of Abraham, and of Moses, as that deceiver taught us, but the everlasting Son of the everlasting Father; the Judge of mankind; the Sovereign of angels; the Lord of all things, both in earth and in heaven!'"

## SIMONIANS.

An infidel sect, organized in France, some years since, whose fundamental principle is, that religion is to perfect the social condition of man; therefore Christianity is no longer suitable for society, because it separates the Christian from other men, and leads him to live for another world. The world requires a religion that shall be of this world, and, consequently, a God of this world. They reject whatever they suppose to have been derived from the philosophy of the East; they consider the Deity neither as spirit nor matter, but as including the whole universe, and are thus plainly Pantheists; and they regard evil as nothing more than an indication of the progress which mankind are doomed to make, in order to be freed from it; in itself, they maintain it is nothing Its members are principally of the higher ranks, and display, not without success, the greatest activity in spreading the venom of their infidel principles. They occupy, in Paris, the largest and most handsomely fitted halls, where they meet in great numbers.

What is very curious in the history of the Simonians is, that they were, at first, merely philosophers, and not at all the founders of a religion. They spoke of science and in dustry, but not of religious doctrines. All at once, however, it seemed to occur to them to teach a religion. Then their school became a church, and their association a sect. It is evident that, with them, religion was not originally the end of their institution, but has been employed by them as the means of collecting a greater number of hearers.

## PAGANS.

A GENERAL term, applied to heathen idolaters, who worship false gods, and are not acquainted either with the doctrines of the Old Testament or the Christian dispensation. The worship of the Grand Lama is of the most extensive and splendid character among the Pagan idolaters. This extends all over Thibet and Mongolia, is almost universal in Bucharia and several provinces of Tartary; it has followers in Cash mere, and is the predominant religion of China.

The Grand Lama is a name given to the sovereign pontiff, or high priest, of the Thibetian Tartars, who resides at Patoli, a vast palace on a mountain, near the banks of Burhampooter, about seven miles from Lahassa. The foot of this mountain is inhabited by twenty thousand Lamas, or priests, who have their separate apartments round about the mountain, and, according to their respective quality, are placed nearer or at a greater distance from the sovereign pontiff. He is not only the sovereign pontiff, the vicegerent of the Deity on earth, but the more remote Tartars are said to absolutely regard him as the Deity himself, and call him *God, the everlasting Father of heaven.* They believe him to be immortal, and endowed with all knowledge and virtue Every year they come up, from different parts, to worship, and make rich offerings at his shrine. Even the emperor of China, who is a Manchou Tartar, does not fail in acknowledgments to him, in his religious capacity, and actually entertains, at a great expense, in the palace of Pekin, an inferior Lama, deputed as his nuncio from Thibet. The Grand Lama, it has been said, is never to be seen but in a secret place of his palace, amidst a great number of lamps, sitting cross-legged upon a cushion, and decked all over with gold and precious stones; where, at a distance, the people prostrate themselves before him, it being not lawful for any so much as to kiss his feet. He returns not the least sign of respect, nor ever speaks, even to the greatest princes, but only lays his hand upon their heads; and they are fully persuaded they receive from thence a full forgiveness of all their sins.

The magnificence and number of the ancient heathen temples almost exceed calculation or belief. At one time, there were no less than 424 temples in the city of Rome. The temple of Diana, at Ephesus, was accounted one of the seven wonders of the world. It was 425 feet in length, 220 in breadth, and was adorned with 100 columns 60 feet high; and, as each column is said to have contained 150 tons of marble, — as the stupendous edifice, outside and in, was adorned with gold, and a profusion of ornaments, — how immense must have been the whole expense of its erection!

At the present day, many of the pagan nations go to immense expense in the support of their religious worship. It is stated, in the Indo-Chinese Gleaner, a paper published by the missionaries in China, that there are, in that empire, 1056 temples dedicated to Confucius, where above 60,000 animals are annually offered. The followers of Confucius form one of the smallest of the three leading sects among the Chinese.

Mr. Ward, a distinguished missionary, was present at the worship of the goddess Doorga, at Calcutta, in 1806. After describing the greatness of the assembly, the profusion of the offerings, and the many strange peculiarities of the worship, he observes, "The whole produced on my mind sensations of the greatest horror. The dress of the singers, their indecent gestures, the abominable nature of the songs, the horrid din of their miserable drum, the lateness of the hour, the darkness of the place, with the reflection that I was standing in an idol temple, and that this immense multitude of rational and immortal creatures, capable of superior joys, were, in the very act of worship, perpetrating a crime of high treason against the God of heaven, while they themselves believed they were performing an act of merit, — excited ideas and feelings in my mind which time can never obliterate."

The vast empire of China, misnamed the *Celestial Empire*, is given up to the vilest idolatry. Idols are encountered at every step, not merely in the temples, but in the houses, and even in the vessels, where a part of the forecastle is consecrated to them, as the most honorable place. The idol is dressed and adorned with a splendor proportioned to the wealth of the captain of the vessel, and daily receives an offering, composed of flesh and fruits, together with the smoke of perfumes. Besides this regular service, the captain makes a solemn sacrifice to his wooden deity, on all important occasions; as, for instance, in passing from one river into another, or in time of tempest, or when the sails flap idly in a calm. The Chinese have likewise a practice of deifying their dead ancestors, and of prostrating themselves before the monumental tablets which are erected to their memory. Yet they appear to have no real veneration for any of their idols; nor do they hesitate to profane the temples, by smoking their pipes, and taking refreshments, and even by gambling, within the consecrated precincts. The priests are shameless impostors. They practise the mountebank sciences of astrology, divination, necromancy, and animal magnetism, and keep for sale a liquid, which, they pretend, will confer immortality on those who drink it.

Tortures of various kinds, burning, and burying alive, are considered religious duties among the pagans.

The festival of Juggernaut is annually held on the sea-coast of Orissa, where there is a celebrated temple, and an idol of the god. The idol is a carved block of wood, with a frightful visage, painted black, and a distended mouth of a bloody color. He is dressed in gorgeous apparel, and his appellation is one of the numerous names of Vishnu, the preserving power of the universe, according to the theology of the Bramins. On festival days, the throne of the idol is placed upon a stupendous movable tower, about sixty feet in height, resting on wheels, which indent the ground deeply, as they turn slowly under the ponderous machine. He is accompanied by two other idols, his brother Balaram, and his sister Shubudra, of a white and yellow color, each on a separate tower, and sitting on thrones of nearly an equal height. Attached to the principal tower are six ropes, of the length and size of a ship's cable, by which the people draw it along. The priests and attendants are stationed around the throne, on the car, and occasionally address the worshippers in libidinous songs and gestures. Both the walls of the temple and sides of the car are covered with the most indecent emblems, in large and durable sculpture. Obscenity and blood are the characteristics of the idol's worship. As the tower moves along, devotees, throwing themselves under the wheels, are crushed to death; and such acts are hailed with the acclamations of the multitude, as the most acceptable sacrifices. A body of prostitutes are maintained in the temple, for the use of the worshippers; and various other systematic indecencies, which will not admit of description, form a part of the service. A number of sacred bulls are kept in the place, which are generally fed with vegetables from the hands of the pilgrims, but, from the scarcity of the vegetation, are commonly seen walking about, and eating the fresh ordure of the worshipping crowds. In the temple, also, is preserved a bone of Krishna, which is considered as a most venerable and precious relic, and which few persons are allowed to see.

The following is an account of the burning of a Gentoo woman, on the funeral pile of her deceased husband: — "We found," says M. Stavorinus, "the body of the deceased lying upon a couch, covered with a piece of white cotton, and strewed with betel leaves. The woman, who was to be the victim, sat upon the couch, with her face turned to that of the deceased. She was richly adorned, and held a little green branch in her right hand, with which she drove away the flies from the body. She seemed like one buried in the most profound meditation, yet betrayed no signs of fear. Many of her relations attended upon her, who, at stated intervals, struck up various kinds of music.

"The pile was made by driving green bamboo stakes into the earth, between which was first laid fire-wood, very dry and combustible; upon this was put a quantity of dry straw, or reeds, besmeared with grease: this was done alternately, till the pile was five feet in height; and the whole was then strewed with rosin, finely powdered. A white cotton sheet, which had been washed in the Ganges, was then spread over the pile, and the whole was ready for the reception of the victim.

"The widow was now admonished, by a priest, that it was time to begin the rites. She was then surrounded by women, who offered her betel, and besought her to supplicate favors for them when she joined her husband in the presence of Ram, or their highest god, and, above all, that she would salute their deceased friends whom she might meet in the celestial mansions.

"In the mean time, the body of the husband was taken and washed in the river. The woman was also led to the Ganges for ablution, where she divested herself of all her ornaments. Her head was covered with a piece of silk, and a cloth was tied round her body, in which the priests put some parched rice.

"She then took a farewell of her friends, and was conducted by two of her female relations to the pile. When she came to it, she scattered flowers and parched rice upon the spectators, and put some into the mouth of the corpse. Two priests next led her three times round it, while she threw rice among the bystanders, who gathered it up with great eagerness. The last time she went round, she placed a little earthen burning lamp to each of the four corners of the pile, then laid herself down on the right side, next to the body, which she embraced with both her arms; a piece of white cotton was spread over them both; they were bound together with two easy bandages, and a quantity of fire-wood, straw, and rosin, was laid upon them. In the last place, her nearest relations, to whom, on the banks of the river, she had given her nose-jewels, came with a burning torch, and set the straw on fire, and in a moment the whole was in a flame. The noise of the drums, and the shouts of the spectators, were such that the shrieks of the unfortunate woman, if she uttered any, could not have been heard."

Instances are related of women eighty years of age, or upwards, perishing in this manner. One case is mentioned, by Mr. Ward, of a Bramin who had married upwards of a hundred wives, thirty-seven of whom were burnt with him. The pile was kept burning for *three days*, and when one or more of them arrived, they threw themselves into the *blazing fire.*

The Pagans worship an immense variety of idols, both animate and inanimate, and very frequently make to themselves gods of objects that are contemptible even among brutes. In Hindoo, the *monkey* is a celebrated god. A few years since, the rajah of Nudeeya expended $50,000 in celebrating the marriage of a pair of those mischievous creatures, with all the parade and solemnity of a Hindoo wedding.

A Bramin of superior understanding gave Mr. Ward

the following *confession of faith*, as the present belief of the philosophical Hindoos, concerning the nature of God, viz.: — "God is invisible, independent, ever-living, glorious, uncor rupt, all-wise, the ever-blessed, the almighty; his perfections are indescribable and past finding out; he rules over all, supports all, destroys all, and remains after the destruction of all; there is none like him; he is silence; he is free from passion, from birth, &c., and from increase and decrease, from fatigue, the need of refreshment, &c. He possesses the power of infinite diminution and lightness, and is the soul of all.

"He created, and then entered into, all things, in which he exists in two ways, untouched by matter, and receiving the fruits of practice. He now assumes visible forms for the sake of engaging the minds of mankind. The different gods are parts of God, though his essence remains undiminished, as rays of light leave the sun his undiminished splendor. He created the gods to perform those things in the government of the world, of which man was incapable. Some gods are parts of other gods, and there are deities of still inferior powers. If it be asked why God himself does not govern the world, the answer is, that it might subject him to exposure, and he chooses to be concealed: he therefore governs by the gods, who are emanations from the one God, possessing a portion of his power: he who worships the gods as the one God, substantially worships God. The gods are helpful to men in all human affairs, but they are not friendly to those who seek final absorption, being jealous lest, instead of attaining absorption, they should become gods, and rival them.

"Religious ceremonies procure a fund of merit to the performer, which raises him in every future birth, and at length advances him to heaven, where he enjoys happiness for a limited period, or carries him towards final absorption A person may sink to earth again by crimes committed in heaven. The joys of heaven arise only from the gratification of the senses. A person raised to heaven is considered as a god.

"When the following lines of Pope were read to a learned Bramin, he started from his seat, begged a copy of them, and declared the author must have been a Hindoo: —

'All are but parts of one stupendous whole,
Whose body Nature is, and God the soul; ......
Warms in the sun, refreshes in the breeze,
Glows in the stars, and blossoms in the trees,
Lives through all life, extends through all extent,
Spreads undivided, operates unspent.'

"Such are the best views of the best of men among the Hindoos. Such a mixture of truth and error, of sense and folly, do they believe and teach."

According to the best accounts that can be obtained from missionaries and others, the number of Pagans, in different countries, exceeds half the population of the globe.

Considerable attempts have been made, of late years, for the enlightening of the heathen; and there is every reason to believe good has been done. From the aspect of Scripture prophecy, we are led to expect that the kingdoms of the heathen at large shall be brought to the light of the gospel. (Matt. 24:14. Isa. 60. Ps. 22:28, 29; 2:7, 8.) It has been much disputed whether it be possible that the heathen should be saved without the knowledge of the gospel; some have absolutely denied it, upon the authority of those texts which universally require faith in Christ; but to this it is answered, that those texts regard only such to whom the gospel comes, and are capable of understanding the contents of it. "The truth," says Dr. Doddridge, "seems to be this — that none of the heathen will be condemned for not believing the gospel, but they are liable to condemnation for the breach of God's natural law: nevertheless, if there be any of them in whom there is a prevailing love to the Divine Being, there seems reason to believe that, for the *sake* of Christ, though to them unknown, they may be accepted by God; and so much the rather, as the ancient Jews, and even the apostles, during the time of our Savior's abode on earth, seem to have had but little notion of those doctrines, which those who deny the salvability of the heathen are most apt to imagine." (Rom. 2:10—22. Acts 10:34, 35. Matt. 8:11, 12.) Grove, Watts, Saurin, and the immortal Newton, favor the same opinion; the latter of whom thus observes: "If we suppose a heathen brought to a sense of his misery; to a conviction that he cannot be happy without the favor of the great Lord of the world; to a feeling of guilt, and desire of mercy; and that, though he has no explicit knowledge of a Savior, he directs the cry of his heart to the unknown Supreme, to have mercy upon him, — who will prove that such views and desires can arise in the heart of a sinner, without the energy of that Spirit which Jesus is exalted to bestow? Who will take upon him to say that his blood has not sufficient efficacy to redeem to God a sinner who is thus disposed, though he have never heard of his name? Or who has a warrant to affirm that the supposition I have made is in the nature of things impossible to be realized?"

"That there exist beings, one or many, powerful above the human race, is a proposition," says Lord Kaimes, "universally admitted as true in all ages and among all nations. I boldly call it *universal*, notwithstanding what is reported of some gross savages; for reports that contradict what is acknowledged to be general among men, require able vouchers. Among many savage tribes there are no words but for objects of external sense: is it surprising that such people are incapable of expressing their religious perceptions, or any perception of internal sense? The conviction that men have of superior powers, in every country where there are words to express it, is so well vouched, that, in fair reasoning, it ought to be taken for granted among the few tribes where language is deficient." The same ingenious author shows, with great strength of reasoning, that the operations of nature and the government of this world, which to us loudly proclaim the existence of a Deity, are not sufficient to account for the universal belief of superior beings among savage tribes. He is, therefore, of opinion that this universality of conviction can spring only from the image of Deity stamped upon the mind of every human being, the ignorant equally with the learned. This, he thinks, may be termed the *sense of Deity.*

## SATANIANS.

A BRANCH of the Messalians, who appeared about the year 390. It is said, among other things, that they believed the devil to be extremely powerful, and that it was much wiser to respect and adore than to curse him.

## ABELIANS, OR ABELONIANS.

A SECT which arose in the diocese of Hippo, in Africa, in the fifth century. They regulated marriage after the example of Abel, who, they pretended, was married, but lived in a state of continence: they therefore allowed each man to marry one woman, but enjoined them to live in the same state. To keep up the sect, when a man and woman entered into this society, they adopted a boy and a girl, who were to inherit their goods, and to marry upon the same terms of not having children, but of adopting two of different

## SUPRALAPSARIANS.

PERSONS who hold that God, without any regard to the good or evil works of men, has resolved, by an eternal decree, *supra lapsum*, antecedently to any knowledge of the fall of

Adam, and independently of it, to save some and reject others; or, in other words, that God intended to glorify his justice in the condemnation of some, as well as his mercy in the salvation of others, and, for that purpose, decreed that Adam should necessarily fall.

## DANCERS.

A SECT which sprung up, about 1373, in Flanders, and places about. It was their custom all of a sudden to fall a-dancing, and, holding each other's hands, to continue thereat, till, being suffocated with the extraordinary violence, they fell down breathless together. During these intervals of vehement agitation, they pretended to be favored with wonderful visions. Like the Whippers, they roved from place to place, begging their victuals, holding their secret assemblies, and treating the priesthood and worship of the church with the utmost contempt.

## EPICUREANS.

THE disciples of Epicurus, who flourished about A. M. 3700. This sect maintained that the world was formed not by God, nor with any design, but by the fortuitous concourse of atoms. They denied that God governs the world, or in the least condescends to interfere with creatures below; they denied the immortality of the soul, and the existence of angels; they maintained that happiness consisted in pleasure; but some of them placed this pleasure in the tranquillity and joy of the mind, arising from the practice of moral virtue, and which is thought by some to have been the true principle of

Epicurus: others understood him in the gross sense, and placed all their happiness in corporeal pleasure. When Paul was at Athens, he had conferences with the Epicurean philosophers. (Acts 17 : 18.) The word *Epicurean* is used, at present, for an indolent, effeminate, and voluptuous person, who only consults his private and particular pleasure.

---

## SKEPTICS.

The word *Skeptic* properly signifies considerative and inquisitive, or one who is always weighing reasons on one side or the other, without ever deciding between them. The word is applied to an ancient sect of philosophers founded by Pyrrho, who denied the real existence of all qualities in bodies, except those which are essential to primary atoms, and referred every thing else to the perceptions of the mind produced by external objects; in other words, to appearance and opinion. In modern times, the word has been applied to Deists, or those who doubt of the truth and authenticity of the sacred Scrip-

---

## WICKLIFFITES.

The followers of the famous John Wickliffe, called "the first reformer," who was born in Yorkshire, in the year 1324. He attacked the jurisdiction of the pope and the bishops. He was for this twice summoned to a council at Lambeth, to give an account of his doctrines, but, being countenanced by the duke of Lancaster, was both times dismissed without condemnation. Wickliffe, therefore, continued to spread his new principles, as usual, adding to them doctrines still more alarming; by which he drew after him a great number of disciples. Upon this, William Courtney, archbishop of Canterbury, called another council in 1382, which condemned 24 propositions of Wickliffe and his disciples, and obtained a declaration of Richard II. against all who should preach them; but while these proceedings were agitating, Wickliffe died at Lutterworth, leaving many works behind him for the establishment of his doctrines. He was buried in his own church, at Lutterworth, in Leicestershire, where his bones were suffered to rest in peace till the year 1428, when, by an order from the pope, they were taken up and burnt. Wickliffe was doubtless a very extraordinary man, considering the times in which he lived. He discovered the absurdities and impositions of the church of Rome, and had the honesty and resolution to promulgate his opinions, which a little more support would probably have enabled him to establish: they were evidently the foundation of the subsequent reformation.

## DIGGERS.

A DENOMINATION which sprung up in Germany, in the fifteenth century; so called because they dug their assemblies under ground, in caves and forests. They derided the church, its ministers, and sacraments.

## ZUINGLIANS.

A BRANCH of the Reformers, so called from Zuinglius, a noted divine of Switzerland. His chief difference from Luther was concerning the eucharist. He maintained that the bread and wine were only *significations* of the body and blood of Jesus Christ, whereas Luther believed in *consubstantiation.*

## SEEKERS.

A DENOMINATION which arose in the year 1645. They derived their name from their maintaining that the true church ministry, Scripture, and ordinances, were lost, for which they were seeking. They taught that the Scriptures were uncertain; that present miracles were necessary to faith; that our ministry is without authority; and that our worship and ordinances are unnecessary or vain.

## WILHELMINIANS.

A DENOMINATION in the 13th century, so called from Wilhelmina, a Bohemian woman, who resided in the territory of Milan. She persuaded a large number that the Holy Ghost was become incarnate in her person, for the salvation of a great part of mankind. According to her doctrines, none were saved by the blood of Jesus but true and pious Christians, while the Jews, Saracens, and unworthy Christians, were to obtain salvation through the Holy Spirit which dwelt in her, and that, in consequence thereof, all which happened in Christ during his appearance upon earth in the human nature, was to be exactly renewed in her person, or rather in that of the Holy Ghost, which was united to her.

## NON-RESISTANTS.

THIS is a name assumed by those who believe in the inviolability of human life, and whose motto is, RESIST NOT EVIL, — that is, by the use of carnal weapons or brute force. They cannot properly be called a religious sect, in the common acceptation of that term, and they repudiate the title; for they differ very widely among themselves in their religious speculations, and have no forms, ordinances, creed, church, or community. Some of them belong to almost every religious persuasion, while others refuse to be connected with any denomination, and to be called by any sectarian name. Like the friends of negro emancipation, or of total abstinence from all intoxicating substances, their eyes are fastened upon a common object, and their hearts united together by a common principle; and whatever calls for the violation of that principle, or for the sacrifice of that object, they feel in duty bound to reject.

In the autumn of 1838, an association was formed in Boston, called the "NEW ENGLAND NON-RESISTANCE SOCIETY," the principles of which are comprehensively imbodied in the second article of its constitution, as follows: —

"The members of this society agree in opinion that no man, or body of men, however constituted, or by whatever name called, have the right to take the life of man as a penalty for transgression; that no one, who professes to have the Spirit of Christ, can consistently sue a man at law for redress of injuries, or thrust any evil-doer into prison, or fill any office in which he would come under obligation to execute penal enactments, or take any part in the military service, or acknowledge allegiance to any human government, or justify any man in fighting in defence of property, liberty, life, or religion; that he cannot engage in or countenance any plot or effort to revolutionize, or change, by physical violence, any government, however corrupt or oppressive; that he will obey 'the powers that be,' except in those cases in which they bid him violate his conscience — and then, rather than to resist, he will meekly submit to the penalty of disobedience; and that, while he will cheerfully endure all things for Christ's sake, without cherishing even the desire to inflict injury upon his persecutors, yet he will be bold and uncompromising for God, in bearing his testimony against sin, in high places and in low places, until righteousness and peace shall reign in all the earth, and there shall be none to molest or make afraid."

On the same occasion, a DECLARATION OF SENTIMENTS was adopted, in which the views of Non-Resistants are set forth in the following positive and argumentative form: —

"We cannot acknowledge allegiance to any human government; neither can we oppose any such government by a resort to physical force. We recognize but one KING and LAWGIVER, one JUDGE and RULER of mankind. We are bound by the laws of a kingdom which is not of this world; the subjects of which are forbidden to fight; in which MERCY and TRUTH are met together, and RIGHTEOUSNESS and PEACE have kissed each other; which has no state lines, no national partitions, no geographical boundaries; in which there is no distinction of rank, or division of caste, or inequality of sex; the officers of which are PEACE, its exactors RIGHTEOUSNESS, its walls SALVATION, and its gates PRAISE; and which is destined to break in pieces and consume all other kingdoms.

"Our country is the world, our countrymen are all mankind. We love the land of our nativity only as we love all other lands. The interests, rights, liberties of American citizens, are no more dear to us than are those of the whole human race. Hence we can allow no appeal to patriotism, to revenge any national insult or injury. The PRINCE OF PEACE, under whose stainless banner we rally, came not to destroy, but to save, even the worst of enemies. He has left us an example, that we should follow his steps. GOD COMMENDETH HIS LOVE TOWARD US, IN THAT, WHILE WE WERE YET SINNERS, CHRIST DIED FOR US.

"We conceive that, if a nation has no right to defend itself against foreign enemies, or to punish its invaders, no individual possesses that right in his own case. The unit cannot be of greater importance than the aggregate. If one man may take life, to obtain or defend his rights, the same license must necessarily be granted to communities, states, and nations. If *he* may use a dagger or a pistol, *they* may employ cannon, bomb-shells, land and naval forces. The means of self-preservation must be in proportion to the magnitude of interests at stake, and the number of lives exposed to destruction. But if a rapacious and bloodthirsty soldiery, thronging these shores from abroad, with intent to commit rapine and destroy life, may not be resisted by the people or magistracy, then ought no resistance to be offered to domestic troublers of the public peace, or of private security. No obligations can rest upon Americans to regard foreigners as more sacred in their persons than themselves, or to give them a monopoly of wrong-doing with impunity.

"The dogma, that all the governments of the world are approvingly ordained of God, and that THE POWERS THAT BE, in the United States, in Russia, in Turkey, are in accordance with his will, is not less absurd than impious. It makes the impartial Author of human freedom and equality unequal and tyrannical. It cannot be affirmed that THE POWERS THAT BE, in any nation, are actuated by the spirit, or guided by the example, of Christ, in the treatment of enemies; therefore they cannot be agreeable to the will of God; and, therefore, their overthrow, by a spiritual regeneration of their subjects, is inevitable.

"We register our testimony, not only against all wars, whether offensive or defensive, but all preparations for war; against every naval ship, every arsenal, every fortification; against the militia system and a standing army; against all military chieftains and soldiers; against all monuments commemorative of victory over a foreign foe, all trophies won in battle, all celebrations in honor of military or naval exploits; against all appropriations for the defence of a nation by force and arms, on the part of any legislative body; against every edict of government requiring of its subjects military service. Hence we deem it unlawful to bear arms, or to hold a military office.

"As every human government is upheld by physical strength, and its laws are enforced virtually at the point of the bayonet, we cannot hold any office which imposes upon its incumbent the obligation to compel men to do right, on pain of imprisonment or death. We therefore voluntarily exclude ourselves from every legislative and judicial body, and repudiate all human politics, worldly honors, and stations of authority. If *we* cannot occupy a seat in the legislature, or on the bench, neither can we elect *others* to act as our substitutes in any such capacity.

"It follows that we cannot sue any man at law, to compel him by force to restore any thing which he may have wrongfully taken from us or others; but, if he has seized our coat, we shall surrender up our cloak rather than subject him to punishment.

"We believe that the penal code of the old covenant, AN EYE FOR AN EYE, AND A TOOTH FOR A TOOTH, has been abrogated by JESUS CHRIST; and that, under the new covenant, the forgiveness, instead of the punishment, of enemies has been enjoined upon all his disciples, in all cases whatsoever. To extort money from enemies, or set them upon a pillory, or cast them into prison, or hang them upon a gallows, is obviously not to forgive, but to take retribution. VENGEANCE IS MINE — I WILL REPAY, SAITH THE LORD.

"The history of mankind is crowded with evidences proving that physical coërcion is not adapted to moral regeneration; that the sinful dispositions of man can be subdued only by love; that evil can be exterminated from the earth only by goodness; that it is not safe to rely upon an arm of flesh, upon man, whose breath is in his nostrils, to preserve us from harm; that there is great security in being gentle, harmless, long-suffering, and abundant in mercy; that it is only the meek who shall inherit the earth, for the violent, who resort to the sword, are destined to perish with the sword. Hence, as a measure of sound policy, — of safety to property, life, and liberty, — of public quietude and private enjoyment, — as well as on the ground of allegiance to HIM who is KING OF KINGS and LORD OF LORDS, — we cordially adopt the non-resistance principle; being confident that it provides for all possible consequences, will insure all things needful to us, is armed with omnipotent power, and must ultimately triumph over every assailing force.

"We advocate no Jacobinical doctrines. The spirit of Jacobinism is the spirit of retaliation, violence, and murder. It neither fears God nor regards man. *We* would be filled with the Spirit of CHRIST. If we abide by our principles, it is impossible for us to be disorderly, or plot treason, or participate in any evil work: we shall submit to every ordinance of man, FOR THE LORD'S SAKE; obey all the requirements of government, except such as we deem contrary to the commands of the gospel; and in no case resist the operation of law, except by meekly submitting to the penalty of disobedience.

"But while we shall adhere to the doctrine of non-resistance and passive submission to enemies, we purpose, in a moral and spiritual sense, to speak and act boldly in the cause of GOD; to assail iniquity in high places and in low places; to apply our principles to all existing civil, political, legal, and ecclesiastical institutions; and to hasten the time when the kingdoms of this world will have become the kingdoms of our LORD and of his CHRIST, and he shall reign forever.

"It appears to us a self-evident truth, that whatever the gospel is designed to destroy at any period of the world, being contrary to it, ought now to be abandoned. If, then, the time is predicted, when swords shall be beaten into ploughshares, and spears into pruning-hooks, and men shall not learn the art of war any more, it follows that all who manufacture, sell, or wield those deadly weapons, do thus array themselves against the peaceful dominion of the SON OF GOD on earth."

Having thus frankly stated their principles and purposes, hey proceed to specify the measures they propose to adopt, in carrying their object into effect, as follows:—

"We expect to prevail through THE FOOLISHNESS OF PREACHING, striving to commend ourselves unto every man's conscience, in the sight of GOD. From the press, we shall promulgate our sentiments as widely as practicable. We shall endeavor to secure the coöperation of all persons, of whatever name or sect. The triumphant progress of the cause of TEMPERANCE and of ABOLITION in our land, through the instrumentality of benevolent and voluntary associations, encourages us to combine our own means and efforts for the promotion of a still greater cause. Hence we shall employ lecturers, circulate tracts and publications, form societies, and petition our state and national governments, in relation to the subject of UNIVERSAL PEACE. It will be our leading object to devise ways and means for effecting a radical change in the views, feelings and practices of society, respecting the sinfulness of war and the treatment of enemies.

"In entering upon the great work before us, we are not unmindful that, in its prosecution, we may be called to test our sincerity, even as in a fiery ordeal. It may subject us to insult, outrage, suffering, yea, even death itself. We anticipate no small amount of misconception, misrepresentation, calumny. Tumults may arise against us. The ungodly and violent, the proud and Pharisaical, the ambitious and tyrannical, principalities and powers, and spiritual wickedness in high places, may combine to crush us. So they treated the MESSIAH, whose example we are humbly striving to imitate. If we suffer with him, we know that we shall reign with him We shall not be afraid of their terror, neither be troubled. Our confidence is in the LORD ALMIGHTY, not in man.

"Having withdrawn from human protection, what can sustain us but that faith which overcomes the world? We shall not think it strange concerning the fiery trial which is to try us, as though some strange thing had happened unto us, but rejoice, inasmuch as we are partakers of CHRIST'S sufferings. Wherefore we commit the keeping of our souls to GOD, in well-doing, as unto a faithful Creator. FOR EVERY ONE THAT FORSAKES HOUSES, OR BRETHREN, OR SISTERS, OR FATHER, OR MOTHER, OR WIFE, OR CHILDREN, OR LANDS

FOR CHRIST'S SAKE, SHALL RECEIVE A HUNDRED FOLD, AND SHALL INHERIT EVERLASTING LIFE."

For entertaining these sentiments, they say that they "have been stigmatized as no human government men," and ranked among disorganizers and anarchists. But they believe that the gospel requires men to suppress every angry emotion, to forgive every injury, to revenge none; and they ask, "Shall we forgive as individuals, and retaliate as communities? Shall we turn the other cheek as individuals, and plunge a dagger into the heart of our enemy as nations? We might as well be sober as individuals, and drunk as nations. We might as well be merciful as individuals, and rob as patriots." They believe that the forgiveness of enemies, whether foreign or domestic, is the essence, the chief virtue, the soul of the gospel; that we should preach our Savior's peace, even if it brings us to our Savior's cross; that Christians should not punish, either to amend those who trespass against them, or to comfort themselves; for they do not amend others by fines and imprisonments, nor do they need any better comfort than that of their Savior, who, on the cross, not only prayed, but apologized for his murderers; that, if the gospel is right in prescribing pardon, the law is wrong in inflicting punishment; that, if a Christian reigns, he reigns by love, not by force; that he cannot smile with frowns, forgive with punishment, love with hatred, bless with the sword, do good with evil, be humble with pride, love God and serve Mammon; that moral power would govern men altogether cheaper and better than physical; that the destruction of every kingdom that has heretofore existed, proves that men will not, cannot be governed by physical force; that the refusal of our Savior to govern, when he had the power of miracles, was his greatest miracle; and that his obedience, forgiveness, sufferings, and death, established the constitution of a government, in which peace on earth and good-will to men will be maintained by the God of peace, the Prince of peace, and the Spirit of peace. They believe that, when Jesus referred his hearers to the law of retaliation, which law constituted the great fundamental principle in the Jewish civil government, and when, in express terms, he repealed that law, he laid the axe at the root of that government, and virtually repealed or abrogated the whole of it; for of what force can any civil government be, which cannot enforce its laws by inflicting evil upon its violators? When Jesus took from the Jewish civil ruler the right to inflict punishment, he declared the only civil government, which God had ever instituted, and recognized as of any rightful authority, to be null and void forever. They think it will be admitted, by all who receive the plain declarations of Scripture as truth, that no man, as an individual, has the right to render evil for evil, or to enforce even his lawful claims, by his fist, the club, or the sword. But if a man has no such right as an individual, he has none as a member of a family, or as the inhabitant of a town, county, state, or nation; hence he cannot delegate any such right to others, called legislators, magistrates, judges, sheriffs, &c. If no man has the right to retaliate with the fist, or club, or sword, it is equally and immutably true that he has no right to render evil for evil, by using laws, or magistrates, or judges, or sheriffs, as the clubs, or swords, or the instruments of such retaliation. When men "resist evil," either by the use of the club, or of human law, the principle upon which they act is the same in both cases; the only difference is in the instruments employed.

## SOUTHCOTTERS.

Dr. Evans gives the following account of the religious views and opinions of Joanna Southcott, who made considerable noise in England, towards the close of the last century: —

"The mission of this prophetess commenced in the year 1792, and the number of people who have joined with her from that period to the present time, as believing her to be divinely inspired, was considerable. It was asserted that she was the instrument, under the direction of Christ, to announce the establishment of his kingdom on earth, as a fulfilment of all the promises in the Scriptures, and of that prayer which he himself gave to his followers; and more particularly of the promise made to the woman in the fall, through which the human race is to be redeemed from all the effects of it in the end. We are taught by the communication of the Spirit of truth to her, that the seven days of the creation were types of the two periods in which the reign of Satan and of Christ are to be proved and contrasted. Satan was conditionally to have his reign tried for six thousand years, shadowed by the six days in which the Lord worked, as his Spirit has striven with man while under the powers of darkness; but Satan's reign is to be shortened, for the sake of the elect, as declared in the gospel; and Satan is to have a further trial at the expiration of the thousand years, for a time equal to the number of the days shortened. At the close of the seven thousand years, the judgment is to take place, and the whole human race will collectively bring forward the testimony of the evil they suffered under the reign of Satan, and of the good they enjoyed under the spiritual reign of Christ. These two testimonies will be evidence, before the whole creation of God, that the pride of Satan was the cause of his rebellion in heaven, and that he was the root of evil upon earth; and, consequently, when those two great proofs have been brought forward, that part of the human race that has fallen under his power, to be tormented by being in the society of Satan and his angels, will revolt from him in that great day, will mourn that they have been deluded, will repent, and the Savior of all will hold out his hand to them in mercy, and will then prepare a new earth for them to work righteousness, and prepare them ultimately to join his saints, who have fought the good fight in this world, while under the reign of Satan.

"The mission of Joanna is to be accomplished by a perfect

obedience to the Spirit that directs her, and so to be made to claim the promise of 'bruising the head of the serpent;' and which promise was made to the woman on her casting the blame upon Satan, whom she unwittingly obeyed, and thus man became dead to the knowledge of the good; and so he blamed his Creator for giving him the woman, who was pronounced his helpmate for good. To fulfil the attribute of justice, Christ took upon himself that blame, and assumed his humanity, to suffer on the cross for it, that he might justly bring the cross upon Satan, and rid him from the earth, and then complete the creation of man, so as to be after his own image. It is declared that 'the seed of the woman' are those who in faith shall join with her in claiming the promise made in the fall; and they are to subscribe with their hands unto the Lord that they do thus join with her, praying for the destruction of the powers of darkness, and for the establishment of the kingdom of Christ. Those who thus come forward in this spiritual war, are to have the seal of the Lord's protection; and if they remain faithful soldiers, death and hell shall not have power over them; and these are to make up the sealed number of one hundred and forty-four thousand, to stand with the Lamb on Mount Sion. The fall of Satan's kingdom will be a second deluge over the earth; so that, from his having brought the human race under his power, a great part of them will fall with him; for the Lord will pluck out of his kingdom all that offend and do wickedly The voice which announces the coming of the Messiah is accompanied with judgments, and the nations must be shaken and brought low before they will lay these things to heart. When all these things are accomplished, then the desire of nations will come in glory, so that 'every eye shall see him,' and he will give his kingdom to his saints.

"It is represented that in the Bible is recorded every event by which the Deity will work the ultimate happiness of the human race, but that the great plan is, for the most part, represented by types and shadows, and otherwise so wrapped up in mysteries, as to be inscrutable to human wisdom As the Lord pronounced that man should become dead to knowledge if he ate the forbidden fruit, so the Lord must prove his words true. He therefore selected a peculiar peo ple as depositaries of the records of that knowledge; and he appeared among them, and they proved themselves dead to every knowledge of him, by crucifying him. He will, in like manner, put the wild olive to the same test; and the result will be, that he will be now crucified in the spirit.

"The mission of Joanna began in 1792, at which time she had prophecies given her, showing how the whole was to be accomplished. Among other things, the Lord said he should visit the surrounding nations with various calamities for fifteen years, as a warning to *this* land; and that then he should bring about events here which should more clearly manifest the truth of her mission, by judgment and otherwise; so that this should be the happy nation to be the first redeemed from its troubles, and be the instrument for awakening the rest of the world to a sense of what is coming upon all, and for destroying *the Beast*, and those who worship his image.

"Joanna Southcott died of a protracted illness. It was given out that she was to be the mother of a *Second Shiloh*. Presents were accordingly made her for the *Babe*, especially a superb cradle, with a Hebrew inscription in poetry. But she expired, and no child appeared on the occasion. A stone placed over her remains in the New Burial-ground, Mary-le-bone, has this mystic inscription:—

IN MEMORY OF
JOANNA SOUTHCOTT,
Who departed this life December 27th, 1814,
Aged 60 years.

While, through all thy wondrous days,
Heaven and earth enraptured gaze,—
While vain sages think they know
Secrets thou alone canst show,—
Time alone will tell what hour
Thou'lt appear in greater power."

## FAMILY OF LOVE.

A sect that arose in Holland, in the sixteenth century, founded by Henry Nicholas, a Westphalian. He maintained that he had a commission from Heaven to teach men that the essence of religion consisted in the feelings of divine love; that all other theological tenets, whether they related to objects of faith or modes of worship, were of no sort of moment, and, consequently, that it was a matter of the most perfect indifference what opinions Christians entertained concerning the divine nature, provided their hearts burned with the pure and sacred flame of piety and love.

## HUTCHINSONIANS.

Hutchinsonians, the followers of John Hutchinson, born in Yorkshire, 1674, and who, in the early part of his life, served the duke of Somerset in the capacity of steward. The Hebrew Scriptures, he says, comprise a perfect system of natural philosophy, theology, and religion. In opposition to Dr. Woodward's "Natural History of the Earth," Mr. Hutchinson, in 1724, published the first part of his curious book, called "Moses' Principia." Its second part was presented to the public in 1727, which contains, as he apprehends, the principles of the Scripture philosophy, which are a plenum and the air. So high an opinion did he entertain of the Hebrew language, that he thought the Almighty must have employed it to communicate every species of knowledge, and that, accordingly, every species of knowledge is to be found in the Old Testament. Of his mode of philosophizing, the following specimen is brought forward to the reader's attention: — "The air, he supposes, exists in three conditions, — fire, light, and spirit; — the two latter are the finer and grosser parts of the air in motion; from the earth to the sun, the air is finer and finer, till it becomes pure light near the confines of the sun, and fire in the orb of the sun, or solar focus. From the earth towards the circumference of this system, in which he includes the fixed stars, the air becomes grosser and grosser, till it becomes stagnant, in which condition it is at the utmost verge of this system, from whence, in his opinion, the expression of *outer darkness*, and *blackness of darkness*, used in the New Testament, seems to be taken."

The followers of Mr. Hutchinson are numerous, and among others the Rev. Mr. Romaine, Lord Duncan Forbes, of Culloden, and the late amiable Dr. Horne, bishop of Norwich.

---

## MORMONITES,

OR

## THE CHURCH OF THE LATTER-DAY SAINTS.

In a little work entitled *Religious Creeds and Statistics*, published in 1836, we gave some account of the origin and faith of the Mormonites, or *Latter-Day Saints*, as they prefer being called. Since that time, we have received an additional stock of the publications of this people, and are now enabled to tell their story in their own words.

In a letter dated Nauvoo, Illinois, March 1, 1842, Prophet Joseph Smith says: —

"On the evening of the 21st of September, A. D. 1823, while I was praying unto God, and endeavoring to exercise faith in the precious promises of Scripture, on a sudden a light like that of day, only of a far purer and more glorious appearance and brightness, burst into the room; indeed, the first sight was as though the house was filled with consuming fire; the appearance produced a shock that affected the whole body

In a moment, a personage stood before me surrounded with a glory yet greater than that with which I was already surrounded. This messenger proclaimed himself to be an angel of God, sent to bring the joyful tidings, that the covenant which God made with ancient Israel was at hand to be fulfilled; that the preparatory work for the second coming of the Messiah was speedily to commence; that the time was at hand for the gospel, in all its fulness, to be preached, in power, unto all nations, that a people might be prepared for the millennial reign.

"I was informed that I was chosen to be an instrument in the hands of God to bring about some of his purposes in this glorious dispensation.

"I was also informed concerning the aboriginal inhabitants of this country, and shown who they were, and from whence they came; a brief sketch of their origin, progress, civilization, laws, governments, of their righteousness and iniquity, and the blessings of God being finally withdrawn from them as a people, was made known unto me. I was also told where there were deposited some plates, on which was engraven an abridgment of the records of the ancient prophets that had existed on this continent. The angel appeared to me three times the same night, and unfolded the same things. After having received many visits from the angels of God, unfolding the majesty and glory of the events that should transpire in the last days, on the morning of the 22d of September, A. D 1827, the angel of the Lord delivered the records into my hands.

"These records were engraven on plates which had the appearance of gold; each plate was six inches wide and eight inches long, and not quite so thick as common tin. They were filled with engravings, in Egyptian characters, and bound together in a volume, as the leaves of a book, with three rings running through the whole. The volume was something near six inches in thickness, a part of which was sealed. The characters on the unsealed part were small, and beautifully engraved. The whole book exhibited many marks of antiquity in its construction, and much skill in the art of engraving With the records was found a curious instrument, which the ancients called 'Urim and Thummim,' which consisted of two transparent stones set in the rim of a bow fastened to a breastplate.

"Through the medium of the Urim and Thummim I translated the record, by the gift and power of God.

"In this important and interesting book the history of ancient America is unfolded, from its first settlement by a colony that came from the tower of Babel, at the confusion of languages, to the beginning of the fifth century of the Christian era. We are informed by these records that America, in ancient times, has been inhabited by two distinct races of people. The first were called Jaredites, and came directly from the tower of Babel. The second race came directly from the city of Jerusalem, about six hundred years before Christ. They were principally Israelites, of the descendants of Joseph. The Jaredites were destroyed about the time that the Israelites came from Jerusalem, who succeeded them in the inheritance of the country. The principal nation of the second race fell in battle towards the close of the fourth century. The remnant are the Indians that now inhabit this country. This book also tells us that our Savior made his appearance upon this continent after his resurrection, that he planted the gospel here in all its fulness, and richness, and power, and blessing; that they had apostles, prophets, pastors, teachers, and evangelists; the same order, the same priesthood, the same ordinances, gifts, powers, and blessing, as were enjoyed on the eastern continent; that the people were cut off in consequence of their transgressions; that the last of their prophets who existed among them was commanded to write an abridgment of their prophecies, history, &c., and to hide it up in the earth, and that it should come forth, and be united with the Bible, for the accomplishment of the purposes of God in the last days. For a more particular account, I would refer to the Book of Mormon, which can be purchased at Nauvoo, or from any of our travelling elders.

"As soon as the news of this discovery was made known

false reports, misrepresentation, and slander flew, as on the wings of the wind, in every direction; the nouse was frequently beset by mobs and evil-designing persons; several times I was shot at, and very narrowly escaped, and every device was made use of to get the plates away from me; but the power and blessing of God attended me, and several began to believe my testimony.

"On the 6th of April, 1830, the 'Church of Jesus Christ of Latter-Day Saints' was first organized in the town of Manchester, Ontario county, state of New York. Some few were called and ordained by the spirit of revelation and prophecy, and began to preach as the Spirit gave them utterance; and though weak, yet were they strengthened by the power of God, and many were brought to repentance, were immersed in the water, and were filled with the Holy Ghost by the laying on of hands. They saw visions and prophesied: devils were cast out, and the sick healed by the laying on of hands. From that time, the work rolled forth with astonishing rapidity, and churches were soon formed in the states of New York, Pennsylvania, Ohio, Indiana, Illinois, and Missouri. In the last-named state, a considerable settlement was formed in Jackson county; numbers joined the church, and we were increasing rapidly; we made large purchases of land, our farms teemed with plenty, and peace and happiness were enjoyed in our domestic circle and throughout our neighborhood; but we could not associate with our neighbors, who were many of them of the basest of men."

After giving an account of their removal from Jackson to Clay, and from Clay to Caldwell and Davies counties, Missouri, with a relation of their persecutions and consequent distresses, the prophet proceeds: —

"We arrived in the state of Illinois in 1839, where we found a hospitable people and a friendly home; a people who were willing to be governed by the principles of law and humanity. We have commenced to build a city, called

'Nauvoo,' in Hancock county. We number from six to eigh thousand here, besides vast numbers in the county around, and in almost every county of the state. We have a city charter granted us, and a charter for a legion, the troops of which now number fifteen hundred. We have also a charter for a university, for an agricultural and manufacturing soci ety, have our own laws and administrators, and possess al the privileges that other free and enlightened citizens enjoy.

"Persecution has not stopped the progress of truth, but has only added fuel to the flame; it has spread with increasing rapidity. Proud of the cause which they have espoused, and conscious of their innocence, and of the truth of their system, amidst calumny and reproach have the elders of this church gone forth, and planted the gospel in almost every state in the Union; it has penetrated our cities, it has spread over our villages, and has caused thousands of our intelligent, noble, and patriotic citizens to obey its divine mandates, and be governed by its sacred truths. It has also spread into England, Ireland, Scotland, and Wales. In the year 1839, where a few of our missionaries were sent, over five thou sand joined the standard of truth. There are numbers now joining in every land.

"Our missionaries are going forth to different nations; and in Germany, Palestine, New Holland, the East Indies, and other places, the standard of truth has been erected. No unhallowed hand can stop the work from progressing. Persecutions may rage, mobs may combine, armies may assemble, calumny may defame, but the truth of God will go forth boldly, nobly, and independent, till it has penetrated every continent, visited every clime, swept every country, and sounded in every ear, till the purposes of God shall be accomplished, and the great Jehovah shall say, 'The work is done!'

"We believe in God, the eternal Father, and in his Son Jesus Christ, and in the Holy Ghost.

"We believe that men will be punished for their own sins, and not for Adam's transgression.

"We believe that, through the atonement of Christ, all mankind may be saved by obedience to the laws and ordinances of the gospel.

"We believe that these ordinances are, 1. faith in the Lord Jesus Christ; 2. repentance; 3. baptism, by immersion, for the remission of sins; 4. laying on of hands for the gift of the Holy Ghost.

"We believe that a man must be called of God by 'prophecy, and by laying on of hands,' by those who are in authority to preach the gospel, and administer in the ordinances thereof.

"We believe in the same organization that existed in the primitive church, viz., apostles, prophets, pastors, teachers, evangelists, &c.

"We believe in the gift of tongues, prophecy, revelation, visions, healing, interpretation of tongues, &c.

"We believe the Bible to be the word of God, as far as it is translated correctly; we also believe the Book of Mormon to be the word of God.

"We believe all that God has revealed, all that he does now reveal, and we believe that he will yet reveal many great and important things pertaining to the kingdom of God.

"We believe in the literal gathering of Israel, and in the restoration of the ten tribes; that Zion will be built upon this continent; that Christ will reign personally upon the earth; and that the earth will be renewed and receive its paradisaic glory.

"We claim the privilege of worshipping Almighty God according to the dictates of our conscience, and allow all men the same privilege, let them worship how, where, or what, they may.

"We believe in being subject to kings, presidents, rulers, and magistrates, in obeying, honoring, and sustaining the law.

"We believe in being honest, true, chaste, benevolent vir

tuous, and in doing good to *all men*. Indeed, we may say that we follow the admonition of Paul, — we 'believe all things, we hope all things;' — we have endured many things, and hope to be able to endure all things. If there is any thing virtuous, lovely, or of good report, or praiseworthy, we seek after these things."

From the *Gospel Reflector*, a volume edited by B. Winchester, presiding elder of the Church of Jesus Christ of Latter-Day Saints, Philadelphia, we extract the following

"HISTORY OF THE ANCIENTS OF AMERICA, AND ALSO OF THE BOOK OF MORMON.

"Six hundred years B. C., according to the Book of Mormon, Lehi, who was a righteous man, was forewarned of he destruction of Jerusalem and the Babylonish captivity who was commanded by the Lord, took his family and fled into the wilderness. He pitched his tent in the wilderness, near the Red Sea, and sent back his sons to Jerusalem, who persuaded one Ishmael and his family to accompany them to their father Lehi. The Lord promised to lead them to a choice land above all lands; therefore they set out on their journey for this land. After a long and tedious journey, they came to the great waters, or the ocean. Nephi, the son of Lehi, who was also a prophet, and their pilot, or leader, in the wilderness, was commanded and instructed to build a ship sufficiently large to transport them over the sea. This work was accomplished in eight years from the time they left Jerusalem. They set sail, and in a proper time they landed, as we infer from their record, somewhere on the western coast of South America. They immediately commenced tilling the earth, and erecting mansions for dwelling-places.

"Lehi had six sons, Laman, Lemuel, Nephi, Sam, Jacob, and Joseph. Laman, Lemuel, and the sons of Ishmael, rebelled against God, and would not keep his commandments, for this they were cursed. Their posterity, in process of time, became a powerful nation, but extremely wicked; and their chief occupations were hunting, plundering, and roving about from place to place. In the Book of Mormon, they are called Lamanites. The other sons of Lehi were obedient to the commands of God. Their posterity, also, in the course of time, became a great nation, and were called Nephites To them God committed his divine oracles, (the holy priesthood,) and they had prophets and inspired men among them. They also kept a record of their prophecies and revelations, and the proceedings of their nation. When they left Jerusalem, they brought with them the law of Moses, and the writings of the former prophets, down to the days of Jeremiah. This accounts for the quotations from Isaiah and others, which are found in the Book of Mormon.

"The Nephites tilled the land, built cities, and erected temples for places of worship; but the Lamanites lived a more indolent life, although, in some instances, they built cities. The Nephites were at times faithful to God at other times they were indifferent, and would not be faithful. They frequently had long and tedious wars with the Lamanites, and were often driven before them. They were constantly emigrating to the north. At length they commenced settlements in the region of country not far from the Isthmus of Darien; and, while in those parts, they advanced further in science and arts than at any time previous, and built more spacious cities and buildings than they did before.

"Six hundred and thirty odd years from the time Lehi left Jerusalem, Christ, after his resurrection, appeared unto many of the Nephites, and established his church, chose disciples, and sent them throughout the land to preach his gospel, thus fulfilling the saying, 'Other sheep I have, which are not of this fold; them I must go and bring also.'

"Individuals of the Lamanites, at times, were obedient to the faith. The Nephites, after Christ's appearance, were faithful for many years; but, in the third or fourth century, iniquity began to abound, and their love began to wax cold. Some dissented, and raised up churches for the sake of gain; and thus they were troubled with the spirit of pride and haughtiness. God commanded Mormon, who ıved in the fourth century, to preach repentance to them, and foretell their destruction if they would not repent. The Lord, fore seeing that they would not repent, commanded Mormon to collect the writings of his forefathers, — their revelations and prophecies, &c., — and make an abridgment of them, and engrave them upon new plates, (their manner of keeping records was to engrave them on metallic plates.) But in consequence of their wars, and their flight to the north, to escape the Lamanites, he did not live to finish this work; and, when the final destruction of the Nephites drew near, he gave the records to his son Moroni, who lived to see their final extermination, or destruction, by the hands of the Lamanites, and they, with his father, left to moulder on the plain.

"Thus a powerful nation, whose fathers were the favorites of Heaven, were cut off, and their names have faded into oblivion!

"The Indians of America are the descendants of the Lamanites, and, according to predictions that are in the Book of Mormon, they will yet lay down their weapons of war, and be converted unto the Lord.

"Moroni finished compiling and abridging the records of his fathers, which he engraved upon new plates, for that purpose, to use his own words, as follows: — 'And now, behold, we have written this record, according to our knowledge, in the characters which are called among us *the reformed Egyptian;* being handed down and altered by us, according to our manner of speech. And, if our plates had been sufficiently large, we should have written in Hebrew; but the Hebrew hath been altered by us also; and, if we could have written in Hebrew, behold, ye would have had no imperfection in our record. But the Lord knoweth the things which we have written, and also that none other people knoweth our language; therefore he hath prepared means for the interpretation thereof.'

"He also engraved on them an account, called the 'Book

of Ether ' of a people who left the old world, and came to this continent at the time the language was confounded at Babel, which was a partial fulfilment of the saying, ' So the Lord scattered them abroad from thence upon the face of all the earth.' (Gen. 11 : 8.)

"Moroni was then commanded to deposit this record in the earth, together with the *Urim and Thummim*, or, as the Nephites would have said, *Interpreters*, which were instruments to assist in the work of the translation, with a promise from the Lord that it should be brought to light by means of a Gentile nation that should possess the land, and be published to the world, and go forth to the Lamanites, and be one of the instruments in the hands of God for their conversion. It remained safe in the place where it was deposited, till it was brought to light by the administration of angels, and translated by the gift and power of God."

The Mormon Bible contains five hundred and eighty-eight duodecimo pages, and purports to have been written at different times, and by the different authors, whose names the parts respectively bear. The following are the names of the different books, in the order in which they occur: —

1. First Book of Nephi.
2. Second Book of Nephi.
3. Book of Jacob, brother of Nephi.
4. Book of Enos, son of Jacob.
5. Book of Jarom, son of Enos.
6. Book of Omni, son of Jarom.
7. Words of Mormon.
8. Book of Mosiah.
9. Book of Alma.
10. Book of Helaman.
11. Book of Nephi, son of Nephi, son of Helaman.
12. Book of Nephi, son of Nephi, one of the disciples of Christ.
13. Book of Mormon.
14. Book of Ether.
15. Book of Moroni.

Two new books have recently been published, — the Prophecies of Enoch, in the *Morning and Evening Star*, and the Book of Abraham, in the *Times and Seasons*.

The Mormons seem to think that revelations from Heaven and miracles wrought, are as necessary now, and as impor tant to the salvation of the present generation, as they were to any generation in any preceding age or period.

In a volume entitled "Doctrine and Covenants," are a great number of revelations, purporting to be from Jesus Christ to Smith and his coadjutors. The following extracts from a revelation given on the 22d and 23d of September, 1832, convey, it is believed, a fair specimen of the whole. We copy *verbatim.*

"Verily, verily, I say unto you, It is expedient that every man who goes forth to proclaim mine everlasting gospel, that, inasmuch as they have families, and receive moneys by gift, that they should send it unto them, or make use of it for their benefit, as the Lord shall direct them; for thus it seemeth me good. And let all those who have not families, who receive moneys, send it up unto the bishop in Zion, or unto the bishop in Ohio, that it may be consecrated for the bringing forth of the revelations, and the printing thereof, and for establishing Zion.

"And if any man shall give unto any of you a coat, or a suit, take the old and cast it unto the poor, and go your way rejoicing. And if any man among you be strong in the Spirit, let him take with him he that is weak, that he may be edified in all meekness, that he may become strong also.

"And the bishop, also, should travel round about and among all the churches, searching after the poor, to administer to their wants by humbling the rich and the proud; he should, also, employ an agent to take charge and to do his secular business, as he shall direct; nevertheless, let the bishop go unto the city of New York, and also to the city of Albany, and also to the city of Boston, and warn the people of those cities with the sound of the gospel, with a loud voice, of the desolation and utter abolishment which awaits them if they do reject these things; for if they do reject these things, the hour of their judgment is nigh, and their nouse shall be left unto them desolate. Let him trust in me, and he shall not be confounded, and a hair of his head shal. not fall to the ground unnoticed.

"And verily I say unto you, the rest of my servants, Go ye forth, as your circumstances shall permit, in your several callings, unto the great and notable cities and villages, reproving the world, in righteousness, of all their unrighteous and ungodly deeds, setting forth clearly and understandingly the desolation of abomination in the last days; for with you, saith the Lord Almighty, I will rend their kingdoms; I will not only shake the earth, but the starry heavens shall tremble; for I the Lord have put forth my hand to exert the powers of heaven: ye cannot see it now; yet a little while and ye shall see it, and know that I am, and that I will come and reign with my people. I am Alpha and Omega, the beginning and the end. Amen."

Joseph Smith is the son of a farmer, and was born in Sharon, Vermont, 23d December, 1805. His father removed to the state of New York about the year 1815, and resided in Palmyra, and afterwards in Manchester.

Smith has many enemies, and his doctrines are warmly opposed; still, it must be acknowledged that, by his talents, or the magic influence his scheme of religion has on the minds of men, or by a union of both, he has acquired an imposing station in the world. He is styled ***Prophet ana High Priest of Jesus Christ***, ***President of the Council of the Church of the Latter-Day Saints***, and ***Lieutenant-General of the Nauvoo Legion.*** He sends his elders, bishops, priests, and teachers, by scores, into all lands, and more than *seventy-five thousand people* bow, with willing subjection, to his mandates.

Nauvoo, Illinois, formerly Commerce, is situated on the east side of the Mississippi River, at the head of Des Moines Rapids, about two hundred and ten miles (by the river) above St. Louis, thirteen hundred and fifty miles above New Orleans, and about three hundred miles below Dubuque, in

Iowa. It comprises two miles square of fertile land. The city of Nauvoo, which was incorporated in 1841, is delightfully located, on rising ground, near the bank of the river. It contains many handsome buildings of brick and stone, among which are the Nauvoo House, a large stone building for the accommodation of travellers, and the Mormon Temple, likewise of stone, measuring on the ground one hundred by one hundred and twenty feet, exclusive of the wings of the building. This place has one of the best landings on the river, and its trade is considerable. The number of inhabitants, at the present time, is about eight thousand, chiefly Mormons. *Nauvoo* is said to signify, THE CITY OF GOD

## DALEITES.

THE followers of David Dale, a very industrious manufacturer, a most benevolent Christian, and the humble pastor of an Independent congregation at Glasgow. At first, he formed a connection with the *Glassites*, in many of whose opinions he concurred, but was disgusted by their narrow and worldly spirit: he therefore separated from them, chiefly on the ground of preferring practical to speculative religion, and Christian charity to severity of church discipline. As he grew rich by industry, he devoted all his property to doing good, and ranks high among the philanthropists of his age. He was founder of the celebrated institution of New Lanark, now under Mr. Robert Owen, his son-in-law. The Daleites now form the second class of Independents in Scotland.

## EMANCIPATORS.

THIS body of Christians was formed in Kentucky, in 1805, by the association of a number of ministers and churches of he Baptist denomination. They differ in no respect from he regular Baptists, except in the decided stand they have taken against slavery, in every branch of it, both in principle and practice, as being a sinful and abominable system, fraught with peculiar evils and miseries, which every good man ought to abandon and bear his testimony against. Their desires and endeavors are, to effect, as soon as it can be done, and in the most prudent and advantageous manner, both to the slaves and to their owners, the general and complete emancipation of this numerous race of enslaved, ignorant, and degraded beings, who are now, by the laws and customs of the land, exposed to hereditary and perpetual bondage. (See Exod. 3:7, 9; 10:3; 6:2; 21:2, 16. Levit. 19:18. Deut. 15: 12, 18; 23:15; 24:7. Job 6:14; 29:11. Ps. 12:5; 103: 6. Prov. 16:8; 22:16. Eccl. 4:1; 5:8. Isa. 1:16; 33: 15; 58:6. Jer. 5:26; 21:12; 22:13; 34:10, 11, 17; 50:33, 34. Ezek. 18:5, 9; 22:29; 27:13. Dan. 4:27. Joel 3:3, 6. Mal. 2:10. Matt. 5:7; 7:12. Luke 4: 18; 6:36. Rom. 12:9. 1 Cor. 7:23. Gal. 5:13. Col. 4:1. 1 Tim. 1:10. Heb. 13:3. James 2:13; 5:4. 2 Pet. 2:2. 1 John 4:20. Rev. 18:11, 13.

The Emancipators say to Christians of all denominations in the United States, in the words of an eloquent philanthropist, "Banish from your land the remains of slavery. Be consistent with your congressional declaration of rights. Remember, there never was, nor will be, a period when justice should not be done. Do what is just, and leave the event with God. Justice is the pillar that upholds the whole fabric of human society, and mercy is the genial ray which cheers and warms the habitations of men. The perfection of our social character consists in properly tempering the two with one another; in holding that middle course which admits of our being just without being rigid, and allows us to be generous without being unjust. May all the citizens of America be found in the performance of such social duties as will secure them peace and happiness in this world, and n the world to come life everlasting!"

## PERFECTIONISTS.

A MODERN sect in New England, who believe that every individual action is either wholly sinful or wholly righteous, and that every being in the universe, at any given time, is either entirely holy or entirely wicked. Consequently, they unblushingly maintain that they themselves are free from sin. In support of this doctrine, they say that Christ dwells in and controls believers, and thus secures their perfect holiness; that the body of Christ, which is the church, is nourished and guided by the life and wisdom of its Head. Hence they condemn the greatest portion of the religion in the world named Christianity, as the work of Antichrist. "All the essential features of Judaism," they say, "and of its successor, Popery, may be distinctly traced in nearly every form of Protestantism; and although we rejoice in the blessings which the reformation has given us, we regard it as rightly named the *reformation*, it being an improvement of Antichrist, not a restoration of Christianity." This last opinion, which has some foundation in truth, has been long held, variously modified, in different parts of the Christian world.

An unsuccessful attempt was made to propagate the views of this sect through the medium of a paper published at New Haven, Conn., entitled the *Perfectionist.*

## METHODISTS' VIEWS OF PERFECTION.

"THE highest perfection which man can attain, while the soul dwells in the body, does not exclude ignorance, and error, and a thousand other infirmities. Now, from wrong judgments, wrong words and actions will often necessarily flow; and in some cases, wrong affections, also, may spring from the same source I may judge wrong of you; I may think more or less highly of you than I ought to think; and this mistake in my judgment may not only occasion something wrong in my behavior, but it may have a still deeper effect; it may occasion something wrong in my affection. From a wrong apprehension, I may love and esteem you either more or less than I ought. Nor can I be freed from a liableness to such a mistake while I remain in a corruptible body. A thousand infirmities, in consequence of this, will attend my spirit, till it returns to God, who gave it; and, in numberless instances, it comes short of doing the will of God, as Adam did in paradise. Hence the best of men may say from the heart,

'Every moment, Lord, I need
The merit of thy death,'

for innumerable violations of the Adamic, as well as the angelic law. It is well, therefore, for us, that we are not now under these, but under the law of love. 'Love is [now] the fulfilling of the law,' which is given to fallen man. This is now, with respect to us, 'the perfect law.' But even against this, through the present weakness of our understanding, we are continually liable to transgress. Therefore every man living needs the blood of atonement; or he could not stand before God.

"What is, then, the perfection of which man is capable while he dwells in a corruptible body? It is the complying with that kind command, 'My son, give me thy heart.' It is the 'loving the Lord his God with all his heart, and with all his soul, and with all his mind.' This is the sum of Christian perfection: it is all comprised in that one word, *love*. The first branch of it is the love of God; and, as he that loves God loves his brother also, it is inseparably connected with the second, 'Thou shalt love thy neighbor as thyself;' thou shalt love every man as thy own soul, as Christ loved us. 'On these two commandments hang all the law and the prophets:' these contain the whole of Christian perfection.

"Another view of this is given us in those words of the great apostle, 'Let this mind be in you which was also in Christ Jesus' For, although this immediately and directly refers to the humility of our Lord, yet it may be taken in a far more extensive sense, so as to include the whole disposition of his mind, all his affections, all his tempers, both toward God and man Now, it is certain that, as there was no evil affection in him, so no good affection or temper was wanting; so that 'whatsoever things are holy, whatsoever things are lovely,' are all included in 'the mind that was in Christ Jesus.'

"St. Paul, when writing to the Galatians, places perfection in yet another view. It is the one undivided *fruit of the Spirit*, which he describes thus: 'The fruit of the Spirit is love, joy, peace, long-suffering, gentleness, goodness, fidelity, [so the word should be translated here,] meekness, temperance.' What a glorious constellation of grace is here! Now, suppose all these things to be knit together in one, to be united together in the soul of a believer, — this is Christian perfection.

HOW TO BE SOUGHT.

"'But what is that faith whereby we are sanctified, saved from sin, and perfected in love?' It is a divine evidence and conviction, first, that God hath promised it in the holy Scripture. Till we are thoroughly satisfied of this, there is no moving one step farther. And one would imagine there needed not one word more to satisfy a reasonable man of this than the ancient promise, 'Then will I circumcise thy heart, and the heart of thy seed, to love the Lord thy God with all thy heart, and with all thy soul, and with all thy mind.' How clearly does this express the being perfected in love! — how strongly imply the being saved from all sin! For as long as love takes up the whole heart, what room is there for sin therein?

"It is a divine evidence and conviction, secondly, that what God hath promised he is able to perform. Admitting, therefore, that 'with men it is impossible' 'to bring a clean hing out of an unclean,' to purify the heart from all sin, and to fill it with all holiness, — yet this creates no difficulty in the case, seeing 'with God all things are possible.' And surely no one ever imagined it was possible to any power less than that of the Almighty! But if God speaks, it shall be done. God saith, 'Let there be light; and there [is] light.'

"It is, thirdly, a divine evidence and conviction that he is able and willing to do it now. And why not? Is not a moment to him the same as a thousand years? He cannot want more time to accomplish whatever is his will. And he cannot want to stay for any more *worthiness* or *fitness* in the persons he is pleased to honor. We may, therefore, boldly say, at any point of time, 'Now is the day of salvation!' 'To-day, if ye will hear his voice, harden not your hearts.' 'Behold, all things are now ready; come unto the marriage.'

"To this confidence that God is both able and willing to sanctify us now, there needs to be added one thing more — a divine evidence and conviction that he doeth it. In that hour it is done: God says to the inmost soul, 'According to thy faith be it unto thee.' Then the soul is pure from every spot of sin; it is clean 'from all unrighteousness.' The believer then experiences the deep meaning of those solemn words, 'If we walk in the light as he is in the light, we have fellowship one with another, and the blood of Jesus Christ his Son cleanseth us from all sin.'

"'But does God work this great work in the soul gradually, or instantaneously?' Perhaps it may be gradually wrought in some: I mean, in this sense, they do not advert to the particular moment wherein sin ceases to be. But it is infinitely desirable, were it the will of God, that it should be done instantaneously; that the Lord should destroy sin 'by the breath of his mouth,' in a moment, in the twinkling of an eye. And so he generally does — a plain fact, of which there is evidence enough to satisfy any unprejudiced person. *Thou*, therefore, look for it every moment." — See *Wesley's Sermons*, vols. i. and ii.

## OBERLIN VIEWS OF SANCTIFICATION.

In the fall of 1836, during an interesting revival of religion in Oberlin, Ohio, the minds of many became deeply interested in the inquiry, "Can we live holy lives? and, if we can, how?" At first, fears were entertained that some would run into the errors of the Perfectionists; but, finally, after much prayer and investigation, they adopted the following views of sanctification: —

"1. That entire obedience to the moral law constitutes entire sanctification or holiness.

"2. That all moral agents are able to render this obedience.

"3. That because all moral agents are able to render this obedience, they are bound to do so.

"4. That sufficient grace for the actual attainment of this state is abundantly in the gospel, and that nothing prevents any Christian from making this attainment in this life, but a neglect to avail himself of the proffered grace of Christ.

"5. That all are bound to aim at and pray for this attainment in this life, and that aiming at this state is indispensable to Christian character.

"6. That obedience to the moral law, or a state of entire sanctification, is in such a sense attainable, as to make it an object of rational pursuit, with the *expectation of attaining it.*

"7. That the philosophy of the mind, the commandments of God, the promises and provisions of the gospel, and the attainments of Paul and many others, should be presented, to induce men to aim at a state of entire sanctification, with the expectation of attaining it."

Since these views were embraced at Oberlin, they have been extensively circulated by many books and pamphlets, and a paper, entitled the *Oberlin Evangelist.* By many

Christians and ministers of different denominations these views have been received; but by others they are opposed.

## WALDENSES.

Many authors of note make the antiquity of this denomination coeval with the apostolic age. The following is an extract from their confession of faith, which is said to have been copied out of certain manuscripts, bearing date nearly four hundred years before the time of Luther:—

"1. That the Scriptures teach that there is one God, almighty, all-wise, and all-good, who made all things by his goodness; for he formed Adam in his own image and likeness; but that, by the envy of the devil, sin entered into the world; and that we are sinners in and by Adam.

"2. That Christ was promised to our fathers, who received the law; that so knowing, by the law, their unrighteousness and insufficiency, they might desire the coming of Christ, to satisfy for their sins, and accomplish the law by himself.

"3. That Christ was born in the time appointed by God the Father; that is to say, in the time when all iniquity abounded, that he might show us grace and mercy, as being faithful; that Christ is our life, truth, peace, and righteousness, as also our pastor, advocate, and priest, who died for the salvation of all who believe, and is risen for our justification; that there is no mediator and advocate with God the Father, save Jesus Christ; that, after this life, there are only two places, the one for the saved, and the other for the damned; that the feasts, the vigils of saints, the water which they call holy, as also to abstain from flesh on certain days, and the like, but especially the masses, are the inventions of men, and ought to be rejected; that the sacraments are signs of the holy thing, visible forms of the invisible grace; and that it is good for the faithful to use those signs, or visible forms, but that they are not essential to salvation; that there are no other sacraments but baptism and the Lord's supper; that we ought to honor the secular powers, by subjection, ready obedience, and paying of tribute."

## ALLENITES.

The disciples of Henry Allen, of Nova Scotia, who began to propagate his doctrines in that country about the year 1778, and died in 1783, during which interval he made many proselytes, and at his death left a considerable party behind him, though now much declined. He published several treatises and sermons, in which he declares that the souls of all the human race are emanations, or rather parts, of the one great Spirit; that they were all present in Eden, and were actually in the first transgression. He supposes that our first parents, in innocency, were pure spirits, and that the material world was not then made; but that, in consequence of the fall, that mankind might not sink into utter destruction, this world was produced, and men clothed with material bodies; and that all the human race will, in their turn, be invested with such bodies, and in them enjoy a state of probation for immortal happiness.

## JOHNSONIANS.

The followers of Mr. John Johnson, many years Baptist minister at Liverpool, in the last century, of whose followers there are still several congregations in different parts of England. He denied that faith was a duty, or even action of the soul, and defined it "an active principle" conferred by grace; and denied also the duty of ministers to exhort the unconverted, or preach any *moral duties* whatever.

Though Mr. Johnson entertained high Supralapsarian notions on the divine decrees, he admitted the universality of the death of Christ. On the doctrine of the Trinity, his followers are said to have embraced the indwelling scheme, with Calvinistic views of justification and the atonement.

## DONATISTS.

A DENOMINATION which arose in the fourth century. They derived their name from Donatus, bishop of Numidia. They maintained that their community was alone to be considered as the true church, and avoided all communication with other churches, from an apprehension of contracting their impurity and corruption. Hence they pronounced the sacred rites and institutions void of all virtue and efficacy among those Christians who were not precisely of their sentiments, and not only rebaptized those who came over to their party from other churches, but, with respect to those who had been ordained ministers of the gospel, they either deprived them of their office, or obliged them to be ordained the second time.

## SE-BAPTISTS.

A SECT of small note, which was formed in England about the beginning of the seventeenth century, by one John Smith, who maintained that it was lawful for every one to baptize himself. There is at this day an inconsiderable sect in Russia who are known by this name, and who perform the rite upon themselves, from an idea that no one is left on earth sufficiently holy to administer it aright.

## RE-ANOINTERS.

A SECT in Russia, which sprang up about the year 1770 They do not rebaptize those who join them from the Greek church, but insist on the necessity of their having the mystery of the chrism or unction again administered to them. They are very numerous in Moscow.

---

## TAO-SE, OR TAOU-TSZE.

THE name of a famous sect among the Chinese, who owe their rise to ***Laou-tsze Lao Kian***, or ***Laokium***, a philosopher, who lived, if we may credit his disciples, about five hundred years before Christ. He professed to restore the religion of *Tao*, (*Taou*,) or Reason. Some of his writings are still extant, and are full of maxims and sentiments of virtue and morality. Among others, this sentence is often repeated in them: " *Tao* hath produced one, one hath produced two, two have produced three, and three have produced all things."

The morality of this philosopher and his disciples is not unlike that of the Epicureans, consisting in a tranquillity of mind, free from all vehement desires and passions. But as this tranquillity would be disturbed by thoughts of death, they boast of a liquor that has the power of rendering them immortal. They are addicted to chemistry, alchemy, and magic, and are persuaded that, by the assistance of demons, whom they invoke, they can obtain all that they desire. The hope of avoiding death prevailed upon a great number of mandarins to study this diabolical art, and certain credulous and superstitious emperors brought it greatly into vogue.

The doctrine of this sect concerning the formation of the world, according to Dr. Milne, much resembles that of the Epicureans. If they do not maintain the eternity of matter, on the other hand, they do not deny it; but, in analogy with the favorite science of alchemy, they represent the first pair as drawn out of the boiling mouth of an "immense crucible,' by a celestial being. The Platonic notion of an *anima mundi*, or soul of the world, is very common; and hence it is that the heavens are considered the body of this imaginary being, the wind its breath, the lights of heaven as proceeding from its eyes, the watery fluids as its spittle and tears.

## QUIETISTS.

THE disciples of Michael de Molinos, a Spanish priest, who flourished in the seventeenth century, and wrote a book called "The Spiritual Guide." They argue thus: — "The apostle tells us, that 'the Spirit makes intercession for,' or *in* 'us.' Now, if the Spirit pray in us, we must resign ourselves to his impulses, by remaining in a state of absolute rest, or quietude, till we attain the perfection of the unitive life" — a life of union with, and, as it should seem, of absorption in, the Deity.

## KNIPPERDOLINGS.

A DENOMINATION in the sixteenth century, so called from Bertrand Knipperdoling, who taught that the righteous, before the day of judgment, shall have a monarchy on earth, and the wicked be destroyed; that men are not justified by their faith in Christ Jesus; that there is no original sin; that infants ought not to be baptized, and immersion is the only mode of baptism; that every one has authority to preach, and administer the sacraments; that men are not obliged to pay respect to magistrates; that all things ought to be in common; and that it is lawful to marry many wives.

## MENDÆANS, MENDAITES,

### *MENDAI IJAHI,*

OR

### DISCIPLES OF ST. JOHN, THAT IS, THE BAPTIST.

From twenty to twenty-five thousand families of this sec still remain, chiefly in the neighborhood of Bassora, a city between Arabia and Persia, on the extremity of the desert of Irac. They are sometimes called *Christians of St. John* — a name which they probably received from the Turks, and to which they contentedly submit for the sake of the toleration it affords them; but they are better known in ecclesiastical history as *Hemero* (or every day) *Baptists,* from their frequent washings.

---

## MUGGLETONIANS.

The followers of Ludovic Muggleton, a journeyman tailor, who, with his companion Reeves, set up for great prophets, in the time of Cromwell. They pretended to absolve or condemn whom they pleased, and gave out that they were the two last witnesses spoken of in the Revelation, who were to appear previous to the final destruction of the world. They affirmed that there was no devil at all without the body of man or woman; that the devil is man's spirit of unclean reason and cursed imagination; that the ministry in this world, whether prophetical or ministerial, is all a lie, and abomination to the Lord; with a variety of other vain and inconsistent tenets.

Muggleton died in 1697, and on his gravestone is this inscription: —

"Whilst mausoleums and large inscriptions give
Might, splendor, and, past death, make potents live,
It is enough briefly to write thy name:
Succeeding times by that will read thy fame;
Thy deeds, thy acts, around the world resound;
No foreign soil where Muggleton's not found."

The raven plume of oblivion hath long ago waved over this prophet's grave.

## YEZIDEES,

### OR

### WORSHIPPERS OF THE DEVIL.

From a very interesting work recently published by Asahel Grant, M. D., a medical missionary to the Nestorians, we copy the following account:—

"The passage of the Tigris transferred me from Mesopotamia into Assyria, and I stood upon the ruins of Nineveh, 'that great city,' where the prophet Jonah proclaimed the dread message of Jehovah to so many repenting thousands whose deep humiliation averted for a time the impending ruin But when her proud monarchs had scourged idolatrous Israe and carried the ten tribes into captivity, and raised the i hands against Judah and the holy city, the inspired strains of the eloquent Nahum, clothed in terrible sublimity as they were, met their full accomplishment in the utter desolation of one of the largest cities on which the sun ever shone. 'Nineveh is laid waste! who will bemoan her? She is empty, and void, and waste; her nobles dwell in the dust; her people are scattered upon the mountains, and no man gathereth them.'

"Where her gorgeous palaces once resounded to the strains of music and the shouts of revelry, a few black tents of the wandering Arab and Tûrkomân are now scattered among the shapeless mounds of earth and rubbish, — the ruins of the city, — as if in mockery of her departed glory; while their tenants were engaged in the fitting employment of weaving 'sackcloth of hair,' as if for the mourning attire of the world's great emporium, whose 'merchants' were 'multiplied above the stars of heaven.' The largest mound, from which very ancient relics and inscriptions are dug, is now crowned with the Moslem village of Neby Yûnas, or the prophet Jonah, where his remains are said to be interred, and over which has been reared, as his mausoleum, a temple of Islâm.

"Soon after leaving the ruins of Nineveh, we came in sight of two villages of the Yezidees, the reputed worshippers of the devil. Large and luxuriant olive-groves, with their rich green foliage, and fruit just ripening in the autumnal sun, imparted such a cheerful aspect to the scene as soon dispelled whatever of pensive melancholy had gathered around me, while treading upon the dust of departed greatness. Several white sepulchres of Yezidee sheiks attracted attention as I approached the villages. They were in the form of fluted cones or pyramids, standing upon quadrangular bases, and rising to the height of some twenty feet or more We became the guests of one of the chief Yezidees of Baa sheka, whose dwelling, like others in the place, was a rude stone structure, with a flat terrace roof. Coarse felt carpets were spread for our seats in the open court, and a formal welcome was given us; but it was evidently not a very cordial one. My Turkish cavass understood the reason, and at once removed it. Our host had mistaken me for a Mahometan, towards whom the Yezidees cherish a settled aversion. As soon as I was introduced to him as a Christian, and he had satisfied himself that this was my true character, his whole deportment was changed. He at once gave me a new and cordial welcome, and set about supplying our wants with new alacrity. He seemed to feel that he had exchanged a Moslem foe for a Christian friend, and I became quite satisfied of the truth of what I had often heard, — that the Yezi dees are friendly towards the professors of Christianity.

"They are said to cherish a high regard for the Christian religion, of which clearly they have some corrupt remains. They practise the rite of baptism, make the sign of the cross, so emblematical of Christianity in the East, put off their shoes, and kiss the threshold when they enter a Christian church; and it is said that they often speak of wine as the blood of Christ, hold the cup with both hands, after the sacramental manner of the East, when drinking it, and, if a drop chance to fall on the ground, they gather it up with religious care.

"They believe in one supreme God, and, in some sense at least, in Christ as a Savior. They have also a remnant of Sabianism, or the religion of the ancient fire-worshippers. They bow in adoration before the rising sun, and kiss his first rays when they strike on a wall or other object near them; and they will not blow out a candle with their breath, or spit in the fire, lest they should defile that sacred element.

"Circumcision and the passover, or a sacrificial festival allied to the passover in time and circumstance, seem also to identify them with the Jews; and, altogether, they certainly present a most singular chapter in the history of man.

"That they are really the worshippers of the devil can only be true, if at all, in a modified sense, though it is true that they pay him so much deference as to refuse to speak of him disrespectfully, (perhaps for fear of his vengeance;) and, instead of pronouncing his name, they call him the 'lord of the evening,' or 'prince of darkness;' also, Sheik Maazen, or Exalted Chief. Some of them say that Satan was a fallen angel, with whom God was angry; but he will at some future day be restored to favor, and there is no reason why they should treat him with disrespect.

"The Christians of Mesopotamia report that the Yezidees make votive offerings to the devil, by throwing money and jewels into a certain deep pit in the mountains of Sinjar, where a large portion of them reside; and it is said that when that district, which has long been independent, was subjugated by the Turks, the pacha compelled the Yezidee priest to disclose the place, and then plundered it of a large treasure, the offerings of centuries. The Yezidees here call themselves Daseni, probably from the ancient name of the district, Dasen, which was a Christian bishopric in early times. Their chief place of concourse, the religious temple of the Yezidees, is said to have once been a Christian church or convent. The late Mr. Rich speaks of the Yezidees as 'lively, brave, hospitable, and good-humored,' and adds that, 'under the British government, much might be made of them.'

"The precise number of the Yezidees it is difficult to estimate, so little is known of them; but it is probable that we must reckon them by tens of thousands, instead of the larger computations which have been made by some travellers, who have received their information merely from report. Still they are sufficiently numerous to form an important object of attention to the Christian church; and I trust, as we learn more about them, sympathy, prayer, and effort, will be enlisted in their behalf. It will be a scene of no ordinary interest when the voice of prayer and praise to God shall ascend from hearts now devoted to the service of the prince of darkness, 'the worshippers of the devil'! May that day be hastened on!"

## GREEK OR RUSSIAN CHURCH.

The Greek church separated from the Latin or Romish church about A. D. 1054. It is under the jurisdiction of the patriarchs or bishops of Constantinople, Alexandria, Antioch, and Jerusalem. The Greek or Russian church is very extensive. Its jurisdiction embraces more territory than that of the Roman see. The population of this church is estimated at about forty millions.

The following are some of the chief tenets held by the Greek or Russian church · — They disown the authority of the pope, and deny that the church of Rome is the true catholic church. They do not baptize their children till they are three, four, five, six, ten, nay, sometimes eighteen years of age: baptism is performed by trine immersion. They insist that the sacrament of the Lord's supper ought to be administered in both kinds, and they give the sacrament to children immediately after baptism. They grant no indulgences, nor do they lay any claim to the character of infallibility, like the church of Rome. They deny that there is any such place as purgatory; notwithstanding, they pray for the dead, that God would have mercy on them at the general judgment. They practise the invocation of saints; though, they say, they do not invoke them as deities, but as intercessors with God. They exclude confirmation, extreme unction, and matrimony out of the seven sacraments. They deny auricular confession to be a divine precept, and say it is only a positive injunction of the church. They pay no religious homage to the eucharist. They administer the communion in both kinds to the laity, both in sickness and in health, though they have never applied themselves to their confessors, because they are persuaded that a lively faith is all which is requisite for the worthy receiving of the Lord's supper. They maintain that the Holy Ghost proceeds only from the Father, and not from the Son. They believe in predestination. They admit of nc images in relief or embossed work, but use paintings ana sculptures in copper or silver. They approve of the marriage of priests, provided they enter into that state before their admission into holy orders. They condemn all fourth marriages. They observe a number of holy days, and keep four fasts in the year more solemn than the rest, of which the fast in Lent, before Easter, is the chief. They believe the doctrine of consubstantiation, or the union of the body of Christ vith the sacramental bread.

The Russians adhere to the doctrine and ceremonies of .ne Greek church, though they are now independent of the patriarch of Constantinople. The church service is contained in twenty-four volumes, folio, in the Sclavonian language, which is not well understood by the common people

## PRIMITIVE CHRISTIANS.

A NEW sect, professing to be an association of Christians to promote the revival and spread of primitive Christianity, has recently sprung up at Bradford, in England. Its originators, or founders, are a Mr. Barker and a Mr. Trother, who have recently been expelled from the ministry of the New Connection of Methodists, by the annual assembly or conference of the members of that body, for some difference of opinion on doctrinal points between them and the conference

## TRINITARIANS.

BY this term we are to understand those who believe that there are three distinct persons in the Godhead, the FATHER, SON, and HOLY SPIRIT, the same in substance, equal in power and dignity, and that these *three* are *one*. Hence it is said they believe in a *triune* God. (See Deut. 6 : 4. 2 Kings 19 : 15. Ps. 19: 1; 83: 18; 139: 7. Isa. 6: 3, 9; 9: 6; 11: 3; 14: 5, 23, 25. Jer. 17 : 10; 23 : 6. Ezek. 8 : 1, 3. Matt. 3 : 16, 17; 9 : 6; 18 : 20; 23 : 19. Luke 1 : 76; 24 : 25. John 1 : 1; 2 : 1; 5 : 19, 23; 10 : 30; 16 : 10, 15. Acts 5 : 4; 28 : 23, 25. Rom. 1 : 5; 9 : 5; 14 : 12, 19. 1 Cor. 2 : 10; 8 : 6. 2 Cor. 13: 14. Phil. 2 : 5, 6, 7, &c.; 3 : 21. Heb. 1 : 3, 6, 10, 11, 12; 9 : 14; 13 : 8. 1 John 5 : 7, 20. Rev. 1 : 4, 5, 6, 8; 3 : 14; 5 : 13, &c.) The Unitarians believe that there is but one person in the Godhead, and that this person is the Father; and they insist that the Trinitarian distinction of persons is contradictory and absurd.

The *unity* of God is a doctrine which both parties consider the foundation of all true religion.

Although the doctrine of the Trinity is ostensibly the main subject of dispute between Trinitarians and Unitarians, yet it is in reality respecting the character of Christ. Those who believe in his proper deity very easily dispose of all the other difficulties in the Trinitarian system; while anti-Trinitarians find more fault with this doctrine than any other in the Trinitarian creed; and the grand obstacle to their reception of the Trinitarian faith is removed, when they can admit that Jesus Christ is God, as well as man; so that the burden of labor, on both sides, is either to prove or disprove the proper deity of the Son of God.

In proof of this doctrine, the Trinitarians urge many declarations of the Scripture, which, in their opinion, admit of no consistent explanation upon the Unitarian scheme; they there find that offices are assigned to Christ, and to the Holy Spirit, which none but God can perform; particularly the creation of the world, and the grand decisions of the day of judgment. As they read the Scriptures, the attributes of *omnipotence, omniscience, omnipresence, unchangeableness*, and *eternity*, are ascribed to Jesus Christ; and they infer that a being to whom all these perfections are ascribed must be truly God, coëqual and coëternal with the Father.

The Unitarians, on the other hand, contend that some of these passages are interpolations, and that the others are either mistranslated or misunderstood. The passage in John, in particular, respecting the *three* that bear record, &c., has been set aside by such high authority, that they consider it unfair to introduce it in the controversy.

The excellent and learned Stillingfleet, in the preface to his Vindication of the Doctrine of the Trinity, says, "Since both sides yield that the matter they dispute about is above their reach, the wisest course they can take is, to assert and defend *what is revealed*, and not to be *peremptory* and quarrelsome about that which is acknowledged to be above our comprehension; I mean as to the *manner* how the *three persons* partake of the *divine nature*."

## MILLENARIANS.

The Millenarians are those who believe that Christ will reign personally on earth for a thousand years; and their name, taken from the Latin *mille*, a thousand, has a direct allusion to the duration of the spiritual empire.

The doctrine of the millennium, or a future paradisaical state of the earth, it is said, is not of Christian, but of Jewish origin. The tradition is attributed to Elijah, which fixes the duration of the world, in its present imperfect condition, to six thousand years, and announces the approach of a Sabbath of a thousand years of universal peace and plenty, to be ushered in by the glorious advent of the Messiah. This idea may be traced in the Epistle of Barnabas, and in the opinions of Papias, who knew of no written testimony in its behalf. It was adopted by the author of the Revelation, by Justin Martyr, by Irenæus, and by a long succession of the fathers. As the theory is animating and consolatory, when it is divested of cabalistic numbers and allegorical decorations, it will no doubt always retain a number of adherents.

However the Millenarians may differ among themselves respecting the nature of this great event, it is agreed, on all hands, that such a revolution will be effected in the latter days, by which vice and its attendant misery shall be banished from the earth; thus completely forgetting all those dissensions and animosities by which the religious world hath been agitated, and terminating the grand drama of Providence with universal felicity. We are not unmindful of the prophetic language of Isaiah, (49 : 22, 23,) together with a sublime passage from the book of the Revelation, (11 : 15,) with which the canon of Scripture concludes — "Thus saith the Lord God, Behold, I will lift up mine hand to the Gentiles, and set up my standard to the people. And kings shall be thy nursing fathers, and their queens thy nursing mothers, [they shall become good themselves, and be the protectors of religion and liberty,] and thou shalt know that I am the Lord, for they shall not be ashamed that wait for me. And the seventh angel sounded, and there were great voices in heaven, saying, The kingdoms of this world are become the kingdoms of our Lord, and of his Christ, and he shall reign forever and ever." (See Matt. 13 : 29, 30 ; 27 : 32. Luke 17 : 29, 30. Acts 3 : 21. Heb. 1 : 12. Phil. 3 : 9, 11. 2 Pet. 3 : 13. Rev. 20 : 1—6, and chaps. 21, 22. Apoc. chap. 21. Ezek. chap. 36.)

## WHITEFIELD CALVINISTIC METHODISTS.

THE *Tabernacle* or *Lady Huntingdon Connection*, formed by Whitefield, is so called from the name given to several places of worship, in London, Bristol, &c. In some of the chapels in this Connection, the service of the church of England is read; in others, the worship is conducted much in the same way as among the Congregationalists; while, in all, the system of supply is more or less kept up, consisting in the employment, for a month or six weeks, of ministers from different parts of the country, who either take the whole duty, or assist the resident minister. Some of the congregations consist of several thousand hearers; and, by the blessing of God on the rousing and faithful sermons which are usually delivered to them, very extensive good is effected in the way of conversion. Most of the ministers now employed as supplies in this Connection are of the Congregational order, to which, of late years, there appears to be a gradual approximation; and it is not improbable that ere long both bodies will coalesce. The number of chapels belonging to this body, at the present time, is about sixty, in all of which the liturgy of the church of England is read, and most of her forms scrupulously kept up. The ministers, who used formerly to supply at different chapels in the course of the year, are now become more stationary, and have assumed more of the pastoral character. They have a respectable college at Cheshunt, in Hertfordshire.

The Calvinistic Methodists in Wales are very numerous. — See *Biographical Sketches* of Whitefield, Wesley, and Lady Huntingdon.

## NONJURORS

Those who refused to take the oaths to government, and who were, in consequence, under certain incapacities, and liable to certain severe penalties. The members of the Episcopal church of Scotland have long been denominated Nonjurors; but perhaps they are now called so improperly, as the ground of their difference from the established church is more on account of ecclesiastical than political principles.

## NONCONFORMISTS.

Those who refuse to join the established church. Nonconformists in England may be considered of three sorts: — 1. Such as absent themselves from divine worship in the established church through total irreligion, and attend the service of no other persuasion. — 2. Such as absent themselves on the plea of conscience; as, Presbyterians, Independents, Baptists, &c. — 3. Internal Nonconformists, or unprincipled clergymen, who applaud and propagate doctrines quite inconsistent with several of those articles they promised on oath to defend. The word is generally used in reference to those ministers who were ejected from their livings by the Act of Uniformity, in 1662. The number of these was about two thousand. However some affect to treat these men with indifference, and suppose that their consciences were more tender than they need be, it must be remembered that they were men of as extensive learning, great abilities, and pious conduct, as ever appeared.

## CHRISTIAN CONNECTION.

This denomination, among themselves, are generally called simply *Christians.* This they do merely to denote their character as the followers of Christ; but, when applied to them collectively, it necessarily becomes the name of a denomination. They are sometimes, by their opposers, called *Christ-ians;* but this pronunciation of the word they universally reject as very improper.

The Christians began to associate and to form a distinct people about the beginning of the nineteenth century, so that they may be said to have existed but about forty years They seem to have sprung up almost simultaneously in different and remote parts of the country, without any interchange of sentiments, concert of action, or even knowledge of each other's views or movements, till after a public stand had been taken in several parts of the country.

The first branch arose in Virginia and North Carolina, and consisted of seceders from the Methodists. At first, there were about one thousand communicants.

The northern branch of this denomination sprung up in New England. It commenced by the formation of several new churches, under the administration of a few ministers who had separated themselves from the Baptists, who were soon joined by several other ministers, and nearly whole churches, from the same denomination.

The western branch arose in Kentucky, and was composed of seceders from the Presbyterians. Some of their ministers were men of strong and well-cultivated minds, who urged forward the reform they had undertaken, till they have spread over most of the Western States.

In all these different sections, their leading purpose, at first, appears to have been, not so much to establish any peculiar or distinctive doctrine, as to assert for individuals and churches more liberty and independence in relation to matters of faith and practice; to shake off the authority of human creeds, and the shackles of prescribed modes and forms; to make the Bible their only guide, claiming for every man the right to judge for himself what is its doctrine, and what are its requirements; and in practice to follow more strictly the simplicity of the apostles and primitive Christians.

This class of believers recognize no individual as a leader or founder, and no man claims this high eminence, although several persons were instrumental in giving rise and progress to the society. They point all to Christ as the Leader and Founder, and professedly labor to bring all to the first principles of original, apostolic Christianity.

Seceding, as the first ministers did, from different denominations, they necessarily brought with them some of the peculiarities of faith and usage in which they had been educated. But the two prominent sentiments that led them out, both kept them together, by rendering them tolerant toward each other, and gradually brought them to be very similar both in faith and practice. These two sentiments were, that the Scriptures *only* should be consulted as a rule of faith and duty, and that all Christians should enjoy universal toleration. Hence scarcely any churches have written creeds, although nearly all record their principles of action. Very few are Trinitarians, though nearly all believe in the preëxistence and proper Sonship of Christ. Perhaps not any believe in or practise sprinkling, but almost all practise immersion; from which circumstance many, though very improperly, call them Christian Baptists.

Perfect uniformity does not exist among all the members of this community, although the approximation to it is far greater than many have supposed it ever could be without a written creed. But there are several important points in which they generally agree fully; and these are regarded as sufficient to secure Christian character, Christian fellowship, and concert of action. Some of these points are the following:—That the Scriptures, including the Old and New Testament, were given by inspiration of God, and are sufficient to teach what men should believe, and what they should practise. That every man has a right to study the Scriptures, and to exercise his own judgment with regard to their true import and meaning. That there is one God, perfect and infinite. That Jesus Christ is the Son of God in the highest possible sense, and that salvation is found in him alone. That all men have sinned and come short of the glory of God, therefore are polluted and guilty. That no transgressor can find pardon but by repentance and faith in Jesus Christ. That the Holy Spirit reproves all sinners, and comforts all Christians. That whoever has sinned has also a way of salvation set before him. That pardon and eternal salvation are found alone through regeneration. That none are proper subjects of church membership, or the ordinances except the regenerated. That God calls men to the ministry, and no others are his true ministers. That perseverance to the end is the only condition on our part that can secure our eternal happiness. That revivals of religion are of the first importance, and should be labored for continually. That every believer should be immersed, and become a public member of some visible church. That every church should continue to observe the Lord's supper. That there will be a resurrection of the dead, both of the just and of the unjust; and that, at the day of judgment, the righteous and the wicked will be separated, and pass, the righteous into everlasting life, and the wicked into eternal damnation.

On all the above points, there is but very little difference of opinion or practice throughout the whole body.

Candidates for baptism and church membership are required to give the reason of their hope, by a relation of their Christian experience; and persons coming from other churches are expected to furnish satisfactory testimonials of their Christian character.

Their communions are always open and free for all Christians of every denomination; but no unconverted or immoral person is invited to the Lord's table.

Each church is so far independent as to have a right to transact all its internal affairs without foreign interference. Every church makes choice of its own minister, agrees on its own principles of action, and administers its own discipline, as they understand the New Testament; but the imposition of hands is invariably administered by ordained ministers.

The connection between the several churches, and between the ministers, is kept up by means of associations called *conferences*, each of which is generally composed of the ministers and churches within a certain district. These hold annual sessions, at which the ministers meet in person, and the churches by delegates. The churches and ministers are generally thus associated; but, if any choose not to do so, the fraternal bonds are not thereby impaired.

Very few of their ministers are thoroughly educated men: but they are generally well acquainted with the Bible, and many of them good sermonizers and powerful preachers. All the important means by which pure Christianity may be advanced are fast gaining favor both in the ministry and the churches.

Within the last few years, there has been a very rapid spread, and great increase; while all has been settling upon a firm and consistent basis. While many are engaged calling sinners to repentance, the churches are set in order, and thus mightily the word of God grows and prevails.

## PUSEYITES.

This school of theology, which has become famous both in England and abroad, had its origin at Oxford, about A. D 1838. Some distinguished members of the university thought that the church of England was in an alarming position, and that irreligious principles and false doctrines had been admitted into the measures of the government of the country on a large scale. To check the progress of these supposed errors and mischievous practices, they published a series of "Tracts for the Times," on such subjects as the *constitution of the church; the authority of its ministers; refutations of the errors of Romanism, and how to oppose it*, &c. &c.

The Puseyites strenuously assert the *apostolical succession;* in other words, that the clergy derive their power from the apostles, through *episcopal* ordination.

In regard to *church polity*, they maintain that the church is an empire and government of its own, — a government appointed by God, — and that its laws, as they are to be found in the Book of Common Prayer, ought to be implicitly obeyed. They deprecate the neglect of the *daily service*, the desecration of festivals, and the scanty administration of the eucharist.

With respect to *sacraments*, the Puseyites hold that they are not subjects of discussion, or for speculation; but "high, mysterious, awful Christian privileges — to be *felt*, reverenced, embraced, realized, acted."

With respect to *church authority*, they hold that human tradition has no place in revelation; that no individuals, since the apostles, can be regarded as expositors of the will of Christ; that the *unanimous witness* of Christendom, as to the teaching of the apostles, is the only and the fully-sufficient guaranty of the whole revealed faith, and that we do possess historically such a guaranty in the remains of the primitive church.

The Puseyites inculcate the necessity of dispensing religious truth with caution and reverence, not throwing it promiscuously before minds ill suited to receive it.

A characteristic feature of the Oxford school of theology, is its opposition to what is called the "popular religionism of the day." The masters of the school grieve that men are sent from the seat of their education with the belief that they are to *think*, not *read; judge*, rather than *learn;* and look to their own minds for truth, rather than to some permanent external standard.

At the head of this school are Dr. Pusey, Regius professor of Hebrew, and canon of Christ Church, Rev. J. Keble, professor of poetry, Rev. J. H. Newman, Rev. J. Williams, and Rev. W. Sewall, professor of moral philosophy.

---

## FREE COMMUNION BAPTISTS.

This denomination of Christians dissent from the regular Baptists on the point that immersion is a prerequisite to the privileges of a church relation, and permit Christians of all denominations, in regular church standing, to partake with them at the Lord's table.

The Rev. Robert Hall, of England, one of the most learned and eloquent Baptist ministers of the age, was an unflinching opposer of the practice of "close communion," which he denounced as "unchristian and unnatural." In a tract written in defence of his views on this subject, he remarks, "It is too much to expect an enlightened public will be eager to enroll themselves among the members of a sect which displays much of the intolerance of Popery, without any portion of its splendor, and prescribes, as the pledge of conversion, the renunciation of the whole Christian world.

In reference to the mode of baptism, Mr. Hall says, "I would not myself baptize in any other way than by immer sion, because I look upon immersion as the ancient mode; that it best represents the meaning of the original term employed, and the substantial import of this institution; and because I should think it right to guard against the spirit of innovation, which, in positive rites, is always dangerous and progressive; *but I should not think myself authorized to rebaptize any one who has been sprinkled in adult age.*"

This class of Baptists are found chiefly in the western and northern parts of the state of New York. They number between forty and fifty churches and ministers.

## TRANSCENDENTALISTS

Transcendent and Transcendental are technical terms in philosophy. According to their etymology, (from *transcendere,*) they signify that which goes beyond a certain limit; in philosophy, that which goes beyond, or transcends, the circle of experience, or of what is perceptible by the senses. Properly speaking, all philosophy is in this sense transcendental, because all philosophical investigations rise above the sensual, even if they start from that which is perceptible by the senses. But philosophical inquiries are to be distinguished according as they proceed from experience, or from principles and ideas not derived from that source. The latter sort are called, in a narrower sense, *pure,* or *transcendental.* The school of Kant makes a still further distinction: it gives the name of *transcendental* to that which does not, indeed, originate from experience, but yet is connected with it, because it contains the grounds of the possibility of experience; but the term *transcendent* it applies to that which cannot be connected with experience, but transcends the limit of possible experience and of philosophizing.

As applied in this country, especially when used as a term of reproach, Transcendentalism would designate a system which builds on feeling, rather than on reason, and relies more on the imagination than on the judgment. In the main, however, the Transcendentalists are persons who hold that man has the power to perceive intuitively truths which transcend the reach of the senses; but they divide, some taking the unction of Sentimentalism, and others of Mysticism.

---

## AUGSBURG CONFESSION OF FAITH.

THE first Protestant Confession was that presented, in 1530, to the diet of Augsburg, by the suggestion and under the direction of John, elector of Saxony. This wise and prudent prince, with the view of having the principal grounds on which the Protestants had separated from the Romish communion distinctly submitted to that assembly, intrusted the duty of preparing a summary of them to the divines of Wittemberg. Nor was that task a difficult one; for the Reformed doctrines had already been digested into seventeen articles, which had been proposed at the conferences both at Sultzbach and Smalcald, as the confession of faith to be adopted by the Protestant confederates. These, accordingly, were delivered to the elector by Luther, and served as the basis of the celebrated Augsburg Confession, written "by the elegant and accurate pen of Melancthon" — a work which has been admired by many even of its enemies, for its perspicuity, piety, and erudition. It contains twenty-eight chapters, the leading topics of which are, the true and essential divinity of Christ; his substitution and vicarious sacrifice; original sin; human inability; the necessity, freedom, and efficacy of divine grace; consubstantiation; and particularly justification by faith, to establish the truth and importance of which was one of its chief objects. The last seven articles condemn and confute the Popish tenets of communion in one kind, clerical celibacy, private masses, auricular confession, legendary traditions monastic vows, and the exorbitant power of the church This Confession is silent on the doctrine of predestination. This is the universal standard of orthodox doctrine among those who profess to be Lutherans, in which no authoritative alteration has ever been made.

## ARMENIANS.

THE chief point of separation between the Armenians on the one side, and the Greeks and the Papists on the other, is, that, while the latter believe in two natures and one person of Christ, the former believe that the humanity and divinity of Christ were so united as to form but *one nature;* and hence they are called ***Monophysites***, signifying *single nature.*

Another point on which they are charged with heresy by the Papists is, that they adhere to the notion that the Spirit proceeds from the Father only; and in this the Greeks join them, though the Papists say that he proceeds from the Father and the Son. In other respects, the Greeks and Armenians have very nearly the same religious opinions, though they differ somewhat in their forms and modes of worship. For instance, the Greeks make the sign of the cross with three fingers, in token of their belief in the doctrine of the Trinity, while the Armenians use two fingers, and the Jacobites one.

The Armenians hold to seven sacraments, like the Latins although baptism, confirmation, and extreme unction, are all performed at the same time; and the forms of prayer for confirmation and extreme unction are perfectly intermingled, which leads one to suppose that, in fact, the latter sacrament does not exist among them, except in name, and that this they have borrowed from the Papists.

Infants are baptized both by triple immersion and pouring water three times upon the head; the former being done, as their books assert, in reference to Christ's having been three days in the grave, and probably suggested by the phrase *buried with him in baptism.*

The latter ceremony they derive from the tradition that, when Christ was baptized, he stood in the midst of Jordan, and John poured water from his hand three times upon his head. In all their pictures of this scene, such is the representation of the mode of our Savior's baptism. Converted Jews, or Mahometans, though adults, are baptized in the same manner.

The Armenians acknowledge sprinkling as a lawful mode of baptism; for they receive from other churches those that have merely been sprinkled, without rebaptizing them.

They believe firmly in transubstantiation, and worship the consecrated elements as God.

Unleavened bread is used in the sacrament, and the broken pieces of bread are dipped in undiluted wine, and thus given to the people.

The latter, however, do not handle it, but receive it into their mouths from the hands of the priest. They suppose it has in itself a sanctifying and saving power. The Greeks, in this sacrament, use leavened bread, and wine mixed with water

The Armenians discard the Popish doctrine of purgatory but yet, most inconsistently, they pray for the dead.

They hold to confession of sins to the priests, who impose penances and grant absolution, though without money, and they give no indulgences.

They pray through the mediation of the virgin Mary, and other saints. The belief that Mary was always a virgin, is a point of very high importance with them; and they consider the thought of her having given birth to children after the birth of Christ, as in the highest degree derogatory to her character, and impious.

They regard baptism and regeneration as the same thing and have no conception of any spiritual change; and they know little of any other terms of salvation than penance, the Lord's supper, fasting, and good works in general.

The Armenians are strictly Trinitarians in their views, holding firmly to the supreme divinity of Christ, and the doctrine of atonement for sin; though their views on the latter subject, as well as in regard to faith and repentance, are somewhat obscure. They say that Christ died to atone for original sin, and that actual sin is to be washed away by penances, — which, in their view, is repentance. Penances are prescribed by the priests, and sometimes consist in an offering of money to the church, a pilgrimage, or more commonly in repeating certain prayers, or reading the whole book of Psalms a specified number of times. Faith in Christ seems to mean but little more than believing in the mystery of transubstantiation. — See *Coleman's Christian Antiquities*

## PRIMITIVE METHODISTS.

THIS sect forms a party in England, which seceded from the Wesleyans in 1817. They differ from the Wesleyans chiefly in church government, by admitting lay representation. They are said to increase rapidly. Their present number is about seventy thousand.

## NOVATIANS.

AN heretical sect in the early church, which derives its name from Novatian, an heresiarch of the third century, who was ordained a priest of the church of Rome, and afterwards got himself clandestinely consecrated bishop of Rome, by three weak men, upon whom he had imposed, and one of whom afterwards did penance for his concern in the business. He was never acknowledged bishop of Rome, but was condemned and excommunicated. He still, however taught his doctrine, and became the head of the party that bore his name. He denied, in opposition to the opinion of the church, that those who had been guilty of idolatry could be again received by the church.

## NESTORIANS.

The branch of the Christian church known by this name is so called from Nestorius, a patriarch of Constantinople, who was born in Germanica, a city of Syria, in the latter part of the fourth century. He was educated and baptized at Antioch, and, soon after his baptism, withdrew to a monastery in the vicinity of that city. His great reputation for eloquence, and the regularity of his life, induced the emperor Theodosius to select him for the see of Constantinople; and he was consecrated bishop of that church A. D. 429. He became a violent persecutor of heretics; but, because he favored the doctrine of his friend Anastasius, that "the virgin Mary cannot with propriety be called the mother of God," he was anathematized by Cyril, bishop of Alexandria, who, in his turn, was anathematized by Nestorius. In the council of Ephesus, A. D. 431, (the third General Council of the church,) at which Cyril presided, and at which Nestorius was not present, he was judged and condemned without being heard, and deprived of his see. He then retired to his monastery, in Antioch, and was afterwards banished to Petra, in Arabia, and thence to Oasis, in Egypt, where he died, about A. D. 435 or 439.

The decision of the council of Ephesus caused many difficulties in the church; and the friends of Nestorius carried his doctrines through all the Oriental provinces, and established numerous congregations, professing an invincible opposition to the decrees of the Ephesian council. Nestorianism spread rapidly over the East, and was embraced by a large number of the oriental bishops. Barsumas, bishop of Nisibis, labored with great zeal and activity to procure for the Nestorians a solid and permanent footing in Persia; and his success was so remarkable that his fame extended throughout the East. He established a school at Nisibis, which became very famous, and from which issued those Nestorian doctors who, in that and the following centuries, spread abroad their tenets through Egypt, Syria, Arabia, India, Tartary, and China.

The Nestorian church is Episcopal in its government, like all the other Oriental churches. Its doctrines, also, are, in general, the same with those of those churches, and they receive and repeat, in their public worship, the Nicene creed. Their *distinguishing* doctrines appear to be, their believing that Mary was not the mother of Jesus Christ, *as God*, but only *as man*, and that there are, consequently, *two persons*, as well as *two natures*, in the Son of God. This notion was looked upon in the earlier ages of the church as a most momentous error; but it has in later times been considered more as an error of words than of doctrine; and that the error of Nestorius was in the words he employed to express his meaning, rather than in the doctrine itself. While the Nestorians believe that Christ had *two natures* and *two persons*, they say "that these natures and persons are so closely and intimately united that they have but one *aspect*." "Now, the word *barsopa*, by which they express this *aspect*, is precisely of the same signification with the Greek word *προσωπον*, which signifies *a person;* and hence it is evident that they attached to the word *aspect* the same idea that we attach to the word *person*, and that they understood, by the word *person*, precisely what we understand by the term *nature*."

The Nestorians, of all the Christian churches of the East, have been the most careful and successful in avoiding a multitude of superstitious opinions and practices, which have infected the Romish and many Eastern churches

Our readers are referred to an interesting volume recently published by Asahel Grant, M. D., in which is contained strong evidence that the Nestorians and the "Lost Tribes" are one people.

## HIGH-CHURCHMEN.

A TERM first given to the Nonjurors, who refused to acknowledge William III. as their lawful king, and who had very proud notions of church power; but it is now commonly used in a more extensive signification, and is applied to all those who, though far from being Nonjurors, yet form high conceptions of the authority and jurisdiction of the church.

## ANCIENT AMERICAN COVENANT OR CONFESSION OF FAITH.

*Copy of the first Covenant, or Confession of Faith, of the First Church in Salem, Massachusetts.*

THE first ordination to the pastoral office, and the first complete organization and erection of a Protestant church, in North America, took place in that town, in the year 1629.

### THE FIRST COVENANT, OR CONFESSION OF FAITH, OF THE FIRST CHURCH IN SALEM.

"We covenant with our Lord, and one with another, and we do bind ourselves, in the presence of God, to walk together in all his ways, according as he is pleased to reveal himself unto us in his blessed word of truth; and do explicitly, in the name and fear of God, profess and protest to walk as followeth, through the power and grace of our Lord Jesus Christ: —

"We avouch the Lord to be our God, and ourselves to be his people, in the truth and simplicity of our spirits.

"We give ourselves to the Lord Jesus Christ, and the word of his grace, for the teaching, ruling, and sanctifying of us in matters of worship and conversation, resolving to cleave unto him alone for life and glory, and to reject all contrary ways, canons, and constitutions of men, in his worship.

"We promise to walk with our brethren, with all watchfulness and tenderness, avoiding jealousies and suspicions, backbitings, censurings, provokings, secret risings of spirit against them; but, in all offences, to follow the rule of our Lord Jesus, and to bear and forbear, give and forgive, as he hath taught us.

"In public or private, we will willingly do nothing to the offence of the church, but will be willing to take advice for ourselves and ours, as occasion shall be presented.

"We will not, in the congregation, be forward, either to show our own gifts and parts in speaking or scrupling, or there discover the weakness or failings of our brethren; but attend an orderly call thereunto, knowing how much the Lord may be dishonored, and his gospel, and the profession of it, slighted by our distempers and weaknesses in public.

"We bind ourselves to study the advancement of the gospel in all truth and peace, both in regard to those that are within or without; no way slighting our sister churches, but using their counsel, as need shall be; not laying a stumbling-block before any, no, not the Indians, whose good we desire to promote; and so to converse, as we may avoid the very appearance of evil.

"We do hereby promise to carry ourselves in all lawful obedience to those that are over us, in church or commonwealth, knowing how well pleasing it will be to the Lord, that they should have encouragement in their places, by our not grieving their spirits through our irregularities.

"We resolve to approve ourselves to the Lord in our particular callings, shunning idleness, as the bane of any state; nor will we deal hardly or oppressingly with any, wherein we are the Lord's stewards.

"Promising, also, unto our best ability, to teach our children and servants the knowledge of God, and of his will, that they may serve him also; and all this, not by any strength of our own, but by the Lord Christ, whose blood we desire may sprinkle this our covenant, made in his name"

"The above is a covenant," says a learned divine, "to which all good Christians, of every denomination, to the end of time, will be able to subscribe their names, — written in a style of touching simplicity, which has seldom been equalled, and containing sentiments which are felt to be eloquent by every amiable and pious heart, — and should form the bond to unite the whole church on earth, as they will unite the church of the redeemed in heaven. This Covenant might well be adopted by all Congregational and Protestant churches; and it will forever constitute the glory, perpetuate the fame, and render precious the memory, of Francis Higginson, the first minister of Salem" *

* See Biographical Sketches.

# STATISTICS OF CHURCHES.

## BAPTISTS.

The following table, from the Baptist Register of 1842, exhibits the statistics of the Regular or Associated Baptists in a perspicuous light: —

### CHURCHES, MINISTERS, &c.

| States. | Churches. | Ministers. | Baptized. | Members. |
|---|---|---|---|---|
| Maine, | 261 | 181 | 2249 | 20490 |
| New Hampshire, | 104 | 77 | 1042 | 9557 |
| Vermont, | 134 | 94 | 784 | 10950 |
| Massachusetts, | 209 | 179 | 2355 | 25092 |
| Rhode Island, | 32 | 25 | 348 | 5196 |
| Connecticut, | 98 | 92 | 559 | 11266 |
| New York, | 814 | 697 | 7533 | 82200 |
| New Jersey,* | 55 | 53 | 961 | 6716 |
| Pennsylvania, | 252 | 181 | 2370 | 20983 |
| Delaware, | 9 | 8 | | 326 |
| Maryland, | 27 | 18 | 661 | 1710 |
| Virginia, | 477 | 238 | 3086 | 57390 |
| North Carolina, | 448 | 193 | 1543 | 26169 |
| South Carolina, | 367 | 192 | 1434 | 34092 |
| Georgia, | 651 | 276 | 1043 | 44022 |
| Alabama, | 503 | 250 | 908 | 25084 |
| Mississippi, | 150 | 64 | 615 | 6050 |
| Louisiana,† | 15 | 9 | | 288 |
| Arkansas, | 43 | 21 | 105 | 798 |
| Tennessee, | 666 | 444 | 938 | 30879 |
| Kentucky, | 627 | 300 | 5842 | 47325 |
| Ohio, | 502 | 284 | 3594 | 22333 |
| Indiana, | 437 | 229 | 1794 | 18198 |
| Illinois, | 351 | 250 | 1227 | 11408 |
| Missouri, | 282 | 161 | 817 | 11010 |
| Michigan, | 130 | 82 | 668 | 6276 |
| Iowa, | 14 | 9 | 10 | 382 |
| Wisconsin, | 15 | 9 | 58 | 385 |
| British Provinces, | 225 | 125 | 4414 | 37127 |
| | 7898 | 4741 | 46958 | 573702 |

* 17 churches, 16 ministers, and 2236 members, in this state, are included in the New York Association.

† 9 churches, 7 ministers, and 526 members, in this state, are included in the Mississippi Association.

Publications. — Quarterly: *Christian Review*, Boston, Mass. — Monthly: *Missionary Magazine*, Boston, Mass.; *Sabbath School Treasury*, Boston, Mass.; *Mother's Monthly Journal*, Utica, N. Y.; *Sabbath School Gleaner*, Philadelphia, Pa.; *Baptist Memorial*, N. Y.; *Michigan Christian Herald*, Detroit, Mich. — Semi-Monthly: *The Register*, Montreal, Ca.; *Baptist Library*, Lexington, N. Y. — Weekly: *Zion's Advocate*, Portland, Me.; *N. H. Baptist Register*, Concord, N. H; *Vermont Telegraph*, Brandon, Vt.; *Vermont Baptist Journal*, Middlebury, Vt.; *Christian Watchman*, Boston, Mass.; *Christian Reflector*, Boston, Mass.; *Christian Secretary*, Hartford, Ct.; *N. Y. Baptist Register*, Utica, N. Y.; *Baptist Advocate*, New York, N. Y.; *Baptist Record*, Philadelphia, Pa.; *Religious Herald*, Richmond, Va.; *The Truth*, Morristown, Pa.; *Christian Index*, Penfield, Ga.; *Banner and Pioneer*, Louisville, Ky.; *Cross and Journal*, Columbus, Ohio; *Christian Messenger*, Halifax, N. S.

## FREE-WILL BAPTISTS.

This denomination of Baptists have in their connection nine hundred and eighty-one churches, six hundred and forty-seven ordained ministers, one hundred and seventy-two licensed preachers, forty-seven thousand two hundred and seventeen communicants, eighty-seven quarterly and fourteen yearly meetings. Of this number of members, thirty-five thousand two hundred and eighty-seven reside in New England and New York. They are most numerous in Maine and New Hampshire.

Publications, &c. — There are two periodicals published by this denomination at Dover, N. H.: the *Morning Star*, a weekly paper, and the *Sabbath School Repository*, published monthly; also the *Christian Soldier*, Providence, R. I., once in two weeks.

The Free-Will Baptists have several benevolent institutions in Maine, and flourishing seminaries of learning at Parsonsfield, Me., Strafford, N. H., Smithfield, R. I., and at Clinton and Varysburgh, N. Y.

These people do not believe in the doctrine of election and reprobation, as taught by Calvin, and invite to the Lord's table all evangelical Christians in good standing in their churches.

## SEVENTH-DAY BAPTISTS.

This people have in the United States about forty-eight churches, thirty-four elders, twenty licentiates, and five thousand communicants

They reside principally in Rhode Island and New York; but have a few churches in New Jersey, Pennsylvania, &c. They are divided into three associations, and meet by delegation annually in general conference. Their government, however, is Independent. They have general *Missionary Society*, a *Society for the Promotion of Christianity among the Jews*, a *Tract* and an *Education Society*. Their principal institution of learning is at De Ruyter, N. Y., and is in a flourishing state, having several teachers, and about two hundred scholars. They are close communionists.

## CHRISTIAN CONNECTION.

This denomination of Christians are found in almost every state in the Union, and in Canada. In 1841, there were in America forty-one conferences, five hundred and ninety-one churches, five hundred and ninety-three ordained preachers, one hundred and eighty-nine unordained preachers, and about thirty thousand church members.

Publications.—This connection has three religious periodicals, viz. The *Christian Palladium*, Union Mills, N. Y.; *Christian Journal*, Exeter, N. H.; and the *Christian Messenger*, Jacksonville, Illinois.

## CALVINISTIC CONGREGATIONALISTS.

So late as the year 1700, eighty years after the landing of the Pilgrims, there were, in all the New England States then settled, but one Episcopal church, no Methodist church, and, with the exception of Rhode Island, not more than half a dozen Baptist churches. At that time, however, there were one hundred and twenty Congregational churches, composed of emigrants from Europe and their descendants, and thirty others composed of converted Indians. The great mass of the descendants of the early settlers of New England are Congregationalists, maintaining, substantially, the same views of church order and religious faith which their venerated ancestry sacrificed home, and country, and life, to maintain and perpetuate.

The present number of Congregational churches in New England is about fifteen hundred; and in the Middle and Western States there are about fourteen hundred and fifty; although the mode of church government adopted by some of them is, in some degree, modified by the "Plan of Union" with Presbyterians. These churches contain, as nearly as can be ascertained, about one hundred and ninety-four thousand communicants.

Recently, symptoms of dissatisfaction with the "Plan of Union have extensively developed themselves, particularly in New York Ohio, Missouri, Illinois, Wisconsin, and Iowa; and the probability now is, that a pure Congregational mode of church government will soon be generally adopted by the descendants of New-England Congregationalists, who are scattered over the great West.

These Congregational churches are more particularly denominated *Orthodox* than any other churches in the United States, and adhere to the doctrines of Calvin or Hopkins.

Publications. — The Orthodox Congregationalists publish a great number of periodicals, the principal of which are the *Boston Recorder*, the *New England Puritan*, Boston, Mass.; the *Christian Mirror*, Portland, Me.; the *Congregational Journal*, Concord, N. H.; the *Vermont Chronicle*, Windsor, Vt.; the *Congregational Observer*, Hartford, Ct.; and several in the Western States, which are sustained partly by Congregationalists and partly by Presbyterians

## DISCIPLES OF CHRIST.

The largest number of this denomination is found in the region of country around where its doctrines were first propagated. There are, however, societies of this class of Christians in other parts of the coun try, some adopting, and others rejecting, its views on baptism. The total number in the United States is about one hundred and fifty thousand.

Publications. The Disciples of Christ publish a periodical, the *Millennial Harbinger*, at Bethany, Va., (edited by Campbell, the founder of the sect,) and another, the *Evangelist*, at Carthage, Ohio.

## EPISCOPALIANS.

We have already given, in the historical account of the Episcopal Church, in this Country, a few brief notices of its condition; and we now present the following additional statistics.

### LIST OF BISHOPS.

It being the essential principle of Episcopacy, that legitimate church authority is not originated by voluntary associations of men, but is of Divine origin, derived from Christ, and transmitted through an unbroken succession of Bishops, who trace their appointment to Him, we here give a list of the names of persons who constitute such succession

### Order of Episcopal Succession.

A. D.
JESUS CHRIST.
44. St. Peter and St. Paul at Rome.
66. Linus.
81. Anacletus
91. Clement.
102. Euarestus.
111. Alexander.
121. Sixtus I.
130. Telesphorus.
141. Hyginus.
144. Pius.
159. Anicetus.
168. Soter.
176. Eleutherius.
193. Victor.
201. Zephyrinus.
218. Callistus.
224. Urbanus.
232. Pontianus.
238. Anterus.
238. Fabianus.
252. Cornelius.
254. Lucius.
255. Stephanus.
258. Sixtus II.
265. Dionysius.
270. Felix I.
275. Eutychianus
283. Caius.
296. Marcellinus.
304. Marcellus.
309. Eusebius.
311. Miltiades.
314. Sylvester.
336. Marcus.
337. Julius.
352. Liberius.
356. Felix II.
366. Damasus.
385. Siricius.
398. Anastasius I.
402. Innocent.

A. D.
417. Zosimus.
419. Boniface I.
423. Celestine.
434. Sixtus III.
443. Leo (the Great.)
464. Hilary.
468. Simplicius.
483. Felix III.
492. Gelasius.
496. Anastasius II.
498. Symmachus
514. Hormisdas.
524. John I.
526. Felix IV.
530. Boniface II.
532. John II.
535. Agapetus.
537. Silverius.
540. Virgilius.
555. Pelagius I.
560. John III.
574. Benedictus.
578. Pelagius II.
590. Gregory (the Great.)
596. Augustine, Missionary Bishop to England.
611. Laurentius
619. Melitus.
624. Justus.
628. Honorius.
656. Adeodatus
668. Theodore.
692. Brithwald.
731. Tatwyn, or Cadwyn
735. Egbright.
736. Nothelmus.
742. Cuthbert.
759. Bregwin.
762. Lambert.
793. Atheland.
806. Wulfred.
830. Theologild.
830. Syred.

| A. D. | | A. D. | |
|---|---|---|---|
| 831. | Ceolneth. | 1349. | Simon Islippe. |
| 871. | Athelredus. | 1366. | Simon Langham. |
| 889. | Plegmund. | 1368. | William Wittlesey. |
| 915. | Athelme. | 1375. | Simon Sudbury. |
| 924. | Wolfhelme | 1381. | William Courtney. |
| 934. | Odo Severus. | 1396. | Thomas Arundel. |
| 957. | Elfin. | 1414. | Henry Chichley. |
| 958. | Brithelme. | 1443. | John Stafford. |
| 959. | Dunstan. | 1452. | John Kemp. |
| 988. | Ethelgarus. | 1454. | Thomas Bourchier. |
| 989. | Siricius. | 1486. | John Morton. |
| 994. | Alfricus. | 1501. | Henry Deane. |
| 1006. | Ælfeagus. | 1504. | William Warham. |
| 1013. | Livingus, or Elstan. | 1521. | John Longland. |
| 1020. | Agelnoth. | 1533. | THOMAS CRANMER.* |
| 1038. | Eadsius, or Eadsinus. | 1536. | Robert Parfew. |
| 1050. | Robert Gemiticensis. | 1537. | John Hodgskins. |
| 1052. | Stigand. | 1559. | Matthew Parker. |
| 1070. | Lanfranc. | 1559. | Edmund Grindal. |
| 1093. | Anselme. | 1577. | John Whitgift. |
| 1114. | Rodolph, or Raphe. | 1597. | Richard Bancroft. |
| 1122. | William Corbel, or Corbois. | 1609. | George Abbott. |
| 1138. | Theobald. | 1617. | George Monteigne |
| 1162. | Thomas a Becket. | 1621. | William Laud. |
| 1173. | Richard. | 1634. | Matthew Wren. |
| 1184. | Baldwin. | 1660. | Gilbert Sheldon. |
| 1191. | Reginald Fitz Joceline. | 1674. | Henry Compton. |
| 1193. | Hubert Walter. | 1677. | William Sancroft. |
| 1207. | Stephen Langton. | 1685. | Jonathan Trelawney |
| 1229. | Richard Weatherhead. | 1715. | John Potter. |
| 1235. | Edmund. | 1737. | Thomas Herring. |
| 1244. | Boniface III. | 1749. | Frederick Cornwallis. |
| 1272. | Robert Kilwarby | 1775. | John Moore. |
| 1278. | John Peckam. | 1792. | Charles Manners Sutton. |
| 1294. | Robert Winchelsey. | 1813. | William Howley, (*now living.*) |
| 1313. | Walter Raynolds. | | ——— |
| 1327. | Simon Mepham. | 1775. | John Moore. |
| 1333. | John Stratford. | 1787. | WILLIAM WHITE.* |
| 1349. | Thomas Bradwardin. | 1811. | Alexander V. Griswold. |

* Archbishop Cranmer was the first in this succession, at and after the Reformation and Bishop White was the connecting link between the English and American successions.

## List of Bishops of the Church in the United States.

Those with an asterisk (*) are deceased.

*1784. Samuel Seabury, D. D., Connecticut, died, 1796.
*1787. William White, D. D., Pennsylvania, died, 1836.
*1787. Samuel Provoost, D. D., New York, died, 1815.
*1790. James Madison, D. D., Virginia, died, 1812.
*1792. Thomas John Claggett, D. D., Maryland, died, 1816.
*1795. Robert Smith, D. D., South Carolina, died, 1801.
*1797. Edward Bass, D. D., Massachusetts, died, 1803.
*1797. Abraham Jarvis, D. D., Connecticut, died, 1813.
*1801. Benjamin Moore, D. D., New York, died, 1816.
*1804. Samuel Parker, D. D., Massachusetts, died, 1804.
*1811. John Henry Hobart, D. D., New York, died, 1830.
1811. Alexander Viets Griswold, D. D., Massachusetts.
*1812. Theodore Dehon, D. D., South Carolina, died, 1817.
*1814. Richard Channing Moore, D. D., Virginia, died, 1841.
*1814. James Kemp, D. D., Maryland, died, 1827.
*1815. John Croes, D. D., New Jersey, died, 1832.
*1818. Nathaniel Bowen, D. D., South Carolina, died, 1839.
1819. Philander Chase, D. D., Illinois.
1819. Thomas Church Brownell, D. D., LL. D., Connecticut.
*1823. John Stark Ravenscroft, D. D., North Carolina, died, 1830.
1827. Henry Ustick Onderdonk, D. D., Pennsylvania.
1829. William Meade, D. D., Virginia.
*1830. William Murray Stone, D. D., Maryland, died, 1838.
1830. Benjamin Tredwell Onderdonk, D. D., New York.
1831. Levi Silliman Ives, D. D., LL. D., North Carolina.
1832. John Henry Hopkins, D. D., Vermont.
1832. Benjamin Bosworth Smith, D. D., Kentucky.
1832. Charles Pettit McIlvaine, D. D., Ohio.
1832. George Washington Doane, D. D., LL. D., New Jersey.
1834. James Hervey Otey, D. D., Tennessee.
1835. Jackson Kemper, D. D., Missionary Bishop, for Wisconsin Iowa, and the Indian territory North of Lat. 36½°.
1836. Samuel Allen McCoskry, D. D., Michigan
1838. Leonidas Polk, D. D., Louisiana.
1839. William Heathcote De Lancey, D. D., Western New York.
1840. Christopher Edwards Gadsden, D. D., South Carolina.
1840. William Rollinson Whittingham, D. D., Maryland.
1841. Stephen Elliott, jun., D. D., Georgia.
1841. Alfred Lee, D. D., Delaware.

The following table contains the statistics of this Church in the United States: —

| States. | Dioceses. | Bishops. | Clergy. |
|---|---|---|---|
| Maine, | 1 | | 7 |
| New Hampshire, | 1 | | 10 |
| Vermont, | 1 | 1 | 24 |
| Massachusetts, | 1 | 1 | 49 |
| Rhode Island, | 1 | | 20 |
| Connecticut, | 1 | 1 | 92 |
| New York, | 1 | 1 | 196 |
| Western New York, | 1 | 1 | 101 |
| New Jersey, | 1 | 1 | 42 |
| Pennsylvania, | 1 | 1 | 107 |
| Delaware, | 1 | 1 | 10 |
| Maryland, | 1 | 1 | 81 |
| Virginia, | 1 | 1 | 94 |
| North Carolina, | 1 | 1 | 30 |
| South Carolina, | 1 | 1 | 47 |
| Georgia, | 1 | 1 | 9 |
| Louisiana, | 1 | 1 | 7 |
| Alabama, | 1 | | 11 |
| Mississippi, | 1 | | 7 |
| Tennessee, | 1 | 1 | 13 |
| Arkansas, | 1 | | 3 |
| Kentucky, | 1 | 1 | 21 |
| Ohio, | 1 | 1 | 58 |
| Illinois, | 1 | 1 | 9 |
| Michigan, | 1 | 1 | 19 |
| Indiana, | 1 | | 17 |
| Missouri, | 1 | 1 | 16 |
| Iowa, | 1 | | 3 |
| Wisconsin, | 1 | | 8 |
| Florida, | 1 | | 4 |
| | 30 | 20 | 1114 |

The Dioceses of Maine, New Hampshire, Massachusetts, and Rhode Island, are under the charge of the same Bishop. Indiana and Missouri are under the charge of the Missionary Bishop for Wisconsin, Iowa, and the Indian territory North of Lat. 36½°. Alabama is under the charge of the Bishop of Louisiana. Mississippi and Arkansas are under the charge of the Bishop of Tennessee.

In the British American Provinces and Islands, there are six dioceses, containing six Bishops, and 454 other clergymen.

There are numerous local Societies for religious purposes, in every Diocese.

Periodical Publications. — Weekly · The *Churchman*, New York; *Gospel Messenger*, Utica; *Gospel Messenger and Southern Episcopal Register*, Charleston, S. C.; *Episcopal Recorder*, Philadelphia *Southern Churchman*, Alexandria, D. C.; *Christian Witness*, Boston, *Western Episcopal Observer*, Cincinnati, Ohio; *Banner of the Cross*,

Philadelphia; *Practical Christian and Church Chronicle*, New Haven, Ct.—MONTHLY: *Journal of Christian Education*, New York; *Children's Magazine*, New York; *Spirit of Missions*, New York; *Church Record*, Flushing, N. Y.

## FRIENDS.

THE Friends are found in most of the states in the Union, and some in the British Provinces. They are most numerous in Pennsylvania, a state first settled by them, under their worthy head and father, in this country, WILLIAM PENN, in 1682.

In England and Ireland, they number about fifty thousand; and in America, about two hundred thousand, and are divided into four hundred and fifty congregations. About half are Orthodox, and the other half Hicksites, or followers of ELIAS HICKS, who died at Jericho, N. Y in 1830, aged 76.

## JEWS.

THE number of Jews in the United States is estimated at about four thousand. They have synagogues in Newport, R. I., the cities of New York, Philadelphia, Charleston, S. C., and in other parts of the country. Their mode of worship is exceedingly interesting. With regard to the number of this people in the world, Blackwood's Magazine says:—

"The statistics of the Jewish population are among the most singular circumstances of this most singular of all people. Under all their calamities and dispersions, they seem to have remained at nearly the same amount as in the days of David and Solomon—never much more in prosperity, never much less after ages of suffering. Nothing like this has occurred in the history of any other race; Europe in general having doubled its population within the last hundred years, and England nearly tripled hers within the last half century; the proportion of America being still more rapid, and the world crowding in a constantly-increasing ratio. Yet the Jews seem to stand still in this vast and general movement. The population of Judea, in its most palmy days, probably did not exceed, if it reached, four millions. The numbers who entered Palestine from the wilderness, were evidently not much more than three; and their census, according to the German statists, who are generally considered to be exact, is now nearly the same as that of the people under Moses—about three millions."

On the above, Judge Noah, of New York, a learned Jew, remarks —

"We apprehend there is some error in the above statistics, and that the number of Jews throughout the world may be estimated at nearer six millions than three. There are more than a million in Poland and Russia; in all Asia, there are full two millions; half a million in Austria; in the Barbary States and Africa, a million; in all Europe, two millions and a half. We do not think, during the most splendid periods of Jewish history, that they ever exceeded four millions; but then their colonies and countries held tributary in Europe and Asia, amounted to many millions more. For example, at one period all Spain paid tribute to King Solomon; and all Spain and Portugal, at this day, are descendants of the Jews and Moors; and there are many thousands of Jews, in both those countries, now adhering in secret to the ancient faith of their fathers, while outwardly professing the Catholic religion. All the familiar Spanish and Portuguese names — Lopez, Mendez, Carvalho, Fonseca, Rodrigues, Peirara, Azavedo, Montefiores, &c. &c. — are of Jewish origin. Their numbers, therefore, will never be accurately known until the restoration, when thousands who, from convenience and pride, and some from apprehension, conceal their religion, will be most eager to avow it when their nation takes rank among the governments of the earth."

## LUTHERANS.

THE government of the Lutherans is somewhat singular. Where it is established by law, the supreme head of the state is also supreme head of the church. They have bishops, but no diocesan episcopacy, except in Denmark and Sweden. These are called *superintendents* in Germany, and *presidents* in the United States. There is but *one* archbishop, and he is the primate of Sweden.

They have in the United States about one thousand churches, four hundred ministers, seventy thousand communing members, and about one hundred and forty thousand which do not commune.

EDUCATION, &c. — They have a college, located at Gettysburg, Pa., and several academies in different parts of the country; also four theological seminaries, located at Gettysburg, Pa.; Columbus, Ohio; Lexington, S. C.; Hartwich, N. Y., a fifth is contemplated in Indiana. Their different education societies support about eighty beneficiaries, preparing for the ministry, at an expense of one hundred dollars each, annually. The *Lutheran Observer* is published weekly, at Baltimore.

The Lutherans are one of the most numerous sects of Christians in the world. The whole number in Europe is estimated at twenty-seven millions, embracing seventeen reigning sovereigns. This estimate, of course, includes the Moravians.

## PROTESTANT METHODISTS.

This infant church is rapidly increasing, especially in the middle States. Its population in the United States exceeds one hundred and fifty thousand.

This class of Christians have twenty-one annual conferences in as many states; nearly four hundred travelling, and a large number of unstationed ministers. They have a general conference, which meets once in four years, consisting of two delegates from every thousand communicants, one a minister, the other a layman: this is their legislative body. The number of communicants is about sixty-five thousand.

Publications. The Protestant Methodists support four religious papers: — the *Olive Branch*, Boston, Mass.; the *New York Luminary*, New York, the *Methodist Protestant*, Baltimore, Md., and the *Western Recorder*, Zanesville, Ohio.

## METHODISTS.

The population of all denominations of Methodists in the United States exceeds three millions.

Publications. — The *Christian Advocate and Journal*, New York city; *Zion's Herald and Wesleyan Journal*, Boston, Mass.; *Northern Advocate*, Auburn, N. Y.; *Christian Repository*, Philadelphia, Pa.; *Richmond Christian Advocate*, Richmond, Va.; *Southern Christian Advocate*, Charleston, S. C.; *South-Western Christian Advocate*, Nashville, Tenn.; *Pittsburg Christian Advocate*, Pittsburg, Pa.; *Western Christian Advocate*, and the *Christian Apologist*, a German paper, Cincinnati, Ohio.

There is also published by this denomination, the *Methodist Quarterly Review*, New York city; *Ladies' Repository*, (monthly,) Cincinnati, Ohio; *Guide to Christian Perfection*, (monthly,) Boston, Mass., *Sunday School Advocate*, (semi-monthly,) New York city; *Sabbath School Messenger*, (semi-monthly,) Boston, Mass. The Methodists have ten colleges, and thirty academies.

In the Methodist church in Canada, are two weekly newspapers viz, *Christian Guardian*, Toronto, U. C.; *The Wesleyan*, Montreal, L. C.

From the "Minutes of the Annual Conferences of the Methodist Episcopal Church, for the Year 1840," we copy the following table: —

CONFERENCES, MINISTERS, &C.

| Conferences. | Whites. | Colored. | Indians. | Total Com. | Trav. Prs. | Loca. Prs. |
|---|---|---|---|---|---|---|
| Troy,............... | 24,488 | 78 | | 24,566 | 144 | 119 |
| New England,....... | 22,319 | 235 | | 22,554 | 157 | 126 |
| New Hampshire,..... | 20,084 | | | 20,084 | 151 | 137 |
| Pittsburg,........... | 35,276 | 474 | | 35,750 | 136 | 172 |
| Maine, ............. | 22,359 | | | 22,359 | 145 | 179 |
| Black River......... | 15,908 | 27 | | 15,935 | 96 | 154 |
| Erie................ | 17,860 | 50 | | 17,910 | 107 | 185 |
| Oneida .............. | 22,909 | 65 | | 22,974 | 142 | 197 |
| Michigan,........... | 11,308 | 12 | 87 | 11,407 | 74 | 116 |
| Rock River,......... | 6,519 | 21 | 45 | 6,585 | 75 | 108 |
| Genesee,............ | 27,931 | 50 | | 27,981 | 162 | 211 |
| North Ohio, ......... | 23,594 | 91 | 213 | 23,898 | 95 | 150 |
| Ohio,............... | 53,621 | 662 | | 54,283 | 168 | 400 |
| Illinois,............. | 24,607 | 80 | | 24,687 | 103 | 435 |
| Missouri,............ | 12,386 | 1,224 | 382 | 13,992 | 66 | 177 |
| Kentucky,.......... | 30,679 | 6,321 | | 37,000 | 114 | 260 |
| Tennessee,.......... | 21,675 | 4,405 | | 26,080 | 95 | 298 |
| Indiana, ............ | 52,208 | 407 | | 52,615 | 156 | 418 |
| Memphis,........... | 12,497 | 1,995 | | 14,492 | 69 | 183 |
| Arkansas,........... | 4,228 | 725 | 1,524 | 6,479 | 41 | 81 |
| Holston,............ | 25,902 | 2,420 | | 28,322 | 68 | 304 |
| Mississippi, ......... | 8,433 | 4,178 | 67 | 12,678 | 81 | 165 |
| North Carolina,...... | 15,983 | 4,480 | | 20,463 | 61 | 116 |
| Texas,.............. | 1,623 | 230 | | 1,853 | 19 | 25 |
| Alabama, ........... | 19,491 | 5,821 | | 25,312 | 87 | |
| South Carolina,...... | 26,945 | 30,481 | | 57,426 | 102 | 243 |
| Virginia,............ | 21,841 | 3,086 | | 24,927 | 94 | 158 |
| Georgia, ............ | 28,868 | 9,989 | | 38,857 | 127 | 386 |
| Baltimore, .......... | 42,789 | 13,904 | | 56,693 | 182 | 261 |
| Philadelphia, ........ | 35,094 | 8,778 | | 43,872 | 128 | 237 |
| New Jersey,......... | 22,733 | 542 | | 23,275 | 108 | 156 |
| New York,.......... | 36,284 | 405 | | 36,689 | 215 | 236 |
| Liberia Mission, ..... | | 922 | | 922 | 19 | |
| Total, 1840,......... | 748,442 | 102,158 | 2,318 | 852,918 | 3,587 | 6,393 |
| Total, 1842,......... | 796,495 | 107,251 | 2,617 | 906,363 | 3,846 | 7,125 |

## PRESBYTERIANS.

THE Protestant faith was introduced into Scotland about 1527; and about 1592 Andrew Melville effected the introduction of the Presbyterian form of church polity. This form, through much persecution, and even bloodshed, has been maintained ever since. Its creed is Calvinistic. This church has nearly a thousand ministers, and about one million five hundred thousand church members. It is the established religion of Scotland, sustained by law. There are also severa bodies of dissenting Presbyterians in Scotland.

Presbyterianism was first introduced into England by those Christians who returned from Frankfort, after the death of Queen Mary For a time, it flourished, but at length lapsed into Socinianism. There are, however, a few churches in England still pure, which are in fellowship with the Scotch Presbyterians.

This denomination began its organized existence in America about the year 1700, and is the offspring of the church of Scotland. Its first ministers were Rev. Francis McKemie, and the Rev. John Hampton, who labored in Virginia.

The first church of this order was organized in Philadelphia, 1703, the first presbytery, 1704, and the first synod in 1716. Since that time, they have steadily increased, and their number in 1840 was ninety-six presbyteries, twelve hundred and thirty-two ministers, eighteen hundred and twenty-three churches, and one hundred and fifty-two thousand four hundred and fifty-one communicants.

The Presbyterians are found chiefly in the Middle, Western, and Southern States. The number of people attached to this form of church government in the United States, is supposed to exceed two millions.

Education. — Within the bounds of the church there are thirteen theological seminaries, three of which are under the care of the General Assembly. They have a board of education, which has about four hundred young men in training for the ministry.

The Calvinistic publications announce their sentiments.

In 1837, a division arose in the Presbyterian church, into Old and New Schools, in consequence of variant views of doctrine and discipline. The friends of the New School were exscinded, or cut off, from the old church, but still claim to be the General Assembly of the Presbyterian church. Unfortunately, the difficulty is not settled; we cannot, therefore, give the strength of the parties.

### OTHER PRESBYTERIAN COMMUNITIES.

The Associate Presbyterians have about one hundred ministers, one hundred and ninety congregations, and twenty thousand communicants. They are principally found south and west of the Hudson River.

The Reformed Presbyterians, or Covenanters, are located principally in Ohio. They have about thirty ministers, fifty congregations, and four thousand communicants.

The Associate Reformed have about one hundred and twenty-five ministers, more than two hundred congregations, and about fifteen thousand communicants. They are located principally in Pennsylvania.

## REFORMED DUTCH CHURCH.

THIS church comprises one general synod, and two particular synods; one at New York, and another at Albany. The two synods comprise eighteen classes, about two hundred ministers, two hundred churches, twenty-seven thousand communicants, and a population of about one hundred and thirty thousand. This denomination of Christians is found almost entirely in the first settlements in the states of New York, New Jersey, and Pennsylvania.

The *Christian Intelligencer*, published at New York, advocates the principles of this church.

## ROMAN CATHOLICS.

THIS denomination is spread over every section of the United States and the British Provinces. They form, it is stated, more than three fourths of the population of the Canadas. They are also found in large numbers in the Provinces of Nova Scotia and New Brunswick. In this Union, they are most numerous in the Middle States; but in consequence of the great influx of this people into North America, and their frequent change of location, it is utterly impossible to state their numbers, in each state, with any degree of accuracy. Their number in the United States is variously stated from five hundred thousand to one million five hundred thousand. Their number, probably, is not less than eight hundred thousand, nor more than one million two hundred thousand. The population of Canada, in 1840, was at least one million.

The first Roman Catholics that came to this country were from England, under Lord Baltimore, a Catholic nobleman, in 1634. They settled the state of Maryland; and, much to their honor, while some of the Protestant provinces were persecuting all those who differed from them on religious subjects, the Catholic Marylanders protected all sects that were moral and civil in their deportment.

We copy from the "Metropolitan Catholic Almanac and Laity's Directory for 1841" the following statistical table: —

STATISTICS OF THE CATHOLIC CHURCH IN THE UNITED STATES

| Diocese. | Churches and Chapels. | Clergymen in the Ministry. | Clergymen otherwise employed. | Ecclesiastical Institutions. | Clerical Students. | Literary Institutions for young Men. | Young Men in College. | Female Religious Institutions. | Female Academies. | Pupils in Female Academies. | Charitable Institutions. |
|---|---|---|---|---|---|---|---|---|---|---|---|
| Baltimore, ... | 68 | 38 | 31 | 4 | 52 | 5 | 633 | 5 | 9 | 530 | 21 |
| Richmond, .. | 7 | 6 | 1 | 0 | 0 | 0 | 0 | 0 | 3 | 100 | 4 |
| Philadelphia, . | 91 | 57 | 2 | 1 | 22 | 2 | 60 | 0 | 1 | 30 | 6 |
| New York, .. | 64 | 65 | 1 | 1 | 14 | 1 | .... | 0 | 2 | 120 | 14 |
| Boston, ..... | 30 | 31 | 0 | 0 | 0 | 1 | 60 | 1 | 1 | .... | 1 |
| Detroit, ..... | 25 | 17 | 1 | 0 | 0 | 1 | .... | 1 | 1 | .... | 2 |
| Cincinnati,... | 38 | 34 | 2 | 1 | .... | 1 | .... | 2 | 2 | 70 | 2 |
| Vincennes, .. | 27 | 25 | 5 | 1 | 9 | 1 | 50 | 1 | 1 | 50 | 2 |
| Du Buque,... | 5 | 8 | 0 | 0 | 0 | 1 | .... | 0 | 1 | .... | .... |
| St. Louis,.... | 56 | 50 | 23 | 2 | 30 | 3 | 320 | 10 | 10 | 640 | 8 |
| Bardstown, .. | 40 | 26 | 25 | 1 | .... | 3 | 300 | 3 | 10 | 528 | 2 |
| Nashville, ... | 1 | 6 | 0 | 1 | 2 | 1 | .... | 0 | 0 | 0 | 0 |
| New Orleans, | 38 | 39 | 11 | 1 | 9 | 1 | 100 | 4 | 4 | 526 | 5 |
| Natchez, .... | 1 | 2 | .... | .... | .... | .... | .... | .... | 0 | 0 | 0 |
| Mobile, ..... | 7 | 12 | 7 | .... | .... | 2 | 70 | 2 | 2 | 60 | 1 |
| Charleston, .. | 14 | 20 | 0 | 4 | 6 | 1 | .... | 2 | 2 | 128 | 4 |
| | 512 | 436 | 109 | 17 | 144 | [illegible] | 1593 | 31 | 49 | 2782 | 72 |

The sacred college of cardinals has fifty-seven members. The total number is seventy.

There are twelve patriarchs in the Christian world. The archbishops and bishops amount to six hundred and seventy-one. The vicars apostolic in different countries are fifty-seven in number, besides whom there are thirty-eight coadjutor-bishops, making the grand total of the Catholic episcopacy amount to seven hundred and sixty-six bishops.

CATHOLIC PERIODICALS.—The *United States Catholic Miscellany*, published weekly in Charleston, S. C.; the *Catholic Telegraph*, published weekly in Cincinnati, Ohio; the *Catholic Herald*, published weekly in Philadelphia; the *Catholic Advocate*, published weekly in Bardstown, Ky.; *Der Wahrheit's Freund*, (German paper,) published weekly in Cincinnati, Ohio; the *New York Catholic Register*, published weekly in the city of New York; *Ordo divini Officii recitandi, Missæque celebrandæ, juxta Rubricas Breviarii ac Missalis Romani*, published annually in Baltimore; the *Young Catholic's Magazine*, enlarged series, published on the first of each month, in New York.

At the time of the reformation, 1517, papal power, or the power of the pope of Rome, had acquired so great a spiritual dominion over the minds and consciences of men, that all Europe submitted to it with implicit obedience. At the present day, the Roman Catholic religion prevails, more or less, in every country in Christendom. Its population is stated to exceed eighty millions. It is the established religion of Austria, France, Portugal, and Spain, and of thirteen other states in Europe.

## POPES OF ROME.*

| A.D. | |
|---|---|
| 33. | St. Peter, martyred. |
| 66. | St. Linus, martyred. |
| 67. | St. Clement, abdicated. |
| 77. | St. Cletus, martyred. |
| 83. | St. Anaclitus. |
| 96. | St. Evaristus, coadjutor to the former, martyred. |
| 108. | St. Alexander I., martyred. |
| 117. | St. Sixtus I., martyred. |
| 127. | Telesphorus, martyred. |
| 138. | Hygenus, martyred. The first called *pope*. |
| 142. | Pius I., martyred. |
| 150. | Anicetus, martyred. |
| 162. | Soter. |
| 171. | Eleutherius, martyred. |
| 185. | Victor I., martyred. |
| 197. | Zephyrinus, martyred. |
| 217. | Calixtus I., martyred. |
| 222. | Urban I., martyred. |
| 230. | Pontianus, martyred. |
| 235. | Anterus, martyred. |
| 236. | Fabian, martyred. |
| 236. | Novatianus, antipope. |
| 250. | Cornelius, beheaded. |
| 252. | Lucius I., martyred. |
| 254. | Stephen I., martyred. |
| 257. | Sixtus II., coadjutor to the former, martyred. |
| 259. | Dionysius. |
| 269. | Felix I. |
| 274. | Eutychianus. |
| 283. | Caius. |
| 295. | Marcellinus, martyred. |
| 304. | Marcellus I., martyred. |
| 310. | Eusebius, martyred. |
| 310. | Melchiades, coadjutor to the former |
| 314. | Sylvester. |
| 336. | Marcus. |
| 337. | Julius I. |
| 352. | Liberius, banished |
| 356. | Felix II., antipope. |
| 358. | Liberius, again, abdicated. |
| 358. | Felix became legal pope but was killed by Liberius. |
| 359. | Liberius, again. |
| 366. | Damasius. |
| 385. | Siricius. |
| 399. | Anastasius. |
| 401. | Innocent I. |
| 417. | Zosimus. |
| 418. | Boniface I. |
| 422. | Celestinus I. |
| 432. | Sixtus III. |
| 440. | Leo I., the Great |
| 461. | Hilary. |
| 468. | Simplicius. |

* The reader will perceive some difference in the dates, and also in the spelling between this list and the list of Bishops, p. 315. This difference arises from the following of different authorities in the chronology and spelling by the compilers of the two lists. It will be seen that they agree in the order of succession, with one or two exceptions. The fourth and fifth names in *this* list are generally considered as the same individual, and the best authorities place him before Clement. The other apparent differences in the succession are caused by the inserting in *this* list of the names of all who were in the see of Rome at any time; while in the other, those who were not lawful bishops of Rome are omitted.

A. D.

483. Felix III.
492. Gelasius.
496. Anastasius II.
498. Symmachus.
514. Hormisdas.
523. John I., died in prison at Ravenna.
526. Felix IV.
530. Boniface II.
533. John II.
535. Agapetus.
536. Sylvester; he was made prisoner by the antipope Vigilius, who enjoyed the papacy.
538. Vigilius, banished, and restored.
555. Pelagius I.
560. John III.
574. Benedict I.
578. Pelagius II.
590. Gregory the Great.
604. Sabiamus.
606. Boniface III.
608. Boniface IV.
615. Deusdedit.
618. Boniface V.
624. Honorius I.
640. Severinus.
640. John IV.
642. Theodorus.
649. Martin I., starved to death.
654. Eugenius I.
657. Vitalianus.
672. Adeodatus.
676. Donus.
679. Agatho.
682. Leo II.
684. Benedict II.
685. John V.
686. Conon.
686. Theodore and Pascan, antipopes.

A. D.

687. Sergius.
701. John VI.
705. John VII.
708. Sisinnius.
708. Constantine
715. Gregory II.
731. Gregory III.
741. Zacharias.
752. Stephen II., governed only four days.
752. Stephen III.
757. Paul I.
768. Stephen IV.
772. Adrian I.
795. Leo III.
816. Stephen V.
817. Paschal I.
824. Eugenius II.
827. Valentinus.
828. Gregory IV
844. Sergius II.
847. Leo IV.
855. Benedict III.
858. Nicholas I.
867. Adrian II.
872. John VIII.
882. Martin II.
883. Adrian III.
885. Stephen VI.
891. Formosus.
896. Boniface VI.
897. Romanus, antipope.
897. Stephen VII.
898. Theodorus II., governed twenty-two days.
898. John IX.
900. Benedict IV.
904. Leo V., killed by Christiphilus.
905. Sergius III.
913. Anastasius III.
914. Laudo.
915. John X., was stifled.

A. D.

928. Leo VI.
929. Stephen VIII.
931. John XI.
936. Leo VII.
939. Stephen IX.
943. Martin III.
946. Agapetus II.
956. John XII.
963. Leo VIII., turned out.
964. Benedict V., banished.
964. Leo VIII.
965. Benedict V., again.
965. John XIII.
972. Benedict VI.
974. Domus.
975. Benedict VII.
975. Boniface VII.
984. John XIV.
985. John XV., died before consecration.
986. John XVI.
996. Gregory V.
999. Silvester II.
1003. John XVI.
1004. John XVII.
1009. Sergius VI.
1012. Benedict VIII.
1024. John XVIII.
1033. Benedict IX., deposed.
1045. Gregory VI.
1046. Clement II.
1047. Benedict IX., again, abdicated.
1048. Damasius II.
1049. Leo IX.
1055. Victor II.
1057. Stephen X.
1058. Nicholas II.
1061. Alexander II.
1073. Gregory VII.
1086. Victor III., poisoned
1088. Urban II.
1099. Paschal II.

A. D.

1118. Gelasius II.
1119. Calixtus II.
1124. Honorius II.
1130. Innocent II
1143. Cælestine II
1144. Lucius II.
1145. Eugenius III.
1153. Anastasius IV., a short time.
1154. Adrian IV., choked by a fly as he was drinking
1159. Alexander III
1181. Lucius III.
1185. Urban III.
1187. Gregory VIII.
1187. Clement III.
1191. Cælestine III.
1198. Innocent III.
1216. Honorius III
1227. Gregory IX.
1241. Cælestine IV.
1243. Innocent IV.
1254. Alexander IV.
1261. Urban IV.
1265. Clement IV.
1271. Gregory X.
1276. Innocent V.
1276. Adrian V.
1276. Vicedominus, died the next day.
1276. John XIX., killed by the fall of his chamber at Viterbium.
1277. Nicholas III.
1281. Martin IV.
1285. Honorius IV.
1288. Nicholas IV.
1294. Cælestine V.
1294. Boniface VIII.
1303. Benedict XI.
1305. Clement V.
1316. John XX.
1334. Benedict XII.

A. D.
1342. Clement VI.
1352. Innocent VI
1362. Urban V.
1370. Gregory XI
1378. Urban VI.
1389. Boniface IX.
1404. Innocent VII.
1406. Gregory XII., deposed.
1409. Alexander V.
1410. John XXI.
1417. Martin V
1431. Eugenius IV
1455. Calixtus III.
1458. Pius II.
1464. Paul II.
1476. Sixtus IV.
1484. Innocent VIII.
1492. Alexander VI
1503. Pius III.
1503. Julius II.
1513. Leo X.
1522. Adrian VI.
1523. Clement VII.
1534. Paul III.
1550. Julius III.
1555. Marcellus II.
1555. Paul IV.
1559. Pius IV.
1566. Pius V.
1572. Gregory XIII.
1535. Sixtus V.

A. D.
1590. Urban VII.
1590. Gregory XIV.
1591. Innocent IX.
1592. Clement VIII.
1605. Leo XI.
1605. Paul V.
1621. Gregory XV.
1623. Urban VIII.
1644. Innocent X.
1655. Alexander VII.
1667. Clement IX.
1670. Clement X.
1676. Innocent XI.
1689. Alexander VIII.
1691. Innocent XII.
1700. Clement XI.
1721. Innocent XIII.
1724. Benedict XIII.
1730. Clement XII.
1740. Benedict XIV.
1758. Clement XIII.
1769. Clement XIV., poisoned.
1775. Pius VI., February 14.
1800. Cardinal Chiaramonte elected at Venice, as Pius VII., March 13.
1823. Annibal della Genga, Leo XII., Sept. 28
1831. Cardinal Mauro Capellari, as Gregory XVI., Feb. 2.

The title of *pope* was originally given to all bishops. It was first adopted by Hygenus, A. D. 138; and Pope Boniface III. procured Phocas, emperor of the East, to confine it to the prelates of Rome, 606. By the connivance of Phocas, also, the pope's supremacy over the Christian church was established. The custom of kissing the pope's toe was introduced in 708. The first sovereign act of the popes of Rome was by Adrian I., who caused money to be coined with his name, 780. Sergius II. was the first pope who changed his name, on his election, in 844. The first pope who kept an army was Leo IX., 1054. Gregory VII. obliged Henry IV., emperor of Germany, to stand three days, in the depth of winter, barefooted, at his castle gate, to implore his pardon 1077. The pope's authority was firmly fixed in England

1079. Appeals from English tribunals to the pope were introduced 1154. Henry II. of England held the stirrup for Pope Alexander III. to mount his horse, 1161, and also for Becket, 1170. "When Louis, king of France, and Henry II. of England, met Pope Alexander III. at the castle of Torci, on the Loire, they both dismounted to receive him, and, holding each of them one of the reins of his bridle, walked on foot by his side, and conducted him in that submissive manner into the castle." Pope Adrian IV. was the only Englishman that ever obtained the tiara. His arrogance was such, that he obliged Frederick I. to prostrate himself before him, kiss his foot, hold his stirrup, and lead the white palfrey on which he rode. Celestine III. kicked the emperor Henry VI.'s crown off his head while kneeling, to show his prerogative of making and unmaking kings, 1191. The pope collected the tenths of the whole kingdom of England, 1226. Appeals to Rome from England were abolished 1533. The words "Lord Pope" were struck out of all English books 1541. The papal authority declined about 1600. Kissing the pope's toe, and other ceremonies, were abolished by Clement XIV., 1773. The pope became destitute of all political influence in Europe, 1787. Pius VI. was burnt in effigy at Paris, 1791. He made submission to the French republic, 1796, was expelled from Rome, and deposed, February 22, 1798, and died at Valence, August 19, 1799. Pius VII. was elected in exile, March 13, 1800; he crowned Napoleon, December 2, 1804; was dethroned May 13, 1809; remained a prisoner at Fontainebleau till Napoleon's overthrow; and was restored May 24, 1814.

## SWEDENBORGIANS.

BELIEVERS in the doctrines of Swedenborg are found in all the states in the Union. In Maine, New Hampshire, Massachusetts, Rhode Island, New York, Pennsylvania, Maryland, Virginia, and Ohio, are eight ordaining ministers, ten priests and teaching ministers, fifteen licentiates, and between thirty and forty societies. There are between two and three hundred towns or places in the United States where the doctrines of the New Jerusalem church are received by some portion of the people.

The number of Swedenborgians in the United States is about five thousand. The societies of this class of Christians in England are more numerous than in the United States. In Sweden they are quite numerous.

PERIODICALS. — The *New Jerusalem Magazine* is issued monthly at Boston, Mass.; the *Precursor* is issued monthly at Cincinnati, Ohio the *New Churchman* is issued quarterly at Philadelphia.

## UNITARIANS.

Of this denomination, there are about three hundred churches and congregations in the United States, and near that number of ministers. In the city of Boston it is one of the most numerous and influential classes of Christians, having eighteen societies, most of which are large and flourishing. In the Middle, Southern, and Western States their congregations are fewer, but gradually multiplying.

Periodicals. — The *Christian Examiner*, the *Monthly Miscellany*, and the *Christian Register*, are published in Boston, Mass.

A favorite project of Christian philanthropy with the Unitarians has been the "ministry to the poor" in large cities and towns. They have established such an institution in Boston, New York, Cincinnati, Louisville, Providence, and elsewhere. In Boston, three large and commodious chapels have been erected, and three ministers constantly employed, by the aid of funds obtained from individual donors and annual subscriptions from associations in the several churches of the denomination

## UNIVERSALISTS.

There are, in the United States and Territories, one United States Convention, one United States Universalist Historical Society, twelve State Conventions, fifty-nine Associations, eight hundred and seventy five societies, five hundred and fifty meeting-houses, and five hundred and forty preachers. Besides these, there are twenty-one periodicals published by the order, and twenty new books have been published within the year, besides reprints. There are also five schools in the patronage of the denomination. There is an Educational Association in Maine, a Sunday School Association in Massachusetts, a Publishing Association in Pennsylvania, a public library of fifteen hundred volumes in Ohio, and two Book Associations in Indiana and Illinois.

By adding the numbers of societies, etc., in the British Provinces, to those in the United States, there are, at present, the grand total of one General Convention, twelve State Conventions, fifty-five Associations, eight hundred and ninety-five societies, five hundred and fifty-six meeting-houses, and five hundred and forty-six preachers.

Periodicals. — *Gospel Banner and Christian Pilot*, Augusta, Me. *Eastern Rose-Bud*, Portland, Me.; *Universalist and Family Visitor*

Contoocookville, N. H.; *Universalist Watchman*, Montpelier, Vt. *Trumpet and Universalist Magazine*, Boston, Mass.; *Christian Freeman and Family Visitor*, Boston, Mass.; *Universalist and Ladies Repository*, Boston, Mass.; *Light of Zion, and Sabbath School Contributor*, Boston, Mass.; *Star and Palladium*, Lowell, Mass.; *Gospel Messenger*, Providence, R. I.; *Universalist*, Middletown, Ct.; *New York Christian Messenger*, New York city; *Universalist Union*, New York city; *Evangelical Magazine and Gospel Advocate*, Utica, N. Y. *Western Luminary*, Rochester, N. Y.; *The Nazarene*, Philadelphia, Pa. *Christian Warrior*, Richmond, Va.; *Southern Universalist*, Columbus Ga. *Star in the West*, Cincinnati, Ohio; *Christian Teacher*, Lafayette, Ind. · *Better Covenant*, Rockford, Ill.

# MISSIONARY STATISTICS.

We have been much assisted in our missionary statistics by the kindness of the secretaries of the several Missionary Boards, and by permission of the proprietor, Mr. F. Rand, for the use of his valuable Missionary Chart, prepared with great care, in 1840, by the Reverend Messrs. Jefferson Hascall and Daniel Wise.

Those of the Congregationalists, Baptists, Methodists, and Episcopalians, are brought down to 1841, and are quite accurate; but the efforts of some of the other denominations in this great and glorious cause are not fully stated, as some of the items have not been reported.

## FIRST PROTESTANT MISSIONS.

The first Protestant mission on record was undertaken in 1559, by Michael, who was sent into Lapland by Gustavus Vasa, king of Sweden.

John Eliot commenced the first mission to the Indians at *Nonan tum*, now Newton, Massachusetts, in 1646. This mission gave rise to a society in England for the propagation of the gospel in New England, and to the formation of several other missionary stations; so that, in 1696, there were thirty Indian churches in New England.

In 1705, Messrs. Ziegenbalg and Plutcho, under the auspices of Frederick IV., king of Denmark, commenced a mission at Tranquebar, in South Hindoostan, which was very successful. Its fruits continue to the present time.

In 1728, a mission was begun by Schultze, at Madras, under the patronage of the Christian Knowledge Society. In the following thirty-three years, fourteen hundred and seventy converts united with the church.

## MORAVIAN MISSIONS.

The Moravians trace their origin to the ninth century, when the king of Moravia united with the Greek church.

West Indian Mission. — The Moravians commenced their mission on the Island of St. Thomas in 1732. Its commencement was occasioned by a conversation between a negro, named Anthony, and some servants of Count Zinzendorf. The negro said he had a sister at St. Thomas, who was deeply anxious to be instructed about religion. This remark was repeated to one of "the *brethren*," named Leonard Dober. He determined to visit St. Thomas, "even," as he said, "if he were obliged to sell himself for a slave to effect his purpose." Dober went; and though, for a time, little good was effected, yet, in 1736, the Lord poured out his spirit, and many of the slaves were awakened. There are now two stations on this island.

In 1734, they began their mission on the Island of St. Croix. It was soon abandoned, but was reëstablished in 1740. In 1754, missions were commenced on the Islands of St. Jan and Jamaica; in 1756, at Antigua; in 1765, at Barbadoes; in 1777, at St. Christopher's; and at Tobago in 1790.

Greenland Mission. — This was commenced in 1733, at New Herrnhut, or Lusatia, by Matthew and Christian Stach, when the congregation of the brethren at home amounted to but six hundred members. They persevered through cold, hunger, and discouragement, though for five years they had no conversions. Greenland is *now* a Christian country.

North American Indian Missions. — These were begun in Georgia, 1735, among the Creeks, at the instigation of Count Zinzendorf. It was followed by numerous other stations, many of which have since become extinct.

South American Missions. — Surinam, a Dutch settlement in Guiana, was the scene of their first operations here, about 1735 or 1738. They began on the invitation of a planter. Several other settlements were attempted, but were subsequently abandoned, for various causes. In 1767, they commenced a prosperous station at Paramaribo.

Labrador Missions. — Supposing that a natural affinity subsisted between this people and the Greenlanders, the brethren commenced their labors here in 1752. This attempt failed; but, in 1770, a settlement was effected at Nain, by the agency of Messrs. Haven, Drachart, and Jensen.

South African Mission. — George Schmidt was the father of this mission. He commenced it in 1737; but it was afterwards abandoned for about fifty years, until, in 1792, a permanent settlement was effected at Gnadenthal, one hundred and thirty-five miles east of Cape Town.

Note. — The brethren have also had missions, at different periods, in Asiatic Russia, Egypt, Persia, Lapland, Guinea, Algiers, Ceylon, and the Nicobar Islands; all of which, for various causes, have been abandoned.

SUMMARY.

In the year 1840, the Moravians had. in the afore-mentioned places and in South Africa, forty-seven stations and out-stations, one hundred and ninety-seven missionaries and assistants, seventeen thousand seven hundred and three communicants, and fifty-seven thousand two hundred and fifty-five souls under their care.

## LONDON MISSIONARY SOCIETY.

THE extensive and splendid missions of this board originated with the Rev. David Bogue, while on a visit to London. From his suggestions, the society was formed, in 1795, by several ministers of various denominations.

SOUTH SEA ISLANDS.—The society commenced their labors among these isles by sending out thirty-six missionaries, in 1796, who arrived safely, and commenced their duties at Otaheite, Tongataboo, and St. Christina, in March, 1797. Subsequently, they spread their influence over nearly all the islands of the Pacific Ocean. These missions have been eminently successful.

NEW SOUTH WALES.—This mission was begun by the labors of Mr. Threlkeld, in 1826, in Bahtabee, on Lake Macquaire.

SOUTH AFRICAN MISSIONS.—The success of the missions in the islands of the Pacific and South Seas, turned their attention to this dark land. Dr. Vanderkemp, who was their first laborer, began his labors on the River Keis Kamma, in Caffraria, in 1799. In 1801, he removed to Graff Reinet, and preached to the Hottentots in that vicinity. These missions afterwards spread very widely among the Caffres and Hottentots.

EAST INDIAN MISSIONS.—The society's missions in this most interesting quarter of the globe were commenced at Calcutta and Chinsura, by the Rev. Mr. Forsyth, in 1798. Subsequently, their stations spread over Northern and Peninsular India, India beyond the Ganges, into China, Siam, and some of the Asiatic Isles.

GUIANA AND WEST INDIES.—At the request of a pious Dutch planter, Mr. Wray was sent to Demerara, in Guiana, in 1807. This was the beginning of the society's operations in South America.

OTHER MISSIONS.—Beside these, are the European and Mediterranean islands missions, which, though of recent date, are promising in their aspects.

EDUCATION.—This society has several presses distributed over the vast field occupied by their agents, by means of which millions of pages are annually scattered among the people. They publish tracts parts of the Scriptures, &c. &c. They have also upwards of four hundred native assistants, which are not mentioned in the following summary.

SUMMARY.

From the best accounts we can obtain, this society had, in 1840, in Asia, the South Sea Islands, Africa, Guiana, and in Europe, about five hundred and fifty missionary stations and out-stations, one hundred and sixty-four missionaries, five thousand communicants, and about twenty-five thousand scholars.

## AMERICAN BOARD OF FOREIGN MISSIONS.

Missions in Asia. — The news of the success of English missionary enterprise, seconded by the zeal and influence of S. J. Mills, originated the germ of the invaluable labors of this board, which was organized in 1810. Their first missions were in Asia. Bombay was the scene of their first labors, in the year 1813, and Messrs. Nott, Newell, and Hall, their first missionaries. From Bombay they extended their influence to Ceylon, in 1816; to China, and South-eastern Asia, and to Siam, in 1830.

Mediterranean Missions. — These missions were begun by sending out Messrs. Parsons and Fisk on a voyage of research. The first station occupied was Beyroot, in Syria, in 1823. To this, stations at Malta, in Greece, at Constantinople, &c., have been added.

Missions at the Sandwich Islands. — A special providence marked the commencement of these missions. Two boys, named Obookiah and Hopu, were, at their own request, brought to America. This gave rise to a train of interesting circumstances, which led to the commencement of the mission, in 1820, by Messrs. Bingham, Thurston, and others. Vast success has attended this mission, especially of late.

North American Indian Missions. — These were commenced in 1816, among the Cherokees, by the Rev. C. Kingsbury. The Choctaws, the Chickasaws, the Osages, and other tribes, have since shared the labors of the board. The late unhappy removal of the Cherokee nation has done much towards the prostration of missionary success among that interesting but deeply-injured tribe.

Missions in Africa. — The efforts of the board in this quarter of the globe are of recent date. Only seven years have elapsed since their commencement. Some native towns on the western coast, and a numerous aboriginal tribe called the Zulus, on the south-east shore, are the chief objects of their labors at present. This field is considered very promising, and it is confidently believed that its occupation will be one effectual aid in the great work of regenerating that darkened, enslaved, and degraded continent.

In 1841, this board had missions to the Zulus in South Africa, the Grebos in West Africa, to Greece, to Turkey, Syria, the Nestorians of Persia, the Independent Nestorians, the Persian Mahometans, to the Mahrattas in Western India, to Madras and Madura in Southern India, to Ceylon, Siam, China Singapore, Borneo, and to the Sandwich Islands.

They have missions to the Cherokee Indians, the Choctaws, Paw nees, to the Oregon Indians, the Sioux, Ojibwas, Stockbridge Indians, New York Indians, and to the Abenaquis.

### SUMMARY OF FOREIGN MISSIONS.

The number of missions in this department is seventeen; of stations, sixty-one; of ordained missionaries, one hundred and eleven, five of whom are also physicians; of physicians, seven; of teachers, eight; of secular superintendents, two; of printers, eleven; of bookbinders, one; of female helpers, married and unmarried, one hundred and thirty-nine; — making a total of laborers beyond sea from this country of two hundred and eighty. To these add four native preachers, and one hundred and thirty-five other native helpers, and the number of laborers who are employed and supported by the board in the missions beyond sea, is four hundred and nineteen.

### SUMMARY OF INDIAN MISSIONS.

Among the Indian nations, there are twenty-five stations; twenty-five missionaries, two of whom are physicians; two other physicians, five teachers; ten other male, and fifty-nine female, assistant missionaries; three native preachers; and three other native assistants; — total, one hundred and seven

### GENERAL SUMMARY.

The number of the missions in 1841 was twenty-six; stations, eighty five; and ordained missionaries, one hundred and thirty-six, ten of whom were physicians. There were nine physicians not preachers, thirteen teachers, twelve printers and bookbinders, and twelve other male and one hundred and ninety-eight female assistant missionaries. The whole number of laborers from this country was three hundred and eighty-one, or sixteen more than were reported in 1840. To these we must add seven native preachers, and one hundred and thirty-eight native helpers, which made the whole number five hundred and twenty-six, thirty-nine more than in 1840. Nine ordained missionaries, three male and seventeen female assistant missionaries, have been sent forth during the year.

The number of mission churches was fifty-nine, containing nineteen thousand eight hundred and forty-two members, of whom four thousand three hundred and fifty were received the year before.

There were fifteen printing establishments, twenty-nine presses five type-founderies, and fifty founts of type in the native languages. The printing for the year was about fifty million pages; the amount of printing from the beginning is about two hundred and ninety million pages. Twenty-four thousand copies of the *Missionary Herald* are now published monthly, and sixty-five thousand copies of the *Day-spring*, a monthly paper, are also issued.

Seven of the thirty-four boarding-schools have received the name of seminaries, and these contain four hundred and ninety-nine boys; the other twenty-seven contain two hundred and fifty three boys and three hundred and seventy-eight girls; — making a total of boarding scholars of one thousand one hundred and thirty. The number of free schools was four hundred and ninety, containing about twenty-three thousand pupils.

The receipts have been two hundred and thirty-five thousand one hundred and eighty-nine dollars, and the expenditures two hundred and sixty eight thousand, nine hundred and fifteen dollars.

## PRESBYTERIAN BOARD OF FOREIGN MISSIONS.

UNTIL within a few years, this body of Christians united with the American board in their operations among the heathen. A distinct society, under the name of the *Western Foreign Missionary Society*, was formed in 1831, by the synod of Pittsburg, which was merged into the present board in 1837.

Three of the missions of the board were begun by this society, namely, the Western Africa, the Hindoostan, and Iowa and Sac missions.

This board is intending to reënforce its missions, and to occupy several new stations, as soon as the requisite arrangements can be made. Its main efforts will be directed towards Hindoostan, where it has now two presses in active coöperation with its missionaries. This denomination of Christians have the following missions: — Iowa and Sac Indians; Chippewa and Ottawa Indians; Texas; Western Africa, *Kroos;* Chinese, *Singapore;* Siam; Northern India, *Lodiana,* Allahabad, Furrukhabad.

### SUMMARY.

This church has now under her care in the foreign field, fifty-seven laborers sent from her own bosom, twenty-three of whom are ministers of the gospel; besides eight native assistants, some of them men of learning, all of them hopefully pious, and in different stages of prep aration and trial for the missionary work among their own benighted people. Through the mission stations occupied by these brethren, the church is brought in direct contact with five different heathen nations, containing two thirds of the whole human race. Annual expenditure about sixty-five thousand dollars.

The Presbyterian Domestic Board of Missions employs or aids two hundred and sixty missionaries and agents, who have under their charge about twenty thousand communicants, and twenty thousand Sabbath school scholars. Annual disbursements about thirty-five thousand dollars.

## ENGLISH BAPTIST MISSIONARY SOCIETY.

East Indies.—A mission was commenced at Serampore in 1793. The English Baptists were just awakening to a sense of their responsibility for the conversion of the world, when Dr. Thomas arrived in London, to solicit missionary aid for Hindoostan. The society took him under their patronage, and sent him back in company with Dr. Cary. After laboring successfully in various places, in 1800 Dr. Cary removed to Serampore, which thenceforward became a central station.

West Indian Missions.—In 1814, a mulatto preacher, named Baker, requested this society to send a missionary to Jamaica. In compliance with this request, Mr. I. Rowe was sent out, who, after laboring with pleasing success, died; and, in 1815, the society sent out Mr. Compere and assistants, who established a mission in Kingston. This was the origin of the Baptist missions in the West Indies.

South American Mission.—On a representation to the society, that much good might be done among the negro population and the Indians in and around Honduras, in the Bay of Mexico, the society, in 1822, sent out Mr. J. Bourne, who succeeded in establishing a church and congregation.

South African Mission.—In 1831, Rev. W. Davies was sent to Graham's Town, at the urgent solicitation of some Baptists, resident at that place.

### SUMMARY.

This society have, in Asia, the Asiatic Islands, West Indies, South America, and South Africa, one hundred and twenty-nine stations and out-stations, one hundred and thirty-four missionaries and assistants, twenty-two thousand four hundred and eighty-eight communicants, and seventeen thousand seven hundred and thirty-five scholars. This statement does not contain the full amount of their labors to the present year.

## AMERICAN BAPTIST BOARD OF FOREIGN MISSIONS.

Missions in Asia.— Rev. A. Judson may be said to be the father of Baptist missions in this country, and, indeed, of the missionary labors of this society. It was his conversion to the principles of the Baptists, while a missionary of the American board in India, that roused them to action. He commenced his labors under discouraging circumstances, at Rangoon, in the Burman empire, 1813. Since then, the operations of this board have become very extensive, embracing immense portions of the Burman empire, Siam, &c. Asia is their principal mission field, and they have laid sure foundations for the evangelization of many parts of that benighted clime.

Indian Missions.—An impression, made, no doubt, by divine influence, of the importance of missions to this people, led, in 1817, to the appointment of J. M. Peck and J. E. Welch to be missionaries to the North American Indians. J. M. Peck commenced their first Indian mission among the Cherokees in 1818. Many tribes are now embraced by the labors of the board, and although the progress of truth has been slow among the "red men," yet the board have cause to rejoice over their Indian missions.

African Mission.—This mission was commenced by the offer of L. Cary and C. Teage, colored men, to become the messengers of the churches in this work. They commenced their duties, in 1821, at Liberia, where the board continues its efforts for the redemption of Africa, with some success, chiefly among the Bassas.

European Missions.—These missions were commenced in 1832. Professor Chase was sent to explore the kingdom of France, and the Rev. J. C. Rostan commenced a course of evangelical demonstrations at Paris; since which, Germany and Greece have shared the attention of the board. These are missions of the first importance

### GENERAL SUMMARY.

This board have missions as follow:—In North America, to the Ojibwas, near Lake Superior; the Ottawas, in Michigan; Oneidas, in New York; Otoes, near the junction of Missouri and Platte Rivers; Shawanoes, including the Delawares, Putawatomies, and Western Ottawas, in the Indian Territory; Cherokees, Creeks, and Choctaws, in the Indian Territory. In Europe, they have missions to France, Germany, Denmark, and Greece;—to the Bassas, in West Africa;—in Asia, to Burmah and the Karens; to Siam and China, Arracan, Asam, and to the Teloogoos.

The number of Indian missions is eight; stations and out-stations, sixteen; missionaries and assistant missionaries, twenty-eight; native assistants, ten; churches, sixteen; baptisms reported the last year, two hundred and seventy-one; present number of church members, one thousand three hundred and twenty-four; schools, seven; scholars, one hundred and ninety-two.

The number of European missions is three; stations and out-stations, twenty; missionaries and assistant missionaries, seven; native preachers and assistants, twenty-three; churches, twenty-seven; baptisms the past year, one hundred and eighty-seven; church members, five hundred and fifty-eight.

In the mission to West Africa there are two stations, five missionaries and assistant missionaries, one native assistant, two churches of twenty-five members, and two schools containing eighty-five scholars.

The number of the Asiatic missions is eight, stations and out-stations, sixty-two; missionaries and assistant missionaries, fifty-nine; native assistants, seventy-seven; churches, thirty-two; baptisms the past year, three hundred and seventeen; church members, one thousand eight hundred and two; schools, thirty-five, scholars, five hundred and sixty.

Grand total, twenty missions, one hundred stations and out-stations, ninety-nine missionaries and assistant missionaries, one hundred and eleven native preachers and assistants, seventy-seven churches, seven hundred and eighty baptisms the past year, more than three thousand seven hundred members of mission churches, forty-four schools, and eight hundred and seventy-seven scholars.

The annual expenditure of the board is about eighty thousand dollars.

## FREE-WILL BAPTISTS.

This flourishing class of Christians have not, until recently, directed their efforts to a foreign field. They now occupy one station in Orissa, where they have two missionaries with their ladies. Two other missionaries are about being located, for which purpose funds are now provided.

## EPISCOPAL MISSIONS.

The Church of England has been actively engaged in missionary operations since the year 1698, when the "Society for Promoting Christian Knowledge" was formed. In 1701, the "Society for the Propagation of the Gospel in Foreign Parts" was instituted. The "Church Missionary Society" was established in 1800. These societies are still in active and vigorous operation They have missions in every quarter of the globe, and their annual expenditures, for the propagation of the Gospel, amount to about one million three hundred and seventeen thousand three hundred and fifty-six dollars.

The Episcopal Church in the United States established a *Domestic and Foreign Missionary Society* in 1820; and the General Convention of 1835 resolved, That the Church itself was the missionary society and that every member of the Church, by baptism, was, of course, bound to support her missions. The missionary field was declared to be THE WORLD; *domestic-missions* being those established within the territory of the United States, and *foreign missions* those without that territory. At each triennial meeting of the General Convention, a Board of Missions, consisting of about one hundred members, is selected from the different dioceses. This Board has the general supervision of all the missionary operations of the Church, and meets annually, or oftener, if necessary.

There are two standing committees of this Board, — the *Committee for Domestic Missions* and the *Committee for Foreign Missions*, to whom, during the recess of the Board, the care and management of the missions is confided. This Society now has under its charge one hundred and forty-five domestic, and twelve foreign stations, employing eighty-five domestic and eleven foreign missionaries, and also eighteen teachers and assistants in the foreign stations.

The expenditures of this Board, for the year 1841, were sixty-one thousand five hundred and eighty-six dollars and thirty-seven cents. This Society has missionary stations in Athens, Crete, Constantinople, China, (Maca,) Cape Palmas and other stations in Western Africa, and in Texas.

## SOCIETY FOR PROPAGATING THE GOSPEL AMONG THE INDIANS AND OTHERS.

THIS society derived its origin among the Puritans, in England, in 1648. The charter under which it now acts was granted by the legislature of Massachusetts, in 1687. Its list of past and present members in 1840, comprised one hundred and twenty-five names of the most eminent divines, jurists, and laymen in Massachusetts, in which state the operations of the society are chiefly confined. The funds of this society, in 1840, amounted to thirty-six thousand three hundred and eighty-seven dollars, the income of which is annually expended for the "propagation of the gospel" among the needy and destitute.

In conformity with the spirit and design of this ancient and venerable society, all measures in any degree of a party or sectarian character, are scrupulously avoided.

## WESLEYAN OR ENGLISH METHODIST MISSIONARY SOCIETY.

Scarcely had Mr. Wesley raised the standard of Methodism in England, before he turned his attention to the wants of other lands America presenting a vast field for missionary labor, he sent over Richard Boardman and Joseph Pilmore, in 1769. These were the first Methodist missionaries. From their labors the Methodist Episcopal church in the United States gradually came into being. Dr. Coke was preëminently useful in establishing missions in various places This society was organized in 1817.

West Indies. — A peculiar providence marked the commencement of this mission. Dr. Coke, with three preachers, was proceeding to Nova Scotia, in September, 1786, but was driven, by stress of weather, to Antigua. Finding a number of serious persons there, he preached Jesus to them, and by his labors laid the foundation for extensive missions.

British North America. — About 1779, several Methodist emigrants were the means of awakening many souls. Among these was Mr. Black, who, after laboring for some time with zeal and success, was appointed the superintendent of the mission in British North America. This mission embraces Nova Scotia, New Brunswick, Canada, Newfoundland, and Honduras.

Missions in Asia. — The plan of establishing missions in Asia originated with Dr. Coke; and, in 1813, he sailed, with Messrs. Harvard, Clough, Ault, Erskine, Squance, and Lynch, for Ceylon. Unfortunately, he died on the passage. The brethren, after many trials, reached Ceylon, and commenced their labors at Jaffna, Batticaloa, and Matura. From Ceylon, the society directed its attention to continental India, where their labors have become very extensive.

Missions in South Africa. — These missions were begun in 1816, by Rev. Barnabas Shaw, among the Namaquas, a tribe of Hottentots. These missions have subsequently spread over large portions of this benighted land.

Missions in the South Seas. — These missions include the Friendly Isles, New Zealand, New South Wales, &c. They were commenced at the latter place, in 1815, by Mr. Leigh, who began his duties and labors at Sydney, with favorable auspices and good success.

Missions in the Mediterranean. — These were commenced in Gibraltar, in 1804, by Mr. McMullen, who died a few days after beginning his labors. The mission was then suspended until 1808, when Mr. William Griffith was appointed to its charge. Besides this mission, the Methodists have stations at Malta, Alexandria, and Zante.

Missions in Europe. — These missions embrace the labors of the society in Sweden, France, Germany, Ireland, and the Norman and

Shetland Isles. Notwithstanding many obstacles, arising from intolerance, ignorance, or superstition, the good work progresses at these missions.

### SUMMARY.

In 1840, this society had, in the West Indies, fifty missionary stations; in British North America, eighty-four stations; in Asia, twenty-two, in the South Seas, twenty-five; in Africa, thirty-one; and in Europe, forty-two stations. In all these countries the society had two hundred and fifty-four stations, six hundred and twenty-three missionaries and teachers, seventy-two thousand seven hundred and twenty-four communicants, and fifty-six thousand five hundred and twenty-two scholars

## MISSIONS OF THE METHODIST EPISCOPAL CHURCH.

### I. Foreign Missions.

1. *The Liberia Mission* was commenced in 1833, by the Rev. M. B Cox, who, in a few short months after, was called to his eternal reward. His dying language was, "Though a thousand fall, Africa must not be given up." Five other missionaries have fallen in the same field. The Liberia mission now includes an annual conference of seventeen preachers, all colored, except the superintendent and the two brethren recently sent out. It has a membership of nearly one thousand, of whom one hundred and fifty are *natives.* There are thirteen day schools, in which from five hundred to six hundred children are instructed, (of whom about forty are natives, preparing for future usefulness,) fourteen churches, eight mission-houses, three school-houses, one academy, (a stone building,) and one printing-office. Total of missionaries, male and female, twenty-four.

2. *The Oregon Mission.*—This mission was commenced by Rev. Messrs. Jason and Daniel Lee, and now numbers twenty-one missionaries, including preachers, teachers, physicians, farmers, mechanics, &c. The greater part of these were sent out in 1840, making, with their wives and children, about fifty souls—the largest missionary expedition going, at one time, from this country. They are now laying the foundations of their future work.

3. *The Texas Mission* was commenced by Rev. Dr. Ruter, assisted by two young preachers, who accompanied him to that country in 1837. An annual conference was established in this mission field in 1840, which now includes three regular presiding elders' districts, and eighteen stations and circuits. It numbers twenty-three travelling preachers, thirty-six local preachers, (i. e., lay preachers, who support themselves, and preach as they have opportunity) and two thousand

seven hundred and ninety-five members. There is a college at Rutersville.

II. Domestic Missions.

1 *German Missions.* — The first German mission was established in Cincinnati, in 1835, by Rev. William Nast. There are now seventeen German missions, containing about one thousand members, in the states of Ohio, Pennsylvania, Kentucky, Indiana, Illinois, Missouri, and New York. A German paper is published at Cincinnati, called *The Christian Apologist*, having eleven hundred subscribers.

2. *Indian Missions* — There are eighteen missions, and one manual labor school, among the Indians located within the bounds of Rock River, Michigan, Holston, Missouri, Mississippi, and Arkansas conferences. These now include two thousand six hundred and seventeen native church members.

3. *Missions among the Slaves.* — There are forty-seven of these missions in successful operation, including twelve thousand three hundred and ninety-three in church fellowship.

4. *Missions in Destitute Portions of the Country.* — There are one hundred and eight domestic missions of this kind, which embrace twenty-three thousand nine hundred and fifty-eight church members.

AGGREGATE.

Foreign missions — sixty-three missionaries, four thousand three hundred and seventeen church members. — Domestic missions — one hundred and seventy-eight missionaries, forty-one thousand church members. — Total — two hundred and forty-one missionaries, forty-five thousand three hundred and seventeen church members.

The whole amount of missionary money collected for the year ending April 20, 1842, is one hundred and five thousand two hundred and eighty-one dollars; expended, one hundred and forty-nine thousand and sixty-five dollars.

## SEVENTH-DAY BAPTIST MISSIONARY SOCIETY.

The operations of this society are confined to the occasional assistance of destitute churches at home. It employs six agents and missionaries. Its receipts for 1838 were one hundred and eighty-six dollars.

The Seventh-Day Baptists have also a *Society for the Promotion of Christianity among the* Jews, at home and abroad. It was organized in 1838.

## FRENCH PROTESTANT MISSIONARY SOCIETY.

This society was formed in 1822, at the house of S. V. S. Wilder Esq , an American merchant, then residing in Paris It has a seminary for the preparation of students. In 1829, it sent out three missionaries to their first field of labor, among the French emigrants of South Africa, and among the surrounding tribes. It had, in 1839, in South Africa, seven stations, twelve missionaries, about one hundred converts, and five hundred scholars.

## NETHERLANDS MISSIONARY SOCIETY.

The principal labors of this society are expended in Dutch India and in Siam. In Dutch India they have eighteen missionaries, at thirteen stations. Of the success of this society, little is known in this country.

## SCOTTISH MISSIONARY SOCIETY.

This society was established, in 1796, by the members of the Episcopal church in Edinburgh. It has had missions in Tartary, Asia, and the West Indies. Some of them are still sustained.

## GERMAN MISSIONARY SOCIETY.

This society was preceded in its formation by the Missionary Seminary at Bâsle, in 1816. In 1821, the Missionary Society was formed by the various pastors and churches of the surrounding country, under he encouragement of Dr. Steinkopff. The scene of their first labors was among the German colonies in Asiatic Russia, in 1822, when seven missionaries were sent to prepare the way of the Lord in that important field. Others followed, and their mission was beginning to promise great results, when, in 1837, by a *ukase* from the emperor of the Russias, they were required to abandon their work.

In 1828, they commenced a mission at Liberia. Death became their opponent here, and seven of their missionaries died through the sickliness of the climate. Two missionaries are still laboring in that field

They have seven missionaries in Hindoostan, who occupy two stations, — Mangalore and Dharwar. They expect to establish another, shortly, at Hoobly, for which five missionaries have been sent out There are several schools, and one seminary, connected with these stations.

## CHURCH OF SCOTLAND MISSIONS.

These missions appear to be of recent date. Most of their labor is expended on Asia.

Calcutta, Bombay, Poonah, and Madras, are their principal stations Their missionaries devote a large portion of their efforts to the promotion of education.

## RHENISH MISSIONARY SOCIETY

The successes of the London Missionary Society inspired the pious inhabitants of the valley of the Rhine with an ardent wish to imitate their zeal. Under this impulse, a society was formed, in 1828, at Barmen, on the Rhine, by a union of the previously-formed societies of Barmen, Elberfield, Cologne, and Wesel.

Messrs. Gottlieb, Leipold, Zahn, and Wurmb, were among their earliest missionaries. Wurmb was formerly a soldier. He fought in the battle of Leipsic as lieutenant, and obtained two medals of honor. He next studied medicine, and gained a diploma; and when he became a subject of religious influence, he laid all his honors and learning at the foot of the cross. He began his labors at Wupperthal, in South Africa, in which country are several missionaries, and four stations.

## MISSIONS OF THE ROMAN CATHOLIC CHURCH.

We regret that it is not in our power to record the missionary efforts of the Roman Catholics. Suffice it to say that their missions extend to all countries, and that they are ardent in their zeal, indefatigable in their labors, and unsparing in their expenditures, in the propagation of the doctrines of this ancient church.

## JEWS' MISSIONARY SOCIETY

This association was formed in England, in 1808. It is patronized chiefly by ministers and members of the established church. It has forty-nine missionaries and agents, who occupy twenty-three stations in Asia and Europe. Of these missionaries, twenty-four are Jewish converts. Its receipts in 1839 were upwards of eighty thousand dollars. Three or four thousand Jews have been converted, by this and other instrumentalities, within a few years.

In England, there is an institution for the purpose of receiving Jewish converts, and teaching them a trade. A considerable number have enjoyed its privileges.

## INDIANS.

As great efforts are making, by almost all classes of Christians to spread the benign influence of the gospel among the red men on our borders, it may not be amiss to state their locations, numbers, &c. &c.

Mr. McCoy, in his valuable "Annual Register of Indian Affairs," published at Shawanoe, in the Indian Territory, makes many important statements respecting this highly-interesting people.

He says that the number of Indians north of Mexico may be fairly estimated at one million eight hundred thousand. He estimates the population of the tribes east and west of the Mississippi as follows: —

TRIBES EAST OF MISSISSIPPI RIVER.

|  |  |
|---|---|
| Indians in New England and New York, | 4,715 |
| Indians from New York, at Green Bay, | 725 |
| Wyandots, in Ohio and Michigan, | 623 |
| Miamies, | 1,200 |
| Winnebagoes, | 4,591 |
| Chippewas, | 6,793 |
| Ottawas and Chippewas of Lake Michigan, | 5,300 |
| Chippewas, Ottawas, and Putawatomies, | 8,000 |
| Putawatomies, | 1,400 |
| Menominees, | 4,200 |
| Creeks, | 22,668 |
| Cherokees, | 10,000 |
| Chickasaws, | 5,429 |
| Choctaws, | 3,500 |
| Seminoles, | 2,420 |
| Appalachicolas, | 340 |
| Total, | 81,904 |

TRIBES WEST OF MISSISSIPPI RIVER.

|  |  |
|---|---|
| Sioux, | 27,500 |
| Iowas, | 1,200 |
| Sauks of Missouri, | 500 |
| Sauks and Foxes, | 6,400 |
| Assinaboines, | 8,000 |
| Crees, | 3,000 |
| Camanches, | 7,000 |
| Crows, | 4,500 |
| Arrepahas, Kiawas, &c., | 1,400 |
| Caddoes, | 800 |
| Snake and other tribes within the Rocky Mountains, | 20,000 |
| Gros-ventres, | 3,000 |
| Arrekaras, | 3,000 |
| Cheyennes, | 2,000 |
| Minatarees, | 1,500 |
| Mandans, | 1,500 |
| Black Feet, | 30,000 |
| Tribes west of Rocky Mountains, | 80,000 |
| Total, | 201,300 |

The above tribes, although within the territory of the United States, are not within what is commonly called the Indian Territory.

Mr. McCoy states the names and numbers of the indigenous and emigrant tribes within the Indian Territory, so called, as follow: —

### INDIGENOUS TRIBES.

|  |  |  |  |
|---|---|---|---|
| Osage, | 5,510 | Pawnee, | 10,000 |
| Kauzau, or Kansas, | 1,684 | Puncah, | 800 |
| Otoe and Missouria, | 1,600 | Quapau, | 450 |
| Omaha, | 1,400 | Total | 21,444 |

### EMIGRANT TRIBES.

|  |  |  |  |
|---|---|---|---|
| Choctaw, | 15,000 | Shawanoe of Kauzau River, | 764 |
| Cherokee, | 4,000 | Delaware, | 856 |
| Creek, | 3,600 | Kickapoo, | 603 |
| Seneca and Shawanoe of Neosho, | 462 | Putawatomie, | 444 |
| Wea, | 225 | | |
| Piankasha, | 119 | Emigrant, | 26,289 |
| Peoria and Kaskaskias, | 135 | Indigenous, | 21,444 |
| Ottawa, | 81 | Total, | 47,733 |

Among the population of the emigrant tribes are included thirteen hundred and fifty negro slaves.

Mr. McCoy estimates that, of the one million eight hundred thousand Indians in North America, about seventy thousand may be classed with civilized man, having in greater or less degrees advanced towards civilization.

By the Indian Territory is meant the country within the following limits, viz.: Beginning on Red River, on the Mexican boundary, and as far west of the state of Arkansas as the country is habitable; thence down Red River, eastwardly, along the Mexican boundary to Arkansas; thence northwardly, along the line of Arkansas, to the state of Missouri; thence north, along its western line, to Missouri River; thence up Missouri River to Puncah River; thence westerly as far as the country is habitable; thence southwardly to the place of beginning.

# BIOGRAPHICAL SKETCHES

OF THE

FATHERS OF THE REFORMATION, FOUNDERS OF SECTS, AND OF OTHER DISTINGUISHED INDIVIDUALS MENTIONED IN THIS VOLUME.

---

## JOHN WICKLIFFE,

a celebrated doctor, professor of divinity at Oxford, and deservedly considered as the forerunner of Luther in the reformation. He was born at Wickliffe, in Yorkshire, about 1324, and educated at Queen's College, and afterwards at Merton, and in 1361 raised to the mastership of Baliol College. In 1365, he was made, by the scholars, head of Canterbury Hall, just founded at Oxford by Archbishop Islip; but his elevation was opposed by the monks, and Langham, the next primate; and the pope, to whom the dispute was referred, displaced him and his secular associates. Thus disgraced by violence, he retired to his living at Lutterworth, in Leicestershire, meditating revenge against the authors of his unjust privation. In the works of Marsilius of Padua, and other bold writers, he found ample room to indulge his opposition; and, well aware of the popularity of attacking a foreign power, which overawed the throne, and submitted the industry and the revenues of the kingdom to its own avaricious views, he loudly inveighed against the errors and the encroachments of the Romish church. His writings alarmed the clergy, and a council was assembled at Lambeth, by Archbishop Sudbury, 1377, and Wickliffe summoned to give an account of his doctrines. He appeared before it, accompanied by the duke of Lancaster, then in power; and he made so able a defence, that he was dismissed without condemnation. His acquittal, however, displeased the pope, Gregory XI., who directed his emissaries to seize the offending heretic, or, if he were protected by the great and powerful of the kingdom, to cite him to Rome, to answer in person before the sovereign pontiff. In consequence of this, a second council assembled at Lambeth, and the nineteen propositions, which the pope had declared heretical, were so ably vindicated by the eloquence of the undaunted reformer, that his judges, afraid of offending the nobles, or of exciting a commotion among the people, who loudly supported the cause of their champion, permitted him to depart in safety, and enjoined on him silence in matters of religion and of controversy. Undismayed by the power of his enemies, Wickliffe continued to preach his doctrines, which were now more universally spread; and a third council, therefore, assembled, under Courtnay, the primate, 1382, and twenty-four propositions of the reformer were condemned as heretical, and fourteen as erroneous. The severity of the church was, at the suggestion of the pope, and the concurrence of the weak Richard II., directed with effect against the supporters of the new heresy; but, while some of his followers suffered punishment for their adherence to his principles, Wickliffe unhappily died at Lutterworth, 1384, at a time when nothing was wanting to emancipate the English nation from the tyranny of Rome, but the boldness, perseverance, and eloquence, of a popular leader. Of the several works which he wrote, his Trialogus is almost the only one which has been printed. The noble struggle which Wickliffe had made against the gigantic power of Rome was almost forgotten after his death, till Martin Luther arose to follow his steps, and to establish his doctrines on a foundation which will last till Christianity is no more. The memory of Wickliffe was branded with ignominy by the impotent Papists, and by the order of the council of Constance, whose cruelties towards John Huss and Jerome of Prague are so well known, the illustrious reformer was declared to have died an obstinate heretic; and his bones were therefore dug up from holy ground, and contemptuously burnt.

---

## JEROME OF PRAGUE,

the celebrated lay reformer, was born at Prague, about the year 1370. Very little is extant relative to the early part of his life; but he was very eager in the pursuit of knowledge, and spent his youth in the universities of Prague, Paris, Heidelberg, Cologne, and Oxford. At the latter university, he became acquainted with the works of Wickliffe, translated them into his native language, professed himself, on his return to Prague, to be an open favorer of him, and attached himself to the Reformed in Bohemia, over whom Huss presided. Before the council of Constance, Jerome was cited on the 17th of April, 1415, when Huss was confined at that place. On his arrival, he found that he could not render any assistance to Huss, and therefore thought it prudent to retire; and, on behalf of Huss, he wrote to the emperor. At Kirsaw, Jerome was seized by an officer of the duke of Sulzbach, who immediately wrote to the council concerning him, and they directed him to send his prisoner to Constance. On his arrival at that place, he was immediately brought before the council, accused of his attachment to Protestant principles, and was remanded from the assembly into a dungeon. As he was there sitting, ruminating on his approaching fate, he heard a voice calling out in these words:—"Fear not, Jerome, to die in the cause of that truth which, during thy life, thou hast defended." It was the voice of Madderwitz, who had contributed to the comfort of Huss; but, in consequence of it, Jerome was conveved to a strong tower, and exposed to torture and want.

This suffering brought on him a dangerous illness, and attempts were then made to induce him to retract his principles; but he remained immovable Unhappily, however, for his subsequent peace of mind, he was at length induced to retract, and acknowledged the errors of Wickliffe and Huss, assented to the condemnation of the latter, and declared himself a firm believer in the church of Rome. But the conscience of Jerome would not allow him to suffer that retraction to remain; and he accordingly recanted, and demanded a second trial.

Accordingly, in the month of May, 1416, Jerome was again called before the council, and charged with his adherence to the errors of Wickliffe, his having had a picture of him in his chamber, his denial of transubstantiation, with other matters of a similar description. On these articles he answered with equal spirit. Through the whole oration he manifested an amazing strength of memory. His voice was sweet, distinct, and full. Firm and intrepid, he stood before the council; collected in himself, and not only despising, but seeming even desirous of death.

His speech did not, however, excite pity; and he was delivered over to the civil power for martyrdom. When surrounded by blazing fagots, he cried out, "O Lord God, have mercy upon me!" and a little afterwards, "Thou knowest how I have loved thy truth." With cheerful countenance he met his fate; and, observing the executioner about to set fire to the wood behind his back, he cried out, "Bring thy torch hither: perform thy office before my face. Had I feared death, I might have avoided it." As the wood began to blaze, he sang a hymn, which the violence of the flames did not interrupt.

Jerome was, unquestionably, an excellent man. His Christianity must have been sincere, thus to have supported him; and the uniform tenor of his virtuous life corroborated the truth of that opinion. His temper was mild and affable, and the relations of life he supported with great piety and benevolence. He was a light set upon a hill; and though for a few moments it was obscured and darkened, yet it again burst forth, and continued to shine with splendor and advantage.

### JOHN HUSS,

a famous divine and martyr, born in Bohemia, 1376, and educated at Prague, where he took his degrees, and entered into the ministry. The writings of Wickliffe converted him from the superstitions of Rome, and, with eloquent zeal, he began to preach against the power and influence of the pope. His efforts proved successful; the Papal authority began to be slighted in Bohemia; but the archbishop of Prague issued two mandates against the heresies of Wickliffe, and the labors of Huss and his followers; and this exertion of power was soon seconded by a bull from Rome, for the suppression of all tenets offensive to the holy see. Huss exclaimed against these proceedings, and, though summoned to Rome to answer for his conduct, he, supported by the favor of Wenceslaus, king of Bohemia, disregarded the pope's authority, and was excommunicated; and, soon after, his friends and adherents were included in the same interdict. After causing, by his opposition to the Papal decrees, various tumults in Prague and Bohemia, Huss was prevailed upon to appear at the council of Constance, to give an account of his doctrines. The emperor Sigismund granted him his protection, and insured security to his person; but when, soon after, he reached Constance, 1414, he was seized as a heretic, and imprisoned, and, after a confinement of severe hardships for six months, he was condemned without a hearing; and, when he refused to recant his errors, he was tumultuously sentenced to be burnt. The emperor indeed complained of the contempt shown to his authority, and of the perfidy used towards the delinquent, but all in vain. Huss was inhumanly dragged to execution; he was stripped of his sacerdotal habit, deprived of his degrees, and, with a paper crown on his head, with pictures of devils round, and the inscription of "Heresiarch," he was burned alive, July, 1415. He endured his torments with uncommon fortitude and truly Christian resignation His ashes were collected, and then sprinkled in the Rhine

## JOHN ŒCOLAMPADIUS,

an eminent German reformer, was born, in 1482, at Weinsberg, in Franconia. He was converted to the Protestant faith by reading the works of Luther; became professor of theology at Básle; embraced the opinions of Zuinglius respecting the sacrament; contributed much to the progress of ecclesiastical reform, and died in 1531.

Œcolampadius was of a meek and quiet disposition; in the undertaking of any business he was very circumspect; nor was there any thing more pleasing to him, than to spend his time in reading and commenting. His publications are numerous, consisting chiefly of annotations on the holy Scriptures.

---

## MARTIN LUTHER,

the celebrated reformer, was born at Isleben, in Saxony, 10th November, 1483. His parents wished him to devote himself to the labors of the bar, but an extraordinary accident diverted his purpose. As he walked one day in the fields with a fellow-student, he was struck down by lightning, and his companion killed by his side; and this had such effect upon his mind that, without consulting his friends, he retired from the world, into the order of the Augustines. In this seclusion he found by accident a Latin Bible, which he never before had seen, and in perusing it he was astonished at the little knowledge of Scripture and of Christianity which the clergy then imparted to the people. From the convent of Erfurt he was removed to Wittemberg University; and here he read lectures on philosophy, for three years, to numerous and applauding audiences. The completion of St. Peter's Church at Rome at this time required extraordinary sums, and the pope, Leo X., to fill his coffers with greater facility, published general indulgences for the forgiveness of sins to such as would contribute to the pious work. The Dominicans were intrusted with the selling of these indulgences in Germany and in paying their money the good friar Tetzel informed the superstitious people that they might release themselves not only from past, but also future sins. This pious imposition did not escape the discerning eye of Luther; he published, in 1517, a thesis, containing ninety-five propositions on indulgences, and challenged opposition. Tetzel was not silent on the occasion; but while he, with the voice of authority, called his opponent a damnable heretic, and whilst he burnt the thesis with all possible ignominy, Luther asserted boldly the inefficacy of indulgences, and regarded penitence and works of mercy and charity alone capable of forming a reconciliation with Heaven. Though attacked by numbers, Luther had the satisfaction to see his sentiments embraced with eagerness by the body of the people; and, when summoned by the pope to appear at Rome to answer for his conduct, he had the firmness to refuse, though he, at the same time, in the most submissive manner, exculpated himself, and deprecated the resentment of the supreme pontiff. Maximilian, the emperor, was anxious to support the cause of Rome; but Luther happily found a protector and friend in the elector of Saxony, and, upon an assurance of personal safety, he did not refuse to appear at Augsburg before the Papal legate, Cajetan. The conference ended by the refusal of Luther to submit implicitly to the pleasure of the Papal see. The pope, however, finding that violence could not destroy the obstinacy of Luther, had recourse to milder means, and his agent Miltitius was employed to visit the reformer, to argue with him, and to offer terms of reconciliation. Luther was struck with the civilities and the temper of the Papal missionary; but, instead of making submission, he was roused to greater opposition by the exhortations of the Bohemians, and the able support of Melancthon, Carolostadius, and other learned men. In 1519, he was engaged in a personal controversy at Leipsic with Eccius, divinity professor at Ingolstadt; but it tended only to sow greater enmity and deeper variance between the disputants. The same year, his book against indulgences was censured by the divines of Louvaine and Cologne; but Luther disregarded their opinions, and appealed for protection to the new emperor, Charles V. Though he had written, at the suggestion of Miltitius, a letter to the pope, not indeed of submission, but rather of exculpation, in language bold and energetic, he was in 1520 formally condemned by a bull from Rome, which, after enumerating forty-one of his heretical opinions, denounces against him the vengeance of the church, and excommunication, if within sixty days he did not make a due submission. This violent conduct Luther answered by "The Captivity of Babylon," a book in which he inveighed bitterly against the abuses of Rome; and then, calling the students of Wittemberg together, he flung into the fire the offensive decree, which he called the *execrable bull of Antichrist.* In 1521, he was summoned to appear before the emperor at the diet of Worms, with a promise of protection; and, though his friends dissuaded him, and told him that, as his opponents had burned his writings, so they would treat him after the manner of Huss, he declared, with fearless voice, "If I knew there were as many devils at Worms as tiles on the houses, I would go." At Worms he was required by Eccius to retract his opinions; but he declared that, except what he advanced could be proved contrary to Scripture, he neither could nor would recant. His obstinacy proved offensive to the emperor; but, as he had promised him his protection, he permitted him to depart. Charles, nevertheless, published his edict against him and his adherents, and placed him under the ban of the empire. Luther, however, remained secure under the protection of the elector, who had thus effected his deliverance, and in the castle of Wittemberg, which he denominated his *hermitage* and his *Patmos*, he held a secret correspondence with his friends, or composed books in defence of his opinions. At the end of ten months, when the emperor was departed for Flanders, he again appeared publicly at Wittemberg, and had the satisfaction to find that, instead of being checked, his doctrines had gained ground, and were universally embraced through Germany. In 1522, he published, in conjunction with Melancthon, a Latin translation of the New Testament; and the work was read with avidity by the German nation. In 1524, he had to contend with Erasmus, a man who had apparently adopted his sentiments, though he had not the manliness to acknowledge them; and he now found in him an able antagonist enlisted in defence of the pope. In 1524, Luther threw aside the monastic habit; and the next year he married Catherine de Bore, a nun who had escaped from a convent; and though he was ridiculed by his enemies, and censured for taking a young wife, he defended his conduct by scriptural texts, and again set at nought the authority of Rome and the cavils of her advocates. In 1525, the emperor called a diet at Spires, in consequence of the war with the Turks, as well as the troubled state of Germany in consequence of religious disputes; and in the sitting of the next year he proposed that the edict of Worms should be duly enforced, the Catholic religion supported, and heretics punished. The new doctrines, though thus openly attacked by the head of the empire, were ably defended by the electors of Saxony and Brandenburg, the landgrave of Hesse, the prince of Anhalt, and others; and in another diet, held again at Spires, these dissentient princes protested against the measures of the empire, and were consequently called ***Protestants.*** In the midst of the confusion of Germany, a confession of faith was drawn up by Melancthon, the mildest and most moderate of Luther's followers, and, as it was presented to the emperor at Augsburg, it has been called the ***Augsburg Confession.*** Thus the opposition raised against the mighty empire of spiritual Rome by an obscure monk, was supported by intelligent princes and powerful nations, and Luther, now regarded as the champion of the faith through Germany, had nothing to apprehend from his persecutors, but had only to labor earnestly to confirm what had been so happily established. His German translation of the Bible appeared in 1535, and was received with grateful raptures by the Germans. He died at Isleben, 18th February, 1546, aged 63. This illustrious man, engaged, as Atterbury has observed, against the united forces of the Papal world, stood the shock with bravery and success. He was a man of high endowments of mind, and great virtues. He had a vast understanding, which raised him to a pitch of learning unknown in the age in which he lived. His works, collected after his death, appeared at Wittemberg, in seven volumes, folio.

---

## ULRICUS ZUINGLIUS,

a zealous reformer, born at Wildehausen, in Switzerland, 1487 He studied the learned languages at Bâsle and Berne, and applied himself to philosophy at Vienna, and took his degree of doctor of divinity, at Bâsle, 1505. For ten years he acquired popularity as public preacher at Glaris, and in 1516 he was invited to Zurich to undertake the office of minister. The tenets of Luther, which were now propagated in Germany, encouraged the Swiss preacher to oppose the sale of indulgences, and to regard them as impositions from the court of Rome upon the superstitious credulity of the people. Undaunted in the publication of his opinions, he continued to increase the number of his adherents, and in 1523 he assembled the senate and the clergy of Zurich, and presented before them in sixty-seven propositions the minute articles of his faith. Though opposed by the bishop of Constance, his doctrines were adopted by the full senate, and he was exhorted to preach the word of God, whilst all pastors were forbidden to teach any thing but what could be proved by the gospel. Another synod still more powerfully favored the cause of Zuinglius and of truth; images and relics were removed from churches, processions were forbidden, and the greater part of the outward worship and ceremonies of the church of Rome was abolished. While, however, successful in the establishment of his doctrines in the canton of Zurich, Zuinglius met with violent opposition in the other members of the Swiss confederacy, and, after the fruitless conferences of Baden between Œcolampadius on the part of Zurich, and of Eckius on the part of the Catholics, both sides had recourse to arms. In one of the first encounters, the great cnampion of the reformation was slain, 11th October, 1531. As a leader, Zuinglius displayed great firmness, deep learning, and astonishing presence of mind. Though he opposed the doctrines of the Romish church, he greatly differed from the German reformer, and each, unhappily, paid little respect to the opinions of the other. His followers continued to increase; and in bearing his name they maintained doctrines on original sin, and on grace, which were rejected by the other seceders from the jurisdiction of Rome. According to Zuinglius, salvation was extended not only to infants, who died before baptism, but to heathens of a virtuous and moral life. Some alterations were afterwards introduced by Calvin, by Beza, and others; but whilst the proselytes to these new opinions acquired the name of *Calvinists* in France, and in other parts of Europe, the Zuinglians, who firmly adhered to the tenets of their founder, assumed the appellation of *Sacramentarians.* The works of Zuinglius, as a controversialist, were respectable, chiefly written in German, and were comprehended in four volumes, folio.

---

## MARTIN BUCER,

a Dominican, born in Alsace, in 1491, who early embraced the tenets of Luther. He afterwards inclined more to the opinions of Zuinglius, and, in his zeal for the reformation, attempted in vain to reconcile these two powerful leaders. For twenty years, his eloquence was exerted at Strasburg to establish the Protestant cause; but the turbulence of the times, and his opposition to the views of the Catholics at Augsburg, rendered him unpopular, so that he received with pleasure the invitations of Cranmer to settle in England. He was received with gratitude by the nation. Edward VI. treated him with great kindness, and he was appointed theological professor at Cambridge, in 1549, where he died two years after Five years after, the persecutions of Mary were extended to his remains, which were ignominiously burned; but the insult was repaired by the good sense of Elizabeth. In learning, judgment, and moderation, Bucer was inferior to none of the great reformers, and, with Melancthon, he may be considered as the best calculated to restore and maintain unanimity among contending churches and opposite sects. His writings, in Latin and German, were very numerous, and all on theological subjects.

---

## PHILIP MELANCTHON,

a celebrated reformer, born 16th February, 1497, at Bretten, in the Palatinate of the Rhine. His father's name was Schwartserdt, which signifies *black earth;* but the word was changed, according to the affectation of the times, by his friend Reuchlin, into Melancthon, which, in Greek, expresses the same meaning. He studied at Bretten, Pfortsheim, and Heidelberg, and with such success that, at thirteen, he wrote a comedy of some merit. He left Heidelberg in 1512, because he was refused a degree on account of his youth, and then passed to Tubingen, where he resided for six years, and gave public lectures on Virgil, Terence, and other classics. In 1518, by the recommendation of his friend Reuchlin, he was appointed, by the elector of Saxony, Greek professor at Wittemberg; and here began that intimacy with Luther, which contributed so much to the progress of the reformation. He was, in 1527, appointed by his patron, the duke, to visit the churches of the electorate, and afterwards he was employed in the arduous labors of preparing those articles of faith which have received the name of the Augsburg Confession, because presented to the emperor at the diet of that city. In the disputes which he maintained in those days of controversial enmity, he displayed great candor and mildness, which his friend Luther attributed more to a spirit of timidity, than to the meekness of the Christian character. His moderation, as well as his learning, was so universally acknowledged, that he received a liberal invitation from Francis I. to come to France, to settle the disputes of the Protestants; but through the interference of the duke of Saxony, the offer was declined, as likewise a similar invitation from the king of England. He was engaged in the various conferences which took place on religious subjects at Frankfort, Reinspurg, Worms, Spires, and Ratisbon, and every where evinced the deepest learning, the most peaceable temper, and the strongest moderation. The character of the times, and not inclination, rendered him a controversialist, and his answer to his mother displayed the great and the good man. When asked by the aged woman, who repeated before him her prayers in a simple but pious manner, what she must believe in this great confusion of creeds, he replied, "Go on, mother, to believe and pray as you have done, and never trouble yourself about controversies." He died at Wittemberg, 19th April, 1560, and was buried by the side of his friend Luther, in the church of the castle. Among the reasons which, on his death-bed, he assigned for considering dissolution as happiness, he said that it delivered him from theological persecutions. His works were very numerous, and, as they were written in the midst of controversy and ecclesiastical avocations, they were not always so correct in language, as they proved useful in advancing the reformation. A chronological catalogue of these was published in 1582, and they appeared altogether in four volumes, folio, at Wittemberg, 1601.

---

## PETER MARTYR,

a celebrated reformer and theologian, whose real name was Vermigli, was born, in 1500, at Florence. He was originally an Augustine monk, and became an eminent preacher, and prior of St. Fridian's, at Lucca. Having, however, embraced he Protestant doctrines, he found it necessary to quit his native country. After having been for some time professor of divinity at Strasburg, he was invited to England, and appointed professor of theology at Oxford. He left England on the accession of Mary, and died in 1561, theological professor at Zurich. He wrote several works, of great erudition, among which are Commentaries upon parts of the Scriptures. His personal character is said to have been extremely amiable.

---

HENRY BULLINGER,

one of the early reformers, was born in the canton of Zurich at Baumgarten, in 1504. The works of Melancthon converted him to Protestantism, and he became closely connected with Zuinglius, to whom he succeeded as pastor of Zurich He was one of the authors of the Helvetic Confession, and assisted Calvin in drawing up the formulary of 1549. Bullinger was a moderate and conscientious man; and it is much to his honor that, on the ground of its being inconsistent with Christianity for any one to hire himself out to slaughter those who had never injured him, he successfully opposed a treaty for supplying France with a body of Swiss mercenaries. He died in 1575. His printed works form ten folio volumes.

---

JOHN KNOX,

the great champion of the Scottish reformation, was born, in 1505, at Gifford, in East Lothian, and was educated at Haddington and St. Andrews. After he was created master of arts, he taught philosophy, most probably as a regent in one of the colleges of the university. His class became celebrated, and he was considered as equalling, if not excelling, his master in the subtilties of the dialectic art. About the same time, although he had no interest but what was procured by his own merit, he was advanced to clerical orders, and ordained a priest before he reached the age fixed by the canons of the church. At this time, the fathers of the Christian church, Jerome and Augustine, attracted his particular attention. By the writings of the former, he was led to the Scriptures as the only pure fountain of divine truth, and instructed in the utility of studying them in the original languages. In the works of the latter he found religious sentiments very opposite to those taught in the Romish church, who, while she retained his name as a saint in her calendar, had banished his doctrine as heretical from her pulpits. From this time he renounced the study of scholastic theology; and, although not yet completely emancipated from superstition, his mind was fitted for improving the means which Providence had given for leading him to a fuller and more comprehensive view of the system of evangelical religion. It was about the year 1535, when this favorable change commenced; but it does not appear that he professed himself a Protestant before the year 1542. He was converted from the Romish faith by Wishart, and became a zealous preacher of the new doctrines. Having been compelled to take shelter in the castle of St. Andrews, he fell into the hands of the French in July, 1547, and was carried with the garrison to France, where he remained a captive on board of the galleys till 1549. Subsequent to his liberation, he was for a short time chaplain to Edward VI., after which he visited Geneva and Frankfort, and, in 1555, returned to his native country. After having for twelve months labored actively and successfully to strengthen the Protestant cause in Scotland, he revisited Geneva, where he remained till 1559. During his residence in Geneva, he published his "First Blast of the Trumpet against the monstrous Government of Women" — a treatise which was levelled against Mary of England, but which gave serious offence to Elizabeth. From April, 1559, when he once more and finally set foot on Scottish earth, till his decease, which took place November 24, 1572, the reformed church was triumphant, and he was one of its most prominent, admired, and honored leaders.

When his body was laid in the grave, the regent of Scotland emphatically pronounced his eulogium, in the well-known words, "There lies he who never feared the face of man."

Knox has been styled the intrepid reformer; and that character he unquestionably deserves. In personal intrepidity and popular eloquence he resembled Luther. His doctrinal sentiments were those of Calvin; and, like Zuinglius, he felt an attachment to the principles of religious liberty. He effected much in the great work of the reformation; but his manners were so severe, and his temper so acrid, that whilst he may be equally respected with Luther and Melancthon, he is not equally beloved. Knox was, however, known and beloved by the principal persons among the reformed in France, Switzerland, and Germany; and the affectionate veneration in which his memory was held in Scotland after his death, evinced that the influence he possessed among his countrymen, during his life, was not constrained, but founded on the high opinion which they entertained. Banatyne has thus drawn his character, and it is unquestionably entitled to consideration: — "In this manner," says he, "departed this man of God; the light of Scotland, the comfort of the church within the same, the mirror of godliness, and pattern and example to all true ministers, in purity of life, soundness of doctrine, and boldness in reproving of wickedness; one that cared not for the favor of men, how great soever they were

---

## JOHN CALVIN,

a celebrated reformer, born at Noyon, in Picardy, 10th July, 1509. His family name was *Cauvin,* which he Latinized into *Calvinus.* He was first intended for the church, and, subsequently, for the profession of civil law. Having embraced the principles of Protestantism, he was under the necessity of quitting France; and he settled at Bâsle, where he published his celebrated "Institutions of the Christian Religion." After having visited Italy, he was returning by the way of Geneva, in 1536, when Farel and other reformers induced him to take up his abode in that city. He was chosen one of the ministers of the gospel, and professor of divinity. A dispute with the city authorities soon compelled him to leave Geneva, and he withdrew to Strasburg; whence he was recalled in 1541. From the time of his recall, he possessed almost absolute power at Geneva; and he exerted himself vigorously in establishing the Presbyterian form of church government. The reformer, who so loudly exclaimed against the tyranny of Rome, directed the whole torrent of his persecution against Servetus, a physician, who had in an ambiguous style written upon the Trinity; and his vengeance was not appeased till the unfortunate heretic had expired in the flames. He died May 26, 1564; and, though he had long enjoyed a high reputation and exercised an unbounded authority, he left only three hundred crowns to his heirs, including his library, the books of which sold afterwards at a great price. The works of Calvin were printed in twelve volumes, folio, Geneva, and in nine, Amsterdam, in 1667.

---

## JEROME ZANCHIUS,

a native of Alzano, who entered in the congregation of the Lateran canons. He embraced the tenets of the Protestants by the conversation of Peter Martyr, who was of the same establishment; and, afraid of persecution, he retired, 1553, to Strasburg, where he taught divinity and the philosophy of Aristotle. He quitted Strasburg, in 1563, for Chiavene, and, in 1568, removed to Heidelberg, where he was appointed professor of theology, and where he died 19th November, 1590, aged eighty-four. He was author of "Commentaries on St. Paul's Epistles," and other works, published together at Geneva, in eight volumes, folio, 1613. In his character he was a man of moderation, learned, benevolent, and pious.

---

## THEODORE BEZA,

one of the most eminent of the reformers, was born at Vezelai, in the Nivernois, in 1519, and was originally a Catholic, and intended for the law. At the age of twenty, he gained an unenviable reputation by the composition of Latin poetry which was at once elegant and licentious, and which, some years afterwards, he published under the title of "Juvenile Poems." Though not in orders, he possessed benefices of considerable value. These, however, he abandoned in 1548, and retired to Geneva, where he publicly abjured Popery. To this he was induced by his having meditated, during illness, upon the doctrines which he had heard from his Protestant tutor, Melchior Wolmar; and perhaps also, in some measure, by his attachment to a lady, whom he carried with him to Geneva, and married. He now accepted the Greek professorship at Lausanne, which he held for ten years. It was while he was thus occupied that he produced his tragedy of "Abraham's Sacrifice," his version of the New Testament, and his hateful defence of the right of the magistrate to punish heretics. In 1559, he removed to Geneva, and became the colleague of Calvin, through whom he was appointed rector of the academy, and theological professor. Two years after this, he took a prominent part in the conference at Poissy, and was present at the battle of Dreux. He returned to Geneva in 1563, succeeded Calvin in his offices and influence, and was thenceforward considered as the head of the Calvinistic church. After an exceedingly active life, he died on the 13th of October, 1605.

---

## LEO X.,

Pope John de Medici, the son of the illustrious Lorenzo, was born in 1475, at Florence, and was nominated a cardinal in his thirteenth year. In 1505, he was made governor of Perugia; was intrusted with the command of the Papal army in 1511; and was made prisoner, in the following year, at the battle of Ravenna. He attained the Papal crown in 1513, on the death of Julius II. He died in 1521. Leo was one of the most munificent patrons of learning and of the arts; but he was prodigal, and on some occasions grossly violated the principles of justice. To his shameless sale of indulgences, to raise money to complete St. Peter's Church at Rome, and other extravagances, the world is indebted for the reformation of the church by Luther and others.

## JUSTIN,

surnamed the MARTYR, one of the fathers of the church, was born at Neapolis, anciently Sichem, in Palestine, and was a philosopher of the Platonic school. He is believed to have preached the gospel in Italy, Asia Minor, and Egypt. He was beheaded at Rome, in 165. Of his works, the principal are two Apologies for the Christians.

---

## ARIUS,

founder of the sect of the Arians, was an African by birth Disappointment made him a sectary. He propagated the opinion that the Word was not a divine person; and the heresy, though condemned by various councils, gained followers, and excited schisms in the Roman empire. The Nicene creed was drawn up to combat his errors. He was a violent enemy of Athanasius. He died at Alexandria, 386.

---

## ATHANASIUS,

the celebrated patriarch of Alexandria, was born in that city about 296. At the council of Nice, though then but a deacon of Alexandria, his reputation for skill in controversy gained him an honorable place in the council, and with signal ability he exposed the sophistry of those who pleaded on the side of Arius. Six months after, he was appointed the successor of Alexander. Notwithstanding the influence of the emperor, who had recalled Arius from banishment, and, upon a plausible confession of his faith, in which he affected to be Orthodox in his sentiments, directed that he should be received by the Alexandrian church, Athanasius refused to admit him to communion, and exposed his prevarication. The Arians upon this exerted themselves to raise tumults at Alexandria, and to injure the character of Athanasius with he emperor, who was prevailed upon by falsehoods to pronounce against him a sentence of banishment. In the begin ning of the reign of Constantius, he was recalled to his happy people, but was again disturbed and deposed through the influence of the Arians. Accusations were also sent against him and other bishops from the east to the west; but they were acquitted by Pope Julius in full council. Athanasius was restored a second time to his see, upon the death of the Arian bishop, who had been placed in it. Arianism, however, being in favor at court, he was condemned by a council convened at Arles, and by another at Milan, and was a third time obliged to fly into the deserts. His enemies pursued him even here, and set a price upon his head. In this situation, Athanasius composed writings full of eloquence to strengthen the faith of believers, and expose the falsehood of his enemies. He returned with the other bishops whom Julian the Apostate recalled from banishment, and, in A. D. 362, held a council at Alexandria, where the belief of a consubstantial Trinity was openly professed. Many now were recovered from Arianism, and brought to subscribe the Nicene creed. But his peace was again interrupted by the complaints of the heathen, whose temples the zeal of Athanasius kept always empty. He was again obliged to fly to save his life. The accession of Jovian brought him back. During the reign of Jovian, also, Athanasius held another council, which declared its adherence to the Nicene faith; and with the exception of a short retirement under Valens, he was permitted to sit down in quiet and govern his affectionate church of Alexandria, until his death, in 373. Of the forty-six years of his official life, he spent twenty in banishment.

Athanasius (says the Encyclopedia Americana) is one of the greatest men of whom the church can boast. His deep mind, his noble heart, his invincible courage, his living faith, his unbounded benevolence, sincere humility, lofty eloquence, and strictly virtuous life, gained the honor and love of all. In all his writings, his style is distinguished for clearness and moderation.

X

## MOSES MAIMONIDES,

or Moses son of Maimon, commonly called Moses Egypticus, because physician to the sultan of Egypt, was a Jewish rabbi, born at Cordova, in Spain, 1131. He opened a school in Egypt, and as his skill, not only in languages, but in all branches of science and of philosophy, was very great, his instructions were attended by numerous and respectable pupils. Thus eminently distinguished as a scholar, as a physician, and also as a divine, so as to be called inferior only to the legislator Moses, he beheld with indifference, and even contempt, the fables and traditions of his countrymen, and applied all the powers of learning, and the vast resources of his mind, in the cause of truth, virtue, and philosophy. Some of his works were written in Arabic, but are extant now in Hebrew only. The most famous of these are his Commentaries on the Misna; Jad, a complete pandect of the Jewish law; More Nevochim, a valuable work, explaining the difficult passages, phrases, parables, and allegories, in Scripture, and several other works. This great and learned man died in Egypt at the age of seventy, and was buried with his nation in the land of Upper Galilee. His death was mourned for three whole days by Jews and Egyptians, and the year in which he died, in respect of his great virtues and learning, was called Lamentum Lamentabile.

---

## JOHN AGRICOLA,

a German divine, born at Isleb. He was the friend and the disciple of Luther, but afterwards violently opposed him, and became the head of the Antinomians, a sect which regarded faith as the whole of the duties of man. He was also engaged in a dispute with Melancthon; but, with the most laudable motives, he endeavored to effect a reconciliation between the Catholics and Protestants. He died at Berlin, 1566, aged seventy-four.

## MICHAEL SERVETUS,

a native of Villanuova, in Arragon, son of a notary. He studied the law at Toulouse, but afterwards applied to medicine at Paris, and took there his doctor's degree. The boldness and pertinacity of his opinions created him enemies, and he left the capital to settle at Lyons, but afterwards he retired to Charlieu. On the invitation of the archbishop of Vienne, in Dauphiny, he was prevailed upon to fix his residence there, and he might have lived in peace and respected, had he been satisfied to seek celebrity in medical pursuits alone. Eager to publish his Arian opinions on religion, he sent three questions to Calvin on the Divinity of Christ, on Regeneration, and on the Necessity of Baptism, and, when answered with civility, he reflected on the sentiments of his correspondent with arrogant harshness. This produced a quarrel, and ended in the most implacable hatred, so that Calvin, bent on revenge, obtained, by secret means, copies of a work in which his antagonist was engaged, and caused him to be accused before the archbishop as a dangerous man. Servetus escaped from prison; but, on his way to Italy, he had the imprudence to pass in disguise through Geneva, where he was recognized by Calvin, and immediately seized by the magistrate as an impious heretic. Forty heretical errors were proved against him by his accusers; but Servetus refused to renounce them, and the magistrates, at last yielding to the loud representations of the ministers of Bâsle, Berne, and Zurich, and especially of Calvin, who demanded the punishment of a profane heretic, ordered the unhappy man to be burnt. On the 27th October, 1553, the wretched Servetus was conducted to the stake, and, as the wind prevented the flames from fully reaching his body, two long hours elapsed before he was freed from his miseries. This cruel treatment deservedly called down the general odium on the head of Calvin, who ably defended his conduct and that of the magistrates. Servetus published various works against the Trinity, which were burnt in disgrace at Geneva, and other places.

---

## SIMONIS MENNO,

an ecclesiastic of Friesland, embraced the tenets of the Anabaptists, and, after being again baptized by Ubbo Philippi, became a powerful leader of his sect. He denied that Jesus Christ received a human shape from his mother, the virgin Mary; and while he maintained the necessity of again baptizing adults, he inveighed against the custom of infant baptism, which he regarded as Popish innovation. His eloquence and his learning were so much admired, that he gained a great number of followers in Westphalia, Guelderland, Holland, and Brabant; but, though a price was set on his head, he had the good fortune to escape his persecutors. He was, in his opinions, more moderate than the rest of the Anabaptists. His followers are still to be found in the Low Countries, under the name of *Mennonites*, divided into two distinct sects. He died at Oldeslo, between Lubec and Hamburg, 1565. His works were published at Amsterdam, 1681.

---

## FRANCIS XAVIER,

denominated the *Apostle of the Indies*, was born, in 1506, at the castle of Xavier, in Navarre; studied at Paris; became one of the first and most zealous disciples of Ignatius Loyola; was sent to the East by John III. of Portugal, to propagate the gospel; performed his mission in Hindoostan, the Moluccas, and Japan; and was on the point of landing in China, when he died, 1552.

---

## FAUSTUS SOCINUS,

from whom the Socinians derive their name, was born, in 1539, at Sienna, and was for a considerable period in the service of the grand duke of Tuscany; after which he went to study theology, at Bâsle. The result of his studies was the adoption of those anti-Trinitarian doctrines, which his uncle Lelio Socinus is believed also to have professed Faustus settled in Poland, gained many followers, endured much persecution, and died in 1604.

---

### ROBERT BROWN

was educated at Cambridge, and was a man of good parts and some learning. He began to inveigh openly against the ceremonies of the church, at Norwich, in 1580; but, being much opposed by the bishops, he, with his congregation, left England, and settled at Middleburgh, in Zealand, where they obtained leave to worship God in their own way, and form a church according to their own model. They soon, however, began to differ among themselves, so that Brown, growing weary of his office, returned to England in 1589, renounced his principles of separation, and was preferred to the rectory of a church in Northamptonshire. He died in prison in 1630. The revolt of Brown was attended with the dissolution of the church at Middleburgh; but the seeds of Brownism which he had sown in England were so far from being destroyed, that Sir Walter Raleigh, in a speech in 1592, computes no less than twenty thousand of this sect.

---

### JAMES ARMINIUS,

a native of Oude-water, in Holland, 1560, founder of the sect of the Arminians. As he lost his father early, he was supported at the university of Utrecht, and of Marpurg, by the liberality of his friends; but when he returned home, in the midst of the ravages caused by the Spanish arms, instead of being received by his mother, he found that she, as well as her daughters, and all her family, had been sacrificed to the wantonness of the ferocious enemy. His distress was for a while inconsolable; but the thirst after distinction called him to the newly-founded university of Leyden, where his industry acquired him the protection of the magistrates of Amsterdam, at whose expense he travelled to Geneva and Italy, to hear the lectures of Theodore Beza and James Zabarella. On his return to Holland, he was ordained minister of Amsterdam, 1588. As professor of divinity at Leyden, to which office he was called 1603, he distinguished himself by three valuable orations on the object of theology, on the author and end of it, and on the certainty of it; and he afterwards explained the prophet Jonah. In his public and private life, Arminius has been admired for his moderation; and though many gross insinuations have been thrown against him, yet his memory has been fully vindicated by the ablest pens, and he seemed entitled to the motto which he assumed, — *A good conscience is a paradise.* A life of perpetual labor and vexation of mind at last brought on a sickness of which he died, October 19, 1619. His writings were all on controversial and theological subjects, and were published in one volume, quarto, Frankfort, 1661.

---

## FRANCIS HIGGINSON,

first minister of Salem, Massachusetts, after receiving his education at Emanuel College, in Cambridge, became the minister of a church at Leicester, in England. While his popular talents filled his church with attentive hearers, such was the divine blessing upon his labors, that a deep attention to religious subjects was excited among his people. Becoming at length a conscientious Nonconformist to the rites of the English church, some of which he thought not only were unsupported by Scripture, but corrupted the purity of Christian worship and discipline, he was excluded from the parish church, and became obnoxious to the High Commission Court. One day two messengers came to his house, and with loud knocks cried out, "Where is Mr. Higginson? We must speak with Mr. Higginson!" His wife ran to his chamber, and entreated him to conceal himself; but he replied, that he should acquiesce in the will of God. He went down, and, as the messengers entered the hall, they presented him with some papers, saying, in a rough manner, "Sir, we came from London, and our business is to convey you to London, as you may see by those papers." "I thought so," exclaimed Mrs. Higginson, weeping; but a woman's tears could have but little effect upon hard-hearted pursuivants. Mr. Higginson opened the packet to read the form of his arrest, but, instead of an order from Bishop Laud for his seizure, he found a copy of the charter of Massachusetts, and letters from the governor and company, inviting him to embark with them for New England. The sudden transition of feeling from despondence to joy, may be better imagined than described.

Having sought advice and implored the divine direction, he resolved to accept the invitation. In his farewell sermon, preached before a vast assembly, he declared his persuasion, that England would be chastised by war, and that Leicester would have more than an ordinary share of sufferings. It was not long before his prediction was verified. It is not meant that he claimed the power of foretelling future events; but he could reason with considerable accuracy from cause to effect, knowing that iniquity is generally followed by its punishment; and he lived in an age when it was usual for ministers to speak with more confidence, and authority, and efficacy, than at present. He sailed from Gravesend, April 25, 1629, accompanied by Mr. Skelton, whose principles accorded with his own. When he came to the Land's End, he called his children and the other passengers on deck to take the last view of their native country; and he now exclaimed, "Farewell, England! farewell, the church of God in England, and all the Christian friends there! We do not go to America as separatists from the church of England, though we cannot but separate from its corruptions." He then concluded with a fervent prayer for the king, church, and state, in England. He arrived at Cape Ann, June 27, 1629, and, having spent the next day there, which was Sunday, on the 29th he entered the harbor of Salem. July the 20th was observed as a day of fasting by the appointment of Governor Endicott, and the church then made choice of Mr. Higginson to be their teacher, and Mr. Skelton their pastor.

Thus auspicious was the commencement of the settlement of Naumkeag, or Salem; but the scene was soon changed. During the first winter, about one hundred persons died, and Mr. Higginson was soon seized with a hectic, which terminated his days in August, 1630, aged forty-two. In his last sickness, he was reminded of his benevolent exertions in the service of the Lord Jesus Christ. To consoling suggestions of this kind he replied, "I have been an unprofitable servant, and all my desire is to win Christ, and be found in him, no having my own righteousness."

---

## RICHARD BAXTER,

a Nonconformist, born at Rowton, Shropshire, 12th November, 1615. He compensated for the deficiencies of a neglected education by unusual application, and was appointed master of Dudley free-school by the interest of Mr. Richard Foley, of Stourbridge, and soon after admitted into orders by the bishop of Winchester. His scruples were raised by the oath which was proposed by the convention at that time sitting, and he was among the number of those who showed their dislike to an unqualified submission "to archbishops, bishops, et cetera," as they knew not what the *et cetera* comprehended. In 1640, he was invited to be minister at Kidderminster; but the civil war, which broke out soon after, exposed him to persecution, as he espoused the cause of the parliament. He retired to Coventry, and continued his ministerial labors till the success of the republicans recalled him to his favorite flock at Kidderminster. The usurpation of Cromwell gave him great offence, and he even presumed to argue in private with the tyrant on the nature and illegality of his power; but in the only sermon which he preached before him, he wisely confined his subject to the dissensions which existed in the kingdom on religious matters. He was in London after

Cromwell's death, and preached before parliament the day before the king's return was voted, and likewise before the lord mayor for Monk's successes. Charles II. made him one of his chaplains, and Chancellor Clarendon offered him the bishopric of Hereford, which he declined. He was, however, soon involved in the general persecution of the Nonconformists His paraphrase on the New Testament drew upon him, in 1685, the vengeance of Jeffreys, and he was condemned to be imprisoned for two years, from which punishment, six months after, he was discharged by the interference of Lord Powis with King James. He died December 8th, 1691, and was interred in Christ Church.

---

## GEORGE FOX,

the founder of the society of Friends, or Quakers, was born, in 1624, at Drayton, in Leicestershire, and was the son of a weaver, a pious and virtuous man, who gave him a religious education. Being apprenticed to a grazier, he was employed in keeping sheep — an occupation, the silence and solitude of which were well calculated to nurse his naturally enthusiastic feelings. When he was about nineteen, he believed himself to have received a divine command to forsake all, renounce society, and dedicate his existence to the service of religion. For five years, he accordingly led a wandering life, fasting, praying, and living secluded; but it was not till about 1648 that he began to preach his doctrines. Manchester was the place where he first promulgated them. Thenceforth he pursued his career with untirable zeal and activity, in spite of frequent imprisonment and brutal usage. It was at Derby that his followers were first denominated *Quakers*, either from their tremulous mode of speaking, or from their calling on their hearers to "tremble at the name of the Lord." The labors of Fox were crowned with considerable success; and, in 1669, he extended the sphere of them to America, where he spent two years. He also twice visited the continent He died in 1690. His writings were collected in three volumes, folio. Whatever may be thought of the tenets of Fox there can be no doubt that he was sincere in them, and that he was a man of strict temperance, humility, moderation, and piety.

---

WILLIAM PENN,

the founder of Pennsylvania, was born in London, 1644 From a private school at Chigwell, Essex, he entered, in 1660, as a gentleman commoner at Christ Church, Oxford; but, as he withdrew from the national forms of worship with other students, who, like himself, had listened to the preaching of Thomas Loe, a Quaker of eminence, who was fined for Nonconformity, and, the next year, as he pertinaciously adhered to his opinions, he was expelled from the college. His father sent him to France, and, on his return, he entered at Lincoln's Inn, as a law student. In 1666, he was sent to manage an estate in Ireland, and, during his residence there, he renewed his acquaintance with Loe, and showed such partiality to the Quakers, that he was, in those days of persecution, taken up at a meeting at Cork, and imprisoned by the mayor, who at last restored him to liberty at the request of Lord Orrery His return to England produced a violent altercation with his father, who wished him to abandon those singular habits so offensive to decorum and established forms; and, when he refused to appear uncovered before him and before the king, he a second time dismissed him from his protection and favor. In 1668, he first appeared as a preacher and as an author among the Quakers; and, in consequence of some controversial dispute, he was sent to the Tower, where he remained in confinement for seven months. The passing of the conventicle act soon after again sent him to prison in Newgate, from which he was released by the interest of his father, who about this time was reconciled to him, and left him, on his decease some time after, a valuable estate of about fifteen hundred pounds per annum. In 1672, he married Gulielma Maria Springett, a lady of principles similar to his own, and then fixed his residence at Rickmansworth, where he employed himself zealously in promoting the cause of the Friends by his preaching, as well as by his writings. In 1677, he went, with George Fox and Robert Barclay, to the continent on a religious excursion; and, after visiting Amsterdam and the other chief towns of Holland, they proceeded to the court of Princess Elizabeth, the granddaughter of James I., at Herwerden or Herford, where they were received with great kindness and hospitality. Soon after his return to England, Charles II. granted him, in consideration of the services of his father, and for a debt due to him from the crown, a province of North America, then called New Netherlands, but now making the state of Pennsylvania. In consequence of this acquisition, he invited, under the royal patent, settlers from all parts of the kingdom, and drew up, in twenty-four articles, the fundamental constitution of his new province, in which he held out a greater degree of religious liberty than had at that time appeared in the Christian world. A colony of people, chiefly of his persuasion, soon flocked to share his fortunes; the lands of the country were cleared and improved, and a town was built, which, on the principle of brotherly love, received the name of *Philadelphia.* In 1682, Penn visited the province, and confirmed that good understanding which he had recommended with the natives; and, after two years' residence, and with the satisfaction of witnessing and promoting the prosperity of the colonists, he returned to England. Soon after, Charles died, and the acquaintance which Penn had with the new monarch was honorably used to protect the people of his persuasion. At the revolution however, he was suspected of treasonable correspondence with the exiled prince, and therefore exposed to molestation and persecution. In 1694, he lost his wife; but, though severely afflicted by the event, he in about two years married again, and afterwards employed himself in travelling in Ireland, and over England, in disseminating, as a preacher, the doctrines of his sect. He visited, in 1699, his province with his wife and family, and returned to England in 1701. The suspicion with which he had been regarded under William's government, ceased at the accession of Queen Anne, and the unyielding advocate of Quakerism was permitted to live with greater freedom, and to fear persecution less. In 1710, he removed to Rushcomb, near Twyford, Berks, where he spent the rest of his life. Three repeated attacks of an apoplexy at last came to weaken his faculties and his constitution, and, after nearly losing all recollection of his former friends and associates, he expired, 30th July, 1718, and was buried at Jordan, near Beaconsfield, Bucks. The character of Penn is truly amiable, benevolent, and humane; his labors were exerted for the good of mankind, and, with the strictest consistency of moral conduct and religious opinion, he endured persecution and malice with resignation; and, guided by the approbation of a pure conscience, he showed himself indefatigable in the fulfilling of what he considered as the law of God, and the clear demonstration of the truth of the gospel. The long prosperity of Pennsylvania, and of his favorite city, Philadelphia, furnishes the best evidence of his wisdom as a legislator.

---

## BENEDICT SPINOZA,

an atheistical writer, son of a Portuguese Jew, born at Amsterdam, 1638. He studied medicine and theology; but his religion was so loose, and his inquiries for the reason of every thing which he was to believe, became so offensive to the rabbies, that he was thrust out of the synagogue. In consequence of this, he became a Christian, and was baptized; but his conversion was insincere, and though, during his life, he did not openly profess himself an atheist, his posthumous works plainly proved him such. He died, of a consumption, at the Hague, February, 1677, aged forty-five. He is the founder of a regular system of atheism, and by his hypothesis he wished to establish that there is but one substance in nature, which is endowed with infinite attributes, with extension and thought; that all spirits are modifications of that substance; and that God, the necessary and most perfect being, is the cause of all things that exist, but does not differ from them. These monstrous doctrines, though not new, were thus built into a regular system by this extraordinary man, who is said in other respects to have been of a good moral character in private life, benevolent, friendly, and charitable. His conduct was marked by no licentiousness or irregularity; but he retired from the tumults of Amsterdam to a more peaceful residence at the Hague, where curiosity led princes, philosophers, and learned men, to see and to converse with this bold assertor of atheism.

---

## ANN LEE

was born in the town of Manchester, in England, in 1736. Her father, John Lee, though not in affluent circumstances, was an honest and industrious man. Her mother was esteemed as a very pious woman. As was common with the laboring classes of people in England at that period, their children, instead of being sent to school, were brought up to work from early childhood. By this means, Ann, though quite illiterate, acquired a habit of industry, and was early distinguished for her activity, faithfulness, neatness, and good economy in her temporal employments.

From early childhood she was the subject of religious impressions and divine manifestations. These continued, in a greater or less degree, as she advanced in years; so that, at times, she was strongly impressed with a sense of the great depravity of human nature, and of the lost state of mankind by reason of sin. But losing her mother at an early age, and finding no person to assist her in the pursuit of a life of holiness, and being urged by the solicitations of her relations and friends, she was married to Abraham Stanley, by whom she had four children, who all died in infancy. But the convictions of her youth often returned upon her with great force, which at length brought her under excessive tribulation of soul. In this situation, she sought earnestly for deliverance from the bondage of sin.

While under these exercises of mind, she became acquainted with a society of people associated under the ministration of James Wardly, who, with Jane, his wife, had been greatly favored with divine manifestations concerning the second appearing of Christ, which they foresaw was near at hand Ann readily embraced their testimony, and united herself to the society in the month of September, 1758.

In this society, Ann found that strength and protection against the powerful influences of evil, which, for the time being, were answerable to her faith; and, by her faithful obedience, she by degrees attained to the full knowledge and experience in spiritual things which they had found. But as she still found in herself the remains of the propensities of fallen nature, she could not rest satisfied short of full salvation; she therefore sought earnestly, day and night, in the most fervent prayers and cries to God, to find complete deliverance from a sinful nature, and to know more perfectly the way of full redemption and final salvation.

After passing through many scenes of tribulation and suffering, she received a full answer to her prayers and desires to God. She then came forward, and, with extraordinary power and energy of spirit, testified that she had received, through the Spirit of Christ, a full revelation of the fallen nature of man, and of the only means of redemption, which were comprised in his precepts and living example while on earth. The astonishing power of God which accompanied her testimony of this revelation to the society, was too awakening and convincing to leave a doubt on the minds of the society of its divine authority. When, therefore, Ann had thus manifested to the society the revelation of light which she had received, she was received and acknowledged as their leader and spiritual *Mother in Christ*. This was the only name of distinction by which she was known in the society. The term *Elect Lady* was given to her by her enemies. Ann, with a number of her followers, visited America in 1774, and formed the first society of Shakers in this country, at Watervliet, N. Y., where she died in 1784

## JOHN GLASS,

Scotch divine, born at Dundee, 1698, and educated at Aberdeen. Upon his publication of a pamphlet on the inconsistency of a civil establishment with Christianity, he was deposed from his church, near Dundee, and then became the founder of a new sect, called the *Glassites* in Scotland, and *Sandemanians* in England. As the discipline of his sect was very rigorous, few embraced his tenets, and the name is scarce known now.

## GEORGE KEITH,

a Quaker, was born at Aberdeen, and was well educated. He came, in 1682, to East Jersey, where he was surveyor-general. In 1689, he taught a school in Philadelphia. After various exertions, writing and travelling for the propagation of the sentiments of his sect, he at first seceded, and at length entirely deserted the society. In England, he became an Episcopalian, and was consecrated as an Episcopal missionary, and in that capacity officiated for a short time in New York and Boston. Returning to England in 1706, he was a rector at Edburton, in Sussex, where he died. His publications were numerous, but almost exclusively controversial.

## NICHOLAS LOUIS, COUNT ZINZENDORF,

the patron of the sect of the Moravians, was born at Dresden, in May, 1700. He studied at Halle and Utrecht. About the year 1721, he purchased the lordship of Bertholdsdorf, in Lusatia. Some poor Christians, the followers of John Huss, obtained leave, in 1722, to settle on his estate. They soon made converts. Such was the origin of the village of Herrnhut. Their noble patron soon after joined them.

From this period Count Zinzendorf devoted himself to the business of instructing his fellow-men by his writings and by preaching He travelled through Germany, and in Denmark became acquainted with the Danish missions in the East Indies and Greenland. About 1732, he engaged earnestly in the promotion of missions by his Moravian brethren, whose numbers at Herrnhut were then about five hundred. So successful were these missions, that in a few years four thousand negroes were baptized in the West Indies, and the converts in Greenland amounted to seven hundred and eighty-four.

In 1737, he visited London, and, in 1741, came to America, and preached at Germantown and Bethlehem. February 11, 1742, he ordained at Oly, in Pennsylvania, the missionaries Rauch and Buettner, and Rauch baptized three Indians from Shekomeco, east of the Hudson, "the firstlings of the Indians." He soon, with his daughter, Benigna, and several brethren and sisters, visited various tribes of Indians. At Shekomeco he established the first Indian Moravian congregation in North America. In 1743, he returned to Europe. He died at Herrnhut, in 1760, and his coffin was carried to the grave by thirty-two preachers and missionaries, whom he had reared, and some of whom had toiled in Holland, England, Ireland, North America, and Greenland. What monarch was ever honored by a funeral like this?

---

## WILLIAM COURTNEY,

archbishop of Canterbury, was the fourth son of Hugh Courtney, earl of Devonshire, by Margaret, granddaughter of Edward I. He was educated at Oxford, and, though possessed of abilities, owed his elevation in the church to the consequence of his family. When twenty-eight, he was made bishop of Hereford, and afterwards translated to London, where he summoned before him the great Wickliffe, in St. Paul's Cathedral, 1377. The bold reformer was on this occasion attended by his friends John of Gaunt and Lord Percy, who, in supporting his tenets, treated the prelate with such asperity, that a tumult was excited among the citizens of London. Courtney was made chancellor, 1381, and afterwards raised to the see of Canterbury. He was a violent persecutor of the Wickliffites, and condemned their tenets in a synod. He died at Maidstone, 1396, aged 55.

---

## RICHARD HOOKER,

an eminent divine of the church of England, was born in 1553, at Heavitree, near Exeter, and, under the patronage of Bishop Jewel, was educated at Corpus Christi College, Oxford, where he was distinguished for his piety and exemplary conduct. An unhappy marriage, which he contracted before he was thirty, with a scold who had neither beauty, money, nor manners, lost him his college fellowship, and was a fertile source of annoyance to him. In 1585, he was made master of the Temple; but, weary of disputes with the afternoon lecturer, — a violent Presbyterian, — and longing for rural retirement, he relinquished this preferment, and obtained the rectory of Bishop's Bourne, in Kent, at which he resided till his decease, in 1600. His great work is the treatise on "Ecclesiastical Polity;" of which Pope Clement VIII. said, "There are in it such seeds of eternity as will continue till the last fire shall devour all learning."

---

## CHARLES CHAUNCEY,

second president of Harvard College, was born in England, in 1589. He received his grammar education at Westminster, and took the degree of M. D. at the university of Cambridge. He emigrated to New England in 1638, and, after serving for a number of years in the ministry at Scituate, was appointed, in 1654, president of Harvard College. In this office he remained till his death, in 1671, performing all its duties with industrious fidelity. He was eminent as a physician, and was of opinion that there ought to be no distinction between physic and divinity.

ROGER WILLIAMS,

the founder of the Providence Plantations, was born in Wales, in 1599, and was educated at Oxford. Being a dissenter he came to America, in the hope of enjoying in freedom his religious opinions. He arrived at Hull, February 5, 1631, and was established at Salem, Massachusetts, as colleague with Mr. Skelton. His peculiar notions soon subjected him to the severest censure. He maintained that the magistrates were bound to grant toleration to all sects of Christians, and in his actions and words avowed the liberality of his principles. After the death of Mr. Skelton, he was sole minister of Salem. Continuing to avow his opinions, which were considered not only heretical, but seditious, he was summoned before the General Court, to answer to numerous charges He, however, refused to retract any of his opinions, and was accordingly banished, 1635. He first repaired to Seekonk: but, being informed that that territory was within the jurisdiction of Plymouth, he proceeded to Mooshausic, where, with others, in 1636, he began a plantation. The land was honestly purchased of the Indians; and the town, in acknowledgment of the kindness of Heaven, was called Providence. Mr. Williams's benevolence was not confined to his civilized brethren; he learned the language of the Indians, ravelled among them, won the entire confidence of their chiefs, and was often the means of saving from injury the colony that had driven him from its protection. In 1643, he was sent to England, as agent for both settlements, and in September, 1644, returned with a patent for the territory with permission for the inhabitants to institute a government for themselves. In 1651, he was again sent to England, in the capacity of agent, and returned in 1654, when he was chosen president of the government. Benedict Arnold succeeded him in 1657. He died in April, 1683, aged eighty-four. Mr. Williams was consistent in his religious doctrines, and set a bright example of that toleration which he demanded from others. His mind was strong and well cultivated; and he read the Scriptures in the originals. After his banishment from Massachusetts, he maintained a correspondence with some of its principal men, and ever entertained for them the highest affection and respect. In his writings, he evinces his power at argument. In 1672, he held a public dispute with the most eminent Quaker preachers, of which he has published an account. He also published a "Key to the Indian Language," octavo, 1643; an answer to Mr. Cotton's letters, concerning the power of the magistrate in matters of religion, with other letters and discourses.

---

## JOHN CLARKE,

a distinguished Baptist minister, and one of the first founders of Rhode Island, was a physician in London, before he came to this country. Soon after the first settlement of Massachusetts, he was driven from that colony with a number of others; and March 7, 1638, they formed themselves into a body politic, and purchased Aquetneck of the Indian sachems, calling it the Isle of Rhodes, or Rhode Island. The settlement commenced at Pocasset, or Portsmouth. The Indian deed is dated March 24, 1638. Mr. Clarke was soon employed as a preacher; and, in 1644, he formed a church at Newport, and became its pastor. This was the second Baptist church which was established in America.

In 1649, he was an assistant and treasurer of Rhode Island colony. In 1651, he went to visit one of his brethren at Lynn, near Boston, and he preached on Sunday, July 20; but, before he had completed the services of the forenoon, he was seized, with his friends, by an officer of the government. In the afternoon, he was compelled to attend the parish meeting, at the close of which he spoke a few words. He was tried before the Court of Assistants, and fined twenty pounds; in case of failure in the payment of which sum he was to be whipped. In passing the sentence, Judge Endicott observed, "You secretly insinuate things into those who are weak, which you cannot maintain before our ministers; you may try and dispute with them." Mr. Clarke accordingly wrote from prison, proposing a dispute upon the principles which he professed. He represented his principles to be, that Jesus Christ had the sole right of prescribing any laws respecting the worship of God which it was necessary to obey; that baptism, or dipping in water, was an ordinance to be administered only to those who gave some evidence of repentance towards God and faith in Jesus Christ; that such visible believers only constituted the church; that each of them had a right to speak in the congregation, according as the Lord had given him talents, either to make inquiries for his own instruction, or to prophesy for the edification of others, and that at all times and in all places they ought to reprove folly and open their lips to justify wisdom; and that no servant of Jesus Christ had any authority to restrain any fellow-servant in his worship, where injury was not offered to others. No dispute, however, occurred, and Mr. Clarke, his friends paying his fine without his consent, was soon released from prison, and directed to leave the colony. His companion Obadiah Holmes shared a severer fate; for, on declining to pay his fine of thirty pounds, which his friends offered to do for him, he was publicly whipped in Boston.

Mr. Clarke died at Newport, April 20, 1676, aged about 66 years, resigning his soul to his merciful Redeemer, through faith in whose name he enjoyed the hope of a resurrection to eternal life.

His life was so pure, that he was never accused of any vice, to leave a blot on his memory. His noble sentiments respecting religious toleration did not, indeed, accord with the sentiments of the age in which he lived, and exposed him to trouble; but at the present time they are almost universally embraced. His exertions to promote the civil prosperity of Rhode Island must endear his name to those who are now enjoying the fruits of his labors. He possessed the singular honor of contributing much towards establishing the first government upon the earth, which gave equal liberty, civil and religious, to all men living under it.

## ANN HUTCHINSON,

woman who occasioned much difficulty in New England, soon after its first settlement, came from Lincolnshire to Boston, 1635, and was the wife of one of the representatives of Boston. The members of Mr. Cotton's church used to meet every week to repeat his sermons, and discourse on doctrines. She set up meetings for women, and soon had a numerous audience. After repeating the sermons of Mr. Cotton, she added reflections of her own; she advocated her own sentiments, and warped the discourses of her minister to coincide with them. She soon threw the whole colony into a flame. The progress of her sentiments occasioned the synod of 1637, the first synod in America. This convention of ministers condemned eighty-two erroneous opinions, then propagated in the country. Mrs. Hutchinson, after this sentence of her opinions, was herself called before the court in November of the same year, and, being convicted of traducing the ministers, and advancing errors, was banished the colony. She went with her husband to Rhode Island. In the year 1642, after her husband's death, she removed into the Dutch country beyond New Haven; and the next year, she, her son Francis, and most of her family of sixteen persons, were killed by the Indians.

---

## MICHAEL MOLINOS,

founder of the ancient sect of Quietists, was a Spaniard, of a rich and honorable family. He entered into priest's orders young, but would accept no preferment in the church. He possessed great talents, and was ardently pious, without any of the austerities of the Romish religious orders. He went to Rome, where, in 1675, he published his "Spiritual Guide,' which gave him universal reputation. The Jesuits and Dominicans, envious at his success, charged him with heresy, and at last succeeded in getting him condemned by the Inquisition. He died of torment in their dungeons, a few years after.

## JOHN WESLEY,

the great founder of Methodism, was born at Epworth, in England, in 1703. In 1714, he was placed at the Charter House; and two years after he was elected to Christ Church, Oxford. In 1725, he was ordained deacon, and the next year became fellow and tutor of Lincoln College.

Wesley's character, says his biographer, is itself a study He equalled Luther in energy and courage, and Melancthon in learning and prudence. All the excellences of both the Wittemberg reformers were combined, if not transcended, in his individual character.

He possessed, in an eminent degree, the power of comprehending at once the general outlines and the details of plans, the aggregate and the integrants. It is this power which forms the philosophical genius in science; it is indispensable to the successful commander and the great statesman. It is illustrated in the whole economical system of Methodism — a system which, while it fixes itself to the smallest localities with the utmost detail and tenacity, is sufficiently general in its provisions to reach the ends of the world, and still maintain its unity of spirit and discipline.

No man knew better than Wesley the importance of small things. His whole financial system was based on weekly penny collections. It was a rule of his preachers never to omit a single preaching appointment, except when the "risk of limb or life" required. He was the first to apply extensively the plan of tract distribution. He wrote, printed, and scattered over the kingdom, placards on almost every topic of morals and religion. In addition to the usual means of grace, he introduced the band meeting, the class meeting, the prayer meeting, the love feast, and the watch nigh Not content with his itinerant laborers, he called into use the less available powers of his people by establishing the new departments of local preachers, exhorters, and leaders. It was, in fine, by gathering together fragments, by combining minutiæ, that he formed that stupendous system of spiritual means which is rapidly evangelizing the world.

It was not only in the theoretical construction of plans that he excelled; he was, if possible, still more distinguished by practical energy. The variety and number of his labors would be absolutely incredible with less authentic evidence than that which corroborates them. He was perpetually travelling and preaching, studying and writing, translating and abridging, superintending his societies, and applying his great plans. He travelled usually *five thousand* miles a year, preaching twice and thrice a day, commencing at five o'clock in the morning. In the midst of all this travelling and preaching, he carried with him the meditative and studious habits of the philosopher. No department of human inquiry was omitted by him. "History, poetry, and philosophy," said he, "I read on horseback."

Like Luther, he knew the importance of the press; he kept it teeming with his publications. His itinerant preachers were good agents for their circulation. "Carry them with you through every round," he would say; "exert yourselves in this; be not ashamed, be not weary, leave no stone unturned." His works, including abridgments and translations, amounted to about two hundred volumes. These comprise treatises on almost every subject of divinity, poetry, music, history,—natural, moral, metaphysical, and political philosophy. He wrote, as he preached, *ad populum;* and his works have given to his people, especially in Great Britain, an elevated tone of intelligence as well as of piety. He may, indeed, be considered the leader in those exertions which are now being made for the popular diffusion of knowledge.

Differing from the usual character of men who are given to various exertions and many plans, he was accurate and profound. He was an adept in classical literature and the use of the classical tongues; his writings are adorned with their finest passages. He was familiar with a number of modern languages; his own style is one of the best examples of strength and perspicuity among English writers. He was ready on every subject of learning and general literature As a logician, he was considered by his enemies, as well as his friends, to be unrivalled.

He was but little addicted to those exhilarations and contrarieties of frame which characterize imaginative minds. His temperament was warm, but not fiery. His intellect never appears inflamed, but was a glowing, serene radiance. His immense labors were accomplished, not by the impulses of restless enthusiasm, but by the cool calculations of his plans, and the steady self-possession with which he pursued them. "Though always in haste," he said, "I am never in a hurry." He was as economical with his time as a miser could be with his gold; rising at four o'clock in the morning, and allotting to every hour its appropriate work. "Leisure and I have taken leave of each other," said he. And yet such was the happy arrangement of his employments, that, amidst a multiplicity that would distract an ordinary man, he declares that "there are few persons who spend so many hours secluded from all company as mvself." "The wonder of his character," said Robert Hall, "is the self-control by which he preserved himself calm, while he kept all in excitement around him. He was the last man to be infected by fanaticism. His writings abound in statements of preternatural circumstances; but it must be remembered that his faults in these respects were those of his age, while his virtues were peculiarly his own."

Though of a feeble constitution, the regularity of his habits, sustained through a life of great exertions and vicissitudes, produced a vigor and equanimity which are seldom the accompaniments of a laborious mind or of a distracted life. "I do not remember," he says, "to have felt lowness of spirits one quarter of an hour since I was born." "Ten thousand cares are no more weight to my mind than ten thousand hairs are to my head." "I have never lost a night's sleep in my life." "His face was remarkably fine, his complexion fresh to the last week of his life, and his eye quick, keen, and active." He ceased not his labors till death. After the eightieth year of his age, he visited Holland twice. At the end of his eighty-second, he says, "I am never tired (such is the goodness of God) either with writing, preaching, or travelling." He preached under trees which he had planted himself, at Kingswood. He outlived most of his first disciples and preachers, and stood up, mighty in intellect and labors, among the second and third generations of his people. In his later years persecution had subsided; he was every where received as a patriarch, and sometimes excited, by his arrival in towns and cities, an interest "such as the presence of the king himself would produce." He attracted the largest assemblies, perhaps, which were ever congregated for religious instruction, being estimated sometimes at more than *thirty thousand!* Great intellectually, morally, and physically, he at length died, in the eighty-eighth year of his age and sixty-fifth of his ministry, unquestionably one of the most extraordinary men of any age.

Nearly one hundred and forty thousand members, upward of five hundred itinerant, and more than one thousand local preachers, were connected with him when he died.

---

## GEORGE WHITEFIELD,

one of the founders of the sect of the Methodists, was born at Gloucester, where his mother kept the Bell inn, 1714. From the Crypt school of his native town, he entered as servitor at Pembroke College, Oxford, and was ordained at the proper age by Benson, bishop of Gloucester. Enthusiasm and the love of singularity now influenced his conduct, and in his eagerness to obtain popularity, he preached not only in prisons, but in the open fields, and by a strong persuasive eloquence, multitudes regarded him as a man of superior sanctity. In 1738, he went to America, to increase the number of his converts; but, after laboring for some time as the friend and the associate of the Wesleys, he at last was engaged with them in a serious dispute, which produced a separation. While he zealously asserted the doctrine of absolute election and final perseverance, agreeably to the notions of Calvin, his opponents regarded his opinion as unsupported by Scripture, and therefore inadmissible; and in consequence of this arose the two sects of the Calvinistic and the Arminian Methodists. Secure in the good opinion of a great number of adherents, and in the patronage of Lady Huntingdon, to whom he was chaplain, he continued his labors, and built two Tabernacles in the city and in Tottenham Court Road for the commodious reception of his followers. He died at Newburyport, Massachusetts, while on a visit to his churches in America, and had the satisfaction to know that his adherents were numerous on both continents

At Newburyport, the Hon. WILLIAM BARTLETT has erected an elegant marble monument, on which is the following inscription: —

"This Cenotaph is erected, with affectionate veneration, to the memory of the Rev. GEORGE WHITEFIELD, born at Gloucester, England, December 16, 1714; educated at Oxford University; ordained 1736. In a ministry of thirty-four years, he crossed the Atlantic thirteen times, and preached more than eighteen thousand sermons. As a soldier of the cross, humble, devoted, ardent, he put on the whole armor of God; preferring the honor of Christ to his own interest, repose, reputation, and life. As a Christian orator, his deep piety, disinterested zeal, and vivid imagination, gave unexampled energy to his look, utterance, and action. Bold, fervent, pungent, and popular in his eloquence, no other uninspired man ever preached to so large assemblies, or enforced the simple truths of the gospel by motives so persuasive and awful, and with an influence so powerful on the hearts of his hearers. He died of asthma, September 30, 1770, suddenly exchanging his life of unparalleled labors for his eternal rest."

During Mr. Whitefield's visit to Philadelphia, he preached often in the evening from the gallery of the court-house in

Market Street. So loud was his voice at that time, that it was distinctly heard on the Jersey shore, and so distinct was his speech, that every word he said was understood at Market Street wharf, a distance of upwards of four hundred feet from the court-house. All the intermediate space was crowded with his hearers. Mr. Whitefield was truly remarkable for his uncommon eloquence and fervent zeal. His eloquence was indeed very great, and of the truest kind. He was utterly devoid of all affectation; the importance of his subject, and the regard due to his hearers, engrossed all his concern. Every accent of his voice spoke to the ear, every feature of his face, every motion of his hands, and every gesture, spoke to the eye; so that the most dissipated and thoughtless found their attention arrested, and the dullest and most ignorant could not but understand. He appeared to be devoid of the spirit of sectarianism; his only object seemed to be to "preach Christ and him crucified."

The following anecdote respecting his manner of preaching will serve to illustrate this part of his character. One day, while preaching from the balcony of the court-house, in Philadelphia, he cried out, "Father Abraham, who have you got in heaven; any *Episcopalians?*" "No!" "Any *Presbyterians?*" "No!" "Any *Baptists?*" "No!" "Have you any *Methodists* there?" "No!" "Have you any *Independents* or *Seceders?*" "No! No!" "Why, who have you, then?" "We don't know those names here; all that are here are *Christians* — believers in Christ — men who have overcome by the blood of the Lamb, and the word of his testimony!" "O, is this the case? then God help me — God help us all — to forget party names, and to become Christians in deed and in truth."

---

## SELINA HUNTINGDON,

countess, second daughter of Washington, earl Ferrers, was born 1707, and married Lord Huntingdon, by whom she had four sons and three daughters. From habits of gayety and scenes of dissipation, she became all at once, after a serious illness, grave, reserved, and melancholy. Her thoughts were wholly absorbed by religion, and she employed the ample resources which she possessed in disseminating her principles by the popular arts of Whitefield, Romaine, and others. Not only her house in Park Street was thrown open for the frequent assembling of these pious reformers, but chapels were built in various parts of the kingdom, and a college erected in Wales for the education of young persons in the future labors of the ministry. After many acts of extensive charity, and with the best intentions, this enthusiastic lady died in 1791.

---

## ROBERT SANDEMAN,

the founder of the sect called *Sandemanians*, was born at Perth, in Scotland, about the year 1718, and was educated at St. Andrews. Instead of entering into the church, for which he was intended, he became a linen manufacturer, and afterwards turned preacher. He came to America in October, 1764, and from Boston he went to Danbury, Connecticut In that town he gathered a church the following year. He afterwards established several societies in New England. Individuals are still found who adhere to his peculiarities, and are known by the name of his sect. He wrote an answer to Hervey's "Theron and Aspasio," said to be a work of talent, but exhibiting great asperity.

The following is copied from the monument of Mr. Sandeman, in the burying-ground at Danbury: —

"Here lies, until the resurrection, the body of Robert Sandeman, a native of Perth, North Britain, who, in the face of continual opposition from all sorts of men, long boldly contended for the ancient faith, that the bare word of Jesus Christ, without a deed or thought on the part of man, is sufficient to present the chief of sinners spotless before God To declare this blessed truth, as testified in the holy Scriptures, he left his country, he left his friends, and, after much patient suffering, finished his labors at Danbury, April 2, 1771, Æ. 53 years.

> Deigned Christ to come so nigh to us,
>   As not to count it shame
> To call us brethren, should we blush
>   At aught that bears his name?
> Nay, let us boast in his reproach,
>   And glory in his cross;
> When he appears, one smile from him
>   Would far o'erpay our loss."

---

## SAMUEL HOPKINS,

an American divine, who, in his sermons and tracts, has made several additions to the sentiments first advanced by the celebrated Jonathan Edwards, late president of New Jersey College. Dr. Hopkins was born at Waterbury, in Connecticut, 1721, and graduated at Yale College, in 1741. Soon after, he engaged in theological studies, at Northampton, Massachusetts, under the superintendence of Jonathan Edwards, and, in 1743, was ordained at Housatonic, now Great Barrington, Massachusetts, where he continued till he removed to Newport, Rhode Island, in consequence of the diminution of his congregation, and his want of support. When he had resided some time in this place, the people became dissatisfied with his sentiments, and resolved, at a meeting, to intimate to him their disinclination to his continuance among them. On the ensuing Sabbath, he preached his farewell discourse, which was so interesting and impressive that they besought him to remain, which he did till his death, in 1803. He was a pious and zealous man, of considerable talents, and almost incredible powers of application. He is said to have been sometimes engaged during eighteen hours in his studies. His doctrinal views are contained in his "System of Divinity," published in a second edition at Boston, in 1811, in two volumes, octavo.

### JONATHAN MAYHEW,

a divine of Boston, was born in Martha's Vineyard, in 1720 and educated at Harvard College. In 1747, he was ordained pastor of the West Church, in Boston, and continued in this station the remainder of his life. He possessed a mind of great acuteness and energy, and in his principles was a determined republican. He had no little influence in producing the American revolution. His sermons and controversial tracts obtained for him a high reputation; and many of them were republished several times in England. He died in 1766.

---

### SAMUEL SEABURY,

first bishop of the Protestant Episcopal church in the Unitea States, was born in 1728, and graduated at Yale College in 1751. After finishing his classical education, he went to Scotland with the view of studying medicine; but soon, having turned his attention to theology, he altered his purpose and took orders in London, 1753. Returning to America, he officiated, first at Brunswick, New Jersey, then at Jamaica, Long Island, next at West Chester, New York, and lastly at New London, Connecticut, where he remained, as rector of the parish in that city, during the remainder of his life. As much as he was esteemed by his parishioners, his influ ence was extended among his brethren throughout the state. Consequently, when the Episcopal church was organized in that diocese, he was elected bishop. He went immediately o England, in order to obtain consecration; but, meeting with some unexpected obstacles, he repaired to Scotland. Here he was able to accomplish the object of his mission. He was consecrated at Aberdeen, November 14, 1784. As soon as he was able to reach home, he resumed his duties as parish minister at New London, in connection with his episcopal functions for the diocese. Bishop Seabury had a vigorous and well-cultivated mind, and acquired a reputation corresponding with his high station. Three volumes of his sermons have been published.

The following is the inscription on Bishop Seabury's monument at New London, Connecticut:—

"Here lyeth the body of SAMUEL SEABURY, D. D., Bishop of Connecticut and Rhode Island, who departed from this transitory scene February 25th, Anno Domini 1796, in the 68th year of his age, and the 12th of his episcopal consecration.

"Ingenious without pride, learned without pedantry, good without severity, he was duly qualified to discharge the duties of the Christian and the Bishop. In the pulpit he enforced religion; in his conduct he exemplified it. The poor he assisted with his charity; the ignorant he blessed with his instruction. The friend of men, he ever designed their good; the enemy of vice, he ever opposed it. Christian, dost thou aspire to happiness? Seabury has shown the way that leads to it."

---

## RICHARD CLARKE,

a clergyman of the Episcopal church, who maintained for many years a high reputation in South Carolina. He was a native of England, and soon after his arrival in Charleston was appointed rector of St. Philip's Church in that city. Here he was greatly admired as a popular preacher, and highly respected as an exemplary, amiable, benevolent, and liberal man. He returned to England in 1759, and was soon afterwards appointed a stated preacher in one of the principal churches in London. In this station, his eloquence and piety attracted a large share of public attention. His publications, chiefly on theological subjects, were numerous, amounting to six or seven octavo volumes. He lived to a late period in the eighteenth century, universally beloved and respected.

## JOSEPH PRIESTLEY

an English philosopher and dissenting divine, born at Field head, Yorkshire, 1733. He was educated at Daventry, under Dr. Ashworth, for the ministry among the dissenters, and at the proper age he took care of a congregation at Needham Market, Suffolk, and afterwards at Nantwich, Cheshire. He became, in 1761, professor of belles lettres in the Warrington Academy. and after seven years' residence there he removed to Leeds, and two years after accepted the office of librarian and philosophical companion to the earl of Shelburne. In this retreat, the philosopher devoted himself laboriously to metaphysical and theological studies, and published various works; and when, at last, he separated from his noble patron, he retired with an annual pension of one hundred and fifty pounds, to settle at Birmingham, as pastor to a Unitarian congregation, in 1780. While here usefully employed in advancing the cause of philosophy, and too often engaged in theological disputes, he became the victim of popular fury; and the conduct of some of his neighbors in celebrating the anniversary of the French revolution, in 1791, with more intemperance than became Englishmen and loyal subjects, excited a dreadful riot. Not only the meeting-houses were destroyed on this melancholy occasion, but, among others, Dr. Priestley's house, library, manuscripts, and philosophical apparatus, were totally consumed; and, though he recovered a compensation by suing the county, he quitted this scene of prejudice and unpopularity. After residing some time at London and Hackney, where he preached to the congregation over which his friend Price once presided, he determined to quit his native country, and seek a more peaceful retreat in America, where some of his family were already settled He left England in 1794, and fixed his residence at Northumberland, in Pennsylvania, where he died in 1804. His writings were very numerous, and he long attracted the public notice, not only by discoveries in philosophy, but by the boldness of his theological opinions. Had he confined his studies merely to philosophical pursuits, his name would have descended to posterity with greater lustre; but he who attempts innovations in government and religion, for singularity, and to excite popular prejudices, must be little entitled to the applauses of the world.

---

## JAMES PURVES,

a learned Arian preacher, born at a little village of Berwickshire, in 1734. His father was only a keeper of cattle, and intended James for the same profession. He, meanwhile, having obtained the loan of some books on mathematics, made himself master of geometry and trigonometry, and afterwards taught these sciences, with other branches of mathematics, and assisted some public authors in compiling mathematical works, which have been well received. He joined a party of the ancient Cameronians, and in 1769, at one of their general meetings, was called to be a pastor among them. To qualify himself for this office, he studied the Greek and Hebrew languages, and compiled a Hebrew grammar, which is still in manuscript. These acquisitions led him into the study of the Arian controversy, when finally he adopted the opinions of Arius, and afterwards became preacher to a small Arian congregation in Edinburgh, where he also kept a school and a book-shop, for many years before he died.

---

## JOHN JEBB,

Bishop of Limerick, was born September 27, 1775, and died December 9, 1833, aged 58. He was educated at the university of Dublin, where he gained a high reputation as a scholar. He was greatly esteemed as a man of a most amiable and gentle spirit; had the reputation of an accomplished orator and a learned and able theologian; and as a clergyman and a bishop he was truly exemplary. His original publications are not numerous, but are of high merit.

## JOHN GASPAR CHRISTIAN LAVATER,

a celebrated writer, born at Zurich, 1741. He was pastor of the church of St. Peter's at Zurich, and as a minister he acquired great reputation both by his eloquent discourses and his exemplary life. He was wounded by a French soldier when Zurich was taken by storm under Massena in 1799, and died there in consequence of it, 12th January, 1801. He acquired deserved celebrity as a physiognomist, and his writings on the subject, possessing great merit, ingenious remarks, and truly original ideas, have been translated into all the languages of Europe. His Christian piety was of the highest order.

---

## JOHN TILLOTSON,

an eminent prelate, was born in 1630, at Sowerby, in Yorkshire, and was educated at Clare Hall, Cambridge. In 1691, after fruitless attempts to avoid the honor, he accepted, with unfeigned reluctance, the see of Canterbury, which was become vacant by the deprivation of Sancroft. This promotion, however, he did not long survive, as his decease took place in 1694.

In his domestic relations, friendships, and the whole commerce of business, he was easy and humble, frank and open, tender-hearted and bountiful, to such an extent, that, while he was in a private station, he laid aside two tenths of his income for charitable uses. He despised wealth but as it furnished him for charity, in which he was judicious as well as liberal. His affability and candor, as well as abilities in his profession, made him frequently consulted in points relating both to practice and opinion. His love for the real philosophy of nature, and his conviction that the study of it is the most solid support of religion, induced him, not many years after the establishment of the Royal Society, to desire to be admitted into that assembly of the greatest men of the age; into which he was accordingly elected on the 25th of January, 1672. His kindness towards the dissenters was attended with the consequence intended by him, of reconciling many of them to the communion of the established church, and almost all of them to a greater esteem of it than they had before entertained.

He died poor, the copy-right of his Posthumous Sermons (which, however, sold for two thousand five hundred guineas) being all that his family inherited. His works form three folio volumes.

---

## ISAAC NEWTON,

a most celebrated English philosopher and mathematician, and one of the greatest geniuses that ever appeared in the world, was descended from an ancient family in Lincolnshire, where he was born in the year 1642. His powers of mind were wonderfully comprehensive and penetrating. Fontenelle says of him, "that in learning mathematics, he did not study Euclid, who seemed to him too plain and simple, and unworthy of taking up his time. He understood him almost before he read him: a cast of his eye on the contents of the theorems of that great mathematician, seemed to be sufficient to make him master of them." Several of his works mark a profundity of thought and reflection that has astonished the most learned men. He was highly esteemed by the university of Cambridge, and was twice chosen to represent that place in parliament. He was also greatly favored by Queen Anne, and by George I. The princess of Wales, afterwards queen consort of England, who had a turn for philosophical inquiries, used frequently to propose questions to him. This princess had a great regard for him, and often declared that she thought herself happy to live at the same time as he did, and to have the pleasure and advantage of his conversation.

This eminent philosopher was remarkable for being of a very meek disposition and a great lover of peace. He would rather have chosen to remain in obscurity, than to have the serenity of his days disturbed by those storms and disputes, which genius and learning often draw upon those who are eminent for them. We find him reflecting on the controversy respecting his optic lectures (in which he had been almost unavoidably engaged) in the following terms: — "I blamed my own imprudence, for parting with so real a blessing as my quiet, to run after a shadow."

The amiable quality of modesty stands very conspicuous in the character of this great man's mind and manners. He never spoke, either of himself or others, in such a manner as to give the most malicious censurers the least occasion even to suspect him of vanity. He was candid and affable; and he did not assume any airs of superiority over those with whom he associated. He never thought either his merit or his reputation sufficient to excuse him from any of the common offices of social life. Though he was firmly attached to the church of England, he was averse to the persecution of the Nonconformists. He judged of men by their conduct; and the true schismatics, in his opinion, were the vicious and the wicked. This liberality of sentiment did not spring from the want of religion; for he was thoroughly persuaded of the truth of revelation; and amidst the great variety of books which he had constantly before him, that which he loved the best, and studied with the greatest application, was the Bible. He was, indeed, a truly pious man; and his discoveries concerning the frame and system of the universe, were applied by him to demonstrate the being of a God, and to illustrate his power and wisdom. He also wrote an excellent discourse, to prove that the remarkable prophecy of Daniel's weeks was an express prediction of the coming of the Messiah, and that it was fulfilled in Jesus Christ.

The testimony of the pious and learned Dr. Doddridge to the most interesting part of this great man's character, cannot be omitted on the present occasion. "According to the best information," says he, "whether public or private, I could ever obtain, his firm faith in the divine revelation discovered itself in the most genuine fruits of substantial virtue and piety, and consequently gives us the justest reason to conclude that he is now rejoicing in the happy effects of it, infinitely more than in all the applause which his philosophical works have procured him, though they have commanded a fame lasting as the world."

He departed this life in the eighty-fifth year of his age, and, in his principles and conduct through life, has left a strong and comfortable evidence that the highest intellectual powers harmonize with religion and virtue, and that there is nothing in Christianity but what will abide the scrutiny of the soundest and most enlarged understanding.

How great and satisfactory a confirmation is it to the sincere, humble Christian, and what an insurmountable barrier does it present to the infidel, to perceive, in the list of Christian believers, the exalted and venerable name of Newton! a man who must be acknowledged to be an ornament of human nature, when we consider the wide compass of his abilities, the great extent of his learning and knowledge, and the piety, integrity, and beneficence, of his life. This eminent character firmly adhered to the belief of Christianity, after the most diligent and exact researches into the life of its Founder, the authenticity of its records, the completion of its prophecies, the sublimity of its doctrines, the purity of its precepts, and the arguments of its adversaries.

---

## CHARLES V.,

emperor of Germany, king of Spain, and lord of the Netherlands, was born at Ghent, in the year 1500.

He is said to have fought sixty battles, in most of which he was victorious, to have obtained six triumphs, conquered four kingdoms, and to have added eight principalities to his dominions — an almost unparalleled instance of worldly prosperity and the greatness of human glory.

But all these fruits of his ambition, and all the honors which attended him, could not yield true and solid satisfaction. Reflecting on the evils and miseries which he had occasioned, and convinced of the emptiness of earthly magnificence, he became disgusted with the splendor that surrounded him, and thought it his duty to withdraw from it, and spend the rest of his days in religious retirement. Accordingly, he voluntarily resigned all his dominions to his brother and son; and, after taking an affectionate and last farewell of the latter, and a numerous retinue of princes and nobility who respectfully attended him, he repaired to his chosen retreat, which was situated in Spain, in a vale of no great extent, watered by a small brook, and surrounded with rising grounds covered with lofty trees

A deep sense of his frail condition and great imperfections appears to have impressed his mind in this extraordinary resolution, and through the remainder of his life. As soon as he landed in Spain, he fell prostrate on the ground, and considering himself now as dead to the world, he kissed the earth, and said, "Naked came I out of my mother's womb, and naked I now return to thee, thou common mother of mankind!"

In this humble retreat, he spent his time in religious exercises and innocent employments, and buried here, in solitude and silence, his grandeur and his ambition, together with all those vast projects, which, for near half a century, had alarmed and agitated Europe, and filled every kingdom in it, by turns, with the terror of his arms, and the dread of being subjected to his power. Far from taking any part in the political transactions of the world, he restrained his curiosity even from any inquiry concerning them, and seemed to view the busy scene he had abandoned with an elevation and indifference of mind which arose from his thorough experience of its vanity, as well as from the pleasing reflection of having disengaged himself from its cares and temptations

Here he enjoyed more complete contentment than all his grandeur had ever yielded him; as a full proof of which he has left this short but comprehensive testimony: — "I have tasted more satisfaction in my solitude, in one day, than in all the triumphs of my former reign. The sincere study, profession, and practice, of the Christian religion have in them such joys and sweetness as are seldom found in courts and grandeur."

---

## FRANCIS BACON,

baron of Verulam, viscount St. Albans, and lord high chancellor of England, was born in the year 1561. He was one of the most remarkable men of whom any age or country can boast; and his writings furnish incontestable proofs that his knowledge, wisdom, and benevolence, were very extraordinary. Lord Bacon died in 1626.

That this illustrious character was deeply influenced by a truly humble and religious spirit, is manifest from the following prayer, which was found amongst his papers, in his own hand-writing:—

"Most gracious Lord God, my merciful Father; my Creator, my Redeemer, my Comforter! thou soundest and searchest the depths and secrets of all hearts; thou acknowledgest the upright; thou judgest the hypocrite; vanity and crooked ways cannot be hid from thee.

"Remember, O Lord, how thy servant has walked before thee; remember what I have first sought, and what has been principal in my intentions. I have loved thy assemblies; I have mourned for the divisions of thy church; I have delighted in the brightness of thy sanctuary; I have ever prayed unto thee, that the vine which thy right hand hath planted in this nation, might have the former and the latter rain, and that it might stretch its branches to the seas and to the floods. The state and bread of the poor and oppressed have been precious in my eyes; I have hated all cruelty and hardness of heart; I have, though a despised weed, endeavored to procure the good of all men. If any have been my enemies, I thought not of them, neither has the sun gone down upon my displeasure; but I have been as a dove, free from superfluity of maliciousness. Thy creatures have been my books, but thy Scriptures much more so. I have sought thee in the courts, the fields, and the gardens; but I have found thee in thy temples.

"O Lord, my strength! I have, from my youth, met with nee in all my ways; in thy fatherly compassions, in thy merciful chastisements, and in thy most visible providences. As thy favors have increased upon me, so have thy corrections; as my worldly blessings were exalted, so secret darts from thee have pierced me; and when I have ascended before men, I have descended in humiliation before thee. And now, when I have been thinking most of peace and honor, thy hand is heavy upon me, and has humbled me according to thy former loving-kindness, keeping me still in thy fatherly school, not as a bastard, but as a child. Just are thy judgments upon me for my sins, which are more in number than the sands of the sea, but which have no proportion to thy mercies. Besides my innumerable sins, I confess before thee, that I am a debtor to thee for the gracious talent of hy gifts and graces; which I have neither put into a napkin nor placed, as I ought, with exchangers, where it might have made best profit; but I have misspent it in things for which I was least fit: so I may truly say, my soul hath been a stranger in the course of my pilgrimage. Be merciful unto me, O Lord, for my Savior's sake, and receive me into thy bosom, or guide me into thy ways."

---

MATTHEW HALE,

lord chief justice of England, was born in Gloucestershire, in the year 1609, and, by the care of a wise and religious father, had great attention paid to his education.

In his youth, he was fond of company, and fell into many levities and extravagances. But this propensity and conduct were corrected by a circumstance that made a considerable impression on his mind during the rest of his life. Being one day in company with other young men, one of the party, through excess of wine, fell down, apparently dead, at their feet. Young Hale was so affected on this occasion, that he immediately retired to another room, and, shutting the door, fell on his knees, and prayed earnestly to God that his friend might be restored to life, and that he himself might be pardoned for having given countenance to so much excess. At the same time, he made a solemn vow that he would never again keep company in that manner, nor "drink a health" while he lived. His friend recovered, and Hale religiously observed his vow. After this event, there was an entire change in his disposition; he forsook all dissipated company, and was careful to divide his time between the duties of religion and the studies of his profession.

He became remarkable for his solid and grave deportment, his inflexible regard to justice, and a religious tenderness of spirit, which appear to have accompanied him through life. His retired meditations on religious subjects manifest a pious and humble frame of mind, and a solemnity well adapted to excite kindred emotions in the breast of the reader.

"True religion," says he, "teaches the soul a high veneration for Almighty God, a sincere and upright walking, as in the presence of the invisible, all-seeing God. It makes a man truly love, honor, and obey him, and therefore careful to know what his will is. It renders the heart highly thankful to him, as his Creator, Redeemer, and Benefactor. It makes a man entirely depend on him, seek him for guidance, direction, and protection, and submit to his will with patience and resignation of soul. It gives the law, not only to his words and actions, but to his very thoughts and purposes; so that he dares not entertain any which are unbecoming the presence of that God by whom all our thoughts are legible. It crushes all pride and haughtiness, both in a man's heart and carriage, and gives him an humble state of mind before God and men. It regulates the passions, and brings them into due moderation. It gives a man a right estimate of this present world, and sets his heart and hopes above it; so that he never loves it more than it deserves. It makes the wealth and the glory of this world, — high places and great preferments, — of but little consequence to him; so that he is neither covetous, nor ambitious, nor over-solicitous, concerning the advantages of them It makes him value the love of God and the peace of his own conscience above all the wealth and honor in the world, and to be very diligent in preserving them. He performs all his duties to God with sincerity and humility; and, whilst he lives on earth, his conversation, his hope, his treasures, are in heaven; and he endeavors to walk suitably to such a hope."

"They who truly fear God, have a secret guidance from a higher wisdom than what is barely human, namely, the Spirit of truth and goodness; which does really, though secretly, prevent and direct them. Any man that sincerely and truly fears Almighty God, and calls and relies upon him for his direction, has it as really as a son has the counsel and direction of his father; and though the voice be not audible, nor discernible by sense, yet it is equally as real as if a man heard a voice, saying, 'This is the way; walk in it.'"

"Though this secret direction of Almighty God is principally seen in matters relating to the good of the soul, yet, even in the concerns of this life, a good man fearing God, and begging his direction, will very often, if not at all times, find it. I can call my own experience to witness, that even in the temporal affairs of my whole life, I have never been disappointed of the best direction, when I have, in humility and sincerity, implored it.

"The observance of the secret admonition of this Spirit of God in the heart, is an effectual means to cleanse and sanctify us; and the more it is attended to, the more it will be conversant with our souls, for our instruction. In the midst of difficulties, it will be our counsellor; in the midst of temptations, it will be our strength, and grace sufficient for us; in the midst of troubles, it will be our light and our comforter."

Chief Justice Hale died on the twenty-fifth of December, 1676.

## PRINCESS ELIZABETH,

of the Rhine, was born in the year 1620. She was the eldest daughter of Frederick V., elector palatine and king of Bohemia, by Anne, daughter of James I., king of England. This excellent princess possessed only a small territory; but she governed it with great judgment and attention to the happiness of her subjects. She made it a rule to hear, one day in the week, all such causes as were brought before her. On these occasions, her wisdom, justice, and moderation, were very conspicuous. She frequently remitted forfeitures, in cases where the parties were poor, or in any respect worthy of favor. It was remarkable that she often introduced religious considerations as motives to persuade the contending parties to harmony and peace. She was greatly beloved and respected by her subjects, and also by many persons of learning and virtue not resident in her dominions; for she patronized men of this character, whatever might be their country or religious profession.

In the year 1677, the famous William Penn paid her a visit, and was treated by her with great respect. The following account of her is taken from his works: —

" The meekness and humility of the princess appeared to me extraordinary: she did not consider the quality, but the merit, of the people she entertained. Did she hear of a retired man, seeking after the knowledge of a better world, she was sure to set him down in the catalogue of her charity, if he wanted it. I have casually seen, I believe, fifty tokens of her benevolence, sealed and directed to the several poor subjects of her bounty, whose distance prevented them from being personally known to her. Thus, though she kept no sumptuous table in her own court, she spread the tables of the poor in their solitary cells; breaking bread to virtuous pilgrims, according to their wants and her ability.

" She was abstemious in her living, and in apparel void of all vain ornaments. I must needs say, that her mind had a noble prospect: her eye was to a better and more lasting inheritance, than can be found below. This made her not overrate the honors of her station, or the learning of the schools, of which she was an excellent judge. Being once at Hamburgh, a religious person, whom she went to see for religion's sake, remarked to her, that 'it was too great an honor for him, that a visitant of her quality, who was allied to so many great kings and princes of this world, should come under his roof:' to whom she humbly replied, 'If they were religious, as well as great, it would be an honor indeed; but if you knew what that greatness was, as well as I do, you would value it less.'

"After a religious meeting which we had in her chamber, she was much affected, and said, 'It is a hard thing to be faithful to what one knows. O, the way is strait! I am afraid I am not weighty enough in my spirit to walk in it.'"

"She once withdrew, on purpose to give her servants, who were religiously disposed, the liberty of discoursing with us that they might the more freely put what questions of conscience they desired to be satisfied in. Sometimes she suffered both them and the poorest persons of her town to sit by her in her own chamber, where we had two meetings. I cannot forget her last words, when I took my leave of her: —'Let me desire you to remember me, though I live at so great a distance, and you should never see me more. I thank you for this good time. Be assured that, though my condition subjects me to divers temptations, yet my soul has strong desires after the best things.'

"She lived till the age of sixty years, and then departed at her house in Herwerden, in the year 1680, as much lamented as she had been beloved by her people. To her real worth I do, with a religious gratitude, dedicate this memorial."

---

ROBERT BOYLE,

an eminent philosopher, and a truly good man, was the son of Richard, earl of Cork, and was born at Lismore, in Ireland, in the year 1627. At Eton School, where he was educated, he soon discovered a force of understanding which promised great things, and a disposition to improve it to the utmost. During his education, and before he was ten years old, he was much afflicted with an ague, which considerably depressed his spirits; and, to divert his attention, he was persuaded to read Amadis de Gaul, and other romantic books. But this kind of reading, he says in his memoirs, produced such restlessness in him, that he was obliged to apply himself to mathematical studies, in order to fix and settle the volatility of his fancy. He died in the sixty-fifth year of his age.

He was a man of great learning, and his stock of knowledge was immense. The celebrated Dr. Boerhaave has passed the following eulogium upon him: — "Boyle was the ornament of his age and country. Which of his writings shall I commend? All of them. To him we owe the secrets of fire, air, water, animals, vegetables, fossils; so that from his works may be deduced the whole system of natural knowledge."

He was treated with particular kindness and respect by Charles II., as well as by the two great ministers Southampton and Clarendon. By the latter he was solicited to enter into orders; for his distinguished learning and unblemished reputation induced Lord Clarendon to think that so very respectable a personage would do great honor to the clergy. Boyle considered the proposal with due attention. He reflected that, in his present situation of life, whatever he wrote with respect to religion, would have greater weight, as coming from a layman; for he well knew that the irreligious fortified themselves against all that the clergy could offer, by supposing and saying that it was their trade, and that they were paid for it. He considered, likewise, that, in point of fortune and character, he needed no accessions; and, indeed, his desire for these was always very limited. But Bishop Burnet, to whom Boyle had communicated memorandums concerning his life, tells us that what had the greatest weight in determining his judgment, was, "the not feeling within himself any motion or tendency of mind which he could safely esteem a call from the Holy

Spirit, and so not venturing to take holy orders, lest he should be found to have lied unto it."

Bishop Burnet, who was Boyle's particular friend, and who, during an acquaintance of twenty-nine years, had spent many happy hours in conversation with him, gives a full account of his genuine piety and virtue, and of his zeal for the Christian religion. "This zeal," he says, "was unmixed with narrow notions, or a bigoted heat in favor of a particular sect; it was that spirit which is the ornament of a true Christian." Burnet mentions, as a proof of this, his noble foundation for lectures in defence of the gospel, against infidels of all sorts; the effects of which have been very conspicuous, in the many volumes of excellent discourses, which have been published in consequence of that laudable and pious design.

The great object of his philosophical pursuits was to promote the cause of religion, and to discountenance atheism and infidelity. His intimate friend Bishop Burnet makes the following observations on this point: — "It appeared to those who conversed with him on his inquiries into nature, that his main design (on which as he had his own eye constantly fixed, so he took care to put others often in mind of it) was to raise in himself and others more exalted sentiments of the greatness and glory, the wisdom and goodness, of God. This design was so deeply impressed on his mind, that he concludes the article of his will, which relates to the Royal Society, in these words: — 'I wish them a happy success in their attempts to discover the true nature of the works of God; and I pray that they, and all searchers into physical truths, may cordially refer their attainments to the glory of the great Author of nature, and to the comfort of mankind.'"

On another occasion, the same person speaks of him thus — "He had the most profound veneration for the great God of heaven and earth that I ever observed in any man. The very name of God was never mentioned by him without a pause and observable stop in his discourse." So brightly did the example of this great and good man shine, through his whole course, that Bishop Burnet, on reviewing it, in a moment of pious exultation thus expressed himself: — "I might challenge the whole tribe of libertines to come and view the usefulness, as well as the excellence, of the Christian religion, in a life that was entirely dedicated to it."

---

JOHN LOCKE,

a very celebrated philosopher, and one of the greatest men that England ever produced, was born in the year 1632. He was well educated; and, applying himself with vigor to his studies, his mind became enlarged, and stored with much useful knowledge. He went abroad as secretary to the English ambassador at several of the German courts, and afterwards had the offer of being made envoy at the court of the emperor, or of any other that he chose; but he declined the proposal, on account of the infirm state of his health. He was a commissioner of trade and plantations, in which station he very honorably distinguished himself. Notwithstanding his public employments, he found leisure to write much for the benefit of mankind. His "Essay on Human Understanding," his "Discourses on Government," and his "Letters on Toleration," are justly held in the highest esteem.

This enlightened man and profound reasoner was most firmly attached to the Christian religion. His zeal to promote it appeared, first, in his middle age, by publishing a discourse to demonstrate the reasonableness of believing Jesus to be the promised Messiah; and, afterwards, in the latter part of his life, by a Commentary on several of the Epistles of the apostle Paul. The sacred Scriptures are every where mentioned by him with the greatest reverence; and he exhorts Christians "to betake themselves in earnest to the study of the way to salvation, in those holy writings, wherein God has revealed it from heaven, and proposed it to the world; seeking our religion where we are sure it is in truth to be found, comparing spiritual things with spiritual."

In a letter written the year before his death, to one who asked this question, "What is the shortest and surest way for a young man to attain the true knowledge of the Christian religion?" he says, "Let him study the holy Scriptures. especially the New Testament: therein are contained the words of eternal life. It has God for its author; salvation for its end; and truth, without any mixture of error, for its matter." This advice was conformable to his own practice "For fourteen or fifteen years, he applied himself in an especial manner to the study of the Scriptures, and employed the last years of his life hardly in any thing else. He was never weary of admiring the great views of that sacred book, and the just relation of all its parts: he every day made discoveries in it that gave him fresh cause of admiration."

The consolation which he derived from divine revelation is forcibly expressed in these words: — "I gratefully receive and rejoice in the light of revelation, which has set me at rest in many things, the manner whereof my poor reason can by no means make out to me."

After he had diligently employed a great part of his life in a variety of occupations, he chose a pleasing retirement for the remainder of his days. This leisure appears to have been productive of solid improvement, by enabling him to look calmly over the scenes of past life; to form a proper estimate of its enjoyments, and to dedicate himself more fully to the cause of piety and virtue.

About two months before his death, in 1704, he wrote a letter to his friend Anthony Collins, and left this direction upon it: — "To be delivered to him after my decease." It concludes with the following remarkable words: —

"May you live long and happy, in the enjoyment of health, freedom, content, and all those blessings which Providence has bestowed on you, and to which your virtue entitles you. You loved me living, and will preserve my memory when I am dead. All the use to be made of it is, that this life is a scene of vanity, which soon passes away, and affords no solid satisfaction, but in the consciousness of doing well, and in the hopes of another life. This is what I can say upon experience; and what you will find to be true, when you come to make up the account. Adieu!"

## JOSEPH ADDISON,

a celebrated English writer, was born at Milston, in Wiltshire, in the year 1672. About the age of fifteen, he was entered at Queen's College, Oxford, where, by his fine parts and great application, he made a surprising proficiency in classical learning. Before he left the university, he was warmly solicited to enter into orders; and he once resolved to do so; but his great modesty, and an uncommonly delicate sense of the importance of the sacred function, made him afterwards alter his resolution. He was highly respected by many of the greatest and the most learned of his contemporaries. He travelled into Italy, where he made many useful observations, and prepared materials for some of his literary works. On his return to England, he was chosen one of the lords commissioners for trade. In 1709, he was appointed secretary to the lord lieutenant of Ireland, and, in 1717, was advanced to the high office of secretary of state. He died in 1729.

His writings have been of great use to the world, and his "Evidences of the Christian Religion" not the least so. Dr. Johnson, in delineating his character as a writer, gives the following amiable picture of him: — "He employed wit on the side of virtue and religion. He not only made the proper use of wit himself, but taught it to others; and, from his time, it has been generally subservient to the cause of reason and truth. He has dissipated the prejudice that had long connected cheerfulness with vice, and easiness of manners with laxity of principles. He has restored virtue to its dignity, and taught innocence not to be ashamed. This is an elevation of literary character above all Greek, above all Roman fame. As a teacher of wisdom, he may be confidently followed. His religion has nothing in it enthusiastic or superstitious; he appears neither weakly credulous nor wantonly skeptical; his morality is neither dangerously lax nor impracticably rigid. All the enchantment of fancy, and all the cogency of argument, are employed to recommend to the reader his real interest — the care of pleasing the Author of his being."

Of his integrity in discharging the duties of his office, there is a striking proof recorded. When he was secretary in Ireland, he had materially promoted the interest of an individual, who offered him, in return, a bank note of three hundred pounds, and a diamond ring of the same value. These he strenuously refused to accept, and wrote to the person as follows: — "And now, sir, believe me, when I assure you I never did, nor ever will, on any pretence whatsoever, take more than the stated and customary fees of my office. I might keep the contrary practice concealed from the world, were I capable of it, but I could not from myself· and I hope I shall always fear the reproaches of my own heart more than those of all mankind."

A mind conscious of its own uprightness, and humbly trusting in the goodness of God, has the best ground to look forward with complacency towards another life. The following lines of Addison are sweetly expressive of the peace and pleasure which he enjoyed in contemplating his future existence: — "The prospect of a future state is the secret comfort and refreshment of my soul. It is that which makes nature look cheerful about me; it doubles all my pleasures, and supports me under all my afflictions. I can look at disappointments and misfortunes, pain and sickness, death itself, with indifference, so long as I keep in view the pleasures of eternity, and the state of being in which there will be no fears nor apprehensions, pains nor sorrows."

---

## ISAAC WATTS,

a learned and eminent dissenting minister, was born at Southampton, in the year 1674, of parents who were distinguished by their piety and virtue. He died in 1748. He possessed an uncommon genius, of which he gave early proofs. He received a very liberal education, which was rendered highly beneficial to him by his own unwearied efforts to improve himself. After the most serious deliberation, he determined to devote his life to the ministry, of the importance of which office he had a deep and awful sense. He labored very dil igently to promote the instruction and happiness of the people under his care, to whom, by his Christian conduct and amia ble disposition, he greatly endeared himself.

Soon after he had undertaken the pastoral office, his health sustained a severe shock by a painful and dangerous illness, from which he recovered very slowly. But, in the year 1712, he was afflicted with a violent fever, that entirely broke his constitution, and left such weakness upon his nerves, as continued with him, in some measure, to his dying day. For four years he was wholly prevented from discharging the public offices of his station. Though this long interval of sickness was, no doubt, very trying to his active mind, yet it proved ultimately a blessing to him; for it drew upon him he particular notice of Sir Thomas Abney, a very pious and worthy man, who, from motives of friendship, invited him into his family, in which he continued to the end of his life, and, for the long space of thirty-six years, was treated with uniform kindness, attention, and respect.

This excellent man was, by his natural temper, quick of resentment; but, by his established and habitual practice, he was gentle, modest, and inoffensive. His tenderness appeared in his attention to children and to the poor. To the poor, while he lived in the family of his friend, he allowed the third part of his annual revenue; and for children, he condescended to lay aside the scholar, the philosopher, and the wit, to write little poems of devotion, and systems of instruction, adapted to their wants and capacities, from the dawn of reason, through its gradations of advance in the morning of life. Few men have left behind them such purity of character, or such monuments of laborious piety. He has provided instruction for all ages, from those who are lisping their first lessons, to the enlightened readers of Malebranche and Locke. His "Improvement of the Mind" is a work in the highest degree useful and pleasing. Whatever he took in hand was, by his incessant solicitude for souls, converted to theology. As piety predominated in his mind, it is diffused over his works. Under his direction, it may be truly said that philosophy is subservient to evangelical instruction: it is difficult to read a page without learning, or at least wishing, to be better.

The virtue of this good man eminently appeared in the happy state of his mind under great pains and weakness of body, and in the improvement which he derived from them. Of those seasons of affliction, he says, with a truly elevated mind and thankful heart, "I am not afraid to let the world know that, amidst the sinkings of life and nature, Christianity and the gospel were my support. Amidst all the violence of my distemper, and the tiresome months of it, I thank God I never lost sight of reason or religion, though sometimes I had much difficulty to preserve the machine of animal nature in such order as regularly to exercise either the man or the Christian."

The sweet peace of conscience he enjoyed under these trying circumstances, and the rational and Christian foundation of his hope and trust in the divine goodness, are beautifully and justly expressed by him, in the following lines:—

"Yet, gracious God, amid these storms of nature,
Thine eyes behold a sweet and sacred calm
Reign through the realms of conscience; all within
Lies peaceful, all composed. 'Tis wondrous grace
Keeps off thy terrors from this humble bosom;
Though stained with sins and follies, yet serene
In penitential peace and cheerful hope,
Sprinkled and guarded with atoning blood,
Thy vital smiles, amidst this desolation,
Like heavenly sunbeams hid behind the clouds,
Break out in happy moments, with bright radiance
Cleaving the gloom; the fair, celestial light
Softens and gilds the horrors of the storm,
And richest cordials to the heart conveys.'

---

## PHILIP DODDRIDGE

was born in London, in the year 1702. His parents, who were persons of great worth, brought him up in an early knowledge of religion; but he had the misfortune to lose them before he was fourteen years old. This circumstance excited in his mind very serious reflections, which, however, were not wholly of a gloomy nature; for he expressed a devout, and even a cheerful trust in the protection of the God of mercies, the universal Parent of mankind.

He diligently improved his time, and was anxious to be daily advancing in knowledge, piety, virtue, and usefulness. He possessed strong powers of mind, and, by unwearied application, acquired a large fund of sound and elegant learning. His publications, which are chiefly on religious subjects, have been eminently useful to the world. By his literary acquisitions, his amiable disposition, and his desire to imbue the young mind with knowledge and virtue, he was qualified, in a peculiar manner, to become the instructor of youth; and for many years he superintended a very respectable academy. As the pastor of a congregation, he manifested a sincere and zealous regard for the happiness of the people under his care, by whom he was greatly honored and beloved.

He possessed many virtues; but the prime and leading feature of his soul was devotion. He was very solicitous to preserve and cultivate an habitual sense of the Supreme Being, to maintain and increase the ardor of religion in his heart, and to prepare himself, by devout exercises, for the important labors of his station. Nor was it to his secret retirements that his piety was limited; it was manifested in every part of the day, and appeared in his usual intercourse with men. In the little vacancies of time which occur to the busiest of mankind, he was frequently lifting up his soul to God. When he lectured on philosophy, history, anatomy, or other subjects not immediately theological, he would endeavor to graft some religious instructions upon them, that he might raise the minds of his pupils to devotion, as well as to knowledge; and, in his visits to his people, the Christian friend and minister were united.

The piety of Dr. Doddridge was accompanied with the

warmest benevolence to his fellow-creatures. No one could more strongly feel that the love of God was to be united with love to man. Nor was this a principle that rested in kind wishes and pathetic feelings for the happiness of others, but it was manifested in the most active exertions for their welfare. No scheme of doing good was ever suggested to him into which he did not enter with ardor. But the generosity of his mind was most displayed when any plans of propagating religion, and of spreading the gospel among those who were strangers to it, were proposed. In every thing of this kind he was always ready to take the lead, and was ardent in endeavoring to inspire his friends with the same spirit.

He was of a weak and delicate bodily constitution; and a severe cold which he caught about the forty-eighth year of his age, brought on a consumption of the lungs. The nearer he approached to his dissolution, the more plainly was observed his continual improvement in a spiritual and heavenly temper. Indeed, he seemed to have risen above the world, and to be daily breathing after immortality. This disposition of his mind was ardently expressed in several of his letters, and is manifest from his will, which was made at this time, and is prefaced in the following language: — "Whereas it is customary, on these occasions, to begin with commending the soul into the hands of God, through Christ, I do it; not in mere form, but with sincerity and joy; esteeming it my greatest happiness, that I am taught and encouraged to do it, by that glorious gospel, which, having most assuredly believed, I have spent my life in preaching to others; and which I esteem an infinitely greater treasure than all my little worldly store, or possessions ten thousand times greater than mine."

A short time before his death, he had been induced to try the mild air of the south; but change of climate did not produce the desired effect, and Dr. Doddridge continued gradually to weaken, till death put a period to his afflictions. In his last hours, he preserved the same calmness, vigor, and joy of mind, which he had felt and expressed through the whole of his illness. The only pain he had in the thought of dying, was the fear of that grief and distress which his wife would suffer from his removal. To his children, his congregation, and his friends in general, he desired to be remembered in the most affectionate manner; nor did he, in the effusions of his pious benevolence, forget the family where he lodged, or his own servant. Many devout sentiments and aspirations were uttered by him; but the heart of his wife was too much affected with his approaching change to be able to recollect them distinctly. Though he died in a foreign land, and, in a certain sense, among strangers, his decease was embalmed with many tears. His age was 49 years

---

## JOHN MURRAY,

a distinguished preacher of Universalism in the United States, was born in Alton, county of Hampshire, England, on the 10th of December, 1741.

When he had attained his eleventh year, the family removed to Ireland, in the vicinity of Cork. While here, he was converted to Methodism, and gained the attention of John Wesley, by whom he was appointed a class-leader. He was very earnest and devout in his religious exercises, and was regarded by his brethren as a valuable accession to their church. About this time his father died, and he shortly after left Ireland for England. He took up his residence in London, and was gradually led into gay society. The secret monitor, however, frequently reproached him, and finally brought him back again to the services of the sanctuary, and quickened the flame of religious devotion. At this time his prejudices against Universalism were very strong; his soul "kindled with indignation" against them. But, shortly after his marriage to a very amiable young lady of London, he was induced to visit Mr. Relly's chapel, the preacher of universal salvation; and, notwithstanding he had been so filled with wrath against Mr. Relly, that, as he subsequently said, he thought it would have been doing both God and man service to kill him, yet he was moved to tenderness by his preaching and subsequently became an attendant on his ministry Rich were the consolations enjoyed by him and his amiable wife in their new faith. But great sorrows awaited him, she sickened and died; and the death-scene is described by himself, in his autobiography, with thrilling effect. He would gladly have accompanied her to the spirit-world. He was now alone; he felt himself a solitary being; he had no taste for the joys of life; his mind dwelt only on death and eternity; he was unfitted for society; and in this state of mind, Providence seems to have directed his thoughts to America. He resolved to embark; and, in the month of September, 1770, he landed upon the shores of New Jersey. Here he became at once acquainted with a philanthropic landholder, by the name of Thomas Potter, who, in the belief that God would send him a preacher, had erected a meeting-house, and who insisted that Murray was the man whom God had sent. In this house Murray commenced his labors as a preacher; and from this time, he is to be contemplated as the public advocate of Universalism, on the system of Relly. He soon visited the city of New York, and various other cities and towns in the Middle States, preaching the gospel whithersoever he went. His first visit to Boston was made in October, 1773, and his second in September, 1774. It was during this second visit that he was stoned in the pulpit of Rev. Mr. Croswell, in School Street. About this time he visited Gloucester, Massachusetts, which was afterwards his residence for many years. In 1775, he was appointed by General Washington chaplain to the Rhode Island troops, in the army then lying around Boston. He soon, however, returned to his charge in Gloucester, where he remained, making frequent visits to different parts of the United States, until October, 1793, when he was ordained pastor of the First Universalist Society in Boston, which had purchased the house of worship formerly occupied by the society of Dr Samuel Mather. His labors were not confined to this society, however; in one respect he was a minister at large he continued his itinerant habits, more or less, until October, 1809, when he was stricken with the palsy. He lived nearly six years after this affliction, and expired on the third day of September, 1815. He was buried in the Granary burying-ground, where his remains were suffered to lie unhonored until 1837, when they were removed to Mount Auburn, and a monument was erected to his memory. The monument is a beautiful fluted column, surmounted by an urn. It is encircled by a belt, or tablet, on which two inscriptions are placed; on one side —

"John Murray, Preacher of the Gospel; born in Alton, England, December 10, 1741; died in Boston, September 3, 1815; reëntombed beneath this stone, June 8, 1837."

On the opposite side —

"Erected at the recommendation of the United States General Convention of Universalists."

---

## ELHANAN WINCHESTER,

a distinguished advocate of Universalism, was born in Brookline, Massachusetts, September 30, 1751. In his nineteenth year, he was converted, under the preaching of the Baptists; and it was by his labors that the present Baptist society in Newton was originally gathered. In the autumn of 1774, he made a journey to the Southern States. Early in 1778, he first saw Siegvolk's "Everlasting Gospel," a work which originally appeared in Holland, but which had been translated and published by the Mennonites of Pennsylvania. It made a very deep impression upon his mind. In 1779, he came back to New England, his convictions of the truth of Universalism increasing upon him daily. He set out on his return to South Carolina in the autumn of 1780, and arrived at Philadelphia on the 7th of October. Here he intended to remain but a few days; but God evidently had a great work for him to do in this place. Even his enemies acknowl edged that his "manner of preaching was popular, his address very fascinating, and his appearance dignified and commanding." The Baptist church in that city invited him to tarry and preach to them, and he at length consented. About this time he read "Stonehouse on Universal Restitution," which served to confirm him greatly in his belief of that doctrine. Notwithstanding his great popularity, a discontent began to show itself in certain members of the church. He foresaw that a storm was rising, and he determined to prepare for it; not (to use his words) "by denying what I had said, but by more fully examining, and determining for myself, whether the sentiment was according to Scripture, or not. If I found it was not, I was determined to retract; but if it was, to hold it fast, let the consequences be what they might." Such was his truly Christian resolution. He avowed his belief in the final happiness of all men.

A majority of the church were in his favor; but, being a man of remarkably peaceful disposition, he did not urge them to press their claims to the meeting-house; but they retired to the hall of the university, where they held their meetings for about four years, until they purchased a place for themselves. During the rest of his life, he is to be viewed as the public advocate of universal restitution. There were several eminent men who adhered to him, and among others, Dr. Redman, and the celebrated Dr. Benjamin Rush, who remained his correspondent when he was in Europe. Added to all his other troubles, his domestic afflictions were very great. At the age of thirty-two, he had buried four wives. The fifth was a desperate fury, who gave him great trouble as long as he lived. After preaching about six years in Philadelphia, he was seized with an irresistible impulse to visit England. No persuasions could divert him from the purpose; and in September, 1787, he arrived, almost penniless, and a total stranger, in the great metropolis of the British empire. He preached in different parts of London, and, by his fervid eloquence and earnest defence of the restoration, he soon gathered a congregation, who took for him the chapel in Parliament Court, in which he held his meetings until his departure for America. He spent six years and a half in this country, laboring assiduously to bring men to the knowledge of the truth; and a deep and wide impression was made by his labors. In consequence of the ill treatment he experienced from his wife, he was obliged to leave her; and he quitted England privately, and came home, filling the friends whom he had left behind with amazement, being ignorant at first what had befallen him. He arrived in Boston in July, 1794. Various were the speculations in this country in regard to his return. But he commenced at once his labors as a preacher, travelling in several of the states, — visited his former friends in Philadelphia, where he was joined by his wife, who had come home to America, and whom he freely forgave. It became evident, about this time, that his health was greatly impaired; and an increasing asthma foretold a fatal termination. He came to Hartford, Connecticut, in October, 1796, and raised a congregation, to which he preached until he could preach no more. In April, 1797, he delivered a sermon, under a strong presentiment that it was his last, from St. Paul's farewell address to the elders of the Ephesian church. He never entered the desk again. He contemplated his death with serenity and joy On the morning of his decease, he commenced singing the hymn with several of his friends, — "Farewell, my friends in Christ below," but his voice soon faltered, and the torpor of death fell on him. His friends became disconcerted, and ceased to sing; but he revived a little, and encouraged them to go on, joining in the first line of each verse, until his voice was actually "lost in death." This was on the 18th of April, 1797, in the 47th year of his age. His funeral sermon was preached by Rev. Dr. Strong, of Hartford, who bore a frank testimony to Mr. Winchester's excellent character, and his final constancy in the doctrine he had preached.

The following is the inscription on the stone erected to his memory: —

"The General Convention of the Universal Churches, in Memory of their dear departed Brother, the REV. ELHANAN WINCHESTER, erected this Monumental Stone.

"He died April 18th, 1797, aged 46 years.

'Twas thine to preach, with animated zeal,
The glories of the resurrection morn,
When sin, death, hell, the power of Christ shall feel,
And light, life, immortality, be born."

---

SAINT GENEVIEVE,

born at Nanterre, about five miles from Paris, in the year 423, about the time of Pharamond, the first king of France. St. Germain, bishop of Auxerre, observing in her, when yet very young, a particular disposition to sanctity, advised her to take a vow of perpetual virginity, which she accordingly did in the presence of the bishop of Paris. After the death of her parents, she went to Paris. The city was about to be deserted, when Attila, with his Huns, broke into France; but Genevieve assured the inhabitants of complete security, if they would seek it by fervent prayers. Attila took his course from Champaigne to Orleans, returned thence into Champaigne, without touching Paris, and was defeated in 451. By this event, Genevieve's reputation was established In a time of famine, she went along the River Seine, from city to city, and soon returned with twelve large vessels loaded with grain, which she distributed gratuitously among the sufferers. This increased her authority, and she was highly honored by Merovæus and Chilperic. Nothing, however, contributed more to her reputation for sanctity, than the circumstance, that, from her fifteenth to her fiftieth year, she ate nothing but barley-bread, except that she took some beans every two or three weeks, and, after her fiftieth year, some fish and milk. In 460, she built a church over the graves of St. Dionysius Rusticus and Eleutherius, near the village of Chasteville, where Dagobert afterwards founded the abbey of St. Denys. She died in 499 or 501, and her body was placed in the subterraneous chapel which St. Denys had consecrated to the apostles Paul and Peter. Clovis, by her request, built a church over it, which was afterwards called by her name, as was also the abbey that was founded there. Another church, consecrated to this saint, was built adjoining to the church of Notre Dame. Her relics are preserved in the former. The church celebrates the third of January, the day on which she died, in honor of her

---

GILBERT BURNET,

bishop of Salisbury, was born at Edinburgh, in the year 1643. He was carefully educated by his father; and, having a strong constitution and a prodigious memory, he applied himself closely to study, and acquired a great portion of learning and knowledge, which he seemed to have ready for all occasions. He travelled through France, Italy, and Holland, where he formed connections with many of the greatest persons of his time, by whom he was much respected for his talents and virtues. At Amsterdam, he became acquainted with the leading men of the different persuasions tolerated in the United Provinces — Calvinists, Arminians, Lutherans, Anabaptists, Brownists, Roman Catholics, and Unitarians; amongst each of which, he used frequently to declare, he met with men of such unfeigned piety and virtue, that he became strongly fixed in a principle of universal charity, and an invincible abhorrence of all severities on account of religious opinions.

The following sentiments, which he solemnly uttered towards the conclusion of his days, are very expressive of the nature and power of true religion, and of its influence upon his own mind: —

"I recommend," he observes, "to all sorts of men, in the most serious manner, the study and practice of religion, as that which is the most important of all things, and which is both the light of the world, and the salt of the earth.

"Nothing so opens our faculties, and composes and directs

the whole man, as an inward sense of God; of his authority over us; of the laws he has set us; of his eye ever upon us; of his hearing our prayers, assisting our endeavors, watching over our concerns; of his being to judge, and reward or punish, us in another state, according to what we have done in this. Nothing will give us such a detestation of sin, and such a sense of the goodness of God, and of our obligations to holiness, as a right understanding and firm belief of the Christian religion.

"By living according to the rules of religion, a man becomes the wisest, the best, and the happiest creature that he is capable of being. Honest industry, the employing of time well, a constant sobriety, an undefiled purity and chastity, with continued serenity, are the best preservatives, too, of life and health; so that, take a man as an individual, religion is his guard, his perfection, his beauty, and his glory. This will make him a light in the world, shining brightly, and enlightening many round about him.

"Thus religion, if truly received and sincerely adhered to, would prove the greatest of all blessings to a nation. But by religion I understand something more than receiving particular doctrines, though ever so true, or professing them, and engaging to support them, even with zeal and eagerness. What signify the best doctrines, if men do not live suitably to them; if they have not a due influence upon their thoughts and their lives? Men of bad lives, with sound opinions, are self-condemned, and lie under a highly-aggravated guilt.

"By religion I do not mean an outward compliance with forms and customs, in going to church, to prayers, to sermons, and to sacraments, with an external show of devotion; or, which is more, with some inward forced good thoughts, in which many satisfy themselves, while these have no visible effect on their lives, nor any inward force to control and rectify their appetites, passions, and secret designs. These customary performances, how good and useful soever when understood and rightly directed, are of little value when men rest on them, and think, because they do them, they have acquitted themselves of their duty, though they still continue proud, covetous, full of deceit, envy, and malice. Even secret prayers, the most effectual means, are designed for a higher end; which is, to possess our minds with such a constant and present sense of divine truths, as may make these live in us, and govern us, and draw down such assistance, as to exalt and sanctify our natures.

"So that, by religion, I mean such a sense of divine truth as enters into a man, and becomes the spring of a new nature within him; reforming his thoughts and designs; purifying his heart; sanctifying and governing his whole deportment, his words as well as his actions; convincing him that it is not enough not to be scandalously vicious, or to be innocent in his conversation, but that he must be entirely, uniformly, and constantly, pure and virtuous, animated with zeal to be still better and better, more eminently good and exemplary.

"This is true religion, which is the perfection of human nature, and the joy and delight of every one that feels it active and strong within him. It is true, this is not arrived at all at once, and it will have an unhappy alloy, hanging long even about a good man; but, as those ill mixtures are the perpetual grief of his soul, so that it is his chief care to watch over and to mortify them, he will be in a continual progress, still gaining ground upon himself; and as he attains to a degree of purity, he will find a noble flame of life and joy growing up in him. Of this I write with a greater concern and emotion, because I have felt it to be the true, and, indeed, the only joy which runs through a man's heart and life. It is this which has been, for many years, my greatest support. I rejoice daily in it. I feel from it the earnest of that supreme joy which I want and long for; and I am sure there is nothing else which can afford any true and complete happiness."

This eminent scholar, Christian, and divine, departed this life on the seventeenth of March, 1714.

## THEOLOGICAL SCHOOLS.

| Name. | Place. | Denomination. | Com. Operation. | No. Prof. | Stud. in 1840–41. | No. educated. | Vols in Lib. |
|---|---|---|---|---|---|---|---|
| Bangor Theol. Seminary, | Bangor, Me. | Cong | 1816 | 3 | 43 | 139 | 7,000 |
| New Hampt. Theo. Inst. | N. Hampt. N.H. | Baptist, | 1828 | 2 | 36 | 75 | 1,000 |
| Gilmanton Theol. Sem. | Gilmanton, do. | Cong. | 1835 | 3 | 26 | 21 | 2,200 |
| Theological Seminary, | Andover, Mass. | Cong. | 1808 | 5 | 142 | 785 | 17,500 |
| Divinity Sch., Harv. Univ. | Cambridge, do. | Cong. Unit. | 1816 | 2 | 27 | 191 | 1,800 |
| Theological Institution, | Newton, do. | Baptist, | 1825 | 3 | 33 | 137 | 4,000 |
| Theol. Dep. Yale College, | N. Haven, Ct. | Cong. | 1822 | 3 | 61 | 245 | 200 |
| Theol. Inst. of Conn. | E. Windsor, do. | Cong. | 1834 | 3 | 29 | 37 | 4,000 |
| Theol. Inst. Epis. Church, | New York, N. Y. | Prot. Epis. | 1817 | 5 | 74 | 186 | 7,200 |
| New York Theol. Sem. | do. do. | Presbyt. | 1836 | 4 | 129 | | 12,000 |
| Theol. Sem. of Auburn, | Auburn, do. | Presbyt. | 1821 | 4 | 71 | 344 | 5,000 |
| Hamilton Lit. and Th. Inst. | Hamilton, do. | Baptist, | 1820 | 4 | 27 | 124 | 2,250 |
| Hartwick Seminary, | Hartwick, do. | Lutheran, | 1816 | 2 | 3 | | 1,000 |
| Theol. Sem. As. Ref. Ch. | Newburgh, do. | Ass. Ref. Ch. | 1836 | 3 | 11 | | 4,000 |
| Th. Sem. Dutch Ref. Ch. | N. Br'wick N. J. | Dutch Ref. | 1784 | 3 | 36 | 179 | |
| Theol. Sem. Pr. Ch. U. S. | Princeton, do. | Presbyt. | 1812 | 5 | 113 | 714 | 7,000 |
| Sem. Luth. Ch. U. States, | Gettysburg, Pa. | Evang. L. | 1826 | 3 | 26 | 130 | 7,000 |
| German Reformed, | York, do. | G. Ref. Ch. | 1825 | 2 | 20 | | |
| West. Theol. Seminary, | Alleghany T. do. | Presbyt. | 1828 | 2 | 31 | 175 | 6,000 |
| Theological School, | Canonsburg, do. | Asso. Ch. | | 2 | 22 | 47 | 1,600 |
| Theological Seminary, | Pittsburg, do. | Asso. Ref. | 1828 | 1 | 19 | | |
| Mercersburg Theol. Sem. | Mercersburg, do. | | | | | | |
| Epis. Theol. School of Va. | Fairfax Co. Va. | Prot. Epis. | 1822 | 4 | 43 | 126 | 4,000 |
| Union Theol. Seminary, | Pr. Ed. Co. do. | Presbyt. | 1824 | 3 | 20 | 175 | 4,000 |
| Virginia Baptist Seminary, | Richmond, do. | Baptist, | 1832 | 3 | 67 | | 1,600 |
| Southern Theol. Seminary, | Columbia, S. C. | Presbyt. | 1831 | 3 | 18 | 62 | 3,730 |
| Theological Seminary, | Lexington, do. | Lutheran, | 1835 | 2 | 10 | 20 | 1,800 |
| Furman Theol. Seminary, | High Hills, do. | Baptist, | | 2 | 30 | 30 | 1,000 |
| Lit. and Theol. Seminary, | Eaton, Ga. | Baptist, | 1834 | | 10 | | |
| South-West. Theol. Sem. | Maryville, Ten. | Presbyt. | 1821 | 2 | 24 | 90 | 6,000 |
| Lane Seminary, | Cincinnati, Ohio. | Presbyt. | 1829 | 3 | 61 | 43 | 10,500 |
| Theol. Dep. Ken. College, | Gambier, do. | Prot. Epis. | 1828 | 3 | 10 | | |
| Theol. Dep. Wes. Res. Col. | Hudson, do. | Presbyt. | | 3 | 14 | 6 | |
| Theological School, | Columbus, do. | Lutheran, | | | | | |
| Granville Theol. Dep. | Granville, do. | Baptist, | 1832 | 2 | 8 | | 500 |
| Oberlin Theol. Dep. | Oberlin, do. | Presbyt. | 1834 | 4 | 58 | | |
| Indiana Theol. Seminary, | S. Hanover, In. | Presbyt. | | 2 | 10 | | |
| Alton Theol. Seminary, | Upper Alton, Il. | Baptist, | 1835 | | | | |
| Carlinville Theol. Sem. | Carlinville, do. | Presbyt. | 1838 | | | | 700 |
| Theol. Dep. Marion Col. | N. Palmyra, Mo. | Presbyt. | | 1 | | | |

For a notice of the Roman Catholic seminaries, see page 325.

## PROGRESS OF CHRISTIANITY.

M. Laffon de Ladebat, of France, computes the number of Christians, in each century, since the Christian era, as follows: —

| | | |
|---|---|---|
| 1st century, | ............ | 500,000 |
| 2d " | .......... | 2,000,000 |
| 3d " | .......... | 5,000,000 |
| 4th " | .......... | 10,000,000 |
| 5th " | .......... | 15,000,000 |
| 6th " | .......... | 30,000,000 |
| 7th " | .......... | 25,000,000 |
| 8th " | .......... | 30,000,000 |
| 9th " | .......... | 40,000,000 |
| 10th century, | ......... | 50,000,000 |
| 11th " | ......... | 60,000,000 |
| 12th " | ......... | 70,000,000 |
| 13th " | ......... | 75,000,000 |
| 14th " | ......... | 80,000,000 |
| 15th " | ........ | 100,000,000 |
| 16th " | ........ | 125,000,000 |
| 17th " | ........ | 155,000,000 |
| 18th " | ........ | 200,000,000 |

Since the commencement of the nineteenth century, the number of Christians has increased, with great rapidity, in all parts of the world.

www.ingramcontent.com/pod-product-compliance
Lightning Source LLC
LaVergne TN
LVHW021145110826
845150LV00005B/1130

* 9 7 8 1 4 2 5 5 4 8 1 5 5 *